Renaissance Art in Venice:
From Tradition to Individualism

Tom Nichols

Laurence King Publishing

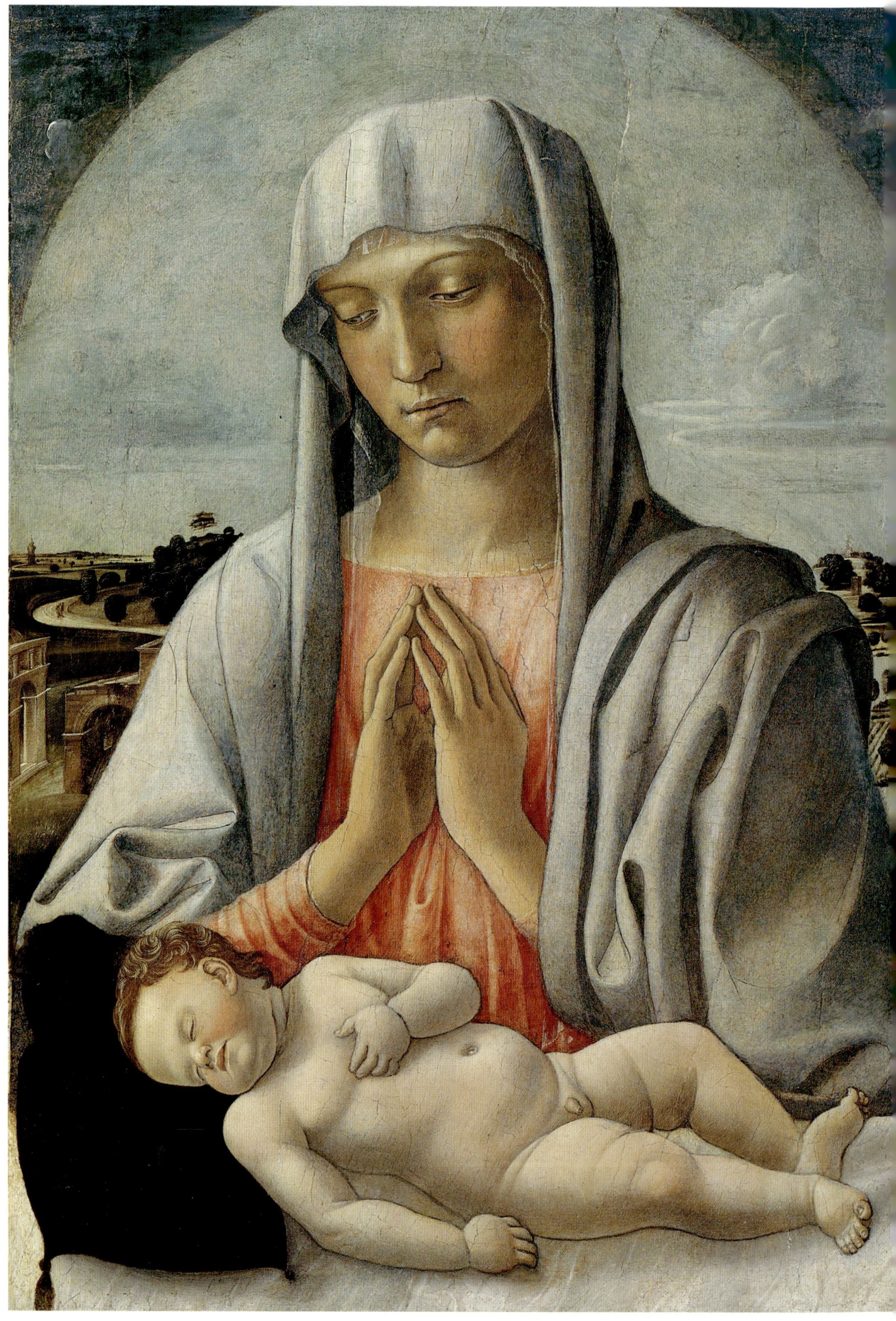

Renaissance Art in Venice:
From Tradition to Individualism

Tom Nichols

Laurence King Publishing

For Kerry

I would like to thank Philip Cottrell,
Debra Strickland, John Richards,
and my colleagues in History of Art
at the University of Glasgow.

Published in 2016 by
Laurence King Publishing Ltd
361–373 City Road
London EC1V 1LR
e-mail: enquiries@laurenceking.com
www.laurenceking.com

Published in 2016 by Laurence King Publishing Ltd.

A catalogue record for this book is available from
the British Library.

ISBN: 978-1-78067-851-1

Series and cover design by Pentagram
Design: Geoff Fennell

Frontispiece: Giovanni Bellini, *Madonna and Child*
(*See* page 45)

This page: Jacopo Tintoretto, *The Brazen Serpent*
(*See* page 196)

Printed in China

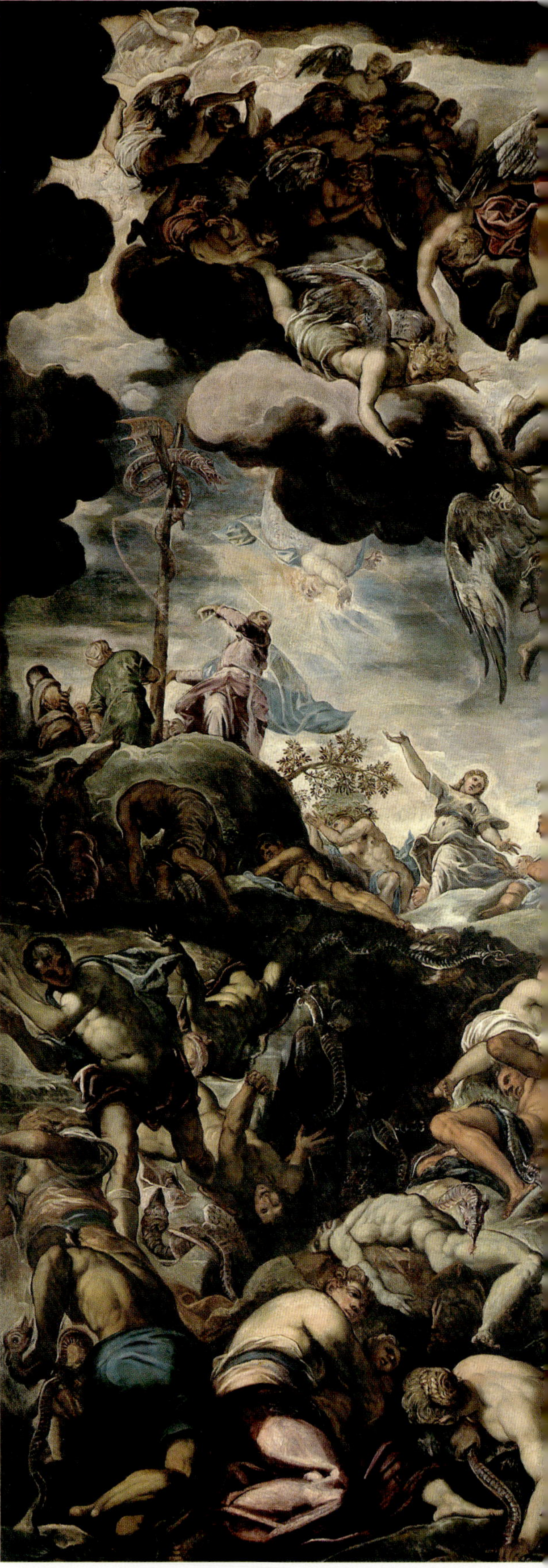

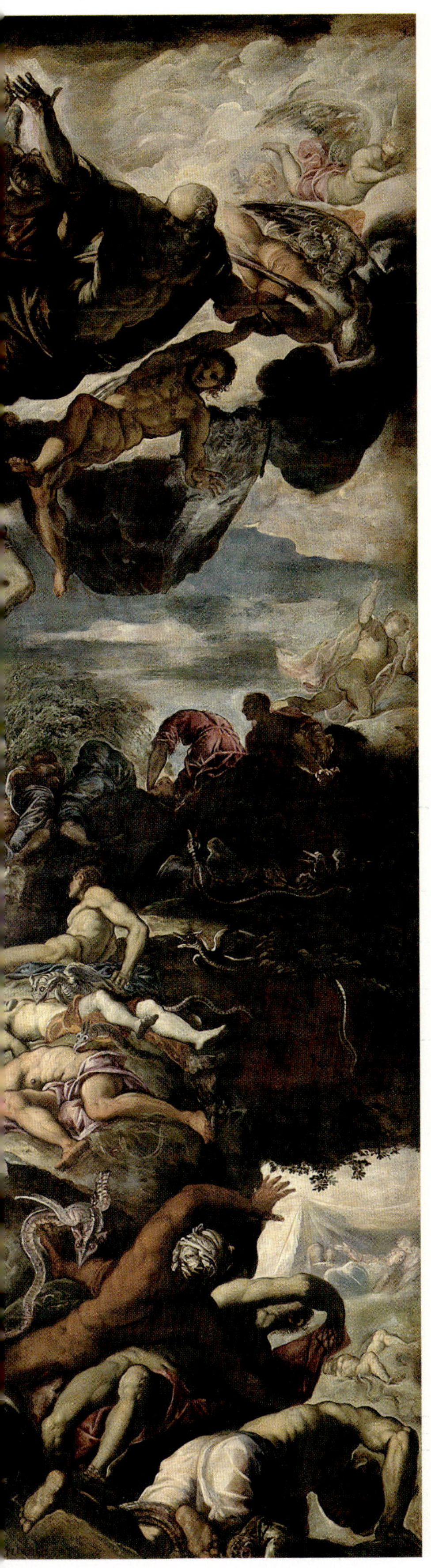

Contents

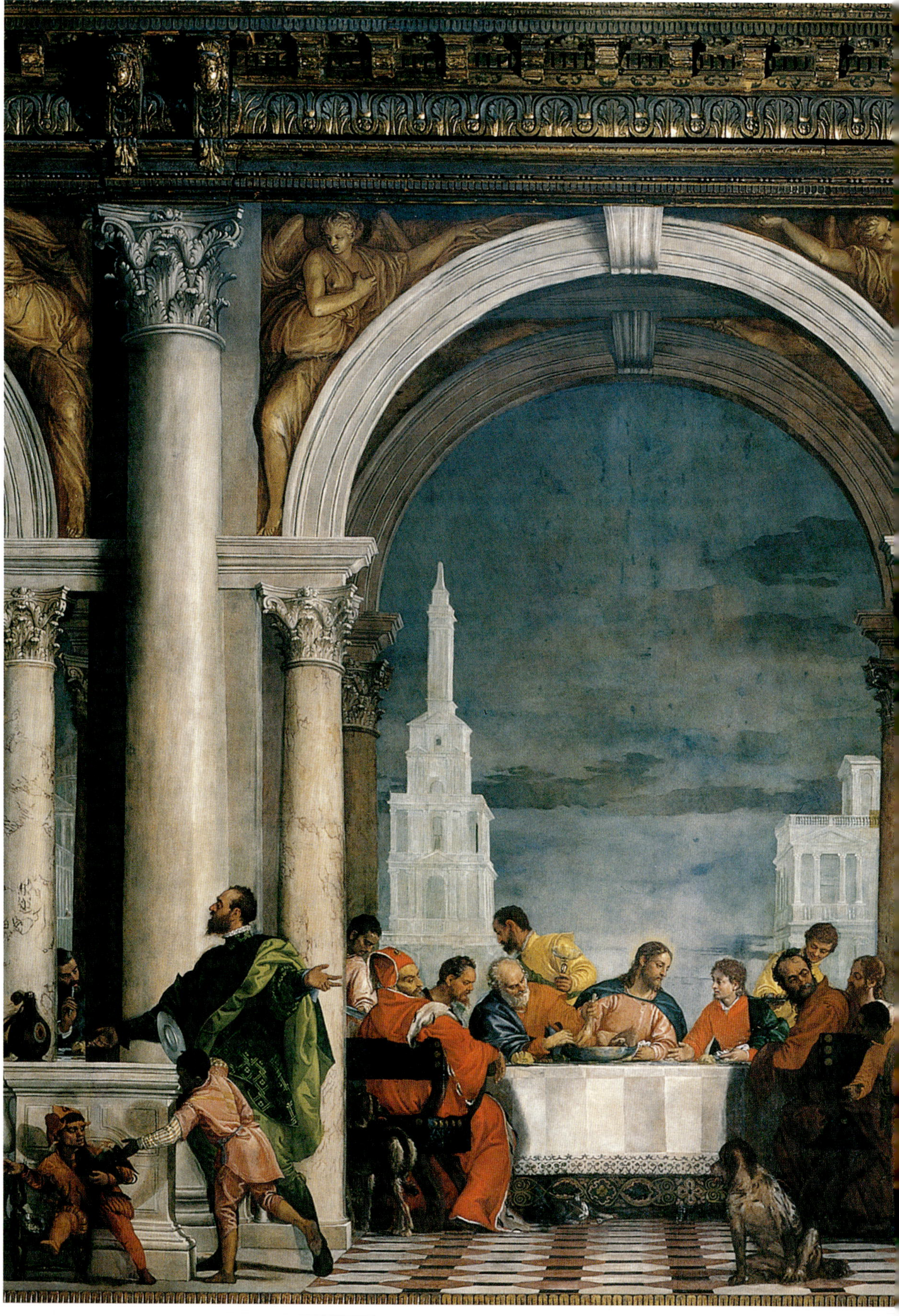

Introduction

see Fig. 103

The title of this book may suggest a distinction between 'Renaissance art' on the one hand, and 'Venice' on the other. These two entities were neither fixed nor separate, and their subtle and creative interaction lies at the heart of the discussion offered here; nonetheless, they did not always sit comfortably together. The coming of the Renaissance style undoubtedly represented a cultural departure in Venice. The roll call of famous 'name' painters, sculptors and architects whose work is discussed below, from the Bellini, the Lombardi and Codussi through to Sansovino, Titian, Tintoretto and Palladio, indicates the new significance of artistic individuals in the Renaissance centuries. These figures introduced personalized styles that marked a change from the traditional Venetian preference for anonymity and collaboration in artistic production.

It is sometimes argued that Venetian artistic culture remained closely tied to the city's medieval state and religious institutions. From this perspective, Venetian art provides a conservative contrast to that in other Italian cities, such as Florence and Rome. In these other centres, emphasis was laid on 'design' or *disegno*: a key concept which referred at once to the use of preparatory drawings; the definition of three-dimensional form and space; and the preconceived idea of the work in the artist's mind. It has been pointed out that this preoccupation with the intellectual or even quasi-scientific aspects of art had less purchase in Venice, where a sensual taste for colour (*colore*) and highly worked surfaces continued, drawing on the traditions of Veneto-Byzantine and Gothic art. Artists and architects offered a more intuitive visual response to the ever-changing play of light on the reflective surfaces of the lagoon city.

Yet it is possible to exaggerate the role of *colore* as the defining aesthetic in Venice, as also the related idea that an all-pervasive 'Venetian-ness' (*Venezianità*) determined artistic developments. Such a view does little to explain the more dynamic dimensions of art and architecture in this period, and fails to account for the radical changes in their appearances. The approach taken in this book highlights the Renaissance as a time of artistic transformation, in which older techniques, materials and conventions were often evoked, but just as often challenged or denied. The discussion below is closely based on key examples, and is presented in a chronological manner, to develop a sense of both continuity and change within the artistic culture of Venice. Two broad consecutive phases of development will be distinguished. In the first of these, lasting until around 1500, Renaissance elements typically co-exist in easy combination with the older styles of Venice. Rather than offering a challenge to the age-old assumption that art should serve the city, these innovations proved particularly well suited to visualizing its political values, cultural myths and sacred aspirations. Thus Renaissance art initially served to intensify the idea of the city as all encompassing cultural horizon.

From the early sixteenth century onwards, however, Renaissance art in Venice quickly came to share certain more progressive characteristics with other leading cultural centres in Italy. It increasingly departed from local patterns, types, models or techniques, in the direction of individual expression, and explored more intimate aspects of personal life. It sometimes possessed a newly monumental order and harmony, in keeping with revered models from classical antiquity or with contemporary Renaissance examples. In its approach to sacred, historical or mythological subject matter, it actively addressed the subjectivity of the viewer in an intellectual, psychological or sensual manner. It engaged directly with ideas about the high cultural status of art itself with reference to literary, poetic or aesthetic values. And it also acknowledged the artist as an independent or even god-like creator. This redefinition of visual art in Venice meant that it was no longer wholly contained within the local envelope of the city's traditional culture.

It is true that the older political and aesthetic ideals of Venice were often referred to or revived within the new approach, but artistic work of the sixteenth century was just as often self-consciously inventive and innovative. Increasingly, figurative artists moved beyond the literal concern with naturalistic accuracy that had helped to realize the perfect image of the city until 1500, introducing references to recent art works, or subjective and original elements. A newly personalized approach to artistic technique, form and iconography emerged that is not always easy to square with the ornate and decorative styles of the past, or with traditional Venetian patriotic or sacred values. The popularity of art itself spread, with the importation or invention of many new image-types, but the determining connection with the immediate local context became less absolute or apparent. Leading painters now often served the aesthetic tastes of private patrons and collectors, or exported bespoke paintings to aristocrats at foreign courts.

Competing against one another for commissions and preferment, sixteenth-century artists in Venice no longer behaved like, or understood themselves as, subservient or nameless artisans. Although no artistic academy emerged in Venice until the early eighteenth century, leading artists and architects of the 1560s were keen to join the recently formed Accademia del Disegno ('Academy of Design') in Florence. Allying themselves with progressive artists from elsewhere in Italy, those working in Venice grew ever more self-confident, depicting themselves in inventive self-portraits while their work became the subject of learned debate in literary texts.

To emphasize these changes is not to argue that Renaissance art and Venice were necessarily or absolutely opposed or contradictory. The evident success of a progressive artistic culture suggests the city's openness to change and development – probably a result of the confidence granted by its unprecedented wealth in this period. It is telling that the progress of the Renaissance only faltered with the economic and political decline of the city after 1550, when its culture began to ossify around a more fixed and backward-looking version of *Venezianità*. Given that the Renaissance approach had gradually dispensed with the security of older communal and collaborative cultural structures in favour of more individualistic forms of expression, its ability to sustain itself now came into question. Although leading artists of the later sixteenth century maintained family workshops, like their forebears in Venice, these did not typically survive the intensely personalized imprint of the masters who had dominated them. The end of the Renaissance in Venice was, to this extent, inscribed in the very success of its leading exponents.

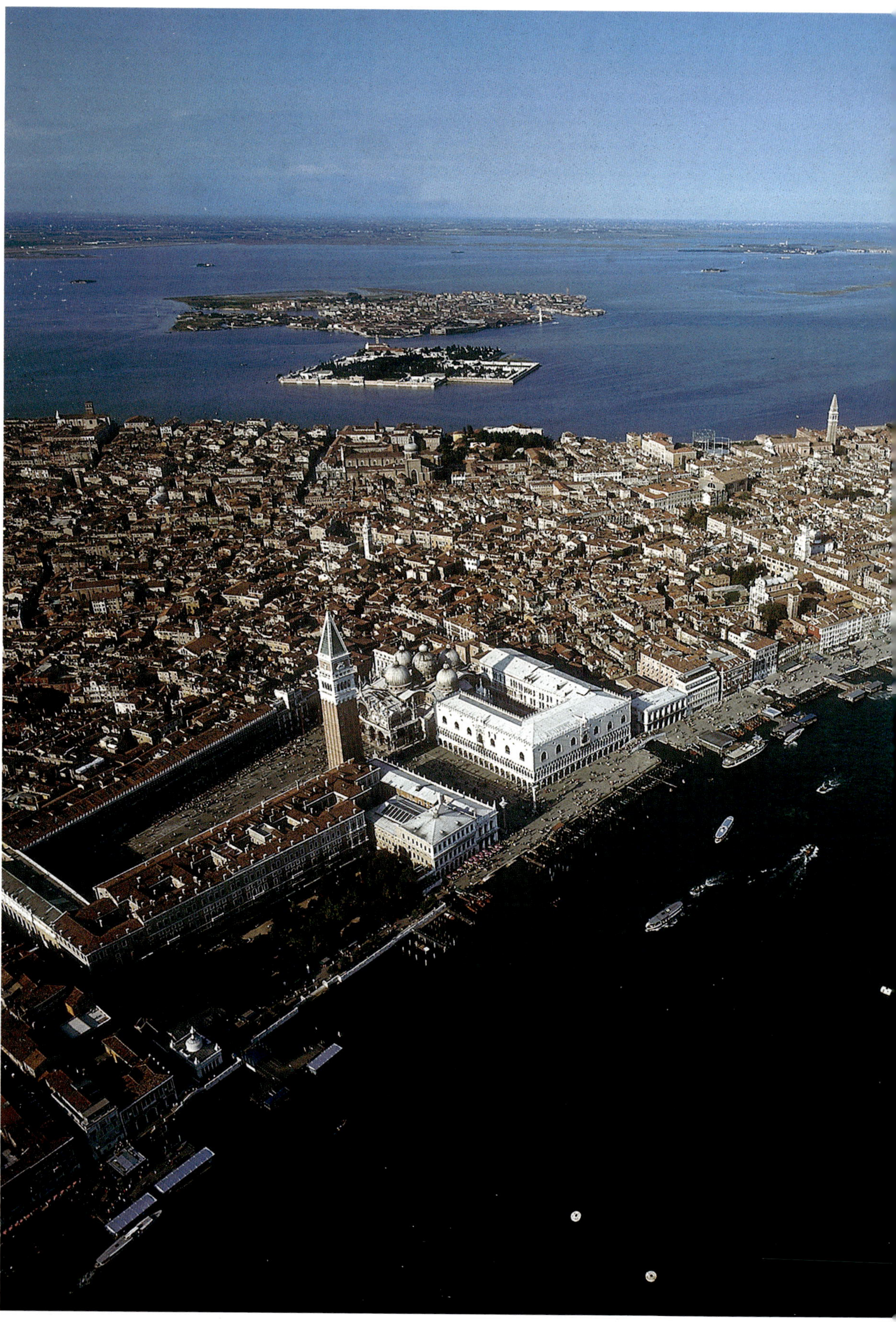

1

'The Most Serene Republic': Venice at the Outset of the Renaissance

Given the unlikely location of Venice among the watery recesses of a lagoon a mile or so off the coast of northeast Italy, it is no surprise that it possessed a unique culture, at some remove from the social mainstream of Europe (FIG. 1). If the city was not quite 'another world', as the fourteenth-century poet Francesco Petrarch described it, it was certainly a mediator between worlds. In the pre-Renaissance centuries, Venice had relied less on a land empire than on the predominance of its merchant fleet at sea. Trading silks and spices from the East with wool and metals from the West, Venice was necessarily dependent on the flow of import and export commodities. The city possessed few raw materials of its own; and it lacked a grand Imperial history, like Rome or Constantinople (modern Istanbul). Perhaps as a result, Venetians developed a heightened sense of the importance of 'tradition' and were particularly active in the invention of stories about their own past. They came to share a series of patriotic narratives or myths that highlighted the city's arbitration between powers and its special sacred destiny.

The city of Venice was built on a series of low islands that were gradually connected via an intricate system of canals, bridges and walkways. Its buildings were erected by driving huge tree trunks into the soft mud of the shallow lagoon. This view features the civic and religious centre of Venice around St. Mark's Square in the foreground (*see* also the plan on page 20).

Origins: Myths of Venice and the basilica of St Mark's

One particularly favoured story focussed on an act of Venetian peace-making between the two most powerful leaders in Europe, Pope Alexander III and the Holy Roman Emperor, Frederick Barbarossa, in 1177. The Venetian doge Sebastiano Ziani (reigned 1172–1178) offered shelter to the pope and then helped to smooth over the conflict between the two rulers. He received a series of ceremonial gifts, or *trionfi*, from Alexander for his efforts, including a sword and an umbrella, which were regularly displayed in centuries to come, especially when the doge processed around the city on Holy Days or in the fulfilment of one or other of the city's many civic rituals (FIG. 2). The story also became a favoured subject in visual art, appearing in illuminated manuscripts and also in large-scale narrative paintings decorating the main room of the city's Ducal Palace, known as the 'Alexander cycle' (*see* FIG. 126).

Another story made the success of Venice appear as predestined from the period of early Christianity. From the twelfth century onwards, it was understood that the city had been founded on 25 March 421, the feast of the Annunciation to the Virgin. This supplied an account of Venice's antiquity and also of its special and continuing protection by the Mother of God herself. The idea of

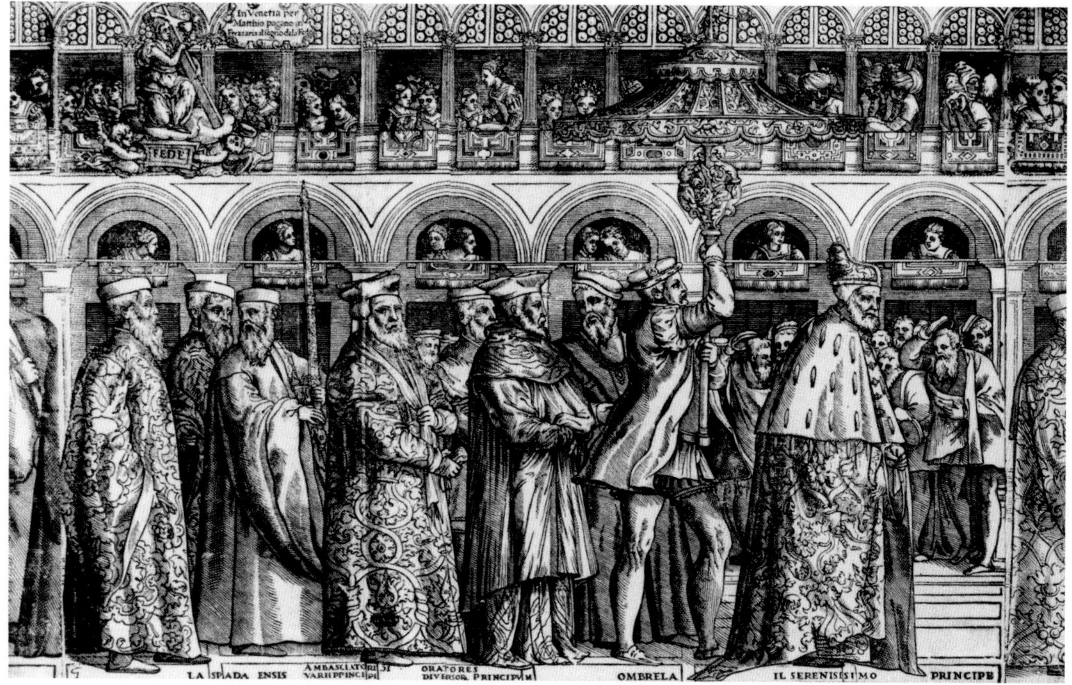

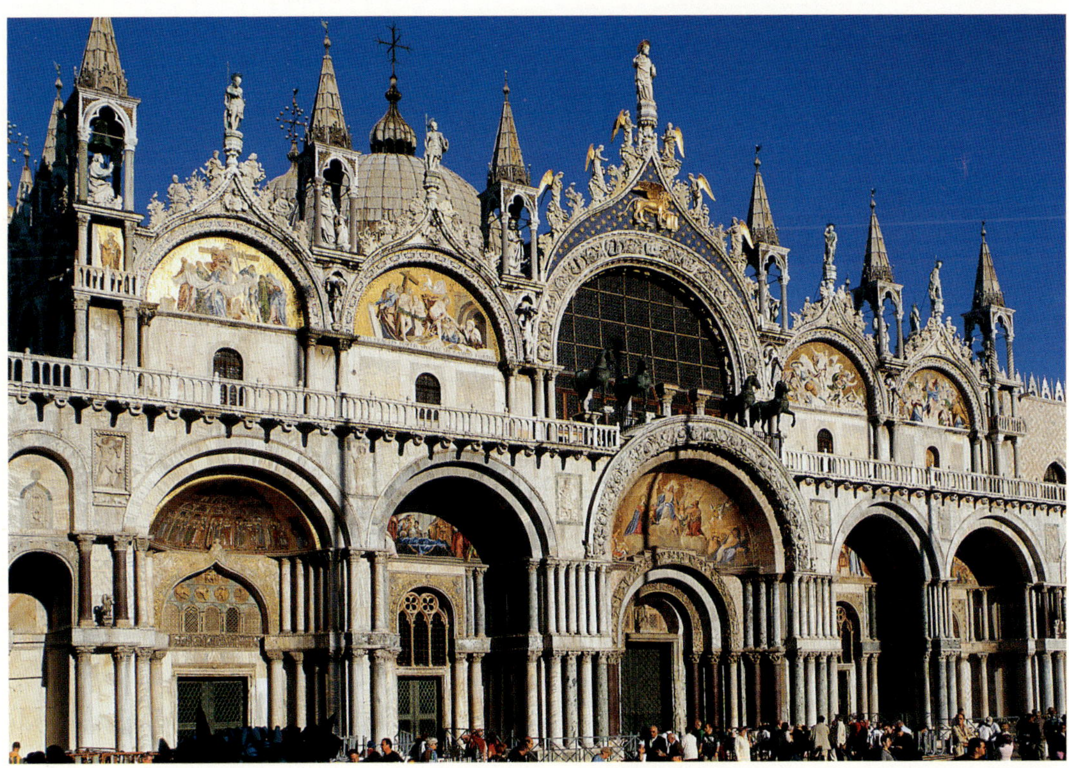

Venice's sacred destiny was reconfirmed by the arrival of the relics of St Mark from Alexandria in Egypt in 829. According to a thirteenth-century legend, Mark had already been told by an angel that his remains would come to Venice. This is the source of the many subsequent images set up around the city showing a winged lion, symbol of St Mark, holding an open book with the words '*Pax tibi Marce, evangelista meus*' ('Peace unto You Mark my Evangelist'). The period between 1100 and 1500 was key to the process of 'mythogenesis' in Venice and was focussed particularly on the great building erected at the eastern end of the city's main piazza to house the relics of the saint: the basilica of St Mark's (FIG. 3).

Many of the Renaissance works discussed in this book owe a debt to the example of St Mark's, or make a definite and explicit reference to the church. Along with the Ducal Palace discussed below, the building stood at the very heart of the city, in both a physical and symbolic sense, functioning as a public monument to its religious and political identity. From the outset this extraordinary building laid more emphasis on the civic power of the city than on the independent identity of the Christian Apostle to whom it was dedicated. St Mark's was not the Cathedral of Venice but rather the

Erected above previous structures between 1043–73; west facade from the thirteenth century, with the six crowns added ca. 1400, Venice. The four bronze horses seen in this photograph are copies, while all but one of the mosaics are from the post-Renaissance period. Late antique marble reliefs featuring Hercules can be seen between the arches.

'doge's chapel', and from the mid-fifteenth century onwards it was physically attached to the Ducal Palace, where the doge lived and the government of Venice was enacted. The ultimate dependence of the church on the seat of city government just to the south is indicative of the Venetian approach to religion, which was carefully controlled by the needs and demands of the state. If Venetian religion was assertively independent of the wider Christian church in both its Roman and Orthodox manifestations, the layout of St Mark's, with its central plan and five domes, drew pointedly on the lost sixth-century church of the Holy Apostles in Constantinople. This was an association which expressed Venice's long-standing connection with the Byzantine Empire of which it had formerly been a part, and with which it remained closely connected, given that its lucrative spice trade in the East was in great part conducted through Byzantine territories.

Much else about the building was intended to appear as ancient or time-hallowed. The extensive cycles of mosaics commissioned to adorn its facade and inner ceilings suggested connection with the similar decorations in early Byzantine churches, such as the sixth-century Basilica of San Vitale in Ravenna (FIG. 4). Although the initial teams of mosaicists employed following the erection of the church in the eleventh century were imported from Byzantium itself, a thriving local school soon grew up who were so skilled in their emulation of the Eastern craftsmen that it is now difficult to tell their works apart. In *The Stones of Venice* (1851–3), the great Victorian John Ruskin noted how the securing of the slabs of multi-coloured marble revetment erected on the lower walls of the church were deliberately left open to view ('the confessed rivet'). Ruskin, who deplored the coming of the individualistic culture of the Renaissance to the city, especially praised this respectful re-use of precious materials imported from abroad as a characteristically Venetian practice. The (unknown) architect at St Mark's, Ruskin went on, readily put his own ideas aside, given his 'care for the preservation of noble work … and more regarded the beauty of his building than his own fame'. For Ruskin, this selfless respect for the past had a quasi-religious dimension; but it also expressed a communal approach that reflected the political and social values of the Republic itself.

There was, however, a much more appropriative dimension to the assemblage of older pre-worked materials from elsewhere at St Mark's: many of the objects displayed on the facade were plunder from the Sack of Constantinople by European Crusaders in 1204, in which Venice had fully participated and from which it subsequently greatly benefited in political and economic terms. As Ruskin

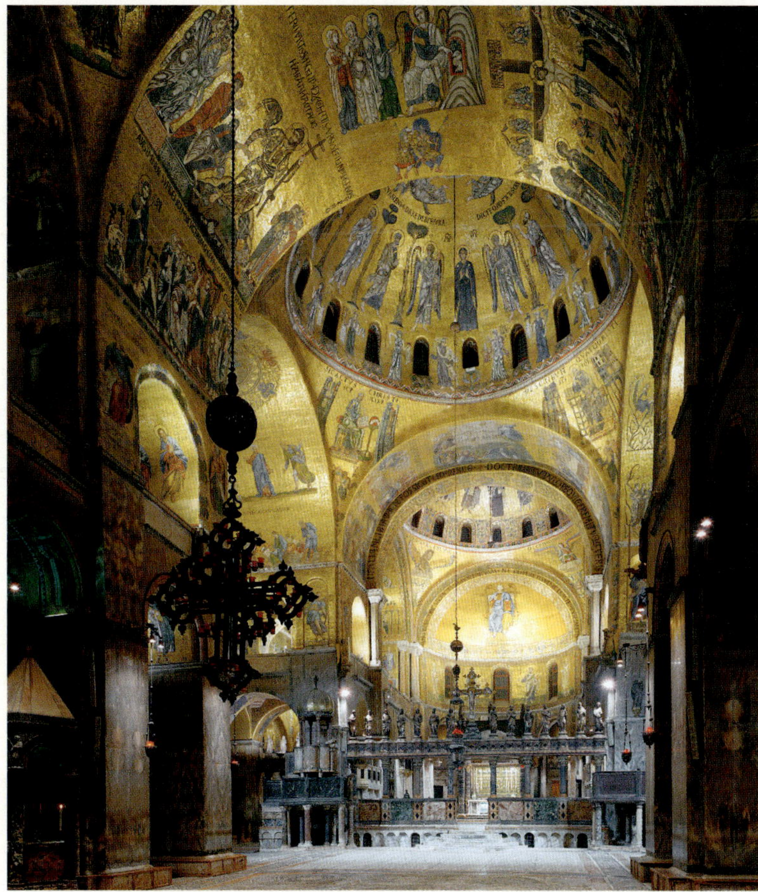

See Fig.3. Interior view from the central nave towards the crossing and apse. The extensive mosaic cycles rising up above the marble revetments on the lower walls were begun in the eleventh century.

acknowledged, these precious objects were elevated as 'the trophies of returning victory', making the facade appear more like 'a shrine at which to dedicate the splendour of miscellaneous spoil, than the organized expression of any fixed architectural law or religious emotion'. The *spolia* displayed at St Mark's proposed an image of ultimate Venetian victory and dominion, but one based on an ideal of social and religious concord between different elements. The plunder from Constantinople reinforced the earlier modelling of the church, giving further credence to the idea that Venice, with its growing empire, was the natural heir to the glories of Byzantium: one that inevitably intensified again following its final fall to the Ottoman Turks in 1453. But this notion did not entail stylistic uniformity. The Venetians proudly displayed classicizing marble reliefs featuring Hercules and four bronze horses from the late antique period on the facade, among the parti-coloured marbles of the portals and a growing forest of Gothic pinnacles, finials and crockets.

The Ducal Palace and the Porta della Carta

Such an approach appeared always to validate 'tradition' and the workmanship of many other cultures of the past, while at the same time suggesting that this ended with the present victory and on-going predominance of Venice itself. The incorporation of different elements or borrowings into the Venetian present discouraged artistic individualism, or sought to accommodate it within a panoply of equally acceptable styles. Diversity, both in the sense of material and form, better expressed the idea of the city as a free and equitable Republican community with a long and illustrious past. Something similar is at play in the Ducal Palace, where the unknown architects engaged in stylistic pluralism from the outset (FIG. 5). If St Mark's was a building in the Byzantine style that was gradually Gothicized over the centuries, the Ducal Palace was only begun in the mid-fourteenth century, and was largely complete a little over a century later. Despite this much shorter gestation, allusions to traditionally distinct architectural traditions were central to its conception, with Gothic and Islamic elements freely combined, probably to suggest overlapping spheres of Venetian influence between West and East. The city's habit of appropriation and amalgamation means that we

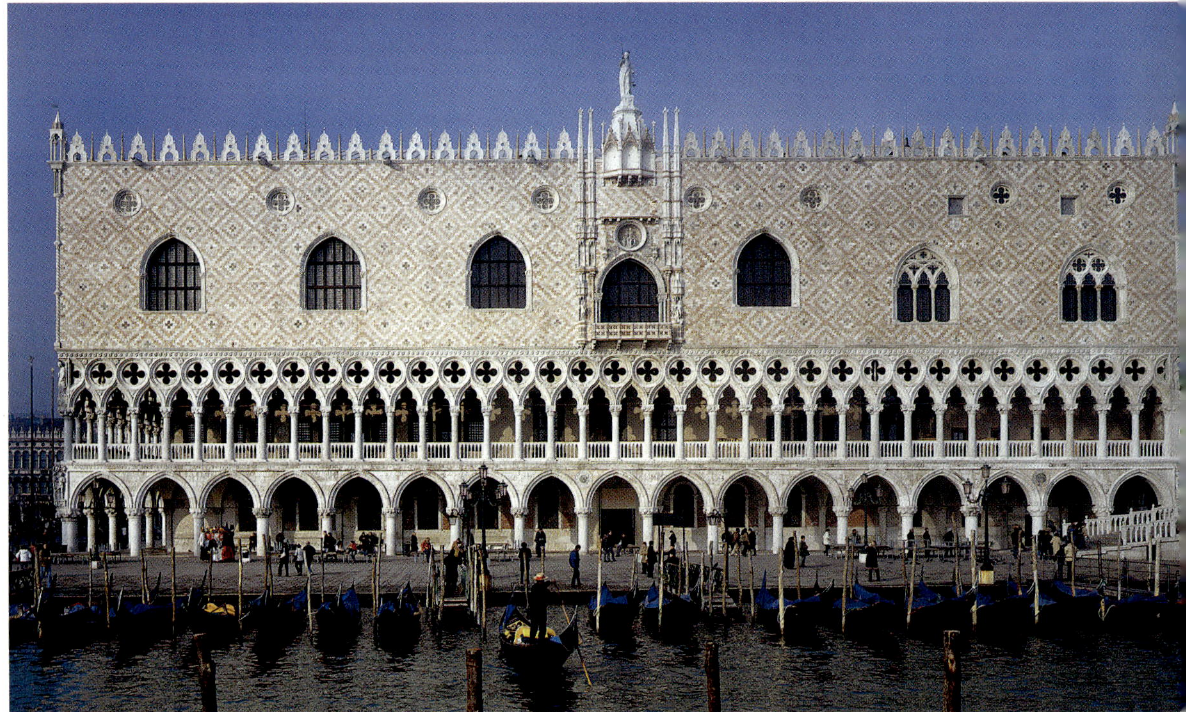

Fig.5
Ducal Palace
View of the south front from
St Mark's Basin, Venice.

Begun in 1341.

cannot precisely pin down the derivation of the different elements included. The traceries above the double rows of colonnades on the lower part of the building, for example, owe something, at least, to Moorish screen walls. And if the overall effect is unmistakably Gothic, the inlaid lozenge pattern of red and white marble tiles on the walls nonetheless has a precedent in Persian decorative tradition. The various elements associate freely together as if they are knowing references or quotations, and this lightness of touch seems actively to deny any sense of the building's inner depth or structure. The dense repetition of elements in the lower colonnades, which contrast in a vibrant two-to-one rhythm, like the subtle variations within a given surface – each pattern of tiles is slightly different – generates a rich and vibrating surface that enters into a fluid relationship with the waters of the Basin beneath.

If the range of Venetian international interests is suggested by the exterior appearance of the Ducal Palace, then its extended box-like shape was a response to the internal politics of the Republic itself. Its effect of low horizontality was quite directly determined by the political arrangement that followed the *serrata* or 'closure' of 1296, when around 200 noble families of the city took control of the Venetian government by hereditary right, with all male members sitting on the so-called 'Great Council' to vote on matters of government (including the election of the doge himself from their number). The need to accommodate a large and inevitably growing number of patrician representatives within a single interior meeting hall governed ideas for building the new palace, and by the 1360s the so-called Sala del Maggiore Consiglio (Hall of the Great Council) was already completed. The long westward extension of the south or 'Molo' facade, where all but the two most easterly windows give onto the vast new room, is indicative of this practical need.

The ideal of Republican assembly was expressed in figurative sculptures placed on the facade suggesting that the palace (and by extension the Venetian state) was the seat of divinely sanctioned justice (FIG. 6). It was also reflected in the colonnades at ground level and on the *piano nobile* (main floor). The colonnades reinforce the illusion of openness or accessibility to the outside world, contrasting with the kind of heavily fortified town halls in city Republics elsewhere in Italy, such as Florence and Siena, or in service of princely courts such

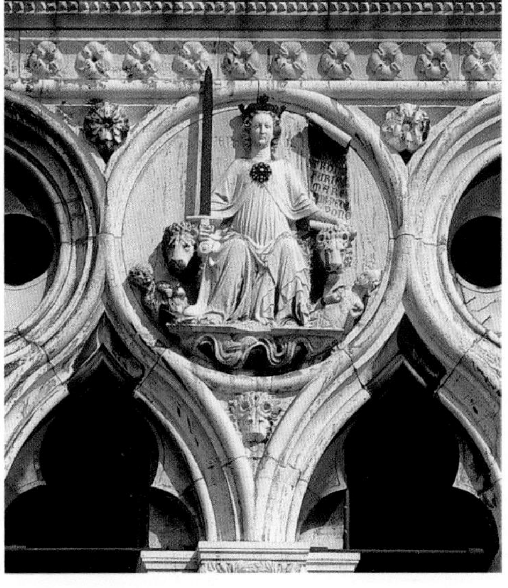

Fig.6
Filippo Calendario (?)
Venecia

Before 1355. Stone relief on the west front of the Ducal Palace, facing the Piazzetta, Venice.

The Venetian state is equated with the cardinal virtue of Justice, shown as a woman holding a sword seated on a Solomonic throne with two lions. The inscription identifies the two defeated figures below her as 'furies of the sea', and the city's maritime power is also indicated by the waves at the bottom.

as Ferrara or Urbino. The decorative crenellations appended to the top of the building, which also have a source in Islamic examples, have a similar kind of meaning. Their visual delicacy appears like an ironic reference to the more functional deployment of such features in the muscular defensive architecture of many medieval castles. Expressing the supreme confidence of a period in which Venetian political power, both on land and sea, rose to unprecedented heights, the Ducal Palace suggests that impregnability need not always appear as a matter of physical strength or social exclusion.

Work on the west front of the Ducal Palace facing the so-called Piazzetta continued into the fifteenth century and involved the physical connection of the building to St Mark's itself via a new ceremonial entrance known as the Porta della Carta (FIG. 7) by the local sculptors Giovanni and Bartolomeo Bon (ca. 1360–1442 and ca. 1400–ca. 1465). Visitors to the palace would now enter through a grand and richly decorated portal. Looking up beyond it, they would encounter an almost life-sized sculpture of the current doge (Francesco Foscari, reigned 1423–1457) kneeling before the symbolic lion of St Mark, who holds open his book with the famous words confirming Venice as the saint's divinely pre-destined resting place. To either side, allegorical sculptures of Virtues re-emphasize the office of the doge as sacred, and as the eye moves further upward beyond the elaborate tracery of the window and the richly decorated pinnacles and crockets to either side, further figurative sculptures intervene to reconfirm the message. St Mark himself appears in the heavenly realm in a round shell niche. Above him, a composite allegorical female figure seated on a throne with lions to either side deliberately recalls Calendario's sculpture of *Venecia* on the west facade of the palace (*see* FIG. 6). Although now identified as 'Justice' by an inscription below her, she is still a composite figure who can stand for both, just as her protective lions refer to the divinely inspired Wisdom of Solomon and to the imagery of St Mark.

These patriotic meanings are developed through the powerful vertical axis of the Porta della Carta, with the current representative of state power placed directly beneath the sacred and allegorical figures in order to suggest that he always acts with their authority. The exaggerated verticality of the new structure was to this extent more than just a response to the narrowness of the given space between church and palace. But there is also an important horizontal dimension, given that the gateway connects the buildings at the heart of Venetian political and sacred authority in Venice. The Ducal Palace (especially the west-faing facade) was seen as the seat of justice, and thus the imagery at the top of the

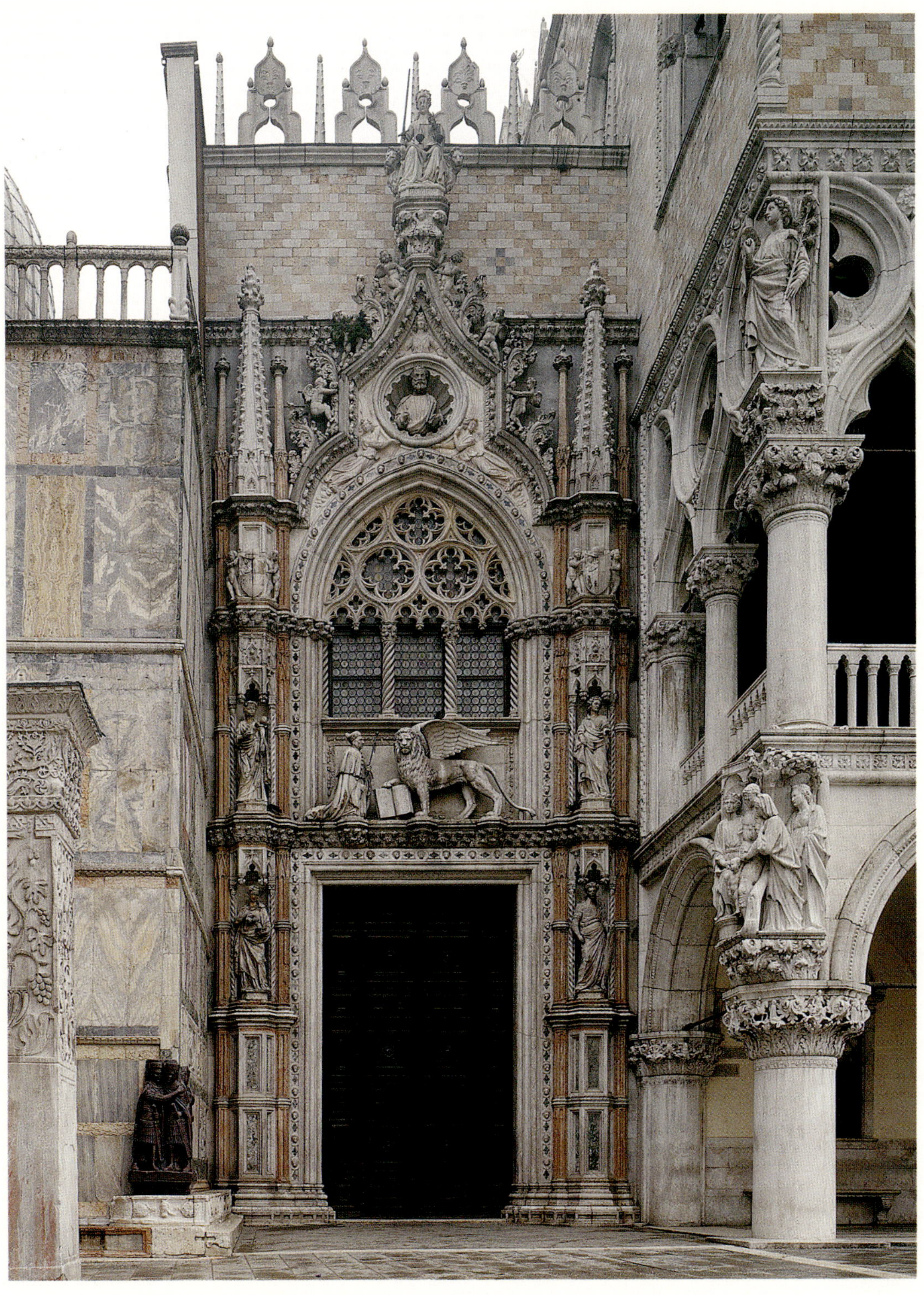

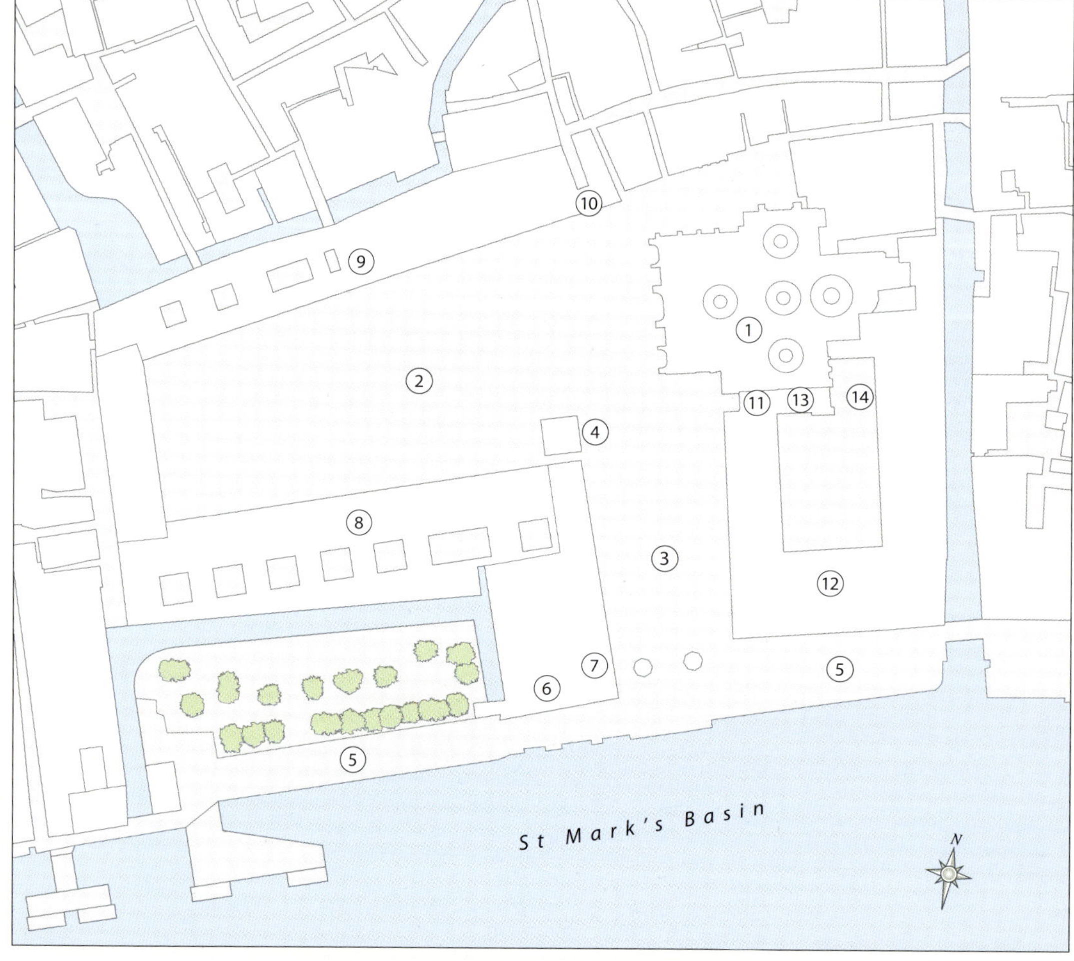

Carta directly extends that already featured on the exterior of the building to the right. The emphasis on the saint, however, refers to St Mark's to the left. Thus the iconography of the Carta reconfirms the authority of the two structures it conjoins, symbolizing their especially intimate connection within Venetian culture. As visitors approached the grand entrance, they could not also fail to notice and engage with the pre-existing sculptures just to the right and left: a corner relief on the palace shows the *Judgement of Solomon*, reconfirming once again that the seat of Venetian government is a place of divinely inspired wisdom and justice. To the left, on the south-facing wall of St Mark's displaying *spolia* from Constantinople, a fifth-century porphyry sculpture featuring the *Four Tetrarchs* now served to express Venetian dominion over the former lands of the Byzantine Empire.

In many ways the Porta della Carta represents a high point in the gradual move away from the severe and reserved monumentality of the older Byzantine style in Venice. And to this extent, it is a prime example of the kind of 'incrustation' of surfaces in the Veneto-Gothic style that Ruskin so admired. Sculpture and architecture combine, such that it is not really possible to think of the one as separate from the other. The Porta also features the intense polychromy typical of the period. The sculptors used a particularly wide range of parti-coloured materials, including pale or white marbles from Istria and Carrara alongside red, green and grey variants from Verona and elsewhere. The sumptuous effect of the highly polished stones was reinforced by gilding and painting in the favoured late-Gothic colours of gold and blue: the former used to pick out the architectural details around the figures, while the latter emphasized the darkness of the recesses behind them.

It is also telling that Ruskin rejected what he saw as the 'insipid confusion' of the Porta, understanding its imagery as already tainted by 'the pestilent art of the Renaissance'. St Mark is presented in the format of a lifelike portrait, and naked putti reminiscent of the art of classical Greece or Rome cavort among the acanthus leaves to either side. The sculpture of the kneeling doge is a nineteenth-century replacement, but the lost original must have allowed Francesco Foscari a newly forceful presence in the public arena at the heart of Venice. We do not know just how lifelike Foscari's image originally was, but it probably introduced a note of naturalism, and perhaps also of self-assertive individualism, that reflected his high profile as an unusually powerful doge who dramatically expanded the Venetian land empire. The confidently eclectic imagery of the Porta draws on the mix of Gothic and early Renaissance styles that had become fashionable in northern mainland Italy by the early 1440s. It might even reflect the beginnings of the Venetian reorientation towards the West: one that was to emerge as a key aspect of the city's politics and artistic culture over the course of the next 150 years.

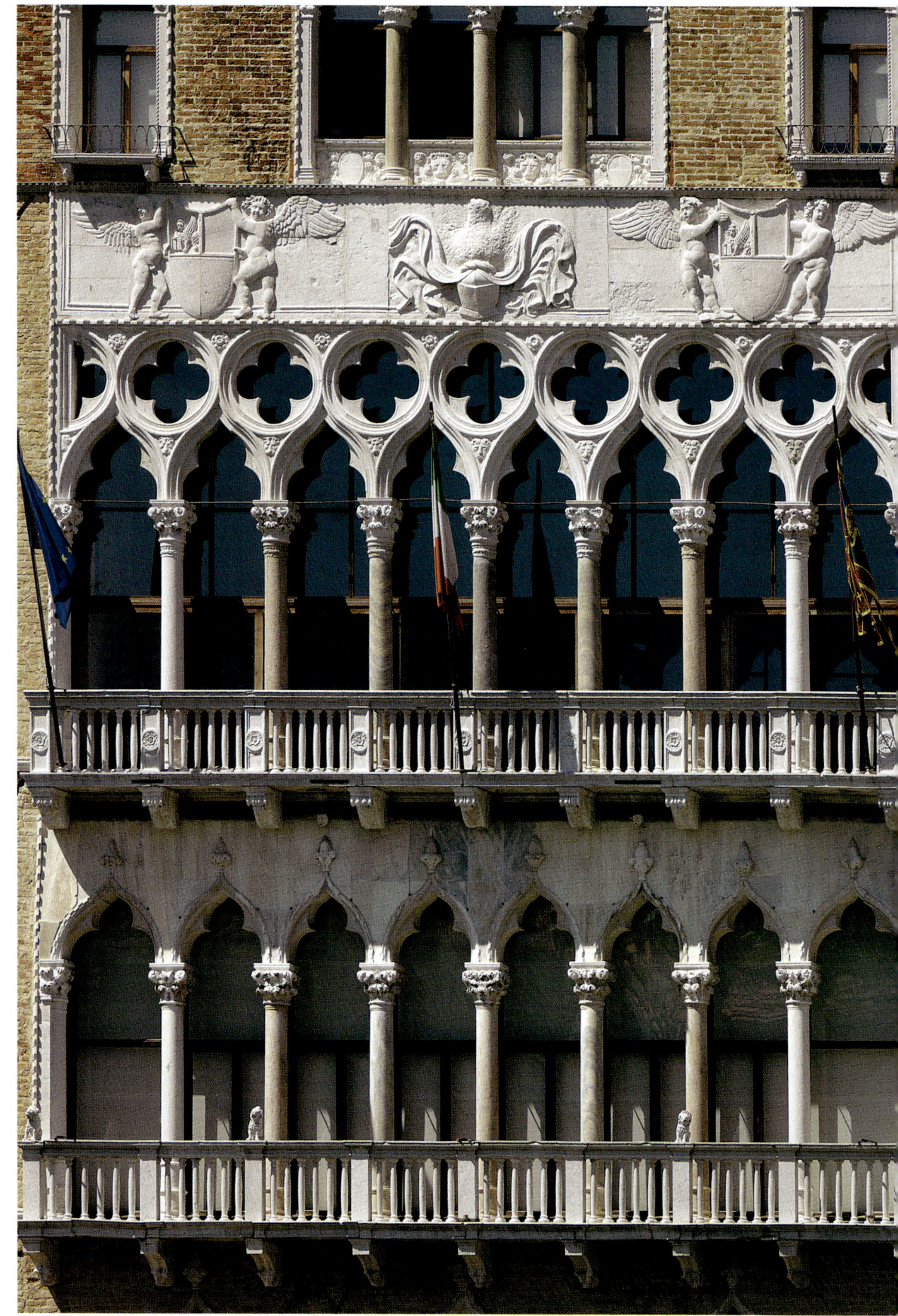

Innovation as Tradition: 1440–75

The imposing palace built by Doge Foscari in the early 1450s, known as Ca'Foscari, appears to continue the pattern of self-assertiveness evident in the Porta della Carta (*see* FIG. 10). Prior to Foscari's acquisition of the site, it had been state-owned for some decades. He now quickly replaced the existing Byzantine building with one in a Gothic style on a larger scale. By comparison with the two adjacent palaces owned by the Giustiniani family, and also rebuilt during the 1450s, Ca'Foscari is larger and grander, with a more extensive and elaborate facade. It features an eight-windowed double window arcade, for example, rather than the rows of six and four that appear on the Giustiniani buildings. If these differences make Foscari's palace appear to be a departure from the communally orientated culture of Venice, nonetheless many of its features reinforce the traditional values of the city. As is the case with many of the works discussed in this and the following chapter, elements of innovation in form or design were understood less as a challenge to 'Venetian tradition' than as an opportunity for its further definition or realization.

Ca'Foscari provides, indeed, a fine example of the kind of domestic palace architecture that had first emerged some two

Fig.9
Bartolomeo Bon (?)
Ca'Foscari

See Fig.10. Detail of the first- and second-storey windows of Ca'Foscari with, above, marble reliefs of putti bearing the Foscari arms.

centuries before, and that had since become characteristic in the city. It features a three-fold division on its facade, with the all-important central part emphasized by the window arcades. These openings front a large living space within, known as the *portego*, while the so-called *androne*, or ground floor, is left relatively plain, reflecting its more humdrum function as a place of business where the family's merchandise was stored. It has a single unadorned water entrance to facilitate the arrival and departure of goods and services. The popularity of this kind of *casa fondaco*, a private residence which also functioned as a warehouse, is an indication that Venetian patricians saw their mercantile activities as wholly consistent with their status as noblemen. This merchant–noble combination was quite anomalous, given that aristocracies across much of Europe were especially concerned to distance themselves from the perceived taint of trade. The visual openness of the facade design of Ca'Foscari, with its emphasis on ornate patterns of fenestration, rather than on the indications of defensive martial power common in equivalent palaces on the mainland of Italy, also gives expression to the open cultural values of the Republic. Although Foscari's new palace is larger than those of the Giustiniani nearby, it remains physically connected to them and shares the same essentials of design. Indeed, the three facades were always intended to make up a single architectural front around the wide curve of the Grand Canal at this point. The effect of physical and decorative unity between the palaces gives visual expression to patrician values of communality and also suggests the limits that this placed on more individualistic forms of expression.

All three facades make particularly insistent reference to the architecture of the Ducal Palace. The cusped Gothic window arches with quatrefoil mouldings above the second storey on Ca'Foscari are particularly derivative. Such borrowings were as relevant to the Giustiniani family as they were to Doge Foscari himself, current leader of the Venetian state. They can also be seen as a sign of the continuing grip of 'official' or public values in Venice in the mid-fifteenth century, even in the apparently more private domain of the family home. The most notable new element on the facade of Ca'Foscari, the large and prominent marble relief insert above the upper row of windows featuring *all'antica* reliefs of naked putti bearing the Foscari coat of arms, is not so radical a departure from precedent as it might first appear (FIG. 9). Stone or marble framing panels had long been used to enclose and highlight the *piano-nobile* (main floor) windows in Venetian palaces, a practice which might have its origin in Islamic architecture. In this case, however, the architect – probably Bartolomeo Bon – more directly adapted the pairs of

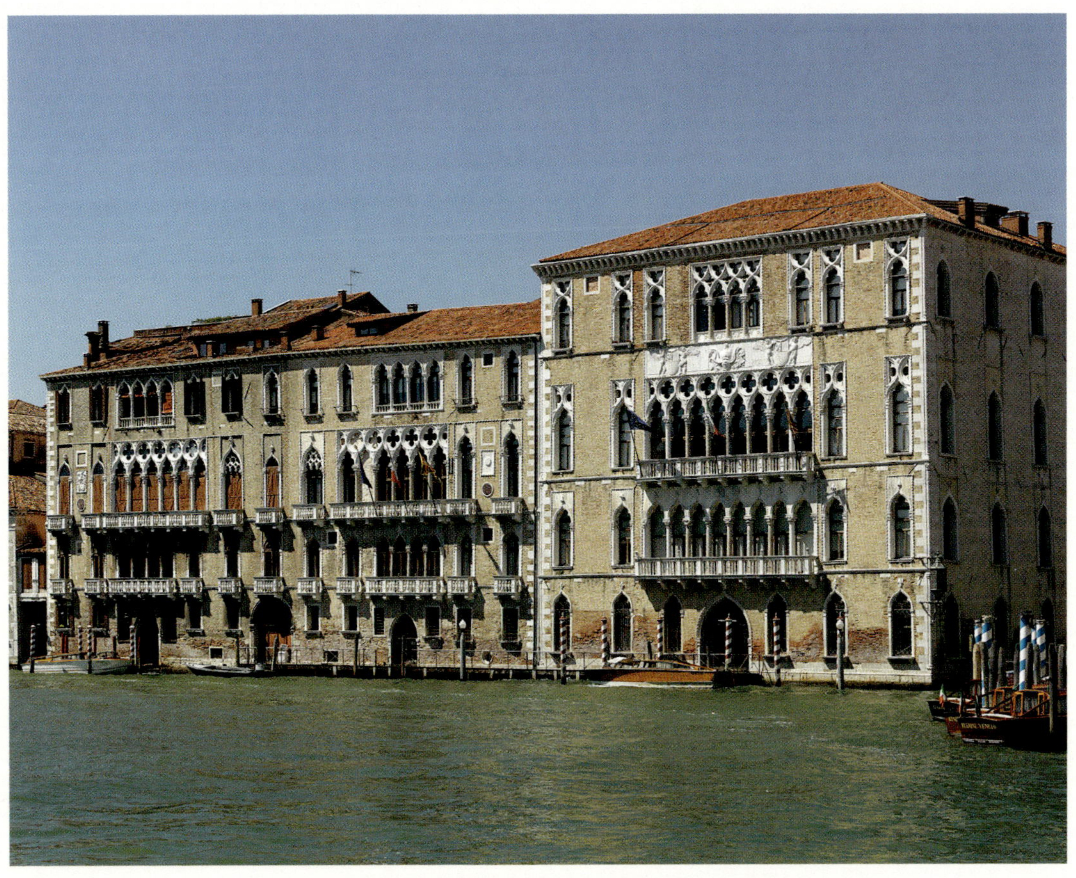

putti he had previously featured on the upper part of the Porta della Carta, where they also hold up the Foscari coat of arms (*see* FIG. 7). The reuse of the motif may be a sign of Foscari's individualistic concern for visibility in Venice. Yet its transfer from an official to a domestic context might equally be understood as a sign of continuity between public and private life in Venice in the mid-fifteenth century. On the facade of Ca'Foscari, as on the Porta della Carta, the *all'antica* putti reliefs are comfortably integrated into a primarily Gothic design. In both cases, classically derived nudes occur on the facades of prominent architectural structures, indicating that the Renaissance in Venice initially showed itself in an essentially open and public context.

Built 1453–7 for Doge Francesco Foscari. Left bank of the Grand Canal, Venice. To the left are the two near-contemporary *palazzi* owned by the Giustiniani family.

Painting in two Venetian chapels of the mid-fifteenth century

A similarly fluid mixture of Gothic and Renaissance styles is apparent in paintings from the period, such as those in the San Tarasio Chapel at the church of San Zaccaria, commissioned under the auspices of the doge's sister, Elena Foscari, abbess of the presiding Benedictine convent. Three altarpieces by the prominent painters Antonio Vivarini (ca. 1418–ca. 1480) and Giovanni d'Alemagna (active 1441–1450) were complemented, in the spaces between the arches above, by a series of ultra-progressive frescoes by the young Florentine Andrea del Castagno (1423–1457) (FIG. 11). The altarpiece illustrated here may deliberately recall the renowned Byzantine Pala d'Oro ('altarpiece of gold') erected on the High Altar in St Mark's in the mid-fourteenth century, insofar as it too is free-standing and painted on both sides. A visual connection to the glittering mosaics and Gothic crockets and pinnacles featured in the 'mother church' was in any case essential to its conception. Like many other Venetian altarpieces of the time, the work shows rows of saints, both painted and sculpted, who are lined up either side of a larger image of the Virgin and Child (though this latter panel, and those of Saints Martin and Blaise to either side, are not original to the ensemble). The sacred figures are presented in a manner that discourages our perception of them as realistic three-dimensional forms in space. Instead, we are made aware of the altarpiece's status as a physical object through the emphasis given to its highly coloured and ornately wrought surfaces. The elaborate mouldings of the frame, covered in expensive gold leaf, dominate the painted field, flattening the surface while also asserting its expressive priority.

The painting of the altarpiece itself also interacts with the stone altar below it, which shares some of its carved features, suggesting that it too was intended as an integral part of the design. The mixed media effect reflects the range of craftsmen involved. Vivarini and d'Alemagna's partnership indicates the collaborative nature of such a pictorial enterprise. We do not know the name of the stone-carver, but that of the frame-maker and gilder, Lodovico da Forlì (active 1425–76), is boldly inscribed on the altarpiece surface, indicating that he was perceived as having an equal part in its creation. Individual authorship was apparently less important than the success of the overall visual ensemble, utilizing a range of artists and materials.

The altarpiece appears to possess its own internally derived illumination, rather than depending on natural light from the windows behind. Nonetheless, the work is conceived in accordance with the verticality of the Gothic architecture of the chapel itself, and

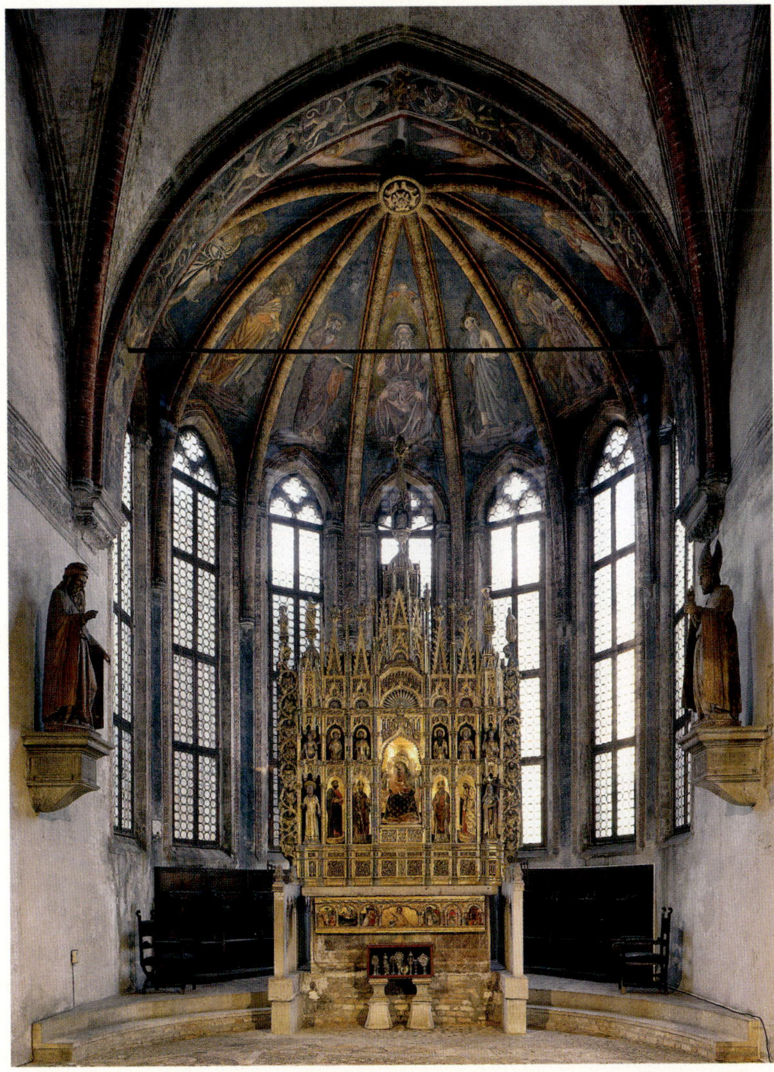

especially with the narrow pointed shapes of the windows behind it. Above these, Castagno painted monumental frescoed figures of God and the saints, his large and powerfully formed figures markedly more three-dimensional than those in the altarpiece below. He had recently arrived from the artistically progressive city of Florence and introduced an emphasis on illusionistic forms that was unprecedented in Venice. There is little evidence that anyone other than the painter himself was involved in making this novel stylistic departure. But Castagno and his patrons probably saw the frescoes simply as part of an on-going programme of unified decoration. His monumental sacred figures supported the altarpieces, just as they respond to the

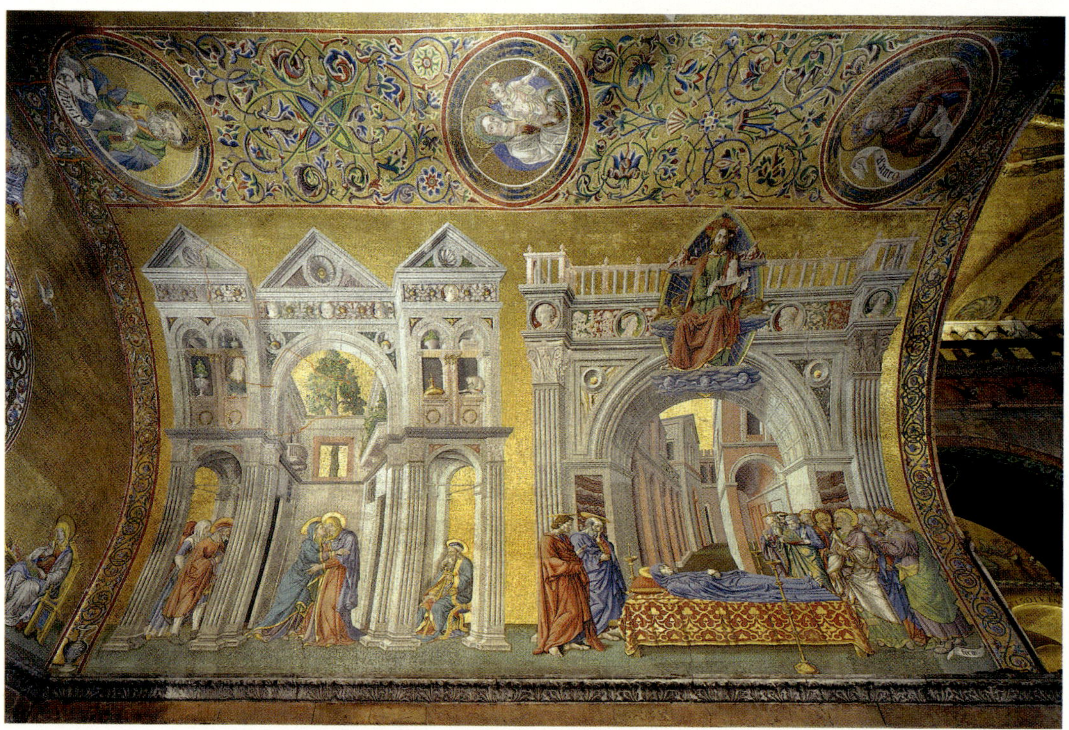

narrow Gothic spaces of the chapel wall itself. It may even be that the severe suppression of colour in Castagno's monumental forms was calculated to offset and highlight the richly decorative approach of the High Altarpiece and other works below. Rather than seeing Castagno as an outsider, whose approach had little to do with the other craftsmen working in the chapel, it would be more accurate to understand his frescoes as extending further the existing local ethos of medium and stylistic diversity. It is no accident that Castagno's enormous seated figure of God the Father appears directly above the Virgin and Child in the altarpiece below, his vast and looming figure quite literally pointed out by the extended central pinnacle of its frame.

Castagno's contribution to the mosaic decorations on the barrel-vaulted ceiling of the Mascoli Chapel in St Mark's was similar in kind (FIG. 12). In this context, too, a range of craftsmen and artists were engaged to complete the decoration, and stylistic variety was central to the overall effect. At a technical level, the use of mosaic immediately related the new work, probably initiated under Doge Foscari's auspices in the 1430s, to the extensive cycles on the ceilings of St Mark's created over the course of the previous centuries. The decoration of the chapel was no longer left to the mosaic specialists alone, however, and is an early example of a division of labour between 'artists' and 'craftsmen' that was to become typical in the Renaissance. Leading painters in the city provided cartoons or designs which the anonymous mosaicists followed. However, in the Mascoli Chapel, the idea of individualized authorship that this proceeding suggests was still offset by the involvement of different painters working in diverse styles. And the work of the mosaicists to create a shimmering surface of glass tesserae on the wall surface remains decisive to the overall decorative effect.

Building on the sense of continuity provided by the mosaic medium, no single artistic style gains the upper hand in the Mascoli Chapel. Thus, if the earlier images featuring scenes from the life of the Virgin on the north side of the chapel were completed by the late Gothic artist Michele Giambono (ca. 1395–1462), then those showing the *Visitation* and the *Dormition* on the opposite wall appear to be based on designs provided by Castagno. The severity of Castagno's manner is apparent enough in the massive architectural settings featuring fluted pilasters and Corinthian capitals: classical features still rarely to be found in the built environment of Venice at this date. In the *Dormition*, in particular, the overall impression is of a monumental Roman triumphal arch. The novel idea of a city-scape of contemporary-looking buildings, whose facades and angled edges recede through a foreground arch, indicates the involvement of a third artist: Jacopo Bellini (ca. 1400–1470/71), the leading painter in the city, who included similar examples in two famous sketchbooks to be discussed below. Few of the figures in the Mascoli mosaics have the simple grandeur of Castagno's San Tarasio frescoes. In the *Dormition*, for example, only the two apostles to the left approach his kind of monumentality, while the less individuated group to the right, supporting the perspective recession, are closer to Bellini's approach. On the other hand, the mandorla (almond-shaped area of light) containing God the Father and the infant Christ above might suggest the contribution of a third hand: perhaps that of Giambono again, whose name, with the date 1451, appears on the wall surface nearby. His dense and linear style has relatively little in common with that of either Castagno or Bellini.

The combination of artists at work in the Mascoli Chapel must owe something, at least, to the start–stop progress of the original commission, which was initially given to Giambono before Castagno intervened in the early 1440s. Castagno's departure from the city in 1442 caused another delay, before Giambono and Bellini brought the decoration to a conclusion. But quite apart from this, there is no sense that the stylistic variation evident in the chapel was perceived as a problem, either by the artists themselves or their patrons.

Elements of Castagno's Florentine solemnity are readily combined with naturalistic motifs introduced by Bellini, while the liquid light reflecting from the mosaics themselves provides a more traditional sense of the integrity of an ornately worked surface. In this regard, too, it is significant that despite the impression of coherent three-dimensional perspective space in the painted architecture, the radical curvature of the vaulted wall intervenes to undermine its planarity.

Space and figure in Jacopo Bellini's drawings

By 1450 Jacopo Bellini's painter's workshop had already superseded that of Vivarini and d'Alemagna as the most prominent in the city. Jacopo had been profoundly influenced by the work of Gentile da Fabriano (ca. 1370–1427), whose florid, late Gothic style had become popular in Venice following his visit to the city earlier in the century. As Jacopo's contribution to the mosaic cycle in the Mascoli Chapel shows, he made attempts to incorporate formal innovations into his public commissions in Venice. He owes his reputation as a founding father of the Renaissance in Venice, however, to two surviving albums of drawings, now housed in the Louvre in Paris (ca. 1435–1440) and in the British Museum in London (ca. 1455–1460), which contain a range of imagery that cannot be matched in the field of contemporary painting. Many drawings in fifteenth-century Italy followed the late medieval pattern-book tradition of carefully made studies used in workshops for training purposes and as a source of motifs for subsequent use in paintings. Artists such as Antonio Pisanello (ca. 1395–ca. 1455) from Verona, whom Jacopo met on a visit to the north Italian court of the d'Este in Ferrara in 1441, had already shown that drawing could offer new opportunities as a medium suitable for the observation of everyday life. Jacopo went further still: if some of his drawings indicate an acute interest in the world around him, others are imaginative artistic inventions. Approaching the medium in this fluid way, Jacopo greatly expanded the range of visual art in Venice, producing images of animals (especially lions); genre scenes and landscapes; urban and architectural views; male and female nudes; recordings of antique fragments and inscriptions; horsemen, jousters and soldiers; corpses, funerary monuments and tombs; as well as more familiar religious subjects from the lives of the saints, or the Old and New Testaments.

Many of Jacopo's drawings feature a carefully constructed linear perspective, along the lines developed in the 1420s and 1430s by Filippo Brunelleschi (1377–1446) and Leon Battista Alberti (1404–

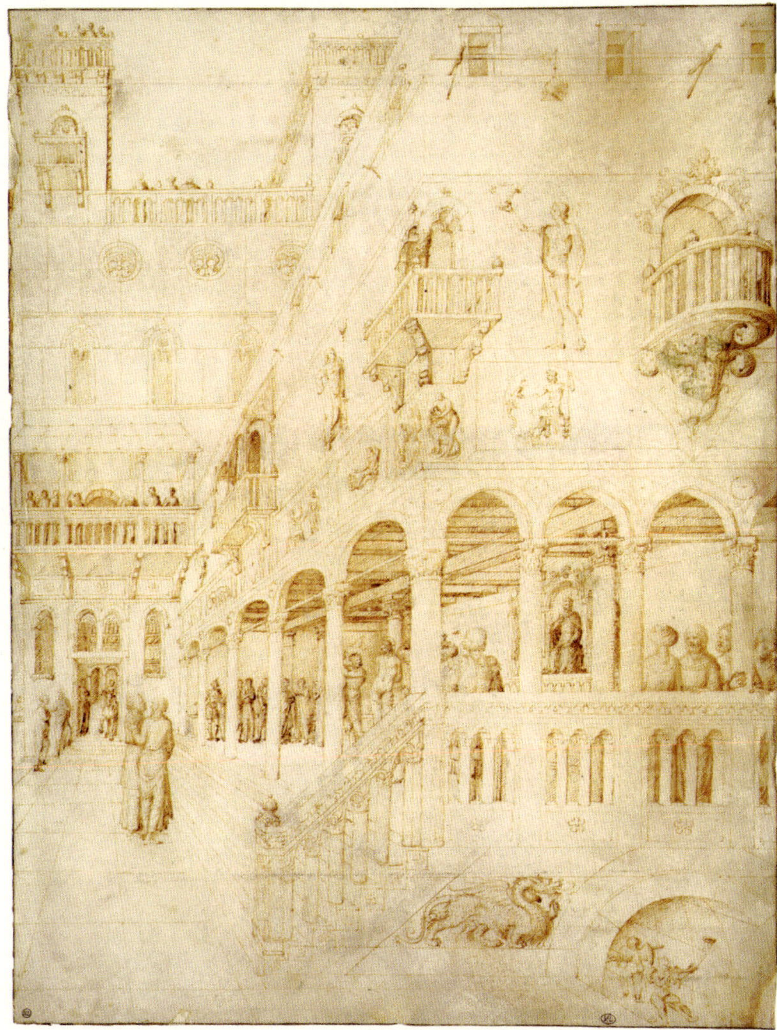

1472) in Florence. Jacopo had met Alberti in Ferrara, and may well have read his recently published treatise on painting, which advocated a mathematically derived use of linear perspective. Jacopo's keen interest in this topic contradicts the later idea that Venetian artists were not concerned with the more scientific aspects of art introduced in the early Renaissance. The importance of line, rather than colour or texture, is a central feature of Jacopo's drawings, the black and white of his medium releasing his imagination to explore new spatial and figurative possibilities. Drawings such as his *Flagellation of Christ* are set in a city-space which certainly recalls the centre of Venice, while never being identifiable with it (FIG. 13). The open loggia at the bottom of the building to the right, with its broad expanse of wall

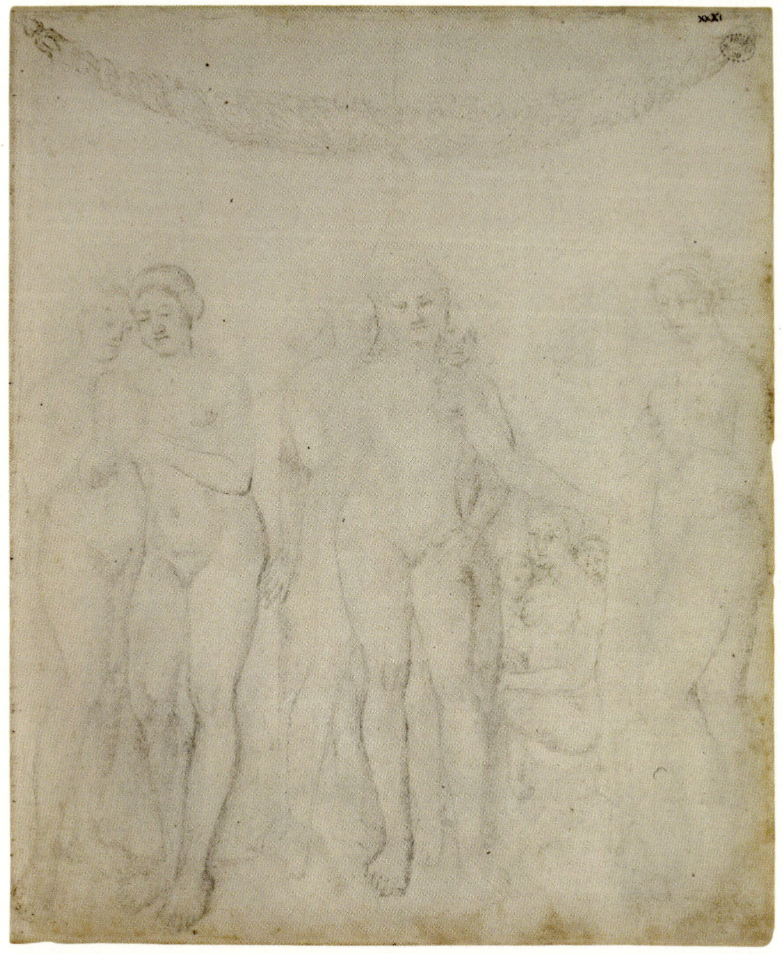

above, punctuated by elaborate balconies, has something in common with the Ducal Palace. However, Jacopo's building has just one arcade and is decorated with frescoes showing pagan subjects. The facades of many buildings in Venice were also covered in paintings, such that on a trip down the Grand Canal in 1495, one visitor dubbed it an '*urbs picta*' or painted city. The classical nudes featured on the walls of Jacopo's building were meant to identify it as a building of Roman antiquity: Pontius Pilate's palace in Jerusalem, where the Flagellation of Christ took place. Pilate is glimpsed seated on his throne to the right, impassively looking on as Christ is beaten. The heroic nudes featured in the fictive facade paintings certainly demonstrate Jacopo's interest in classical relief sculpture. They also serve to distance his imagined pagan city from the pious Christian present of Venice, while also generating a sense of the work as an accurate 'history' or *istoria*.

Jacopo's perspective serves to present the narrative in a way that was to become particularly fashionable in Venice. It is clear enough from the receding pavement to the left that Jacopo establishes a Florentine-style system of linear transversals and orthogonals to establish spatial recession. His figures are also dispersed with reference to this grid-like system, their relative sizes and positions in space plotted with almost naïve accuracy along the lines receding from the picture plane. But there is something more meaningful going on in Jacopo's construction of pictorial space. The vanishing point towards which these lines recede is moved to the left, deliberately drawing the viewer's eye away from the figures of Christ and Pilate to the right, so that we do not immediately realize that there is a significant event occurring. In this regard, Jacopo might appear not to understand the kind of classical painted *istoria* proposed by Alberti, in which the main action was placed in the centre foreground; but Jacopo repeatedly returned to this idea of burying the narrative within a carefully depicted environment in his drawings. This approach was subsequently taken up in large-scale history paintings by his sons Gentile and Giovanni and their followers. By embedding the core sacred or miraculous subject matter of their paintings into carefully elaborated compositions, these artists sought also to supply it with an added sense of validity or truth.

In drawings of religious subjects such as the *Flagellation*, Jacopo's recovery of classical types went alongside his interpretation of them as false pagan idols. In others, Jacopo took a more objective interest in surviving fragments of classical relief sculpture. In works such as the *Nude Women and Children*, he evinces a more independent kind of interest again (FIG. 14). Although the lead-point lines have faded, it is clear that the scene was set within a curving three-dimensional space that was not based on a classical relief. Jacopo's feminine figures remain upright and those to left and right, holding a mirror and an orb, possess an air of allegorical abstraction. But they nonetheless evoke a quality of immediate physical presence and a sense of intimacy. The young women confidently occupy and command the space, even if their exact identities and location remain uncertain. Is this Venus, the classical goddess of love, who suddenly enters with her two acolytes through the vulva-like rent of the curtain at centre stage, to catch our eye? Or are we presented with a more voyeuristic genre-type view of a contemporary Venetian bath house, where women and their children gather to bathe? In either case, it is clear that the young protagonists have already escaped their imaginative moorings in the distant classical past to confront the viewer in a way that looks forward to the erotic nudes often featured in Venetian paintings of the following century.

Despite the immediacy and spontaneity in examples such as this, the majority of Jacopo's drawings are careful finished studies. Those in the London book are meticulously laid out using fine metalpoint, while those in Paris are drawn on expensive parchment. Some, at least, were intended as models for future use in large-scale public paintings. In 1472, just a year or two after his death, Jacopo's workshop completed a painting for St Mark's based on a drawing of the *Lamentation over Christ at the Tomb* (FIGS 15, 16). It may be that both drawing and painting involved collaboration between father and sons. Like the other drawings in the Louvre book, the *Lamentation* appears to have been reworked in pen and ink, probably by Gentile (ca. 1429–1507), who inherited both sketchbooks on his father's death. The related painting is an example of the two sons completing an unfinished work begun by their recently deceased father. The broad but powerfully focussed lighting of Christ's body and head may indicate the input of Giovanni (ca. 1431–1516), Jacopo's especially talented younger son, whose name was once visible on the *cartellino* (tag) attached to the front of Christ's tomb. The more minute and detailed style of his elder brother is evident in the tightly handled forms of the two saints to either side.

Jacopo's *Lamentation* drawing was particularly influential. Giovanni had already drawn closely on it in his recent *Pietà* (ca. 1467–8, Milan, Pinacoteca di Brera) and it continued to influence both him and other painters in subsequent versions of this theme from the 1470s. Such threads of influence indicate just how important Jacopo's extraordinary sketchbooks were to the development of

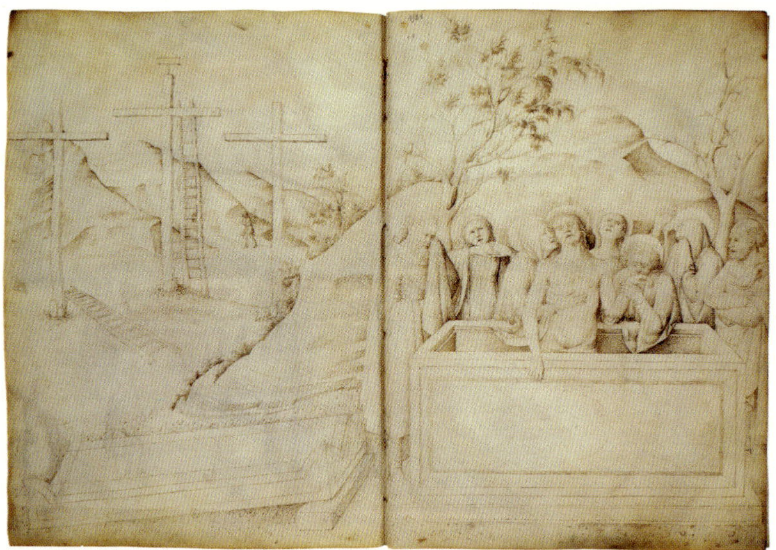

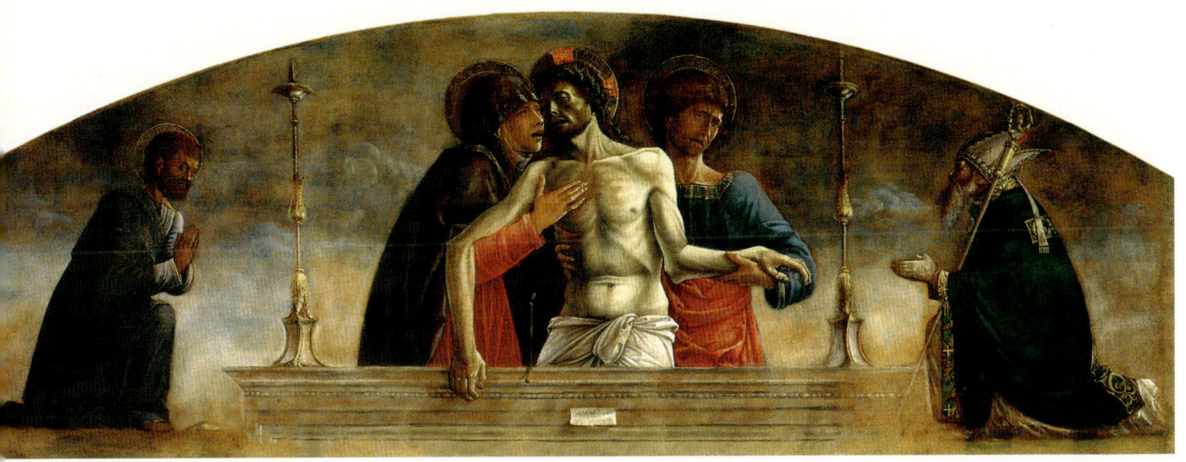

painting in Venice in the later fifteenth century. Long afterwards, in the mid- and later sixteenth century, it was claimed by hostile Central Italian artists and writers that the Venetians cared little about drawing, or *disegno*, when making a painting. Jacopo's sketchbooks and their influence suggest otherwise, indicating that drawing was very important to their artistic process. In Jacopo's hands, drawing was not merely a way of getting closer to nature; it was also a means of realizing a powerful artistic idea or conception. The *Lamentation* was one of Jacopo's two-page spreads, including a naturalistic landscape with trees and hills to the left, but it is nonetheless a carefully contrived and monumental work. Focussing on the sacred figures, Jacopo used affective detail to heighten religious meaning. The Virgin's action – pressing her face against that of her dead Son – indicates her spontaneous grief, while providing the viewer with a model response to Christ's death. Only Christ's limp arm, symbolically pointing downwards towards the earth, is allowed to break through the forward plane of the composition established by the front of the tomb. Although its presence is now difficult to see, it is likely that Christ's revealed hand insistently presented his stigmata, insisting on immediate recognition and emotional response from the viewer.

Padua and its impact

The work of the great Florentine sculptor Donatello (ca. 1386–1466) in nearby Padua also had a major impact on art in Venice in these decades. Padua had only recently (in 1406) come under Venetian control, and continued to possess a very independent 'mainland' or westward-facing culture. Humanistic studies were well established at its famous University, and a keen interest in the literature and art of classical Greece and Rome had been evident for more than a century. Artistic influence from Tuscany was significant, from the time of Giotto's frescoes in the Scrovegni Chapel (ca. 1305) onwards. Donatello's work on the *Gattamelata* monument and on the High Altar of the nearby pilgrimage church of the Santo between 1443 and 1453 now produced a sense of the artistic possibilities raised by the three-dimensionality of sculptural form that was quickly registered in Venice. Jacopo Bellini's drawings, like certain of his paintings, were influenced by the mix of formal monumentality and human expressiveness that Donatello's sculptural example provided. Donatello's work demonstrated a newly heroic model for art that ignored the sensual allure of the highly wrought and encrusted surfaces in the Gothic tradition.

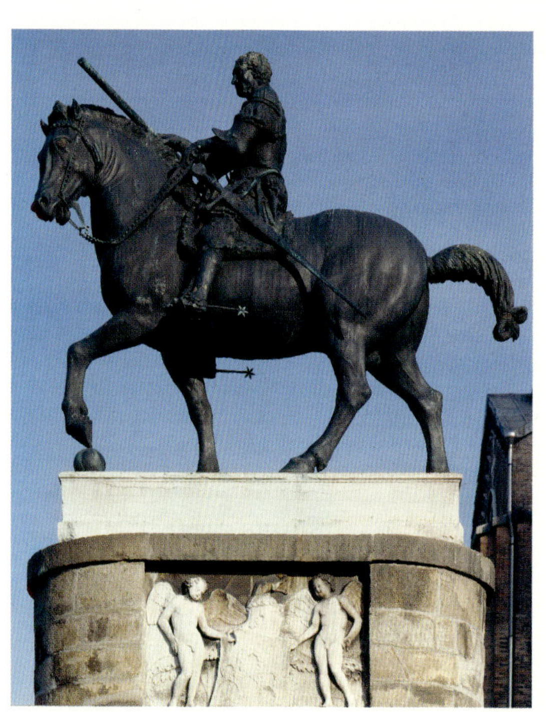

Fig. 17
Donatello
Equestrian statue of
Gattamelata with base

1453. Bronze, height ca.
340cm (11ft 1⅞in). Piazza
del Santo, Padua.

Standing in the centre of the town square, the statue of *Gattamelata* did not rely on a supporting structure or wall beyond its base (FIG. 17). To this extent, it offered a radical departure from the usual habit of embedding sculptural forms into the architectural fabric (*see* FIG. 7). In Venice, this intimate relationship was reflected in the professional organization of the artists concerned. Sculptors and architects were not clearly distinguished from one another and belonged to the same stonemasons' guild (the *arte dei tagliapietra*). Donatello, on the other hand, offered an example of how sculpture could be released from architecture into a state of fully independent three-dimensionality. Although the monument honoured 'Gattamelata' (Erasmo di Narni), the famous mercenary who had won many battles in the service of Venice, in Donatello's hands it served as a vehicle for an intense expression of individual will and power. With its boldly contrasting vertical and horizontal elements, which seem to reflect the essentials of nature itself, Donatello's sculpture was very far from expressing the peaceable collective and mercantile values of the Republic.

It also revived the antique type of the life-sized equestrian bronze, known from surviving examples such as the *Marcus Aurelius* monument in Rome. The studied aspect of Donatello's horseman, as a self-conscious modern recreation of an antique model, owes much to the humanist atmosphere in mid-fifteenth-century Padua, where a parallel concern with the recovery of accurate

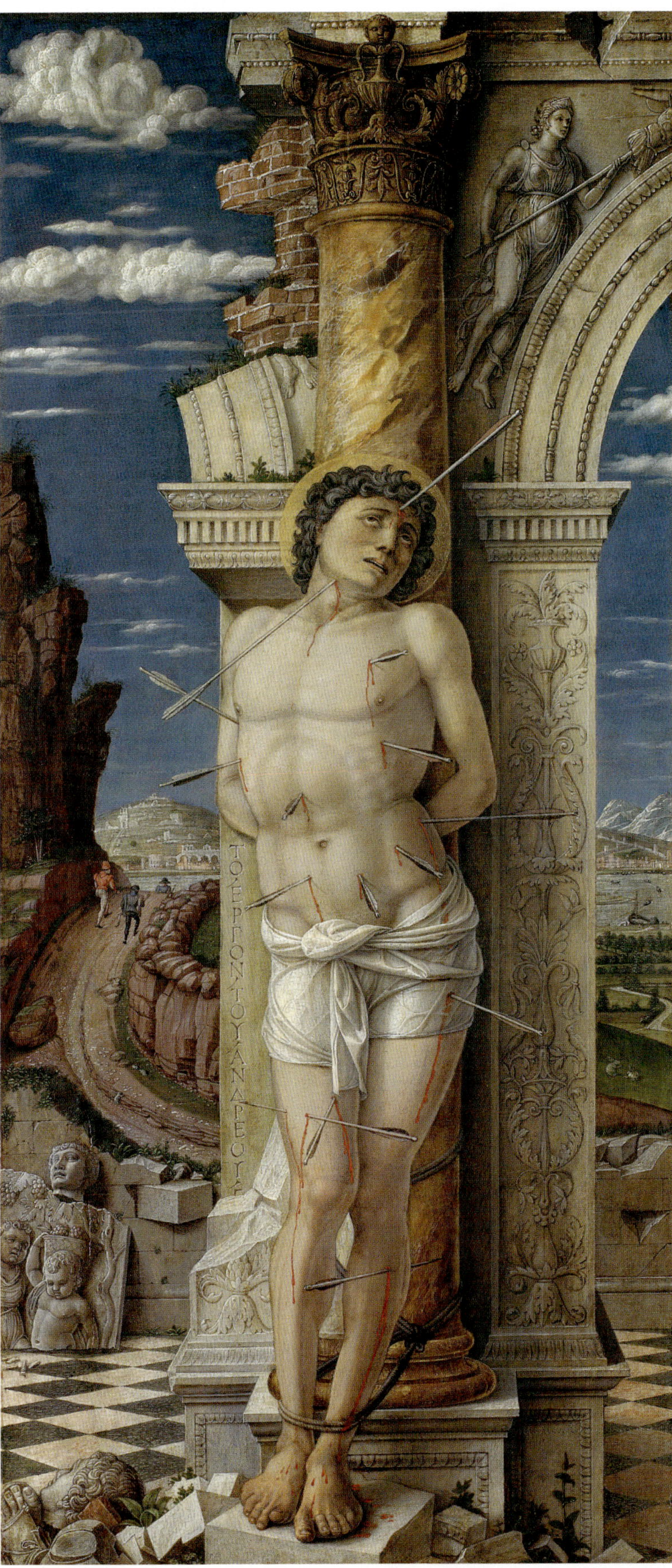

Fig. 18
Andrea Mantegna
St Sebastian

ca. 1459. Tempera on panel,
68 × 30cm (2ft 2¾in × 11¾in).
Kunsthistorisches Museum,
Vienna.

This painting is probably a
private devotional work made
for the patrician collector
Jacopo Marcello, and may
have been painted shortly
before Mantegna left Padua
to become court painter
to the Gonzaga family in
Mantua. Details such as the
Victory in the spandrel
of the arch, and the rider
in the cloud at the upper
left, probably allude to the
Christian conquest of the
pagan world.

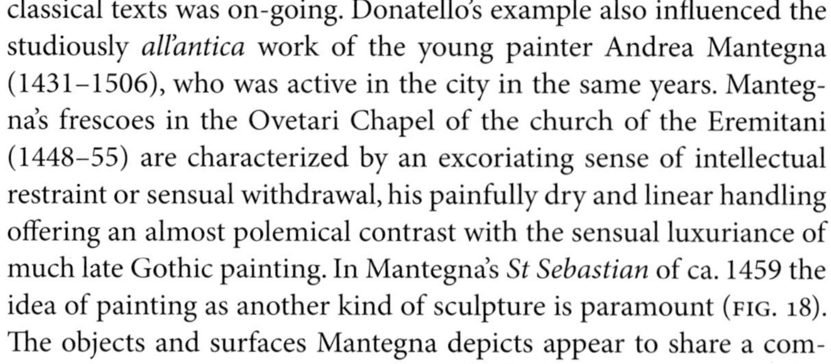

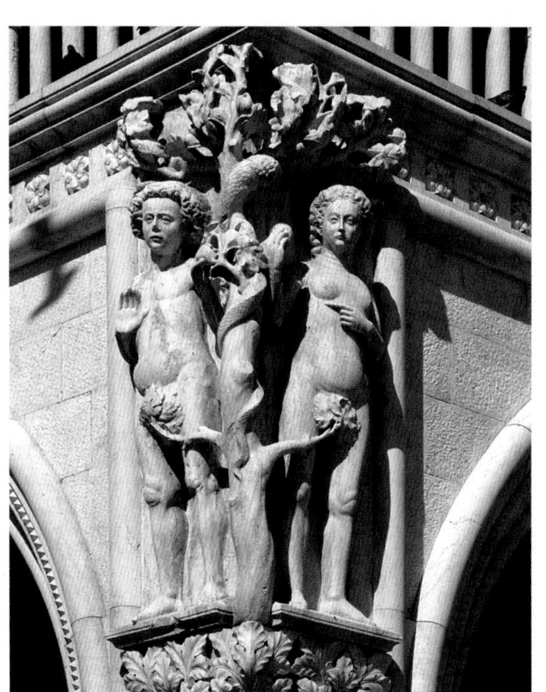

classical texts was on-going. Donatello's example also influenced the studiously *all'antica* work of the young painter Andrea Mantegna (1431–1506), who was active in the city in the same years. Mantegna's frescoes in the Ovetari Chapel of the church of the Eremitani (1448–55) are characterized by an excoriating sense of intellectual restraint or sensual withdrawal, his painfully dry and linear handling offering an almost polemical contrast with the sensual luxuriance of much late Gothic painting. In Mantegna's *St Sebastian* of ca. 1459 the idea of painting as another kind of sculpture is paramount (FIG. 18). The objects and surfaces Mantegna depicts appear to share a common stony quality, which also serves to express the religious theme. He generates tragic meaning from the continuity between the saint's tortured flesh and the fragmented architecture and sculpture that surround it. Only when the Christian martyr Sebastian finally dies, and is no longer a part of this ruined and broken physical world, will he escape its agonies. Classical ruination (with special reference to Ancient Rome, where Sebastian was martyred) also tells the story of Christian spiritual victory over pagan worldly pretension. Yet it appears, too, that Mantegna was independently enraptured with the classical remains he depicts, recording their appearance with the painstaking attention of a painter-cum-archaeologist. His striking depiction of Sebastian's body tellingly uses the kind of *contrapposto* (a pose contrasting relaxed and tensed limbs) found in ancient sculpture.

Mantegna married into the Bellini family in 1453, and both he and Donatello were subsequently influential on the early development of Giovanni's painting. Their influence was perhaps more lasting on the development of sculpture in Venice, as is evident from two marbles made by Antonio Rizzo (before 1430– after 1499) for the inner side of the entrance to the Ducal Palace known as the Arco Foscari. A brief comparison with the earlier relief sculptures on the corner of the palace facade, probably by Filippo Calendario (before 1315-1355) shows just how far Rizzo had been influenced by the Renaissance examples from Padua. Despite the hint of classicism given in the large heads and tightly curled hair of Calendario's figures, their flattened bodies fundamentally conform to the dictates of the supporting walls, emphasizing the change of direction at the southwest corner of the palace (FIG. 19). As with the sculptures on the Porta della Carta, the integrity of surface remains sacrosanct, and this planar conception is also supported by the lack of internal variation between the figures' limbs. In contrast, Rizzo's two near-life-size figures confidently represent three-dimensional nude bodies in movement (FIGS 20, 21). Although they stood in niches, their mobile forms assert an independence from this architectural structure that remind us of Donatello's precedent. Rizzo's figures are, indeed, shot through with a new sense of the lesson to be learned from the antique, appearing as fully fledged sensuous nudes, whose bodies are realistic physical entities made up of bones, sinews and muscles.

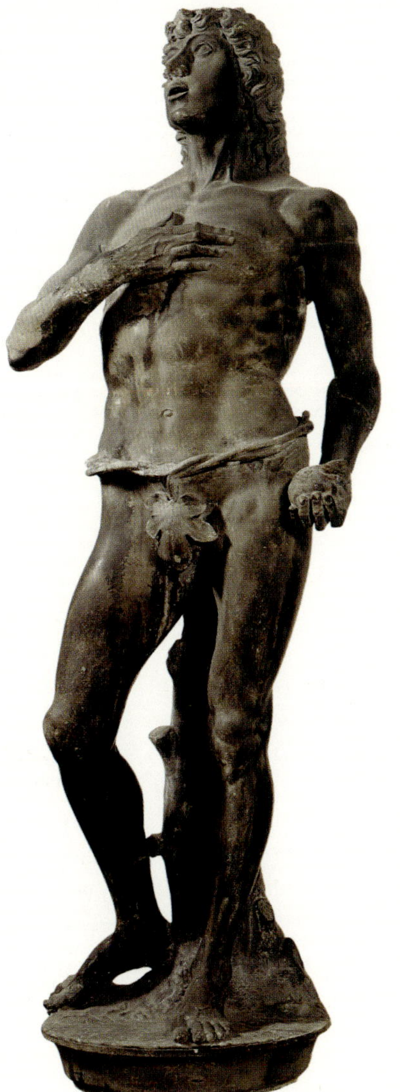

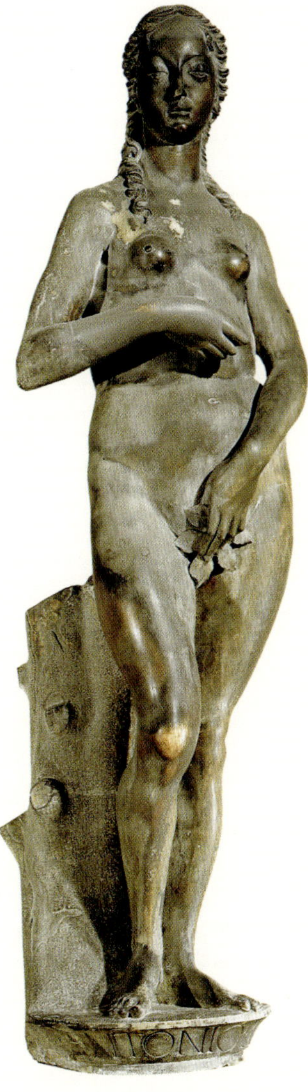

Fig. 20
Antonio Rizzo
Adam

ca. 1471–4. Marble, height 205cm (6ft 8¾in). Sala del Maggior Consiglio, Ducal Palace, Venice.

Fig. 21
Antonio Rizzo
Eve

ca. 1471–4. Marble, height 202cm (6ft 7½in). Sala del Maggior Consiglio, Ducal Palace, Venice.

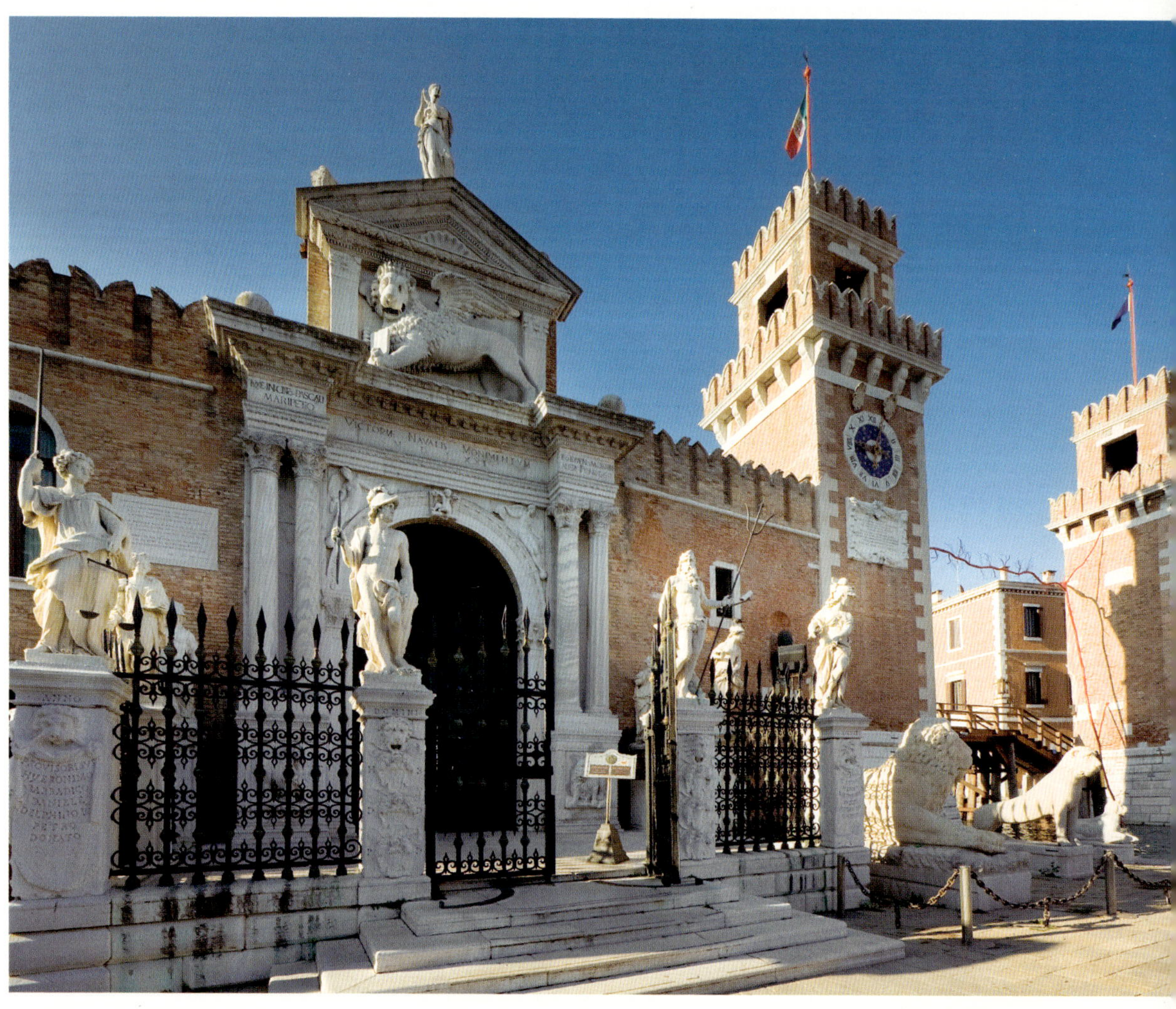

Rizzo's sculptures feature a carefully articulated antique-style *contrapposto* between arms and legs that was essentially new to sculpture in Venice, allowing their forms to move independently in space. Eve is modelled on the antique type of the *Venus pudica* (the 'Venus of modesty', who covers her genitals with one hand), well known in the period from works such as the so-called *Medici Venus* in Florence. She is, however, carefully contrasted with Adam, who looks up to God the Father in heaven like a pleading saint with an expression of intense remorse. His posture, with head turned away from his body and imploring upward gaze, is similar to that of Mantegna's *St Sebastian*. Similar, too, is the way in which the outward movements of the body are made to express the figure's inner feelings, even though Adam's suffering is psychological rather than physical. Like other artists in Venice, however, Rizzo's response to classicism was not narrowly contained by accuracy to antique type or protocol. It was warm and sensual rather than intellectual or programmatic, and also asserted continuity with the late Gothic tradition that it appeared to rebel against. A measure of stylistic eclecticism is still evident in his work. The upper part of Eve's body, with its small oval head and narrow sloping shoulders, is closer to Netherlandish models than to art in Padua, and might even indicate the sculptor's awareness of the naked figure of Eve in Jan van Eyck's Ghent altarpiece (1432, Ghent, St Bavo's Cathedral). In contrast to Adam, she looks down towards the viewer, suggesting worldly complicity, half-concealing the apple in her right hand as if still unable to realize the consequences of her actions. The contrast this provides with Adam's open upward posture might be a sign of Rizzo's continuing attachment to the moralistic (and misogynistic) late medieval tradition of negative representations of Eve. To this extent, Rizzo's figure remains far from the sensual female nudes that became fashionable in Venice after 1500. Rizzo's two figures occupied a prominent position within the ensemble of visual imagery erected around the entrance to the Ducal Palace, indicating again that classicism in Venice first emerged in public and officially sanctioned locations. The same point is relevant to another grand official entrance: the gateway to the Arsenal erected in 1460 (FIG. 22). This was where the city's many merchant and military galleys were built, and it had tellingly been described as 'the foundation of our State' by the Great Council in 1444. The new entrance, built under the auspices of Doge Pasquale Malipiero (reigned 1457–1462), was intended to serve as a tangible sign of the power of the Venetian state, and coincided with the period of maximal expansion of the city's merchant galley fleet. It has long been seen as reflecting the arrival of Renaissance architecture proper in Venice, especially as it is partially based on a specific classical model: the triumphal arch known as the Arco dei Sergi in Pola, a town in Istria (now Croatia) then under Venetian rule.

The architect – probably Antonio Gambello (active 1458–1481) – followed his model insofar as he included two pairs of free-standing columns on pedestals flanking a central archway. Other aspects of the new gateway are independent of the apparent prototype, however, having more in common with the established eclectic approach of Venice. Following a practice first used for the portals at St Mark's, the highly polished marble column shafts are reused from an older building, as are the capitals above them, which reflect the 'basket' type common in Byzantine architecture rather than Roman prototypes. The upper level has no clear precedent in Roman architecture, and Gambello may even have intended it to be seen as a later (though still 'ancient') addition. While the gateway certainly represents a landmark response to classical architecture in Venice, it is equally telling that the chosen model was a building in a non-Italian territory to the east. The Venetian state was well aware of the new threat posed by the warlike Ottoman Turks following their final destruction of the Byzantine Empire in 1453. The erection of a new triumphal gateway at the very hub of its trading and military power does not indicate that Venice had suddenly adopted the culture of the Italian mainland. Rather, it showed that Venice now saw itself as the guardian of Christendom at its newly defined frontiers to the east. If Venice did not yet imagine itself as a new Rome, it could certainly aspire to be another Byzantium.

Icons and images: early Giovanni Bellini

The impact of Donatello and Mantegna on Venetian artists is also evident from the linear and sculptural values in the early work of Giovanni Bellini. In a depiction of the *Dead Christ Supported by Two Angels*, Giovanni drew particularly closely on a bronze relief by Donatello from the High Altar of the Santo in Padua, emulating its naturalism of treatment, telling use of outline and high-pitched emotionality (FIGS 23, 24). Donatello placed a standing Christ in his tomb: an object which also serves as a parapet defining the frontal plane at bottom of the image. Two winged and haloed child angels hold up Christ's winding sheet, which also functions as a cloth of honour (a length of material often shown behind sacred figures). The derivation of Donatello's design from classical sources is evident enough in these figures, whose tunics and wet drapery style, like their symmetrical arrangement, recall the putti often featured in antique reliefs. But features such as their intense emotion and Christ's non-heroic, caved-in body owe more to late Gothic tradition. The angels appear to cry out at the dolorous sight, making them appear as the viewer's surrogates within the image, who indicate what our response should be.

In Giovanni's painting, the placement of Christ in a tomb between child angels is similar. Now, though, these figures appear to hold Christ up, their tiny hands encircling or pressing his soft flesh. In his translation of a sculptural idea into painting, Bellini also further heightens its naturalism. His Christ is less central to the picture space and the forms of the supporting angels less schematically symmetrical. He also deepens the space of the image by raising the viewpoint so that the three-dimensionality of the tomb (with its

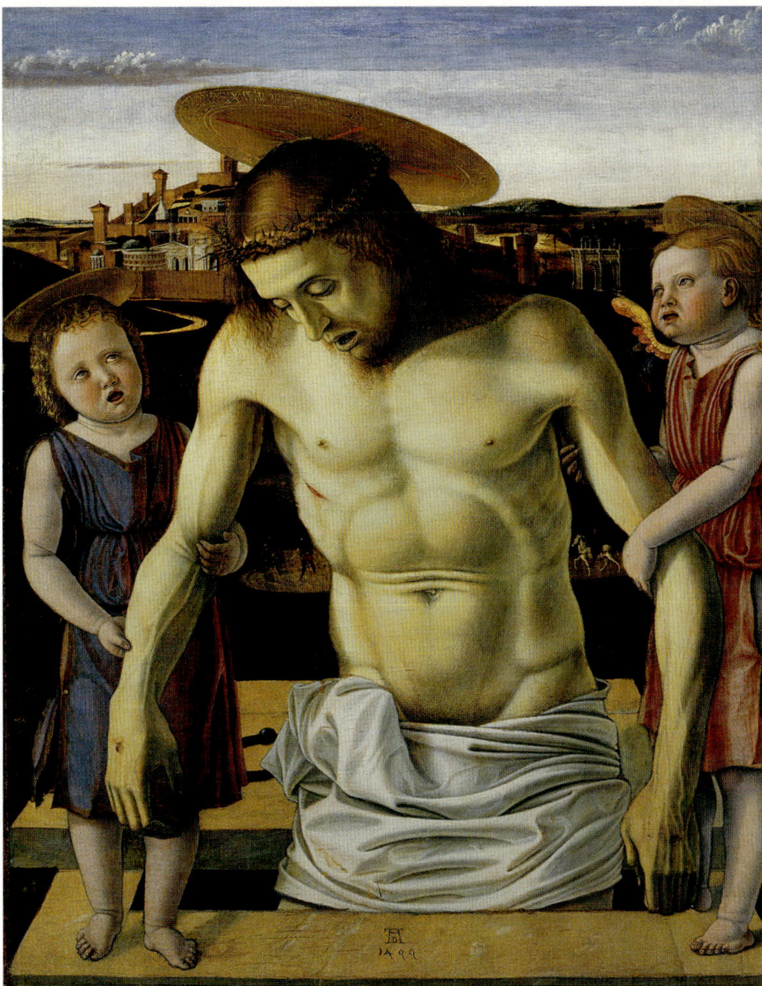

Fig. 23
Giovanni Bellini
*Dead Christ Supported by
Two Angels*

ca. 1460. Tempera on panel,
74 × 50cm (2ft 5⅛in × 1ft
7⅝in). Museo Correr,
Venice.

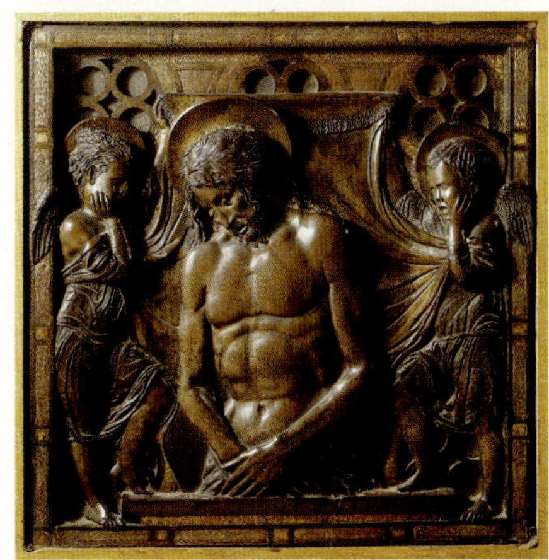

Fig. 24
Donatello
Pietà

ca. 1447–50. Bronze, 58 × 56cm
(1ft 11in × 1ft 10in).
Basilica of Il Santo
(Sant'Antonio), Padua.

displaced lid behind) becomes visible. Behind the figures is a carefully depicted landscape featuring a walled town reminiscent of those on the Venetian *terraferma* (mainland). A suggestive evening sky lightens towards the horizon and contains flecks of cloud touched by a low sun about to set. In this early painting, as in many others dating from before the 1470s, Bellini uses the traditional painting medium of tempera. That he was already able to evoke such poetic effects of light and surface suggests that his interest in such naturalistic innovations preceded his use of oil paint.

Giovanni also quickly developed the half-length Madonna and Child picture type (FIG. 25). Rather than closely following examples by his father Jacopo, he turned to the severe and sculptural style of his brother-in-law Mantegna. In the painting illustrated here, the Madonna's form is made massive and commanding by the tubular, relief-creating folds of her drapery, which recall classical statuary rather than the delicacy of Gothic painting. The unusual paleness of her robe might also be a reference to marble sculpture and supports the sombre or even funereal tone. The Madonna prays respectfully before her Son who is shown asleep, as if already dead, on a structure that follows Donatello's idea, doubling as an illusionistic parapet and a marble tomb. Resting his head on a dark cushion, and with his form pointedly turned out towards us, it is hard not to see an allusion to Christ's forthcoming sacrifice, his fleshly naked body as a sacramental offering, and the parapet as an altar. It is the Madonna who becomes our proxy within the painting, appearing to mirror the correct prayerful response of the devout viewer before the image. In many other such works by Giovanni, she is less impassive and accepting, seeking to protect the Child from his fate with hands placed across his body, or where his wounds will be on the Cross.

Throughout his long career Giovanni frequently returned to this picture type, in each work varying the same simple formal elements. A cloth of honour was typically included; a distant landscape often glimpsed; and a parapet that could be taken as a tomb or altar placed at the lower front. Using his naturalistic style, based on a close understanding of the fall of light on surfaces, the familiar type became a vehicle for a subtle exploration of a range of possible physical, psychological and symbolic relationships between the two protagonists and also between the image and the viewer. It is not entirely clear who many of the patrons for these works were, but the majority were certainly made for private locations in the home, and this is reflected in their intimate tone. Some, at least, might have hung in women's bedrooms, and it is tempting to read Giovanni's soft and delicate pictorial handling, as well as his intimate

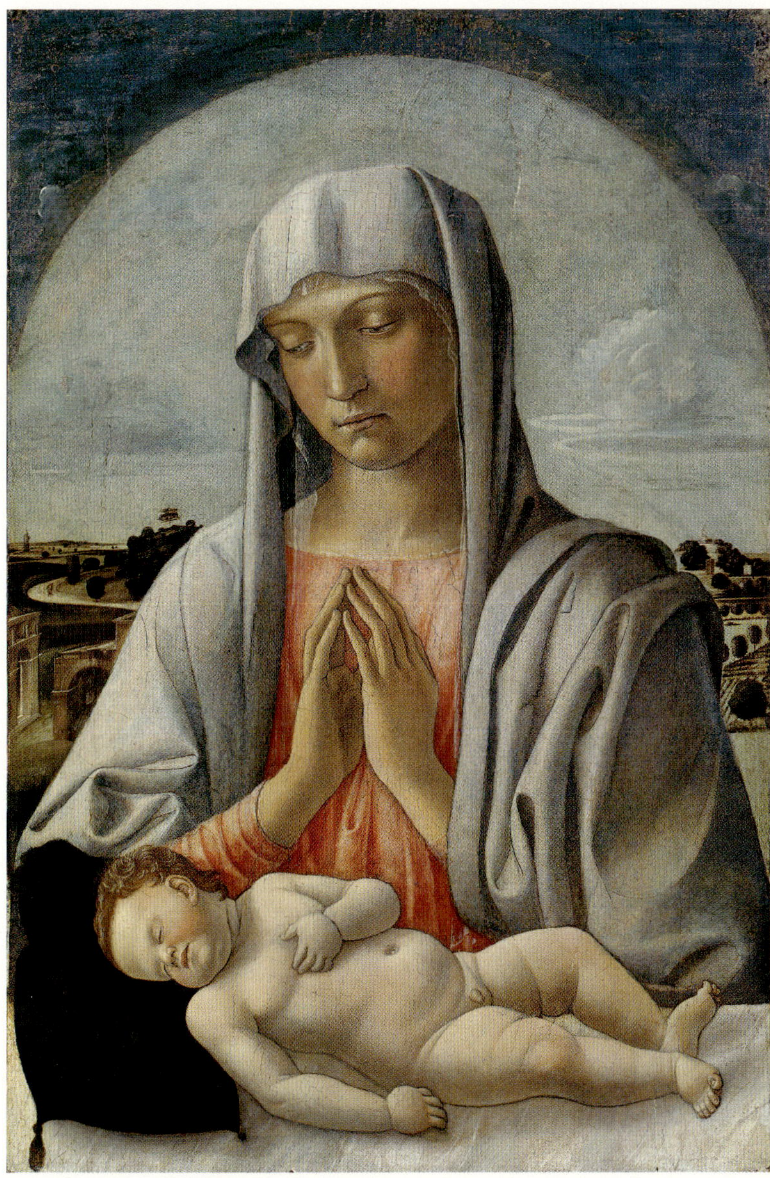

Fig. 25
Giovanni Bellini
Madonna and Child

ca. 1460–5. Tempera on
panel, 72.4 × 46.4cm
(2ft 4½in × 1ft 6¼in).
Metropolitan Museum of
Art, New York. Bequest of
Theodore M. Davis, 1915,
30.95.256.

examination of the relationship between mother and child, as a 'gendered' response to this feminine context. But the *Madonna and Child* illustrated above is indicative of the sometimes austere approach Giovanni took to this kind of picture type. The retreat of the Madonna from any direct physical or emotional contact with her Son must be taken as an indicator of his divine destiny as the saviour of mankind, as also of her doctrinal foreknowledge and acceptance of this as the mother of God.

It is sometimes assumed that Giovanni moved smoothly and progressively towards a naturalistic and forward-looking Renaissance style, jettisoning earlier Gothic and Byzantine traditions in the process. This, however, is to radically underestimate his intense imaginative engagement with such sacred subject matter, and also the sophisticated relationship of his work with earlier stylistic conventions. Like many other artists discussed in this chapter, Giovanni sought to make his formal innovations appear as traditional, integrating his newly naturalistic style with more established approaches. In many of his depictions of the Madonna and Child, the protagonists are shown in a privileged space behind a parapet, but also above and beyond the distant landscape: devices that

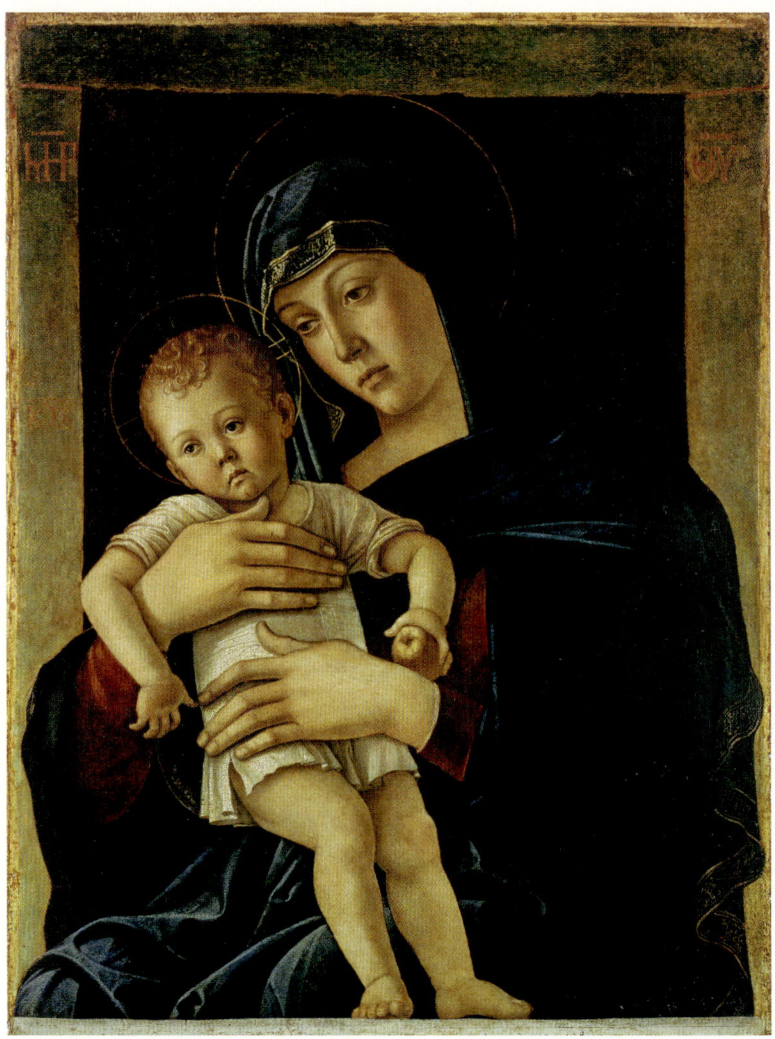

Fig. 26
Giovanni Bellini
Madonna and Child (Madonna Greca)

ca. 1470. Oil on panel, 82 × 62cm (2ft 8¼in × 2ft⅜in). Pinacoteca di Brera, Milan.

insist on a degree of separation of the divine pair from the world beyond the frame. In a painting tellingly known as the *Madonna Greca*, Giovanni downplayed the more Renaissance approach noted in the works discussed above in order to evoke the older tradition of sacred icons (FIG. 26). This painting reinstates something of the abstract flatness typical of such works, abandoning or minimizing space-defining features. The lowered viewpoint, limited model-ling of drapery, dark colouring and relatively sche-matized facial features all insistently recall the con-ventions of a Byzantine icon.

Giovanni's approach in this work can be seen as a response to another wave of cultural appropriation in Venice: one which saw the city promote itself as the natural political heir and spiritual successor to the Byzantine Empire. The donation to the Republic of a reliquary contain-ing fragments of the True Cross and a collection of Greek manuscripts by the leading Byzantine scholar and Cardinal, Johannes Bessarion, only re-emphasized this growing sense of rightful continu-ity and succession. This new 'Byzantinizing' phase further intensified a centuries-old process that, as discussed in Chapter 1, culminated in the Sack of Constantinople in 1204 and the subsequent display of items of plunder in and around St Mark's. In addition to serving as a signs of present Venetian power and dominion, these plundered items were redeployed to further intensify the city's aura of age-old religious power and sanctity. The especially precious Byzantine *Virgin Nikopoios*, for example, was held in the treasury of St Mark's, but also processed around the city during civic rituals twice a year (FIG. 27). In response to the key role of the Virgin herself in the foun-dation myth of Venice, this icon had come to be seen as an important protector of the city. It was also understood as an ancient work: a true depiction of the Virgin painted by St Luke, and acknowledged to have miraculous healing properties. When Giovanni Bellini re-called the style of such icons in the *Madonna Greca*, he did so with the especially high sanctity granted to such works fully in mind.

On the other hand, it is unlikely that Giovanni's new work was ever mistaken for a Byzantine icon. The inclusion of Greek lettering referring to Mary as the Mother of God does not take us in, given that other details, such as the cleverly handled illusion of an un-seen parapet and Christ's sharply foreshortened right foot, are more

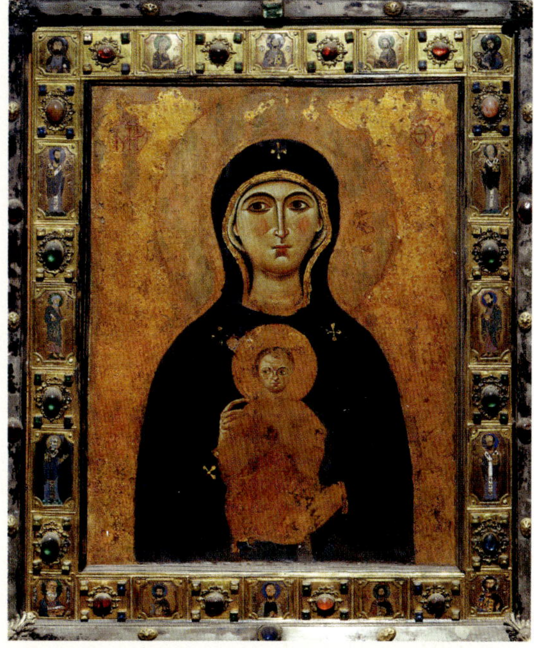

Fig. 27
Anonymous (Byzantine)
Virgin Nikopoios

Eleventh century. Tempera and gold on wood, 48 × 36cm (1ft 6⅞in × 1ft 2⅛in). St Mark's, Venice.

The suitability of the 'Virgin Nikopoios' or 'Victory-maker' type to serve as symbolic of Venetian victory and dominion is evident enough. Such works influenced many of Giovanni Bellini's depictions of the Madonna and Child. Even his most naturalistic versions typically refer to the Byzantine tradition by showing the Madonna with high cheekbones, aquiline nose and a small closed mouth.

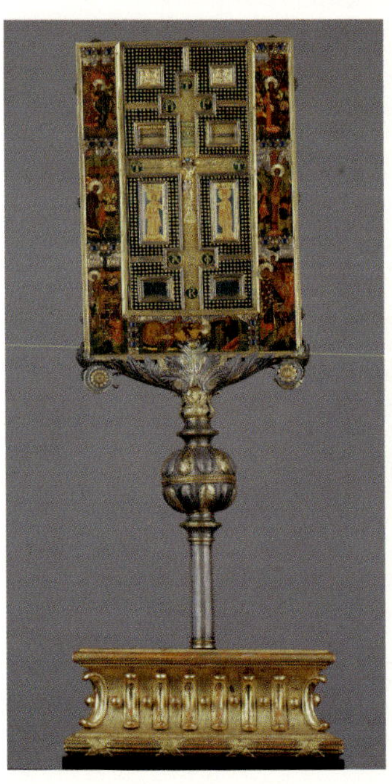

Late fourteenth century–
1460s. Byzantine. Silver,
silver-gilt, enamel, glass,
jewels, wood, tempera, 47 ×
32cm (1ft 6½in × 1ft⅝in).
Gallerie dell'Accademia,
Venice.

The reliquary, which once
belonged to a Byzantine
princess, features a crucifix
attached to a box containing
relics of the True Cross and
Christ's robe. Portraits on
glass of Emperor Constantine
and his mother Helena,
along with seven tempera
paintings in a Byzantine
style featuring Christ's
Passion, adorn its surface.
The jewelled frame and stand
made it suitable to be
carried in procession.

Renaissance in style. We must take it that the viewer's perception that this painting was an archaizing recreation of a Byzantine work was always part of the pleasure it gave. Such an understanding would not have diminished the viewer's response. The perception of Giovanni's painting as a finely wrought illusionistic work of art, in which an older style was knowingly recreated, does not necessarily distance us from its subject-matter, or undermine its validity as a sacred work. Rather than contrasting icon with image, we might lay stress on the way that one category blends seamlessly with the other. In common with many other works discussed in this chapter, Giovanni's adaptation to another mode of presentation only served to intensify the present meaning and value of his work.

A similarly respectful approach to the Byzantine inheritance in Venice is evident in a work by Giovanni's elder brother Gentile, made as a direct response to the first of the two great Bessarion donations mentioned above. Gentile's painting originally decorated a cupboard built to house the precious reliquary the Cardinal had donated to a Venetian lay confraternity in Venice: the Scuola della Carità. As such, it was intended to be seen in immediate proximity to the sacred object it depicted, its merely artistic status constantly revealed by the comparison (FIGS 28, 29). As a skilfully illusionistic representation painted on a flat surface, Gentile's painting was not to be confused with the three-dimensional reality of the reliquary, and this distinction may have granted the painter a certain creative licence. There are, in fact, marked differences between Gentile's depiction and the object itself, especially in his representation of the small Byzantine paintings to each side, which Gentile carefully translated into his own distinctively naturalistic artistic language. His depicted reliquary is pictured in three-dimensional space, between a donor portrait of Cardinal Bessarion in the foreground and two brothers of the Scuola behind, whose kneeling and prayerful attitudes demonstrate the ideal pious response to the relic. This was to go decisively beyond a merely mechanical representation; but Gentile's painting also served to heighten the viewer's anticipation of the precious object contained within the cupboard. In this persuasive image of an icon, Gentile's 'modern' style served to intensify rather than usurp the spiritual significance of the sacred object it represents.

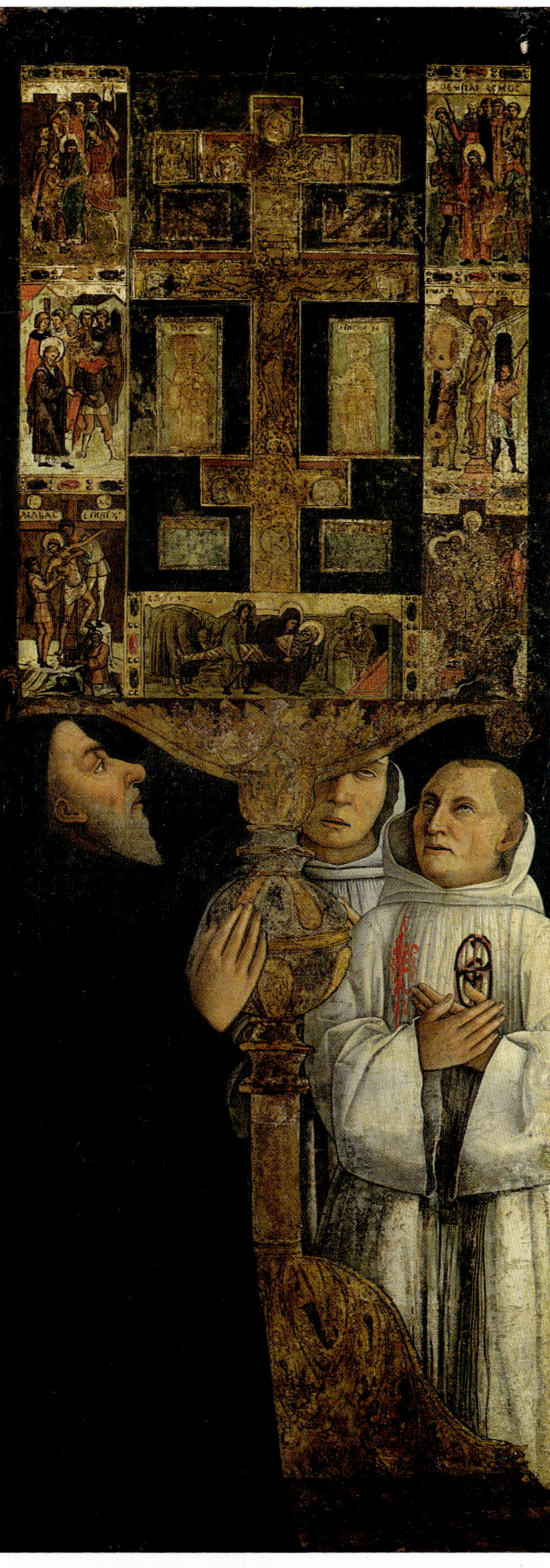

Fig. 29
Gentile Bellini
*Cardinal Bessarion in
Prayer with the Reliquary
and two Brothers of the
Scuola della Carità*

ca. 1472–3. Egg tempera with
gold and silver on panel,
102 × 37cm (3ft 4⅛in × 1ft
2⅝in). National Gallery,
London.

Gentile greatly enlarged
the size of the reliquary,
making it appear to dwarf
its human devotees, probably
in order to emphasize its
great spiritual significance.
In the upper part of his
painting, the reliquary
appears to press forward
against the picture
plane, contradicting the
indications of spatiality
below, and recalling the
effect of a Byzantine icon.

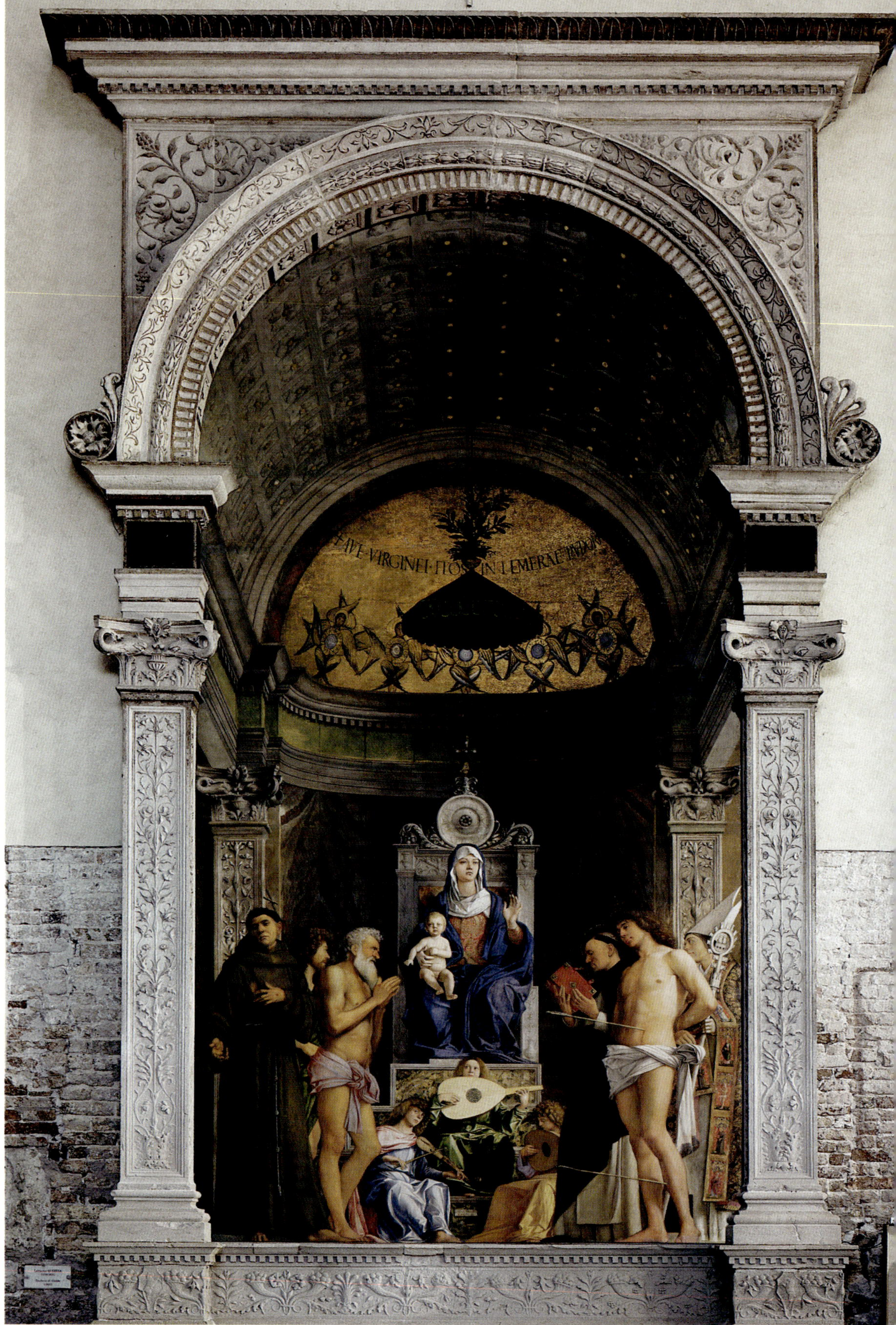

A Perfected Image of Venice: 1476–1500

A new kind of altarpiece, featuring an enlarged and single painted field, emerged in the 1470s, coinciding with the spread of oil painting to Venice. This concurrence may be significant as both medium and picture type offered opportunities to create a more naturalistic kind of painting, and both can be taken as signals of the further development of the Renaissance in Venetian art.

Oil painting and naturalism in the San Giobbe Altarpiece

The golden light permeating Giovanni Bellini's San Giobbe Altarpiece of ca. 1480 was set to become a trademark of his mature style (FIG. 30). Its softening action on the surfaces it touches is dependent on the painter's use of oil paint instead of the egg tempera he had employed in his earlier works (*see* FIGS 23, 25). Later fifteenth-century Venice was a rich emporium of imported luxury goods from the East, and an especially wide range of precious and other paint pigments were sold by so-called *vendecolori* or 'colour merchants' around the city. The subtle effect of Giovanni's mature paintings,

Fig. 30
Giovanni Bellini
San Giobbe Altarpiece

ca. 1480. Oil on panel, 471 × 258cm (15ft 5⅜in × 8ft 5⅝in). Gallerie dell'Accademia, Venice. Photomontage showing Bellini's painting reunited with its original frame in the church of San Giobbe.

In this painting, Bellini may have followed Mantegna's San Zeno Altarpiece (1456–9, San Zeno, Verona) in making his painted architecture appear as a continuation of the frame (designed by Pietro Lombardo). The altarpiece was especially renowned as a masterpiece of pictorial perspective for several centuries after its creation, but is now more often seen as typical of the Venetian predilection for sensuality and naturalism.

however, was dependent less on the variety of colours he used than on his active manipulation of them on the picture surface. The use of slower-drying linseed or walnut oil as a binding agent allowed him to build up translucent layers of paint that were blended into one another to give an impression of the textures of objects, and also of the variety of tones produced when light strikes them.

Giovanni's interest in oil painting was stimulated by the arrival in 1475 of Antonello da Messina (ca. 1430–1479), a Sicilian painter who had absorbed the Netherlandish approach to the medium, based on the manner of Jan van Eyck (1390–1441). In a large altarpiece for the Venetian church of San Cassiano, Antonello exploited translucent qualities to depict the action of light falling on a myriad of different surfaces (FIG. 31). Only a fragment of Antonello's work survives, but his special skill in the depiction of different manufactured materials and textures is still evident. At the lower left, for example, he distinguishes between the soft luxuriance of the threads on St Nicholas of Bari's stole and the hard metallic quality of the golden balls that were this saint's identifying attribute. Nearby he showed the way that transparent objects and liquids refract light and distort form: the spectacular illusionism of his depiction of the glass held by St Mary Magdalene was wholly unprecedented in Venetian art.

Comparison with Giovanni's San Giobbe (*see* (FIG. 30) painting indicates that the Venetian master retreated from Antonello's virtuosic concern with such details in order to build a more monumental and generalized composition. Both works shared a new format in which a much-enlarged single painting (upright and round-topped in shape) replaced the conventional multi-panelled form of the altarpiece (*see* FIG. 11). In the older type, the painted imagery played a secondary role to ornate moulded frames covered in gold leaf. Now, in the single-field altarpiece, a continuous painted illusion becomes predominant. One consequence of this is that the viewer's relationship with the work is made a matter of identification with the figures depicted. If the typical Veneto–Gothic altarpiece was conceived as a sacred intervention against empirical reality or experience, then the new type suggested continuity with the real world beyond its frame.

In these works the previously separated saints were gathered together within a unified space, and closer attention was paid to the details and variety of their depiction. The idea of a gathering of saints from different eras and places (a *sacra conversazione*) was not new, but the conception of these actors as 'real people' certainly was. Giovanni includes two full-length nudes as Saints Job and Sebastian, showing his mastery in the depiction of contrasting old and young bodies. In both figures Giovanni uses a classicizing

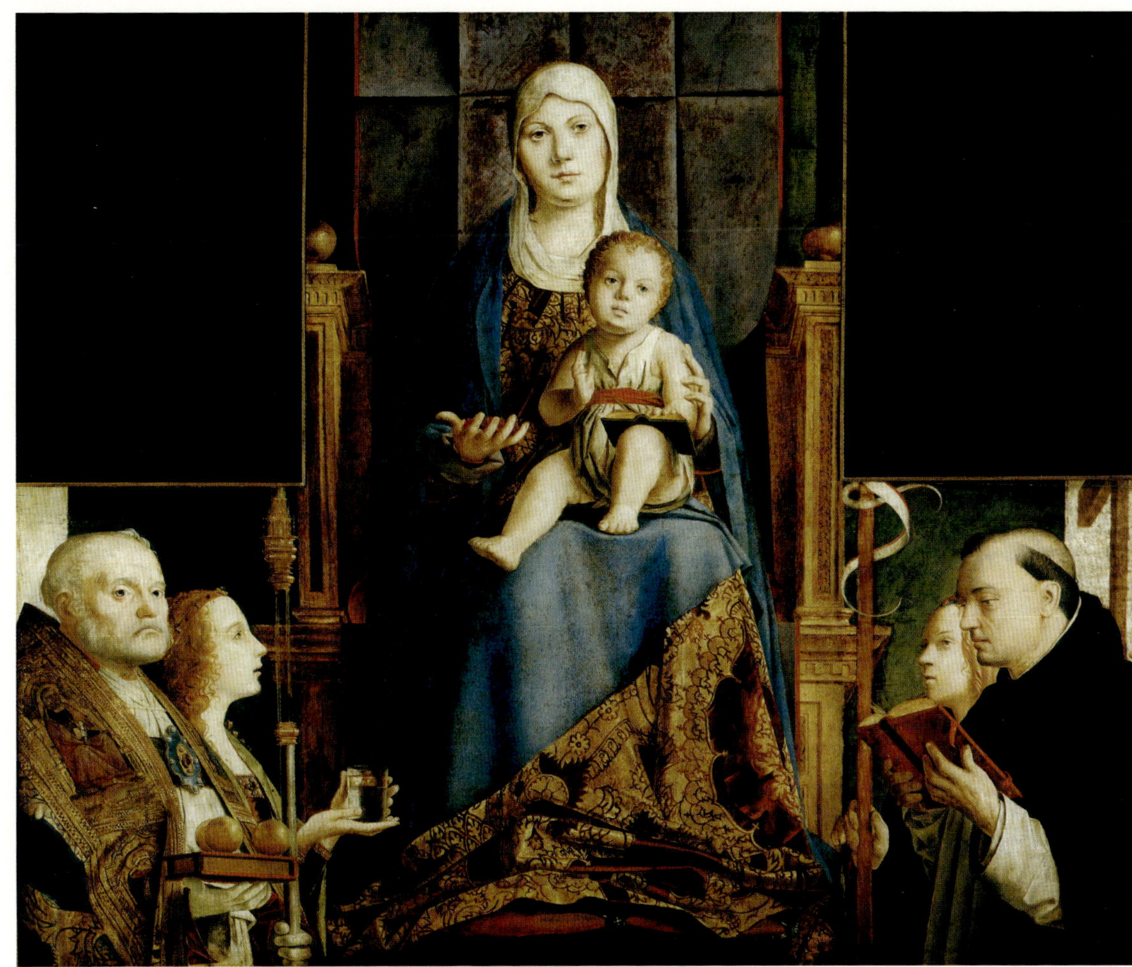

contrapposto stance, with the weight on one leg, to impart an even more lifelike quality. Sebastian, to the right, superficially recalls works such as the Mantegna discussed in the previous chapter (FIG. 32, and *see* FIG. 18). Yet the dreamy introspection of Giovanni's sensuous figure is very far from the severe intellectual approach of his brother-in-law. Rather than contrasting Sebastian's spiritual yearning with the harshness of the world, Giovanni makes it appear that his saint is already released from any hint of physical suffering, the two arrows entering his body appearing to give him no pain or discomfort.

In Giovanni's painting we are invited to think that we are looking into an actual chapel. This was certainly a novel idea in the Venetian context, but it would nonetheless be easy to exaggerate the realism of his altarpiece. As with his devotional paintings, Giovanni's naturalistic style serves here to intensify rather than contradict

Fig. 32
Giovanni Bellini
San Giobbe Altarpiece,
detail of St Sebastian

See Fig. 30

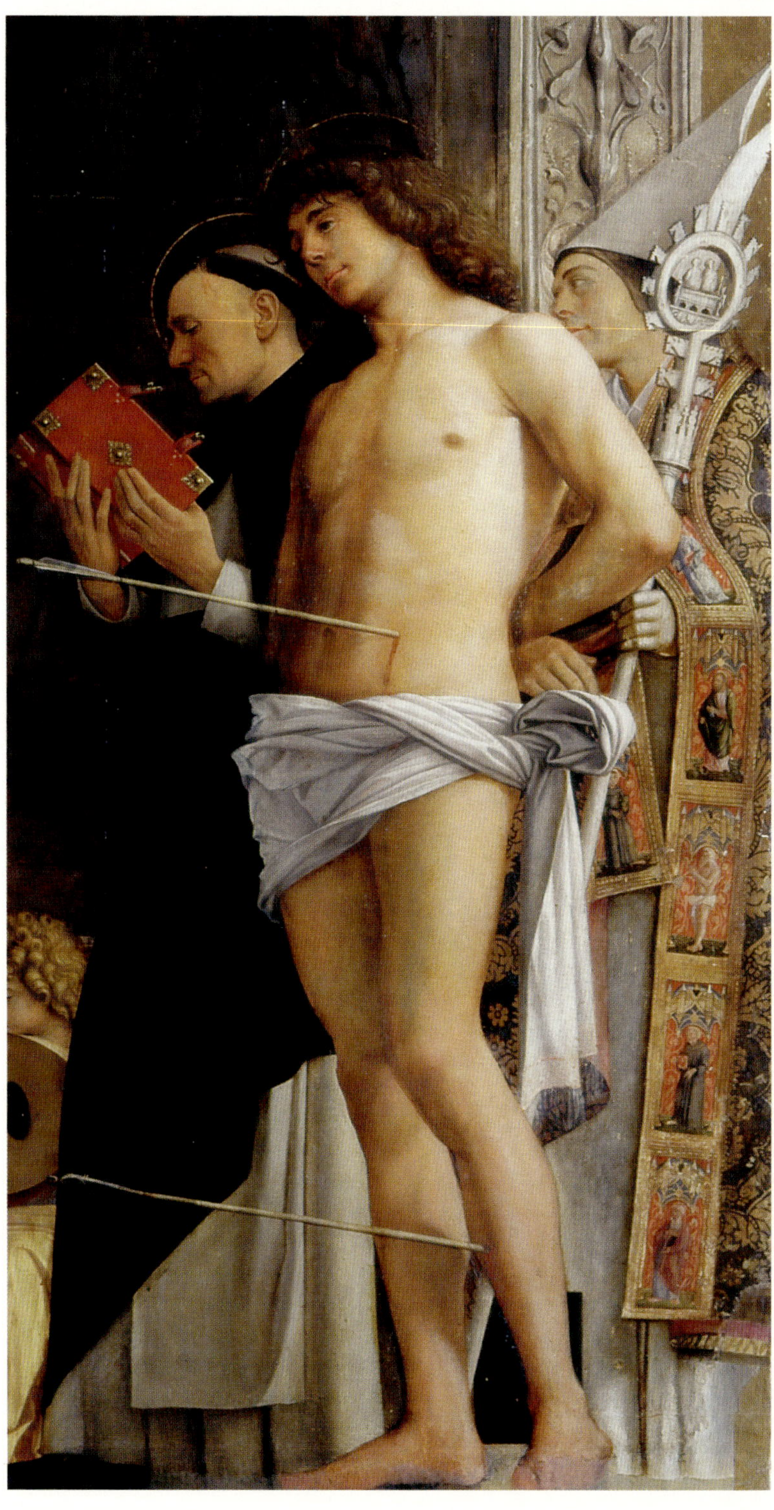

conventional religious values. The fictive chapel recalls the interior of St Mark's itself. The half-dome apse with mosaics featuring Byzantine seraphim above the Virgin's throne, like the variegated marble revetment immediately behind it, are particularly reminiscent of the interior of the city's 'mother church' (*see* FIG. 4). Though Giovanni demonstrates his artistic skill by creating a convincing illusion of these traditional artistic materials in the progressive medium of oils, this nonetheless serves to celebrate and further highlight their lasting spiritual significance and value. In other ways, too, Giovanni seeks to define his role as an upholder or continuator of tradition. The enthroned Virgin is raised above the other saints, as in many earlier altarpieces, towering over them on her throne, a reference to her role as Queen of Heaven. She remains aloof, wrapped in her own narrative, raising her left hand as if to acknowledge the arrival of a being from a still higher unseen realm beyond the painting. Perhaps she sees the Archangel Gabriel, whose words to her at the Annunciation are inscribed on the mosaic above. The golden tones that pervade the painted chapel might be a reference to the divine light of heaven rather than to nature, and the otherworldly location of the scene seems to be confirmed by the presence of the three music-making angels. The gathered saints do not communicate with one another, remaining solemn, still and meditative. To this extent, they are recognizable as descendants of the remote figures featured in Veneto–Gothic altarpieces. St Francis, to the left, turns outward towards the viewer, inviting us to emulate the devotional meditations of the sacred actors. Nonetheless, we must look up into the chapel from a position well below the level of the saints: a viewpoint that can be taken as a sign of our lowly position within the sacred hierarchy. Giovanni's naturalism may seem to bring the saints down to earth, but in many ways his work reconfirms the existence of a perfected spiritual realm that is subtly distinct from ours: one which takes on the appearances of nature without compromise to its vision of timeless eternity.

Pietro Lombardo and Mauro Codussi

Giovanni's altarpiece originally stood in the nave of the church of San Giobbe, then under completion by Pietro Solari, known as 'Lombardo' (ca. 1435–1515), originally from Carona in Lombardy, who had arrived in Venice around 1467. Giovanni's painting was set into a monumental stone frame designed by Lombardo, which still survives in situ in the church. The painter's close response to this frame is evident enough from the photomontage reuniting the two elements, which shows how his painted architecture was conceived as a direct illusionistic extension of it (*see* FIG. 30). Lombardo's frame was, in its turn, modelled directly on the entrance to the chancel of the church, which was conceived as a classicizing triumphal arch. His work at San Giobbe indicates, in fact, his familiarity with the work of Tuscan architects such as Filippo Brunelleschi and Michelozzo di Bartolomeo Michelozzi (1396–1472), though he also covered the surfaces of both frame and chancel arch with the decorative foliage and densely patterned mouldings that were to become the hallmark of his work in Venice.

Lombardo's architectural masterpiece was the little votive church of Santa Maria dei Miracoli, completed between 1481 and 1489 (FIG. 33). In this work, he made insistent reference to Tuscan religious architecture, perhaps because the church was built to house a miracle-working painting owned by the Amadi family, now citizens (*cittadini*) of Venice, but originally silk weavers from Lucca. Following examples such as the Baptistery in Florence, Lombardo completely covered his new building with marble facing on all sides. He also adopted the use of two orders from the Baptistery facade, while the *tondo* (circular) busts of prophets between the arches of the arcade recall those on its famous bronze doors by Lorenzo Ghiberti (1378–1455). Still, the overall effect of Lombardo's little building is far from classical. The Florentine Baptistery was a Romanesque building, though it was widely understood to be 'antique' in the fifteenth century. In keeping with this understanding, but also in common with many of his predecessors working in Venice, Lombardo sought to evoke a generalized impression of ancientness at Santa Maria dei Miracoli, rather than any more specific or accurate kind of reference to the buildings of ancient Greece or Rome.

Purists have noted, in this regard, that the main portal disrupts the rhythm of the arcades above, and that the orders of capitals are used incorrectly, with Corinthian on the ground floor and Ionic above. This casual reversal indicates that Lombardo strived for an overall richness of effect rather than classical correctness. The simple barrel-vaulted shape of the new church had a recent local model in the Mascoli Chapel (*see* FIG. 12), while the lavishness of the parti-coloured marble revetments recall those in St Mark's rather than Tuscan predecessors (see detail opposite). The use of especially rich materials was, indeed, a condition of Lombardo's contract, which specified that he seek out the very finest available Greek, Carrara and red Verona marbles, as well as precious porphyry and *verde antico*, a dark green stone mottled with white that gives a

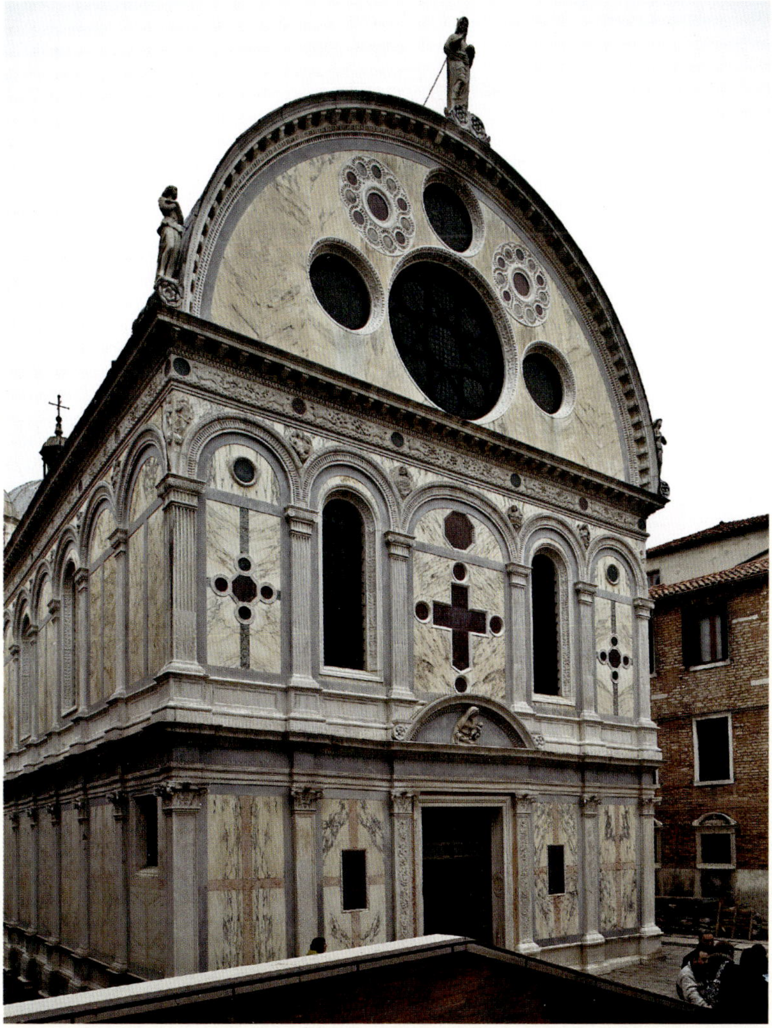

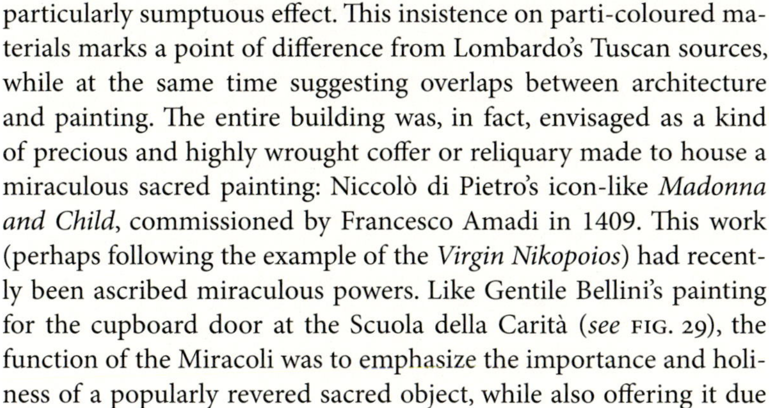

particularly sumptuous effect. This insistence on parti-coloured materials marks a point of difference from Lombardo's Tuscan sources, while at the same time suggesting overlaps between architecture and painting. The entire building was, in fact, envisaged as a kind of precious and highly wrought coffer or reliquary made to house a miraculous sacred painting: Niccolò di Pietro's icon-like *Madonna and Child*, commissioned by Francesco Amadi in 1409. This work (perhaps following the example of the *Virgin Nikopoios*) had recently been ascribed miraculous powers. Like Gentile Bellini's painting for the cupboard door at the Scuola della Carità (*see* FIG. 29), the function of the Miracoli was to emphasize the importance and holiness of a popularly revered sacred object, while also offering it due

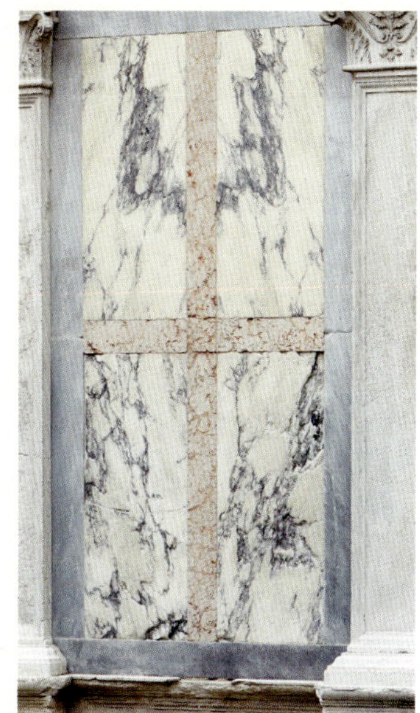

protection. The city's on-going traditions of popular devotion had only intensified after 1450, and provided the raison d'etre, as well as the funds, for Lombardo's new building.

The brilliantly original architecture of San Michele in Isola by Mauro Codussi (ca. 1440–1504) might superficially appear to inaugurate a fully realized Renaissance architectural style in Venice in the early 1470s (FIG. 34). But while Codussi's approach in this building is undoubtedly original, he was careful to align his architecture with more conventional approaches. Codussi was another

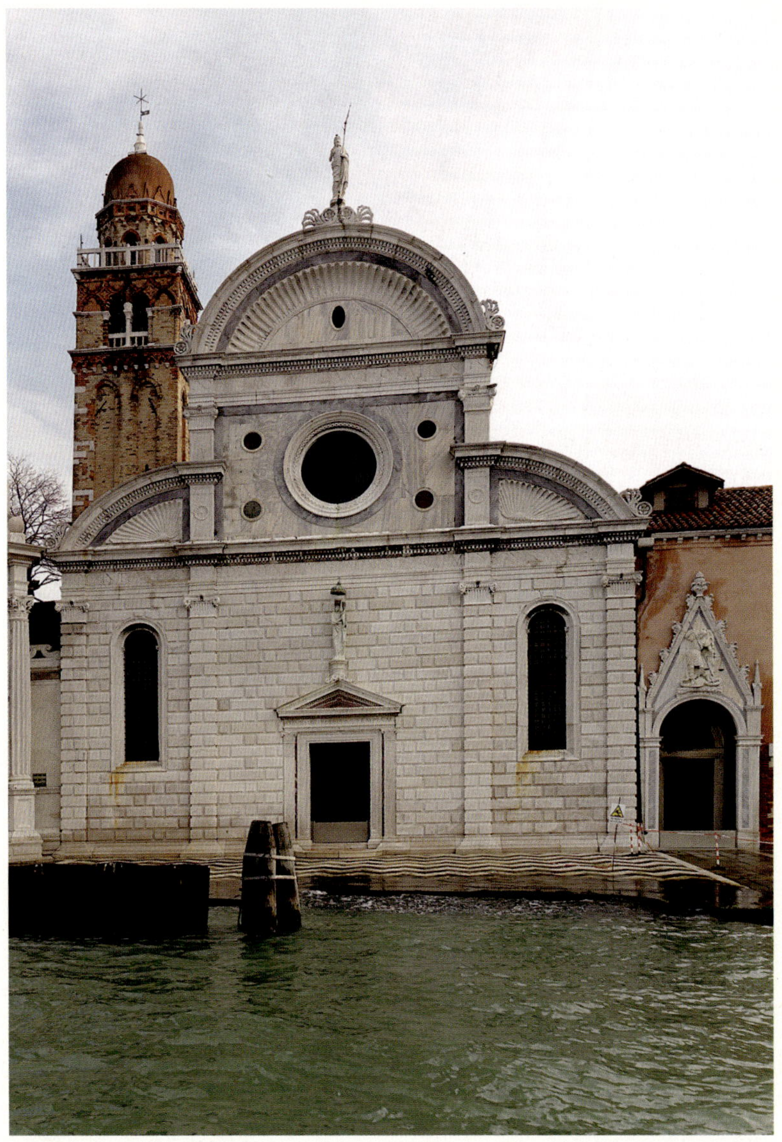

member of the group of stonemasons from Lombardy and the Bergamo area of northern Italy who had recently arrived in Venice, and whose immediate successes initially led to conflicts with local craftsmen. Like Pietro Lombardo, Codussi brought with him a keen awareness of the progressive recent work of Tuscan architects. At San Michele, he drew on examples such as Leon Battista Alberti's Tempio Malatestiano (ca. 1450) in Rimini, offering local stonemasons an object lesson in classicizing restraint. The whiteness of the Istrian stone used by Codussi may have been intended to symbolize the spiritual purity of this isolated church, positioned on the small island between Venice and Murano that served as a hermitage for the reclusive Camaldolese branch of the Benedictine Order. However this may be, it was certainly a departure from the warm brickwork typical of the Gothic churches of the religious orders in Venice. Codussi's facade contains few windows and avoids a dense repetition of elements. The four main apertures that he does include are, however, enlarged, allowing them greater emphasis in the overall effect. Their simplified shapes and strictly symmetrical arrangement serve to articulate the inner structure of the building, with its three-aisled nave.

The subtlety of Codussi's approach, with its balanced combination of restraint and freedom, is best indicated by the contrast his design allows between an ordered lower part and a more freely conceived or playful upper section. Powerful block-like horizontal and vertical elements dominate the lower storey, an effect supported by the rustication of the surface, which Codussi borrowed from recent examples of domestic architecture in Florence, such as Alberti's Palazzo Rucellai. He might also have adapted the idea of flattened pilasters with a classicizing entablature from Alberti's building. In the area above, Codussi was less closely tied to Tuscan examples, evoking the large lunettes on the facade of St Mark's (*see* FIG. 3), while making the central oculus serve as the defining feature. If the four roundels encircling the oculus help assert its importance, then the two quadrant arches to either side are distinct in shape and scale, challenging its authority. Neither do they exactly correspond with the larger semi-circular lunette above. The single ellipse placed in the centre of the tympanum offers a further distortion of the circular theme, restating something of the verticality of the lower part of the facade with reference to the main portal directly below it. However tempting it is to see Codussi's San Michele as a future-orientated precursor to Palladio's work in the sixteenth century, it remains a work of its time and place. Despite his innovations, the earlier architect remained closely concerned with the values of surface evident in existing traditions of building in the city. Like Lombardo at the Miracoli,

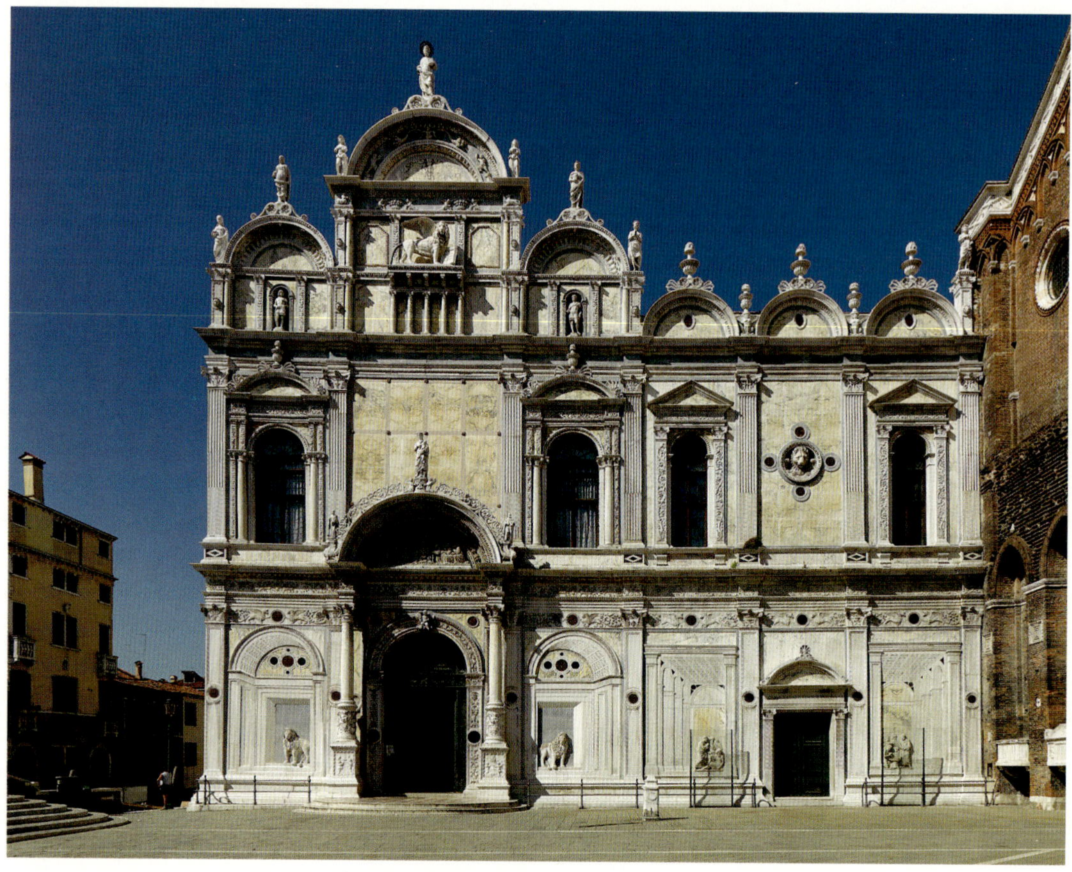

he incorporated rich materials such as porphyry and *verde antico* (in the roundels); and the cornices of the mouldings in the upper area are edged with subtle blue-grey marble. Texture remained important too, with the delicate repetitions of the shell patterns and radial fluting of the tympanum recalling (if only by generic association) local approaches. Even his correct use of inscribed ancient Roman letters in the frieze of the entablatures, which follows Alberti's example again, served to decorate an otherwise blank surface.

Further evidence of Codussi's engagement with local predilections is evident from his completion of the Meeting House of the Scuola Grande di San Marco (FIG. 35), the leading religious confraternity in Venice. Following a fire in 1485, Pietro Lombardo and Giovanni Buora (1450–1513), along with Pietro's talented son Tullio (ca. 1455–1532), were employed to rebuild the Scuola, with substantial funding supplied by the Venetian state itself. This artistic team only completed the lower part of the facade, before a dispute allowed Codussi the opportunity to take over the commission around 1490.

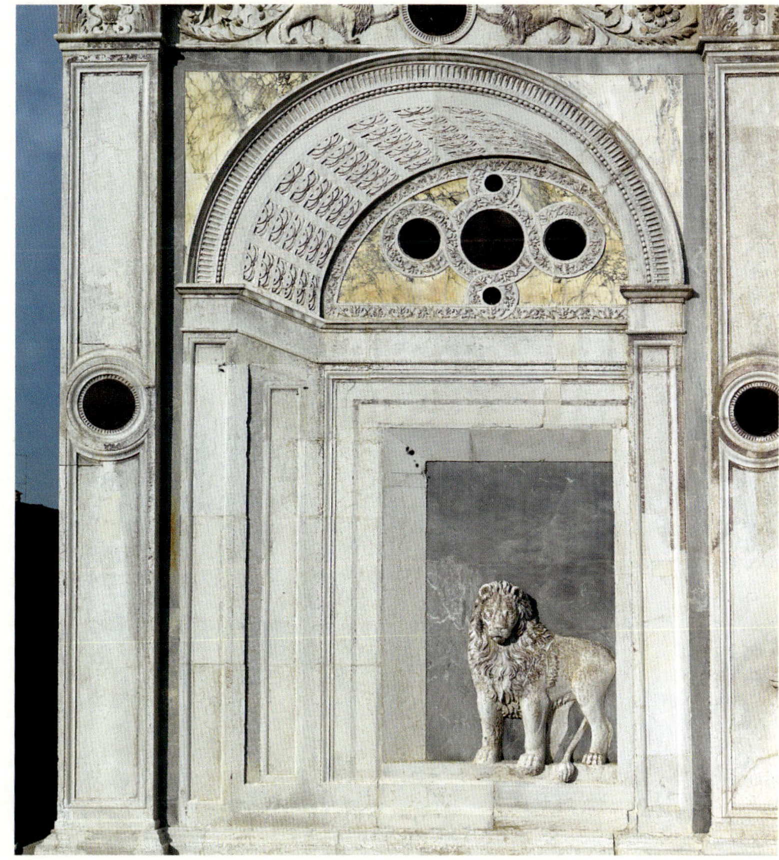

Codussi paid careful attention to the Lombardi's insistent classical references, developing their order of pilasters and entablature on the second storey and enriching the effect by making it reappear on a smaller scale at the sides of the windows. On the lower level, self-consciously *all'antica* illusionistic perspectives, probably by Tullio Lombardo, compensate in a brilliantly original way for the lack of windows (FIG. 36). Codussi responded by adding triangular and segmental pediments over the *piano-nobile* windows that appear as precursors to the fully achieved classical Renaissance architecture of the sixteenth century. Just as the classical effect of the Lombardi's lower order was undermined by the insertion of delicately coloured marble inlays and a profusion of carved patterns of foliage and flowers, so the *all'antica* elements of Codussi's upper storey finally give way to a repeated sequence of variously sized lunettes along the roofline to establish an overriding link to the Veneto–Byzantine architecture of St Mark's (*see* FIG. 3). At the Scuola, they support the repeated sculptural images of St Mark himself and his symbolic lion featured on the facade. The maintenance of the foundations of the old Scuola in the new building had, from the outset, denied any possibility of the kind of ordered symmetry evident at San Michele. Codussi's ultimate subservience to the patriotic requirements of the Scuola and its official backers dictated the way in which classical elements were finally absorbed into a more traditional ethos of stylistic diversity which prioritized the Republic of Venice itself.

Two Venetian tombs

A tradition of commemorating the doges in large and imposing tombs in Venice dates back to the thirteenth century. These monuments were typically placed against the walls of the large brick-built Gothic churches of the religious orders, particularly the Franciscan church of the Frari (ca. 1250–1338) and the Dominican Santi Giovanni e Paolo (1333–1430). They feature a sarcophagus surrounded by elaborately shaped architectural structures with sculptures in niches. Two examples from the later 1470s show how *all'antica* elements were incorporated into an on-going visual type. Antonio Rizzo's *Nicolò Tron* indicates the continuing hold of Republican values in the city, while Pietro Lombardo's near-contemporary *Pietro Mocenigo* presses the boundaries of these traditional values, without finally undermining them (FIGS 37 and 38). Such monuments had always been ambiguous insofar as they served to both celebrate and downplay the role of the given individual depicted. Though typically commissioned by family heirs, the ducal tombs had a quasi-official status and closely represented the very particular socio-political tradition of the Venetian dogeship.

The doges were elected from the ruling patriciate via an extraordinarily elaborate voting process, designed to eliminate any possibility of corruption. Those elected were typically elderly, with long and distinguished careers in the service of the Republic behind them. This policy reflected both the gerontocratic tendencies of a conservative state, and also the more pragmatic imperative to limit the duration of any one ducal reign. Nicolò Tron was doge for just two years (reigned 1471–1473), though the monument erected in his honour is lavish enough. Its upright, round-topped shape might remind us of the single-field altarpieces that became popular in the same decade, although Rizzo's complex compartmentalization of space, with its myriad of smaller elements, was Gothic in character. Although Rizzo had recently indicated his awareness of the spatial possibilities of free-standing sculpture (*see* FIGS 20, 21), in this monument his figures were defined by their relation to the architectural

Fig. 37
Antonio Rizzo
Tomb monument of Doge Nicolò Tron

1475–6. Marble. Santa Maria Gloriosa dei Frari, Venice.

Rizzo was evidently helped by his workshop in the completion of this monument, the largest surviving tomb in Venice from the late fifteenth century. The style of the sculptures is primarily Gothic, although certain of the figures recall examples from Mantegna's oeuvre, indicating again Rizzo's interest in Renaissance innovations.

niche. The Tron monument includes 22 figural sculptures and six reliefs. Although the doge himself appears twice, the sheer quantity of
images mitigates against his visual dominance in the ensemble.

Although Tron's importance is supported by a lengthy inscription describing his reform of the local currency, the wider
meaning of the tomb is supra-personal, presenting the sacred office
of the Venetian dogeship as an expression of the underlying religious schema. The iconography of the tomb is read from bottom to
top, with the consecutive horizontal levels depicting life, death and
afterlife. Tron appears as a living presence in his full ducal regalia
at the bottom centre, with two allegorical sculptures of Charity to
either side, indicating his love of God (*amor Dei*) and of his fel-
low men (*amor proximi*). Immediately above him, reliefs featuring
putti with funeral urns guarded by warriors refer to the inevitability
of death and prepare us for the sarcophagus level itself. Another

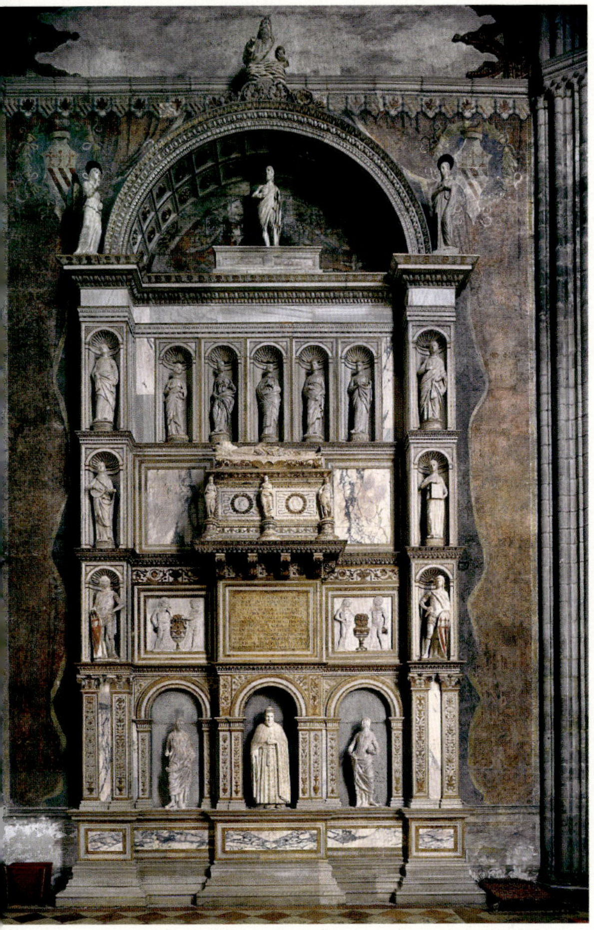

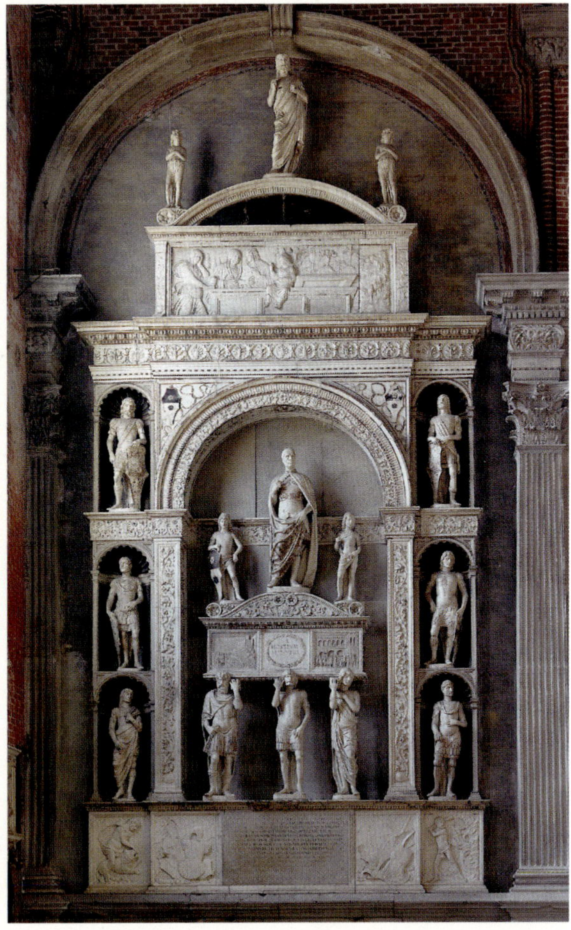

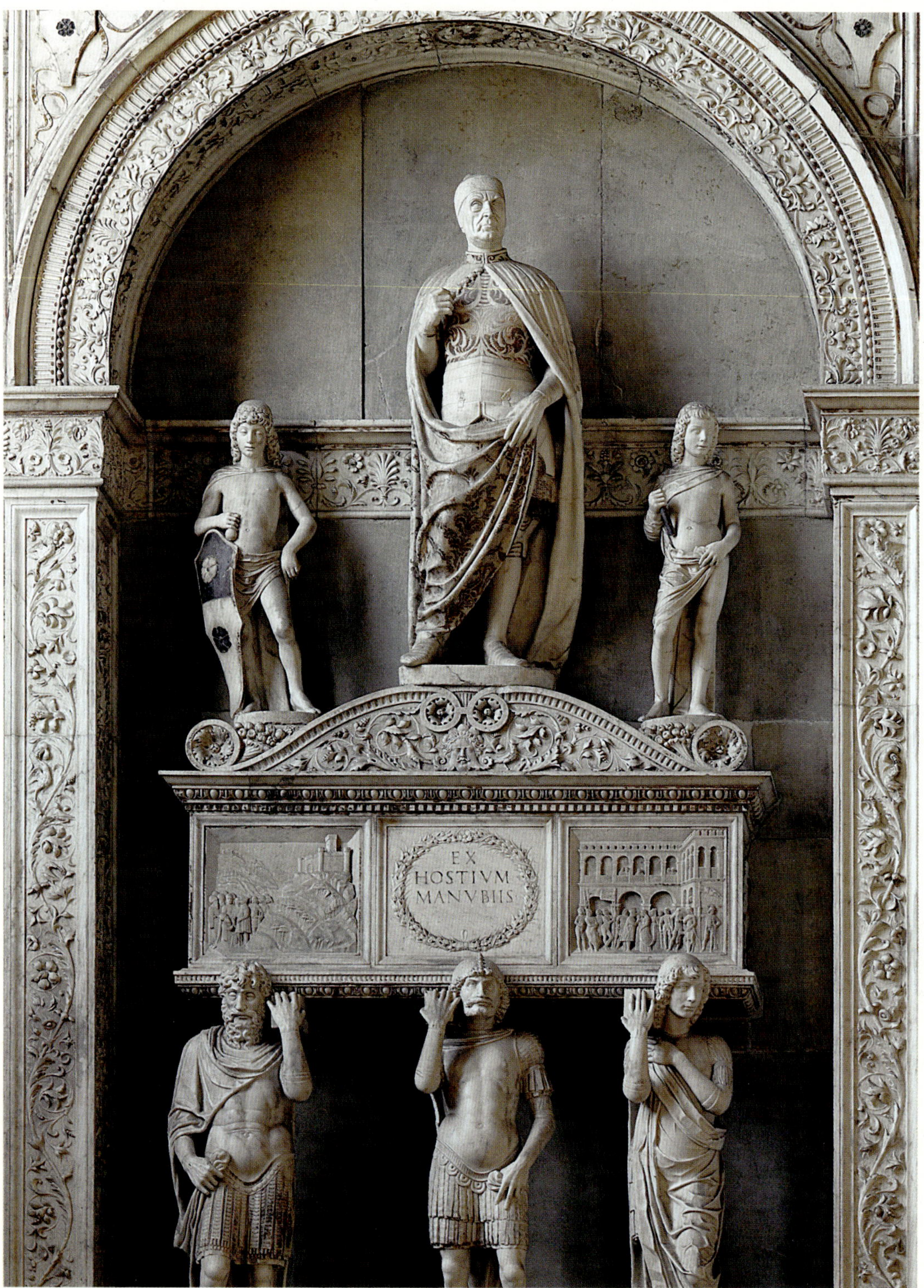
EX
HOSTIVM
MANVBIIS

sculptural portrait of Tron appears here, but is almost invisible from our viewpoint below, his dead body turned upwards towards the heavenly sphere above. Significantly, Tron's own reign is downplayed in this zone. Though the profile heads on the sarcophagus may refer to the Tron coin, struck during his dogeship, the surrounding imagery generates an ideal image of Venice as the perfect state. Female figures holding a lute and a book symbolize the underlying influence of divine harmony and laws, while the small statues on the front of the sarcophagus advertise the city's civic virtues: Security, Concord and Abundance. The seven Virtues in shell niches above return us to Tron's personal fate again, their presence suggesting the imminent ascension of his soul towards the Resurrected Christ, shown standing on his tomb in the sacred zone above. Beyond the dome, which might represent the created universe itself, are the Archangel Gabriel and the Virgin (a reference to the Annunciation, and thus to the foundation myth of Venice) and God the Father.

Although Rizzo included Renaissance elements, such as the putti reliefs, these are not allowed to disturb the Gothic effect of the whole. In contrast, Lombardo's monument was more emphatically influenced by recent humanist examples from Tuscany, such as Bernardo Rossellino's *Leonardo Bruni Monument* (1450, Florence, Sta Croce), where the emphasis falls on the virtues of the given individual commemorated, rather than on his place within the wider sacred and political order. Lombardo dispenses with the usual panoply of supportive virtues, introducing an armed guard of warriors who serve to reiterate Mocenigo's military prowess. If Rizzo focussed on Tron's achievement during his short time as doge, then Lombardo laid emphasis on Mocenigo's career as admiral of the Venetian fleet (*capitano generale da mar*) before he was elected. He had heroically resisted the advances of the Ottoman Turks on a number of occasions, two of which are featured on the sarcophagus reliefs. The simple inscription 'Ex Hostum Manubiis' ('from hostile booty'), refers to the fact that his heirs used the funds won from his infidel enemies to pay for the monument.

Lombardo's artistic language follows a more thorough going *all'antica* approach. Each figure stands in a *contrapposto* pose, while the warriors sport classicizing tunics and have tightly curled hair reminiscent of Roman statuary. The powerfully individuation of Mocenigo himself had few precedents in Venetian ducal imagery. His commanding figure, standing on his tomb, directly mirrors that of Christ above him, beneath what appears to be his own Roman-style triumphal arch (*see* detail opposite). Although Mocenigo sports the ducal *corno* (hat) and cloak, this only partially conceals his

See Fig. 38

The doge originally held a standard of St Mark in his right hand. The reliefs show scenes from Mocenigo's pre-Ducal naval career: the *Siege of Scultari* and the *Surrender of the Keys of Cyprus*. The monument was commissioned by Pietro's relatives, Niccolò and Giovanni, the latter of whom was himself elected doge in 1478.

armour beneath. The martial and masculine tone of the monument seems also to have encouraged a clearer separation of secular and sacred space within it, with a marked expansion of the former at the expense of the latter. Indeed, the sacred zone above the triumphal arch at the top takes a secondary role, supplying Christian justification for the self-proclaiming imagery below.

The current impression of individualism and secularity may, however, be exaggerated by the loss of sculptures featuring the patron saints of the city (Mark and Theodore), once placed on the upper part of the monument. These would have provided the ensemble with a strongly patriotic imprimatur. The reliefs featuring episodes from Mocenigo's career as *capitano generale* emphasized his dutiful and heroic service to the Republic rather than his more personal qualities. Even the especially close link between the standing figures of Mocenigo and Christ, with their matching child/angel guards, may evoke the standard association between sacred and secular leaders familiar from earlier Venetian monuments such as the Porta della Carta (*see* FIG. 7). Lombardo's fundamental idea of the monument as a triumphal arch is offset by the continued use of Gothic side niches. And, in common with many of his works, the architectural surfaces are overrun with floral patterns, which have a decorative effect that softens the severity of the martial tone. Closer examination of the somewhat squat bodies of Lombardo's warrior caste reveals that his knowledge of, or interest in, the proportions of Roman statuary was limited. Even the *all'antica* reliefs featuring the ancient hero Hercules, featured at the bottom of the monument, offered the viewer a link to the well-known imagery on the facade of St Mark's, where the battles of the classical hero were featured on marble reliefs .

Ruler imagery

Lombardo's depiction of Mocenigo was, nonetheless, unusual, given that the Venetian authorities typically maintained strict control over representations of the doges. Official images of the incumbents were traditionally commissioned to hang in the frieze of the Sala del Maggior Consiglio (Hall of the Great Council) of the Ducal Palace. These were destroyed in the disastrous fire of 1577, but works such as Gentile Bellini's portrait of Pietro's brother, *Doge Giovanni Mocenigo*, probably commissioned as a replica of a lost original in the Palace, indicate that the painter very deliberately maintained the traditional type (FIG. 39). Gentile pointedly ignored recent examples of more naturalistic portraits in oil in the Flemish manner by Antonello da

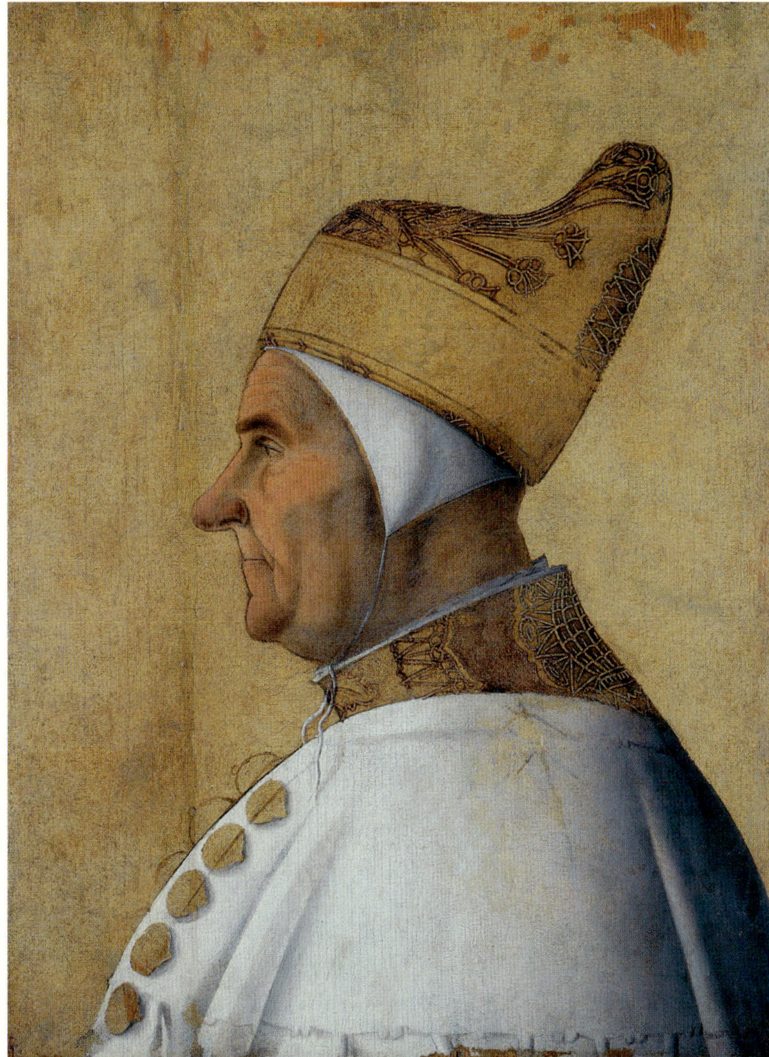

Fig. 39
Gentile Bellini
Doge Giovanni Mocenigo

ca. 1480. Tempera on panel,
62 × 45cm (2ft ¼in × 1ft
5¾in). Museo Correr,
Venice.

Messina, returning instead to the older profile view, with its evocation of the ruler portraits featured on coins and medals. Using the traditional medium of tempera, Gentile laid careful emphasis on the delicate floral details of the doge's *corno* and collar. The coloration may recall the use of gold leaf in traditions of religious imagery, in accordance with the idea of dogeship as a sacred office. Despite this, Gentile also emphasizes the individual facial characteristics of his sitter: his depiction of Mocenigo is distinctly un-idealized, carefully recording the dark stubble and loose folds of flesh around his jaw, his pinched mouth and bulbous nose. Gentile's work is typical of its time in the way that no tension emerges between the effect of naturalism

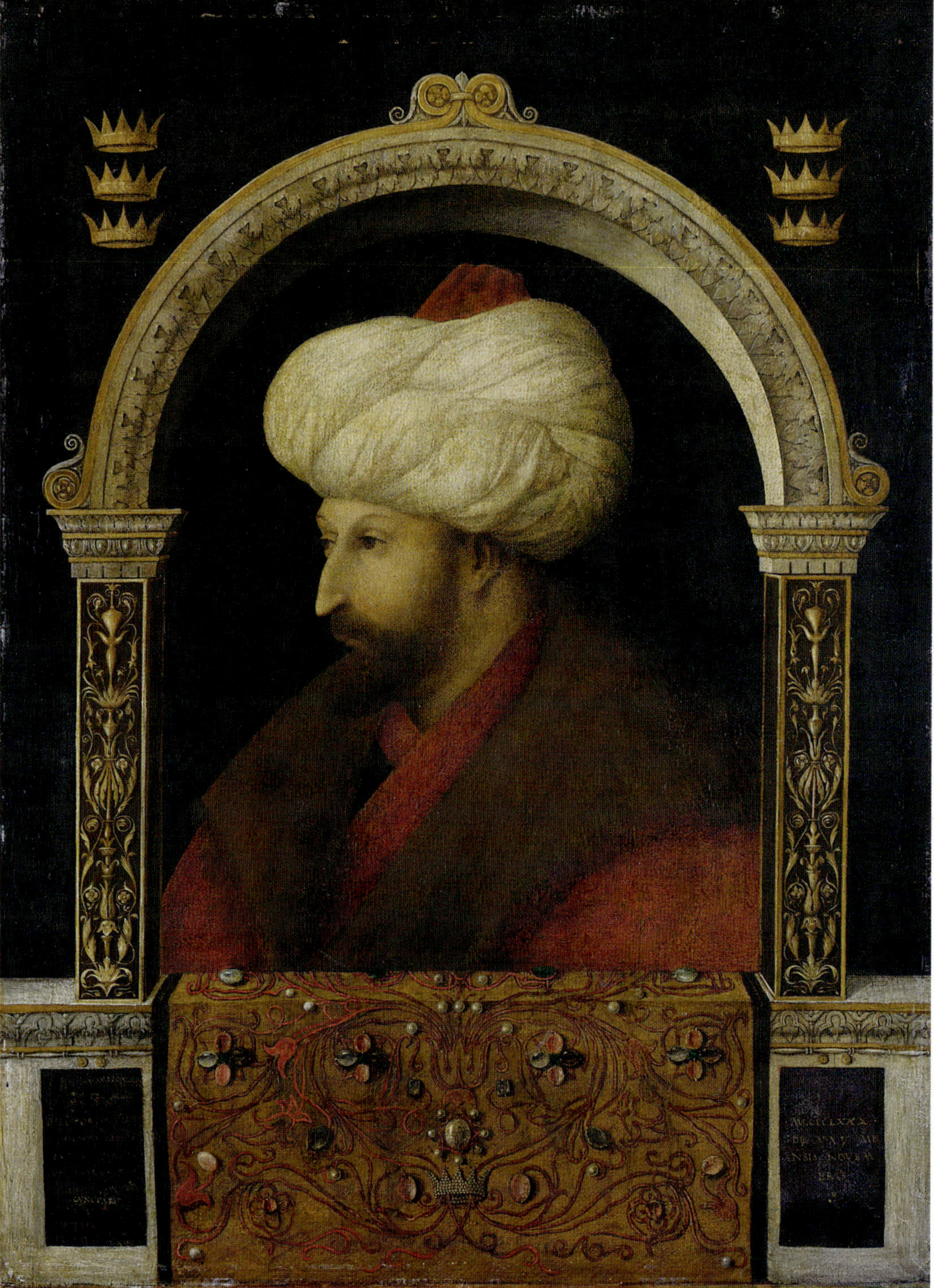

given in these details and the conventionality of the presentation; or between the potentially conflicting demands of individualizing Mocenigo and characterizing him as the leader of the Venetian state.

Though Gentile's reputation has since waned in comparison with that of his younger brother, he was certainly seen as the more high-profile artist in the 1470s and 1480s. He gained the so-called *sansaria*, a salary of over 100 ducats paid by the state to its official painter, as early as 1474, and in this capacity took a leading role in the on-going pictorial decorations at the Ducal Palace. He had also been knighted by the Holy Roman Emperor Frederick III, and it is no surprise that in 1479, following a request from the court of Mehmet II at Constantinople (modern Istanbul), he was chosen to represent Venice and sent to the Sultan's court to make a portrait. This was certainly a difficult and tricky assignment, given that Venice had been at war with the Ottoman Turks for the past 16 years, and that figurative art was prohibited under Muslim religious law. Mehmet, however, took a more liberal view, and commissioned Gentile to paint a portrait which showed him as a powerful international ruler, equivalent not just to those in Europe, but also to Alexander the Great in antiquity (FIG. 40). His Alexander-like victories over Greece, Trebizond and Asia may be symbolized in the three crowns motif, while his turban and the richly threaded and bejewelled cloth draped over the parapet indicate his status as an Eastern potentate. Gentile showed Mehmet in the familiar three-quarter profile he sometimes used in his ducal portraits in Venice. To the lower left and right he included fictive engraved stone tablets which recall the kind of ancient Roman inscriptions found in his father's sketchbook (now in the Louvre), which he is rumoured to have presented as a gift to the Sultan. The ornate architecture surrounding Mehmet has no precedents in Gentile's portraiture: but it might reflect Lombardo's recent *Mocenigo* monument. Despite its effect of oriental delicacy, it probably serves a similar symbolic function. Like Pietro Mocenigo, the Sultan appears under a triumphal arch that refers to his many military victories. At the same time, Gentile uses his naturalistic technique to soften the portrait. The arch and Mehmet's turban feature an illusionistic fall of light and shadow, while comparison with contemporary medals shows that Gentile subtly idealized his sitter's features, lending him the appearance of youthfulness and perspicacity.

In the *Mehmet* portrait, Gentile pressed Renaissance naturalism into the service of Venetian diplomacy, providing a perfect image of the seamless interface with the East that had long been key to Venetian cultural aspirations and identity. Gentile quickly returned to Venice to resume his duties as leading painter for the city's public

Fig. 40
Gentile Bellini
Sultan Mehmet II

1480. Oil (nineteenth-century repaint) on canvas, perhaps transferred from panel, 69.9 × 52.1cm (2ft 3½ in × 1ft 8½ in). National Gallery, London.

institutions, and his portrait of the Sultan apparently followed him home relatively quickly, after it was sold off to Venetian merchants by Mehmet's less tolerant son, Bayezid II. However, the integration of Western and Eastern elements that Gentile arrived at during his stay in Constantinople, based on avoidance of any hint of negativity or judgement, was destined to have a lasting effect: the oriental mode that he and his followers further developed in Venice continued to be popular into the following century. A further portrait of a military leader from these decades tells a different story (FIG. 41). When the mercenary and leader of the Venetian land forces, Bartolomeo Colleoni, died in 1475, he bequeathed a fortune to the Republic on the condition that an equestrian statue was raised in his honour in St Mark's Square. Colleoni's request was undoubtedly made with Donatello's *Gattamelata* (*see* FIG. 17) in mind. Venice was not Padua, though, and there had always been an implicit embargo on the raising of monuments to powerful individuals in St Mark's Square: the very heart of communal public space in the city. The age-old Republican mistrust of free-standing three-dimensional sculpture came to the fore, alongside an equally traditional pragmatism which suggested a solution. Colleoni's monument could be built in a Venetian piazza, but away from St Mark's Square itself, in front of the Scuola Grande di San Marco and the grand Dominican church of Santi Giovanni e Paolo.

Perhaps even more significant than the state's objection was its readiness to compromise. If the new location was less highly charged than St Mark's, it was still very prominent, with work on-going in the creation of the lavish new building for the Scuola (*see* FIG. 35). To this extent, the monument marks a new stage in the arrival of the Renaissance style in Venice. Though the work was designed by the Florentine Andrea del Verrocchio (1435–1488) it was cast by a local craftsman, Alessandro Leopardi (active from 1482, died 1522), who signed it on the horse's girth. Leopardi also designed the high socle in an assertively *all'antica* style, a work of which he was apparently very proud, alluding to it in an inscription on his tomb. Recognition of Venetian input may have been important to local acceptance of the work, which in many ways ran counter to established tastes and cultural values. The muscular self-assertiveness of the rider and his

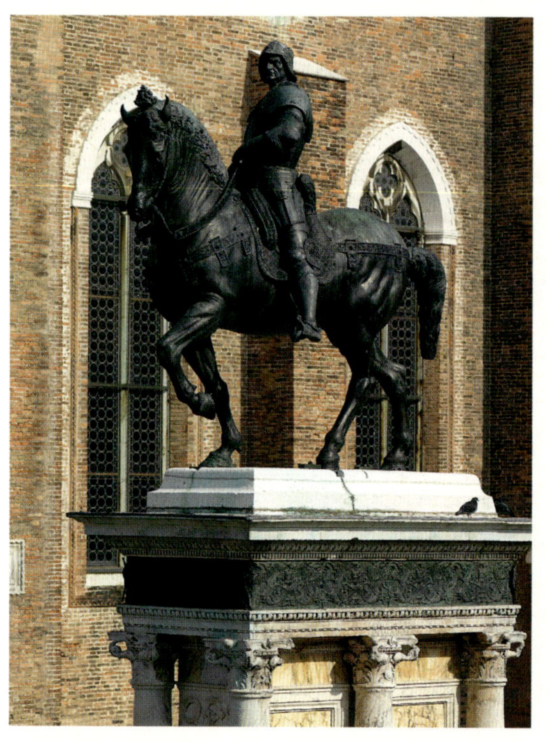

Fig. 41
Andrea del Verrocchio and
Alessandro Leopardi
Colleoni Monument

1481–88/96. Gilded bronze on marble base, height 400cm (13ft 1½in), (395cm without the socle). Piazza di Santi Giovanni e Paolo, Venice.

Having won a competition in 1479 to make both horse and rider, Verrocchio was then told he should only complete the horse. A dispute apparently followed, though Verrocchio did finally produce a clay model for the entire sculpture. Following his death, Leopardi cast the sculpture.

horse in the Colleoni monument went further than any other work discussed so far in its contradiction of the Venetian values of collaboration, its bristling individualism appearing to offer a direct challenge to the collective identity of the city. Yet it too might finally be understood as a patriotic work. Colleoni, like many other *condottieri* or mercenaries, had served other states as well as Venice during his career, and had even fought against the city on several occasions; but when his image was erected in a Venetian piazza, the city could lay special claim to him as an expression of the power of the Republic and as a potent symbol of its military might on the mainland of Italy.

The cultural dynamics of space: maps and history paintings

The naturalism of many paintings and sculptures discussed in this chapter is sometimes taken as a sign of the rise of a newly rational or scientific approach to the world, and thus also of the coming of modernity itself. There can be no doubt that by the late fifteenth century, figurative art in Venice had become intensely and convincingly illusionistic, such that the actors featured within the given work appear real, and as if existing within a three-dimensional space that is a continuous extension of the viewer's own. Key works, such as Giovanni Bellini's San Giobbe Altarpiece, were lauded as masterpieces of perspective painting, and he and Gentile had become renowned for their special expertise in this area. The leading mathematician Luca Pacioli made special mention of his fruitful discussions with the brothers on

Fig. 42
Jacopo de'Barbari
Map of Venice

1500. Woodcut, 140 × 282 cm
(4ft 7in × 9ft 3in). Museo
Correr, Venice.

The image was printed on
six large woodblocks, and
covered nearly 2 square
metres. The publisher,
Anton Kolb, was a merchant
from Nuremberg, which might
explain the orientation of
the map towards the Alps to
the north. In any case, the
production was certainly
intended to appeal to an
international audience.

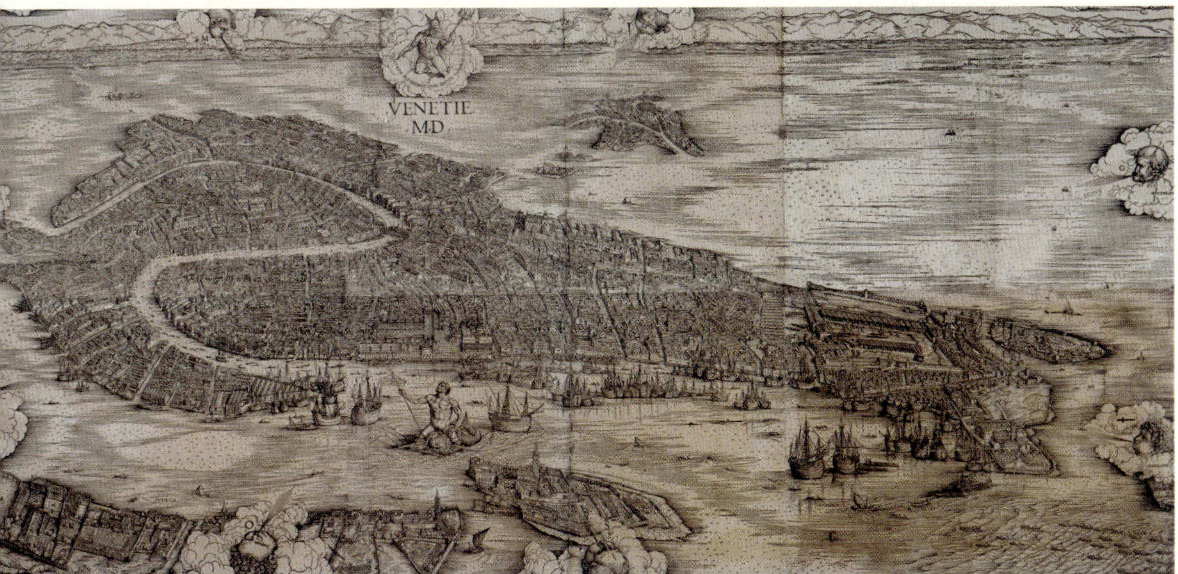

this topic in his *De divina proportione* (1493). Though they must have known of Alberti's injunction to painters regarding the use of perspective in his *De pictura* (1435), their father's sketchbooks provided them with more immediate models. Giovanni's composition of the San Giobbe Altarpiece draws quite closely, in fact, on certain of his father's drawings featuring a box-like receding space seen through a round-topped archway. Gentile demonstrated his own special abilities as a master of linear perspective in works such as the *Procession in St Mark's Square* of 1496. But the effect of visual accuracy that perspective generated does not mean that the brothers sought to be scientific or objective, in our sense of these words. Indeed, their skill in giving an illusionistic effect typically served traditional symbolic meanings.

The extraordinary map of Venice by Jacopo de'Barbari (ca. 1460/70–1516) uses perspective in a similar way to these painters (FIG. 42). Comparison with older depictions of the city, such as that featured in a manuscript of Marco Polo's travels of ca. 1400, reveal de'Barbari's accuracy (FIG. 43). The late medieval illuminator

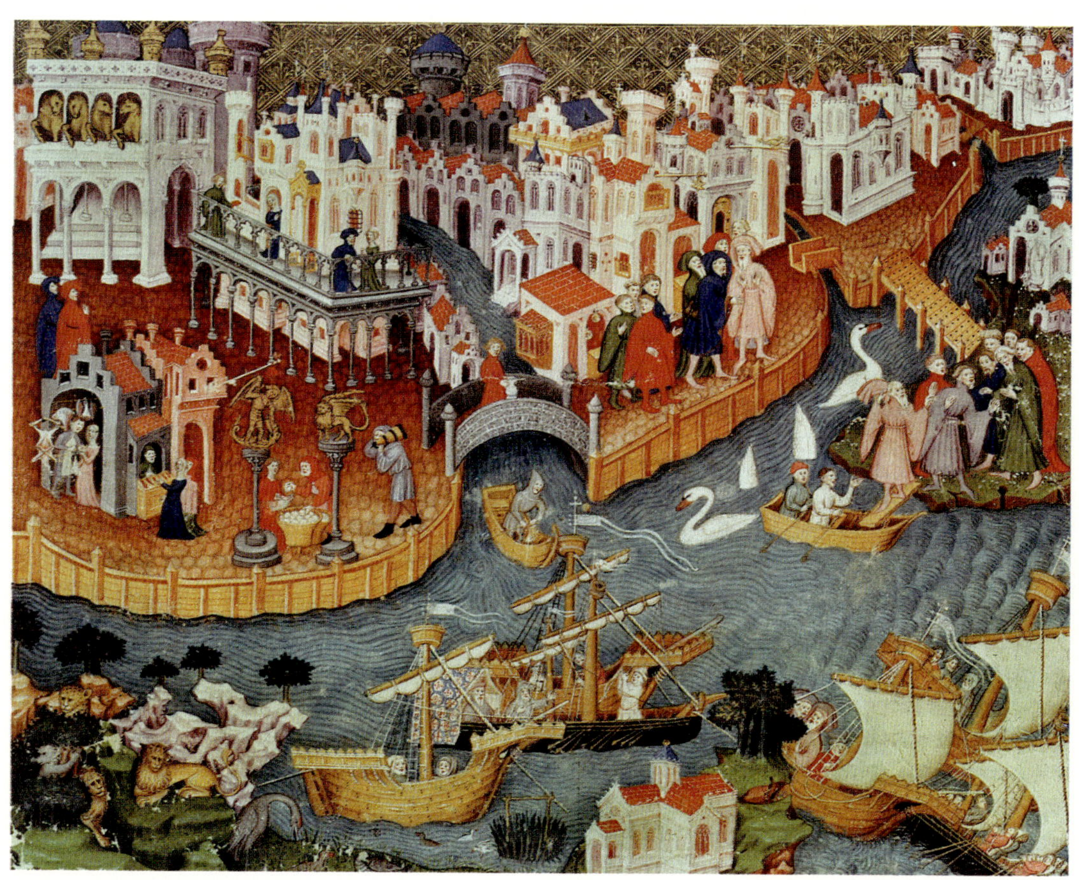

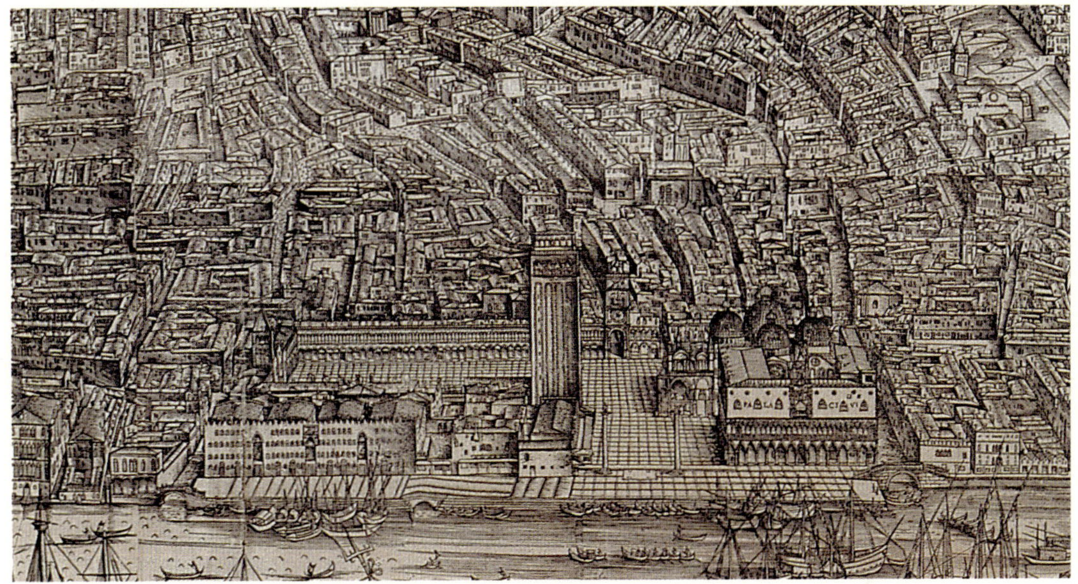

was aware of Venice's maritime location, with canals and bridges, and also knew that two columns topped by sculptures of the city's patron saints had been erected near its entrance, and that four bronze horses stood on the upper facade of its main church nearby; but he had clearly never visited the city. De'Barbari, on the other hand, was a Venetian, and used a determinedly non-generic approach in the creation of his bird's eye view. With its uncompromisingly accurate record of the city's individual buildings and myriad waterways, the print is still used by historians today as a rich source of documentary knowledge about the appearance of the city in 1500. Despite this, de'Barbari evidently took liberties with the urban topography. Many houses and even *calli* (alleyways) were omitted towards the left (west) part of the map in order to provide a more orderly composition, while key buildings at the heart of the city, such as the Ducal Palace, were enlarged for symbolic purposes (*see* detail above). The unified perspective of de'Barbari's bird's eye view is not a product of scientific survey techniques, but of imaginative projection. The chosen direction of view, from south to north, has a cultural significance, given that it follows the city's main line of trade from the Adriatic to Northern Europe. This conception is reiterated by the presence of Neptune, god of the sea, in the Bacino next to Venetian galleys; and Mercury, god of commerce, directly in front of the distant view of the Alps. It may be that de'Barbari went further still in the symbolic fashioning of his map: his Venice is shaped like a dolphin, commonly regarded by mariners as an emblem of good fortune.

Jacopo de'Barbari
Detail of the Ducal Palace
from Map of Venice

See Fig.42.

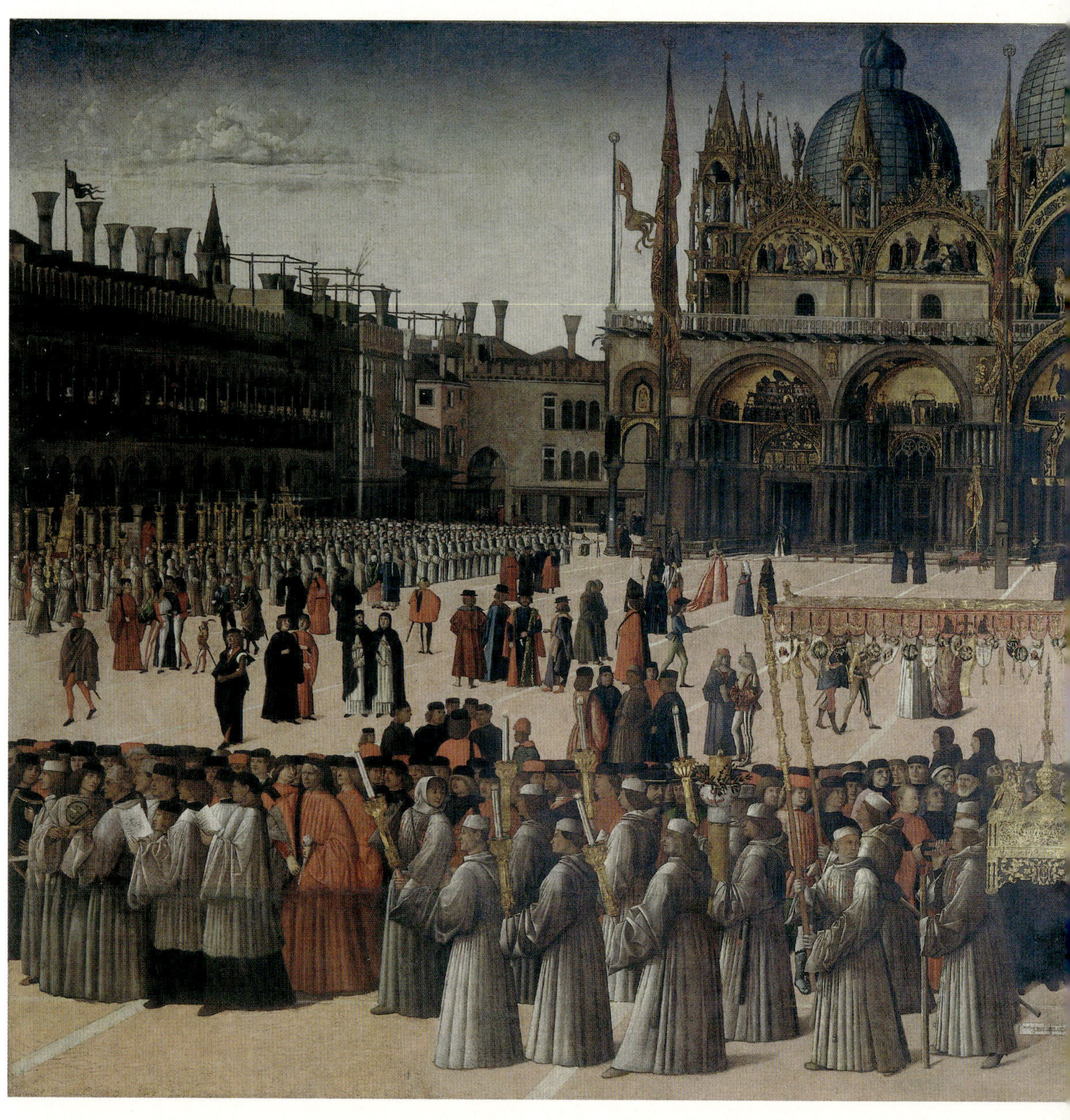

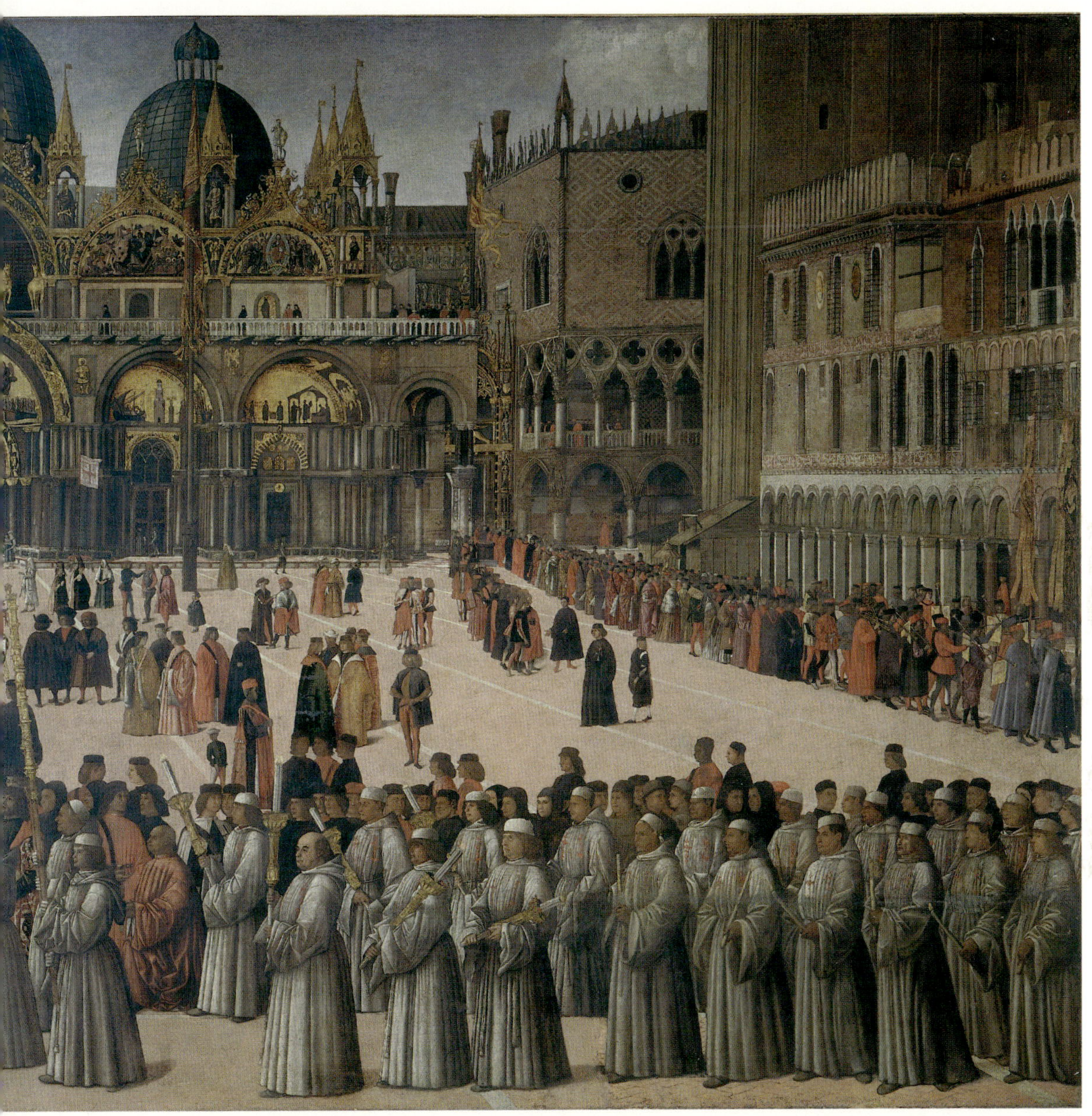

Fig. 44
Gentile Bellini
*Procession in St Mark's
Square*

1496. Tempera on canvas,
367 × 745cm (12ft ½in ×
24ft 5½in). Gallerie
dell'Accademia, Venice.

To the left of the painting,
members of the other Scuole
Grandi have assembled,
while a wide range of
social types mill around
in the Piazza itself,
their apparent randomness
giving an impression of
'happenstance'. Among the
five lunette mosaics on the
facade of St Mark's, only
that over the left-hand
portal of Sant'Alippio now
survives, its closeness
to Gentile's depiction
attesting to the accuracy of
his painting.

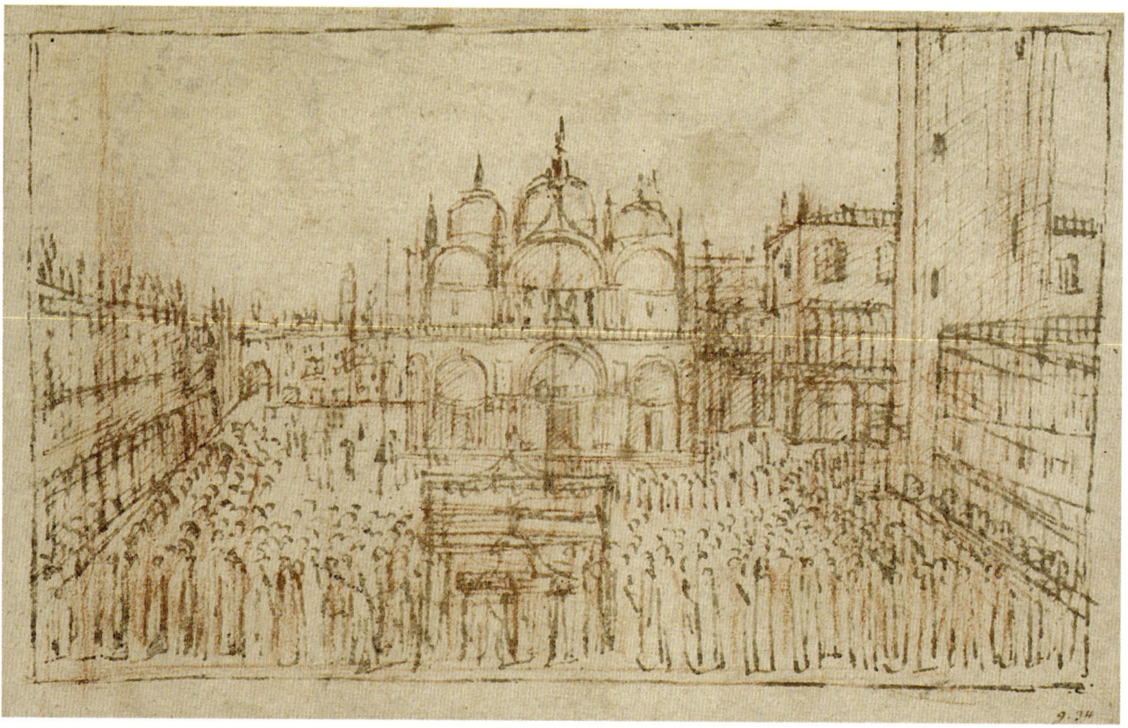

Fig. 45
Gentile Bellini
Drawing for *Procession in
St Mark's Square*

1496. Pen and brown ink,
over red chalk on paper,
13 × 19.6cm (5⅛ × 7¾in).
British Museum, London.

Gentile Bellini is said to have made a bird's eye view of Venice on his visit to Constantinople in 1479, and there is an evident overlap with cartography in the *Procession* (FIG. 44). In this painted history, as with de'Barbari's map, the impression of objectivity is made central to the overall effect. With his almost miniaturist precision of technique, Gentile pays particular attention to the richly encrusted facade of St Mark's itself, such that it is possible to reconstruct the compositions of the four lost mosaics in the arches above its portals on the basis of his painted record. It does not follow, however, that Gentile's rendering of St Mark's Square is the documentary representation that it appears. A surviving preparatory drawing shows his readiness to take radical liberties with the reality of the view from the west end of the Square (FIG. 45). In order to accommodate his rearrangement of the buildings at the right, where the bell tower is moved back to allow a view of the Porta della Carta and the Ducal Palace, the facade of St Mark's is shrunk from five bays to three. In the final painting, the solution for the bell tower is retained, but St Mark's has regained its actual shape. Lowering the viewpoint, Gentile now made this hallowed building the centrepiece of his composition: it appears as an enormous outsized structure, its onion domes extending beyond the picture margin at the top.

The *Procession* formed part of the 'True Cross' cycle commissioned by the Scuola Grande di San Giovanni Evangelista: one of the city's many lay confraternities. These peculiarly Venetian public institutions were dominated by non-nobles of citizen rather than patrician rank. These *cittadini*, who were carefully distinguished from the wider populace (the so-called *popolani*) of the city, comprised the often extremely wealthy rentiers, merchants and civil servants. They were forever excluded from political power by the *serrata* of 1296 (a ruling which had made seats on the Great Council hereditary), but were still very concerned to play a role in the on-going public life of the city. The Scuole provided them with an opportunity to do so, and 200 or more confraternities of this kind were active. The largest, most prestigious and richest were the six so-called Scuole Grandi, who had come to play a central role in the city's cultural life, and were widely seen as special guardians of its popular traditions of piety and patriotism. One observer aptly described them as 'mini-Republics', given that their strict internal organization consciously mirrored that of the Venetian state itself. In their art patronage of the late fifteenth century, the *cittadini* of the Scuole carefully emulated their patrician masters, filling their increasingly lavish Meeting Houses with large narrative histories (*istorie*), often modelled on those being commissioned in official buildings such as the Ducal Palace. Although these latter cycles of *istorie* were largely destroyed in two fires in the later sixteenth century, many of the works for the Scuole have survived.

In addition to providing social and financial benefits to their members, the Scuole also provided a focus for intense religious devotions and frequently processed through the city on Holy Days. It is one such procession that Gentile depicts in the painting illustrated here. The Scuole provided a vital stabilizing measure of social cohesion between the noble and non-noble sectors of the population in Venice, as is also evident from Gentile's painting. As the procession continues around the Square, it is the white-robed brothers (*fratelli*) of the commissioning Scuola who dominate proceedings at the front of the painting. They carry their precious relic of the True Cross housed in a golden tabernacle, which is symbolically positioned before the main portal of St Mark's to demonstrate the Scuola's piety and patriotism. Emphasizing the shared white costume of the *fratelli*, Gentile downplays the individuality of each Scuola

Gentile Bellini
Detail from *Procession in St Mark's Square*

See Fig. 44.

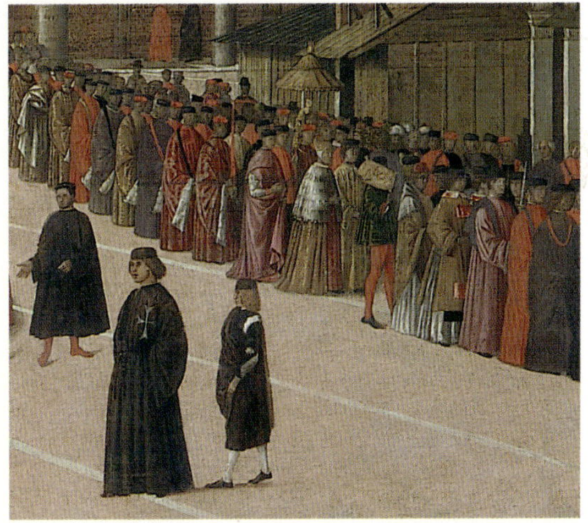

member in favour of a group representation in which no one person predominates. Among the procession at the background right, we glimpse the current doge, Agostino Barbarigo (*see* detail on previous page). The manner in which the leader of the state is buried in the crowd towards the picture margins offers a perfect expression of Venice's favoured cultural ideal of *mediocritas* (modesty or moderation). Rather than an open display of magnificence and power, such as one would find in an image of a princely court, the core values of the Republic are represented by the doge's show of deference to the city's on-going popular devotional and patriotic traditions.

Following his father's example in the sketchbooks (*see* FIG. 13), Gentile also carefully buried the given narrative of his *istoria* within its richly documented environment, to increase the sense of its validity and truth. The line of processing *fratelli* part just slightly at the foreground right, opening our view of the merchant Jacopo de'Salis,

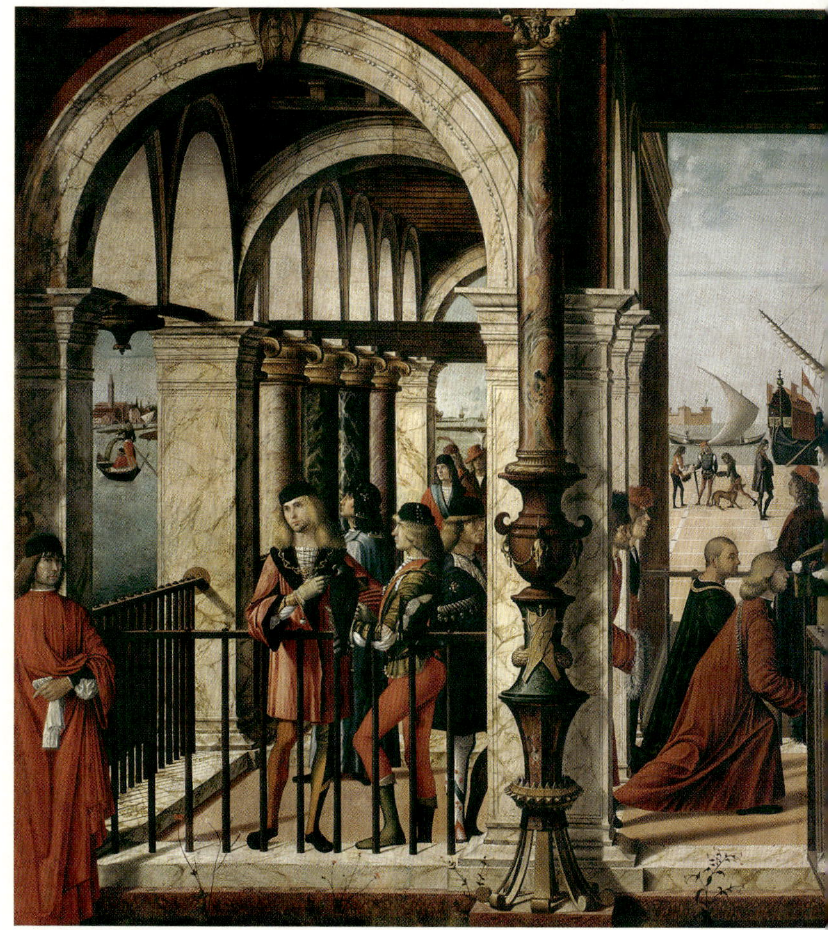

who is praying on his knees before the Scuola's relic, and whose sickly son is immediately healed in far-away Brescia. The point is that this miracle does not disturb the on-going ritual devotions in St Mark's Square, even if it is a direct result of them. Supported by Gentile's special abilities with linear perspective and his naturalistic depiction of the built and human environment of the city, in this work the mythic image of Venice as the home of cultural and spiritual perfection was brought to a new level of realization.

Carpaccio: past and present life

It was fitting enough that Gentile's *Procession* was set in Venice, given that this was (according to the Scuola's *incunabula* or printed handbook) where the various miracles of the relic of the True Cross occurred. In their further contributions to the cycle, Gentile and

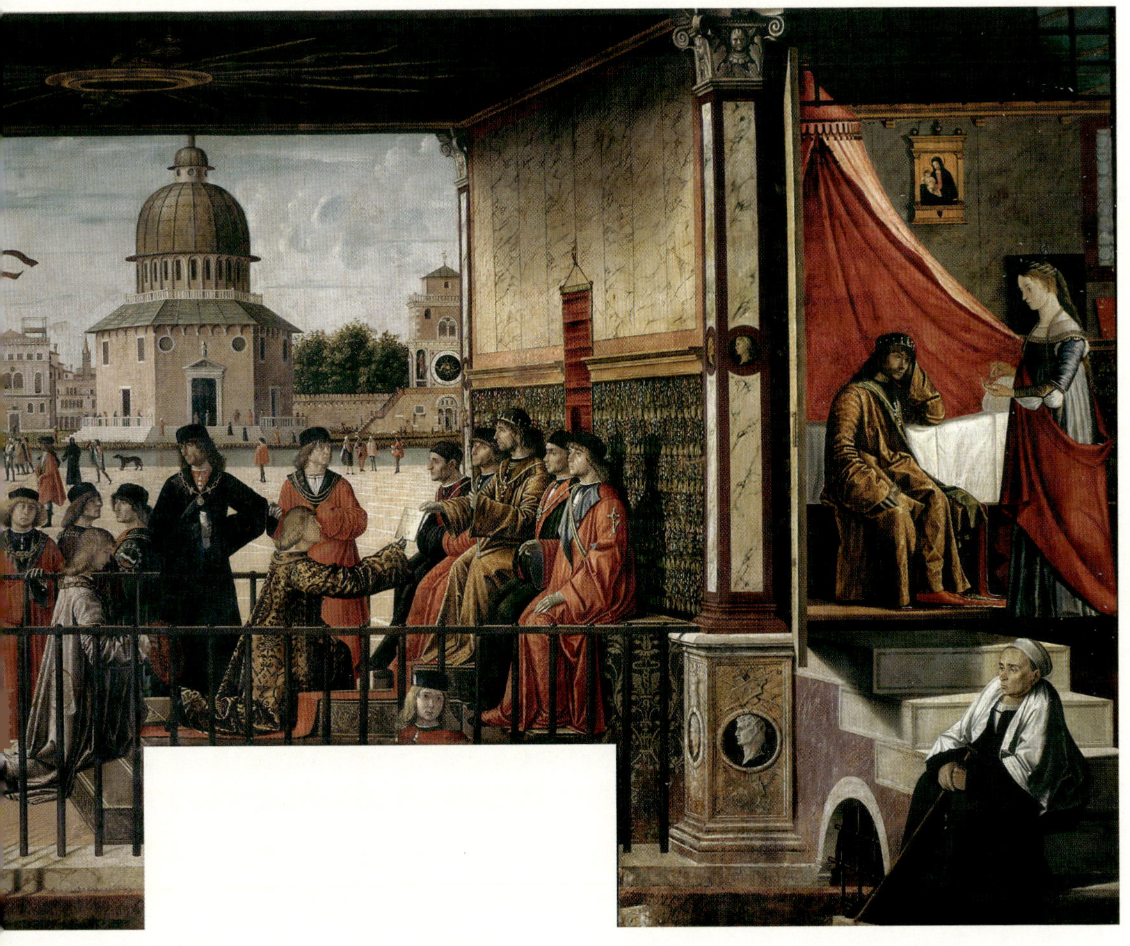

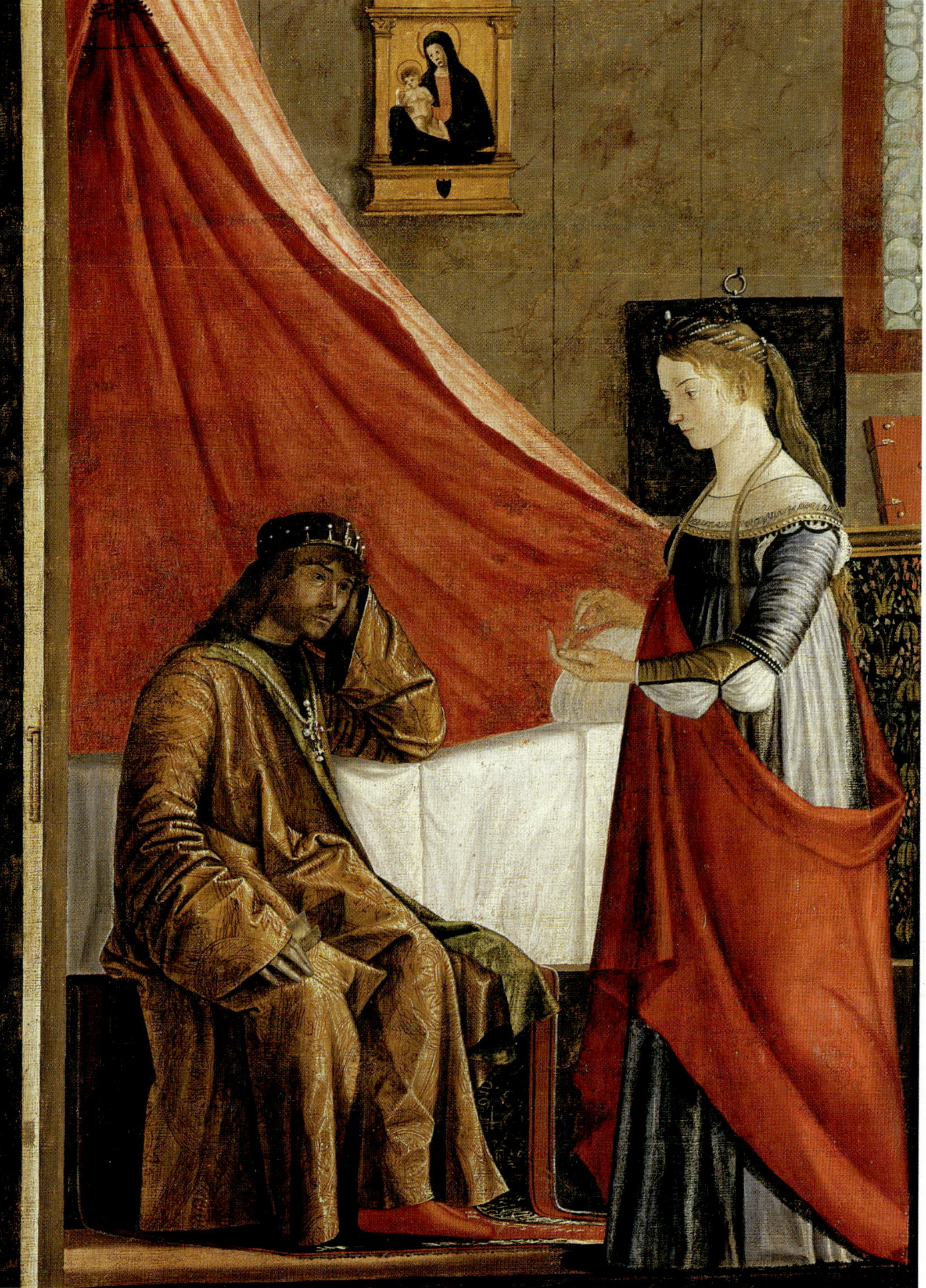

his followers, including Vittore Carpaccio (1460–1520), developed the 'eyewitness' style of history painting, burying the given event within richly documented depictions of specific streets, bridges and canals of the city. This approach is much less evident in equivalent *istorie* commissioned by the city's other Scuole from this period. In Carpaccio's cycle for the Scuola di Sant'Orsola, for example, also dating from the 1490s, the painter still pays careful attention to the detailed elaboration of the setting, including a dazzling array of exotic architectural structures and costumes (FIG. 46). Although these sometimes recall local or foreign examples, the setting is no longer geographically specific, and the main narrative scene is often set on a stage-like space at the front. Carpaccio was more like Gentile in his evident discomfort with the immediacy of unanticipated dramatic events. In several of his paintings for this cycle, nothing more occurs than the arrival or departure of important dignitaries: in the painting illustrated here, ambassadors from England are received at the French court in Brittany. The careful spacing between the three men, whose kneeling postures appear as carefully choreographed variations on one another, express an ideal of public life at the end of the fifteenth century in which timeless ceremonial predominates.

Although Carpaccio imagines a fairy-tale world of chivalric courts from long ago in the St Ursula cycle, his paintings still express contemporary (perhaps even progressive) values. Venetian ambassadorial culture was renowned across Europe, and contemporary-looking Venetians in their typical long-sleeved high-necked togas feature prominently among the onlookers. The aristocratic world presented is a matter of formal public display, in which details of dress, action and gesture are closely observed to establish position within a hierarchical and ritualized reality that always appears as predestined and fixed. But that is certainly not the end of the story, either in the St Ursula cycle or in Carpaccio's work more widely. The painter constantly punctuated his superficially static vision with reference to the dynamic and proactive heroine of his narrative: St Ursula. This kind of juxtaposition is evident from the contrast between the right-hand section of the composition (see detail opposite) and the imagery to the left. Here we are afforded a view into a more private, intimate and feminine world, dominated not by the king and his court, but by Ursula herself. Standing in her bedroom, she is counting out on her fingers the conditions which might lead her to consent to the English offer of marriage. Meanwhile the king has lost much of the grandeur of his public appearance on his throne just to the left, reappearing slumped down on a chair listening to his dominant daughter's demands. This role inversion was certainly in keeping with the demands of the Christian narrative depicted, and Ursula's sacred authority is supported by the depiction of the Virgin herself in a devotional painting hanging on the wall nearby. In making her demands, Ursula was in fact beginning her emulation of the Mother of God as a Virgin Martyr. Despite these very serious meanings, it is difficult not to see this scene as a humorous aside against the male-dominated public world of the image on the main stage.

Such genre-like vignettes also indicate that it would be a mistake to see Carpaccio as naïve or unknowing. In combination with the elements of unreality that are introduced, it appears that he sought to move beyond Gentile's insistent documentary-style naturalism and perhaps also to depart from the patriotic platitudes this so often served. The light or playful tone of Carpaccio's work, with the implicit sense that he knows that the stories he tells are fairy tales or myths, is sophisticated rather than simple, and released him into a more independent kind of enjoyment of incidental elements than is evident in the solemn and meaningful world of the Bellini. In this sense, Carpaccio looks forward rather than back. The discovery that his famous painting of *Two Women* is the lower half of a scene showing Venetian men hunting in the lagoon does little to contradict the sense that Carpaccio often reached beneath the facade of public life in the fifteenth century (FIG. 47). The distant men, wholly absorbed in their pursuit of other prey, may be the absent husbands or clients of the ladies that they have left behind on the balcony, and on whom Carpaccio focuses our attention. These women, dressed up in ultra-fashionable finery with no detail overlooked, are waiting to be noticed: but to no avail. For all the possible symbolism of the many objects, birds and animals that surround them, it is their overriding feeling of boredom that interests the painter most. The special allure of Carpaccio's painting lies in its telling focus on a private but familiar moment in which nothing happens. Capturing the commonplace experience of ennui, he also introduced a more recognizable and distinctly modern kind of reality into Venetian art.

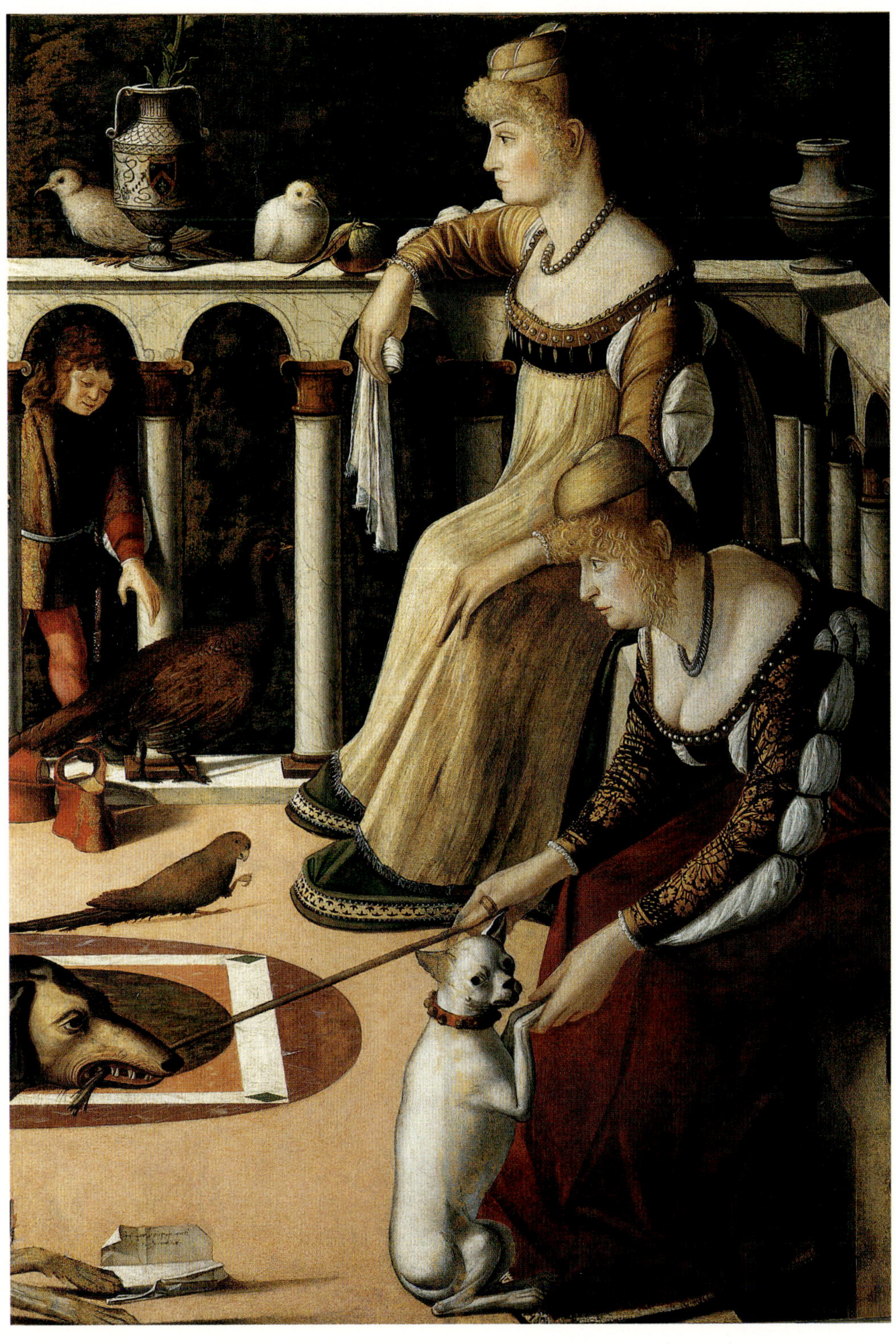

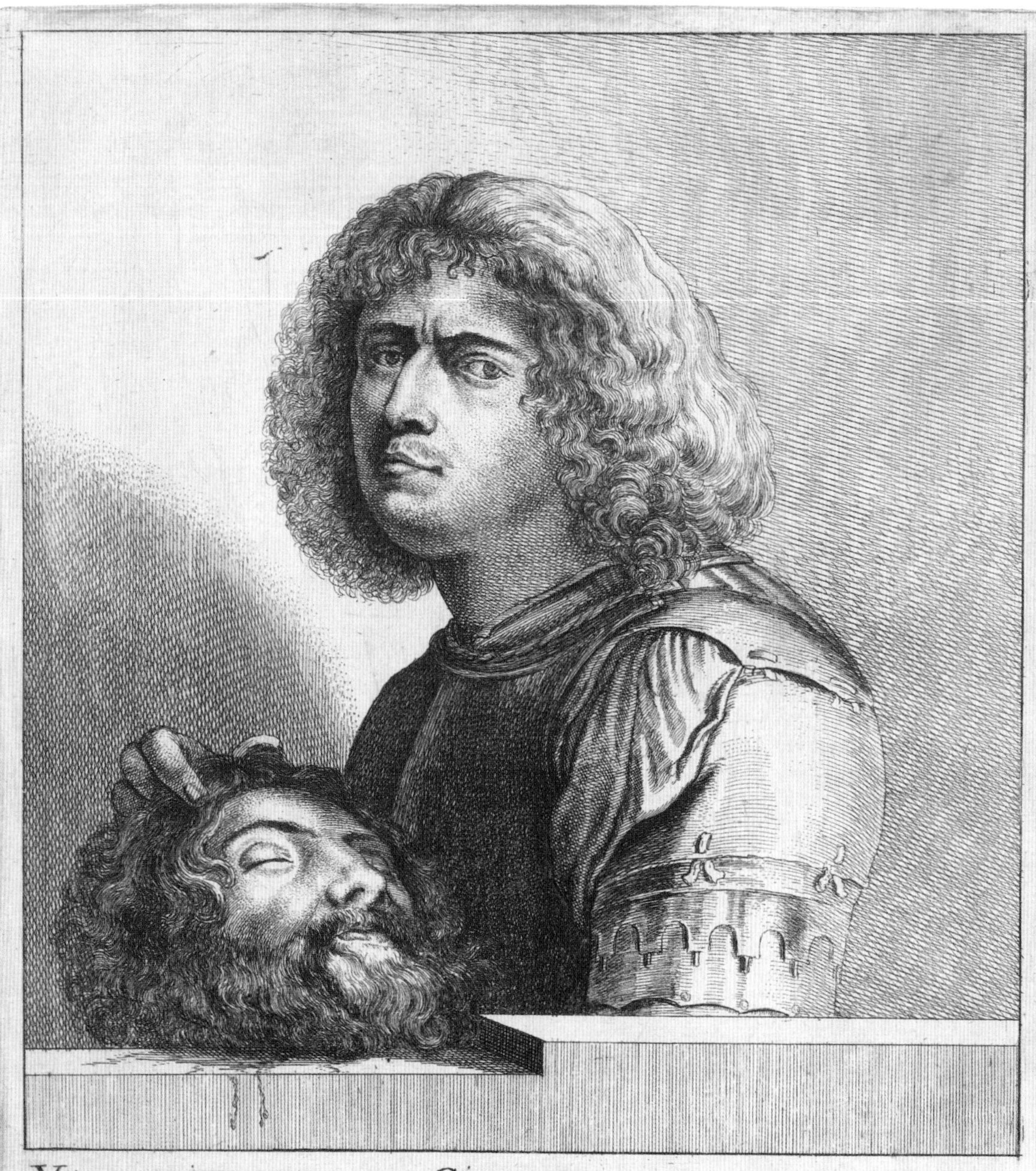

VERO RITRATTO DE GIORGONE DE CASTEL FRANCO
da luy fatto come lo celebra il libro del VASARI.

W. Hollar fecit ex Collectione Iohannis, et Iacobi van Verle, 1650.   F. van den Wyngarde excudit.

4

Individualism, Internationalism, Secularization: 1501–25

n his *Lives of the Artists* (Florence, 1550), Giorgio Vasari (1511–1574) noted that a significant change occurred in the art of Venice around the turn of the sixteenth century. The painter Giorgione (ca. 1477/8–1510), he proclaimed, ushered in a new 'modern age' that could be paralleled in artistic developments elsewhere in Italy at this time. The Tuscan Vasari was sceptical of all Venetian painters, given their supposed lack of *disegno* (design) and carefully ascribed Giorgione's innovations to the influence of a compatriot: Leonardo da Vinci (1452–1519). Yet his perception that Giorgione's 'blending of tones and tremendous impression of movement' represented a fundamental departure from the art of the past was accurate enough. The previous chapters have shown that the Renaissance approach had been readily incorporated within a fluid spectrum of styles in Venice, in order to support and intensify the city's social, political and religious values. It now began to be developed in more individualistic and less integrated ways, often proposing departure from earlier visual conventions or expectations. Its previously intimate relationship to the public culture of the city became less clear or pronounced in the process.

New artistic identities

Giorgione ('Big George'), whose real name was Giorgio Barbarelli, died of the plague in his early thirties, and precious little is known about the progress of his short career. He seems initially to have been a pupil in Giovanni Bellini's crowded workshop: one which also harboured major painters such as Sebastiano del Piombo (1485–1547) and Titian (ca. 1488/90–1576). The special success of Giovanni's workshop in his later career may have been based on his willingness to incorporate elements of his pupils' progressive styles into his own, as can be seen in certain of his works from the decade or so before his death in 1516. But Giovanni went only so far in this regard, and his approach to painting after 1500 remained tied in many ways to that which he had developed in previous decades. Even the suggestion in a contemporary humanist poem that Giovanni was homosexual does not undermine the sense that he had become the respectable father figure of painting in Venice. Although he was exempted from membership of the Venetian painters' guild (the *Arte dei pittori*) in 1480, his work remained focussed on service to the city's main institutions and public buildings, such as the Ducal Palace, the Meeting Houses of the Scuole, and the city's numerous churches. Giorgione, on the other hand, only rarely produced large-scale or public paintings. He appears to have worked primarily for a small clique of sophisticated patrician patrons who were in a position to withdraw from their humdrum mercantile and political duties into a world of refined leisure and contemplation. This private and elite patronage encouraged Giorgione to develop a poetic or pastoral kind of painting, and might also have led him to develop a quite different identity as an artist.

Comparison of a medal featuring Giovanni Bellini with an engraving after a lost self-portrait by Giorgione demonstrates the younger artist's new persona very well. While in contemporary Florence the idea that leading artists were innately talented geniuses found favour among the cognoscenti, in Venice they continued to be considered as artisans who ran family-based or collaborative workshops in the service of the city. Both Giovanni's medal and Giorgione's self-portrait indicate that the social profile of leading painters was on the rise. As members of the highest rank of the citizenry – the so-called 'original citizens' or *cittadini originarii*, who could demonstrate three generations of residency in Venice – the Bellini family enjoyed a position much further up the social scale than other painters of their time. The very fact of having *all'antica* medals cast (Gentile commissioned one too) is a measure of the

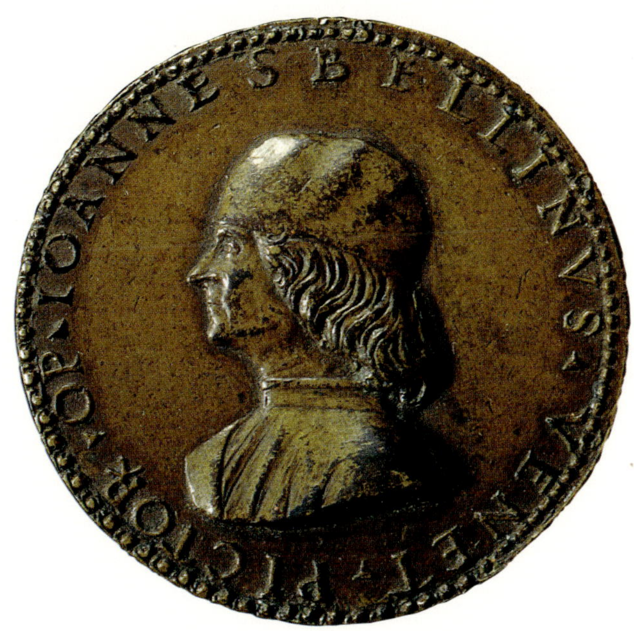

family's social prominence. Yet Giovanni's shows him as a faithful and patriotic civil servant rather than as an individualistic creator (FIG. 49). Scant attention is paid to the definition of his personal features: the hat pulled down firmly over his forehead does little to suggest his intellectual power, and he sports the *stola* (stole) often worn by Venetian citizens. The border legend identifies him simply as 'Ioannes Bellinus Venet Pictor' ('Giovanni Bellini, Venetian Painter), confirming his trade as also his close identification with the city that he served.

In Giorgione's self-portrait, on the other hand, there is no direct reference either to his profession or to Venice (*see* FIG. 48). If Giovanni's persona was defined in these outward terms, then Giorgione's projected identity is altogether more ambiguous and is made a matter of sophisticated literary association or analogy. Giorgione presents himself in the guise of the Old Testament hero David, who has recently slain the giant Goliath. The identification with David (which Giorgione apparently shared with the young Michelangelo in Florence) undoubtedly served to symbolize the artist's tussle with the 'Goliath' of nature. It also presented the artist as divinely inspired, an idea which was destined to become an important topos in leading artistic centres across Italy during the sixteenth century. In his self-portrait Giorgione still maintained the parapet familiar from his master's portraits, but the emphasis now falls directly on the sitter's expression with its suggestion of his troubled or conflicted state of mind. As the fingers of his right hand absent-mindedly caress the tousled hair of his decapitated victim, and trickles of blood spill down the front of the parapet, the painter's knitted brows serve to suggest something about the undertow of struggle or even violence involved in the creative act and in the making of a modern artist.

International cross-currents

The arrival of Albrecht Dürer (1471–1528) in the autumn of 1505, to work on a painting for the altar of the German merchants in the church of San Bartolomeo al Rialto, had an immediate impact on the development of painting in Venice. In his letters home to Nuremberg, Dürer identified Giovanni Bellini as the best painter in Venice, and feared poisoning by other (unnamed) artists in the city, jealous of his success and reputation. In fact his example was of more interest to Giovanni's followers than to the old master himself. A *Christ among the Doctors* by Cima da Conegliano (1459/60–1517/18) has certain features in common with Dürer's painting of the same subject of 1506 (FIGS 50, 51). Cima's painting probably precedes Dürer's (which may have been begun in Venice, but completed in Rome), and both works were apparently

Fig. 50
Cima da Conegliano
Christ among the Doctors

ca. 1504–5. Oil on panel, 54.5 × 87cm (1ft 9½in × 2ft 10¼in). Muzeum Narodowe, Warsaw. From the collection of Potoccy of Krzeszowice.

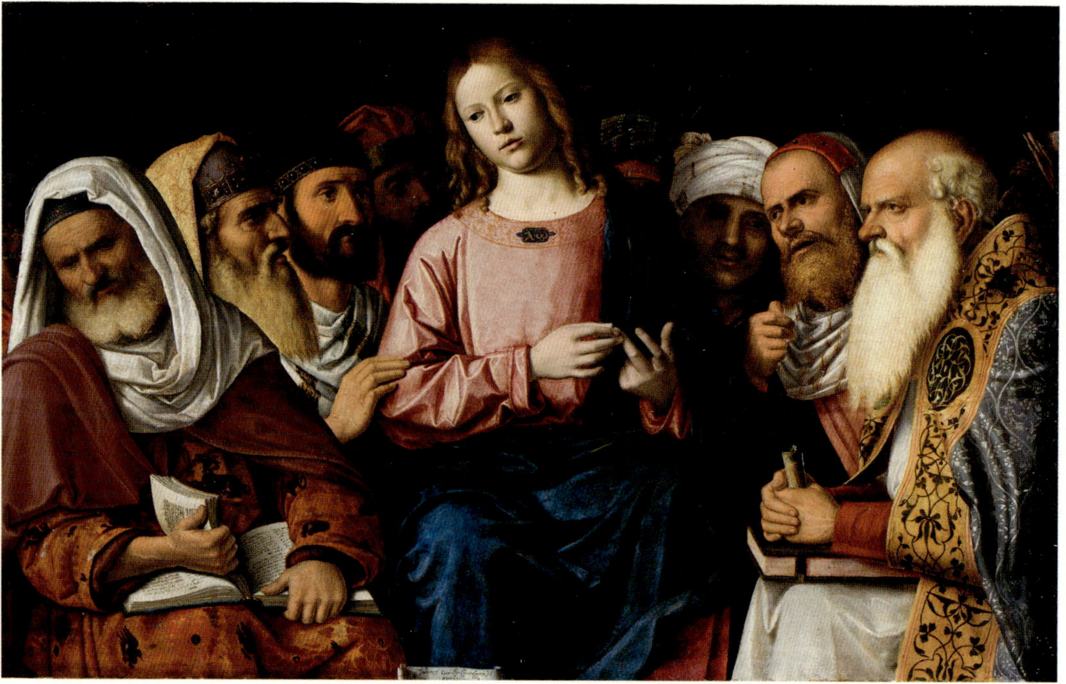

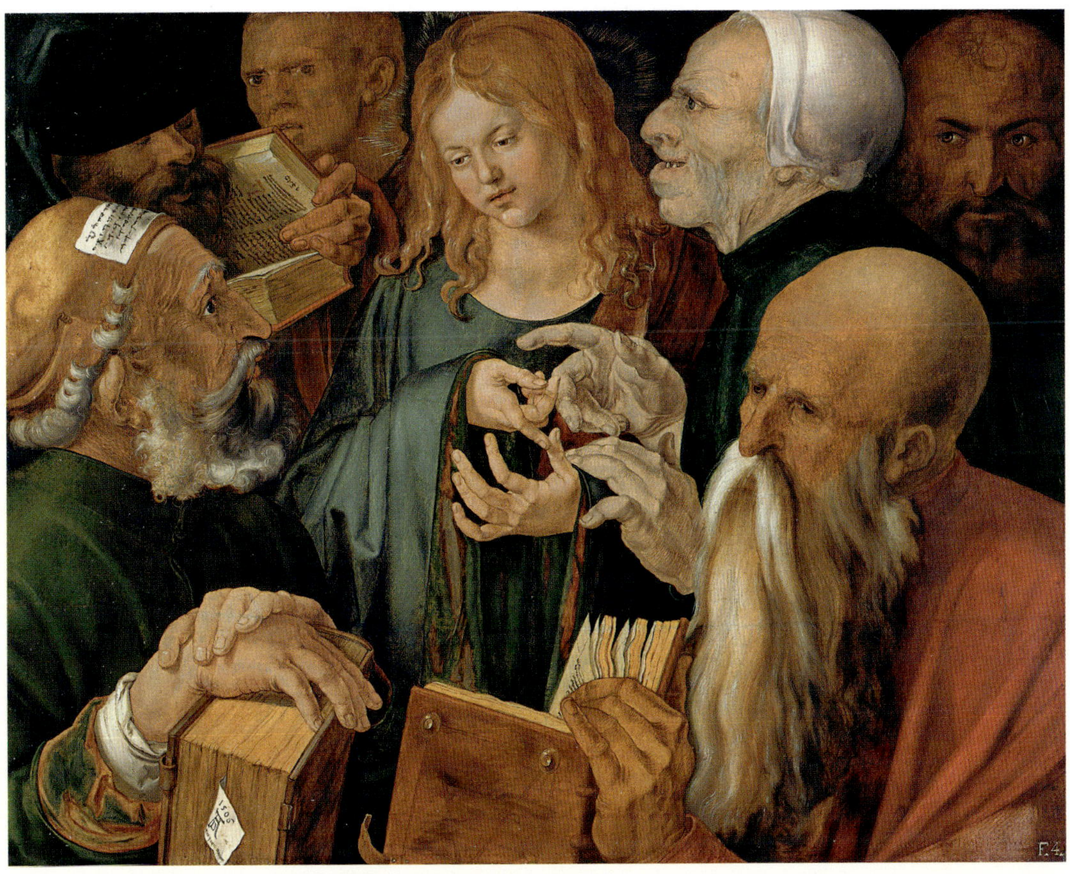

dependent on a common source: a lost painting by Leonardo da Vinci. They feature half-length figures treated with portrait-like intensity, using a chiaroscuro treatment which allows the forms to emerge out of a dark background into the light, and to this extent follow Leonardo's example. But Cima had long remained faithful to the style of Giovanni Bellini first established in the 1470s, and attempted to absorb progressive Leonardesque features into the more familiar local idiom. Thus, his figures are placed at a decorous distance from us, with Christ placed on a raised seat and the Doctors forming a semi-circle to each side: an arrangement which recalls the Bellinesque type of the *sacra conversazione* (gathering of saints) that Cima had often adopted in his altarpieces. Despite the meticulous rendering of details, Cima carefully idealizes his figures, allowing Christ to appear as a young man (according to Luke's gospel, he was just 12 when he visited the temple) and softening the facial differences between the surrounding figures.

Dürer, on the other hand, moves his figures disturbingly close to the picture plane, setting their overlapping forms into a cramped and expressively ambiguous space. He laid powerful emphasis on the individualization of their features, as also on extremes of

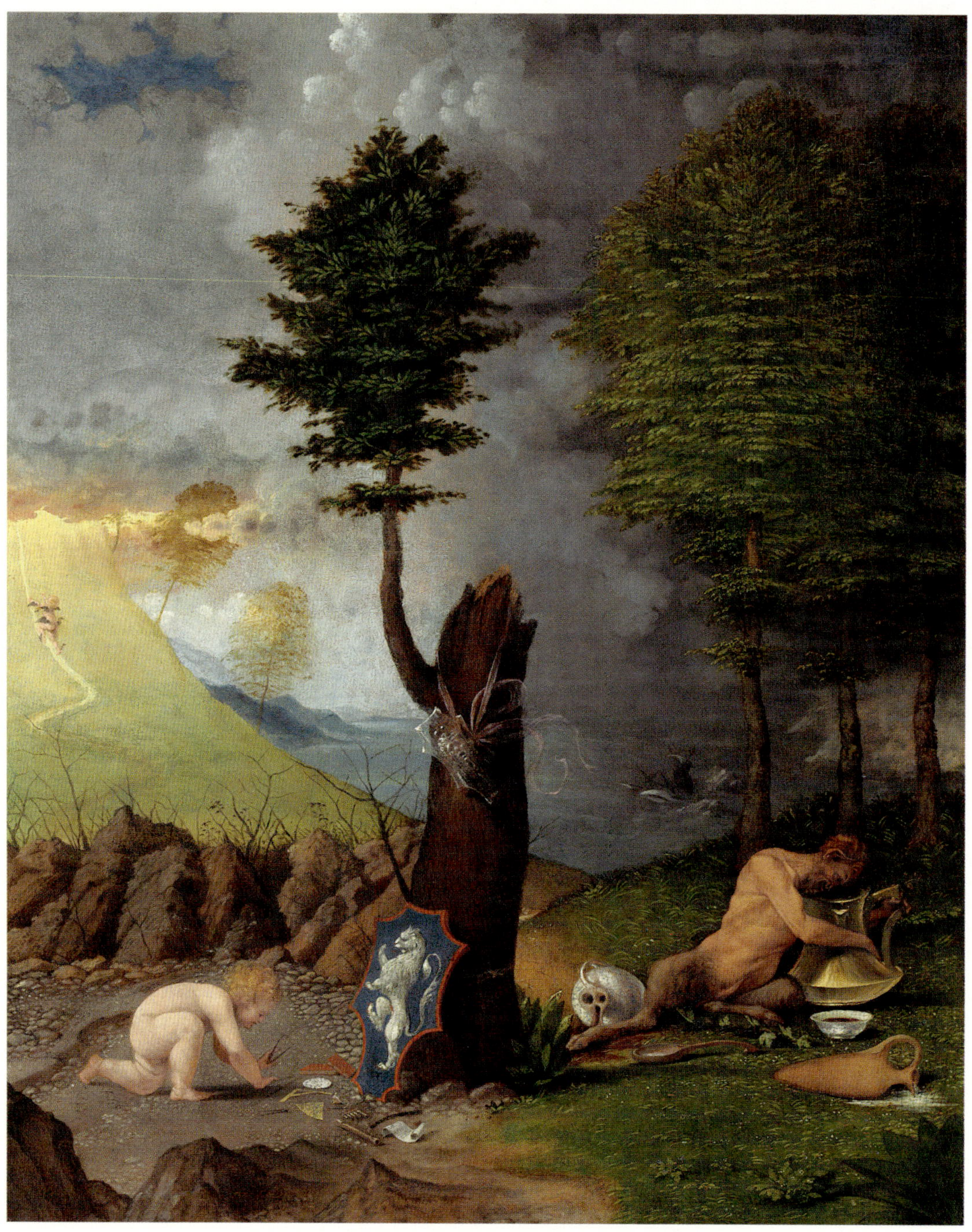

physiognomic contrast, most obviously between the beautiful young Christ and the deformed features of the Doctor to his left. In doing so, he apparently followed Leonardo more directly than did Cima. Although we do not know what Leonardo's original work looked like, it probably drew on his many drawings featuring expressively contrasting heads (young and old; beautiful and ugly; good and bad). Dürer appears to have understood Leonardo's concern that a painting should be 'accurate' not only to the outward forms of nature but also to its inward, unseen qualities. Dürer's closer understanding of Leonardo's lesson in this regard also suggests the more radical nature of his impact in Venice. Though his work undoubtedly opened a further vista onto the naturalistic tradition of art in Northern Europe, it also brought cutting-edge knowledge of progressive Renaissance ideas from elsewhere in Italy. He must have appeared challengingly cosmopolitan to those brought up on a local diet of Bellinesque painting and still tied to quattrocento (fifteenth century) conventions. If Cima instinctively sought to absorb the international cross-currents at play in the art of Dürer into the Venetian approach, others were more alive to the potential it offered to press beyond established boundaries.

The young Lorenzo Lotto (1480–1556/7), whose workshop was then based in Treviso on the *terraferma* (mainland), was more closely responsive to Dürer's example than either Giovanni Bellini or Cima, and may even have visited the German artist's temporary studio in Venice to observe him at work. A number of Lotto's early religious paintings draw strongly on Dürer's example, featuring exaggerated physiognomic juxtapositions. Cima may have ignored Dürer's use of ugliness to generate expressive power, but Lotto readily included stark contrasts between grizzled old saints and the beautiful young Christ, using acidic colours and jagged, sharp-edged drapery folds to add further drama to his compositions. Similar formal contrasts were included in his early secular works, where they could take on an assertively moral dimension. In a small painting produced as a cover for a portrait of the controversial bishop of Treviso, Bernardo de' Rossi, the entire composition is generated through a contrast between opposing elements (FIG. 52). The details included in Giovanni's Bellini's landscape backgrounds had often served to express religious meaning, though this was typically concealed beneath an appearance of nature based on close observation of the local topography of the *terraferma*. Lotto's landscape was more overtly constructed around visual symbols that serve the underlying allegory, and does not suggest an immediate association with the countryside near to Venice.

1505. Oil on panel, 56.5 × 42.2cm (1ft 10¼in × 1ft 4⅝in). National Gallery of Art, Washington D.C. Samuel H. Kress Collection, 1939.1.156.

Lotto developed a twofold 'moral' landscape divided by a symbolic tree placed at the centre, basing his composition on a Dürer print featuring *Hercules at the Crossroads*, in which the landscape is divided in a similar fashion. The hard work of the foreground cupid, operating mathematical and musical instruments, is contrasted with the debauched satyr to the right, whose blind sensuality is established by his myopic stare into a wine vat and his associated state of sexual arousal. The satyr's connection with pagan antiquity reconfirms the point of contrast, as does the depiction of the sea storm behind him, which contrasts with the sunlit mountain ascending towards heaven at the background left. Lotto's painting served to emphasize the virtuous path followed by his patron, as is evident from the coat of arms placed at the base of the tree on the 'good' side near to the industrious putto. The painting probably functioned as a kind of *impresa* or emblem interpreting the portrait below, and may have been more specifically intended to answer the charges of political corruption that had recently been raised against de' Rossi by the Venetian authorities. Quite apart from its symbolic or political meanings, Lotto's painting reflects an intensifying interest in landscape as an expressive pictorial form in its own right. Given its more abstract structuring around moral ideas, it is something of a surprise to find that his landscape also features subtle transitions of light, colour and air, still managing to convince as an observation of rapidly changing atmospheric effects.

Poetic painting and printmaking

Giorgione was also influenced by Dürer, as is evident from the little painting known as the *Tempest* (FIG. 53). He might also have known Lotto's painted cover, given that both works feature dramatically contrasting conditions of light caused by the arrival of a violent storm. Both also possess an allegorical quality, but if the symbolism in Lotto's work is apparent enough, then the meaning of Giorgione's work remains mysterious. Although many strenuous attempts have been made to establish the precise subject-matter, it may be that it was intentionally ambiguous or open-ended. This quality distinguishes the *Tempest* from the predominantly public face of painting in fifteenth-century Venice, with its overriding concern to be explicit and meaningful. Giovanni Bellini had fostered a taste for a more private kind of painting in the city in his devotional imagery, and had painted a small number of allegories and other works in which landscape dominates over figure. These latter paintings, however,

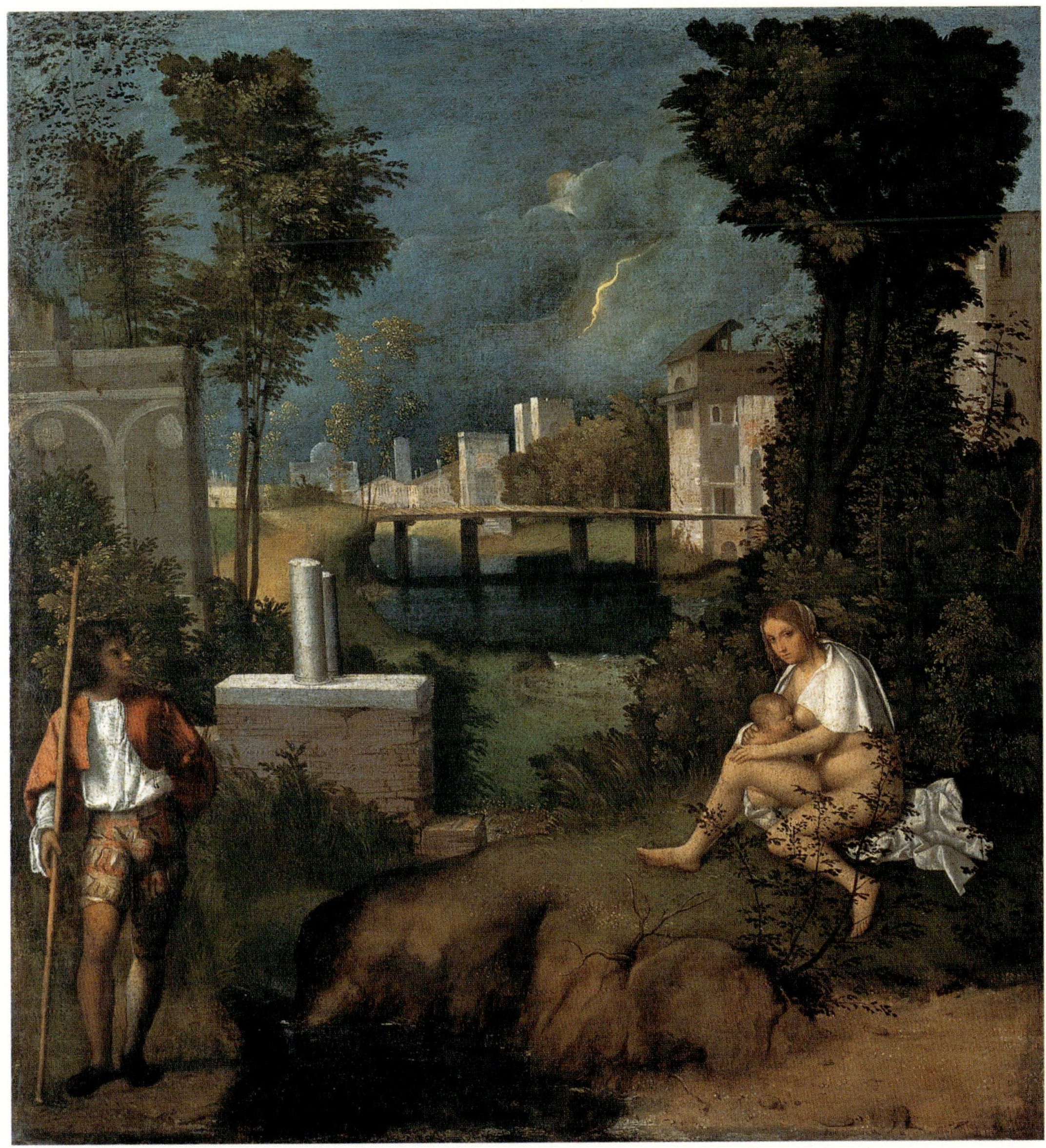

Fig.53
Giorgione
Tempest

ca. 1509–10. Oil on canvas,
82 × 73cm (2ft 8½in ×
2ft 4¼in). Gallerie
dell'Accademia, Venice.

This little painting has
provided art historians with
a great opportunity to show
off their ingenuity. It has
been variously interpreted
as a mythology (the Infancy
of Paris, the Birth of
Apollo and others); as an
allegory of the forces of
Nature or Fortune; and as
a religious painting showing
the Finding of Moses, or
Adam and Eve following the
Fall.

typically feature still and placid depictions of nature that support the underlying religious meaning of the picture. They do not prepare us for the radical sense of movement and temporariness in the *Tempest*: a painting in which the concern to evoke the peculiarly charged and livid atmosphere that immediately precedes a violent thunderstorm is paramount.

A contemporary-looking man with a pike and a semi-naked woman suckling a child occupy the foreground, but their precise identity and relationship to one another remain uncertain. In 1530, the painting was described by the Venetian patrician art collector Marcantonio Michiel as the 'little landscape with the storm and the gypsy'. Gypsies had become well known across Europe during the fifteenth century, and were sometimes shown semi-naked, suckling children and wandering through landscapes to suggest their vagrancy, or a more general sense of worldly transience. Michiel says nothing about the man standing to the left, and the generic quality of his description suggests he was already uncertain about what the painting depicts. He listed the *Tempest* in the private art collection of Gabriele Vendramin, and also saw Giorgione's *Three Philosophers*

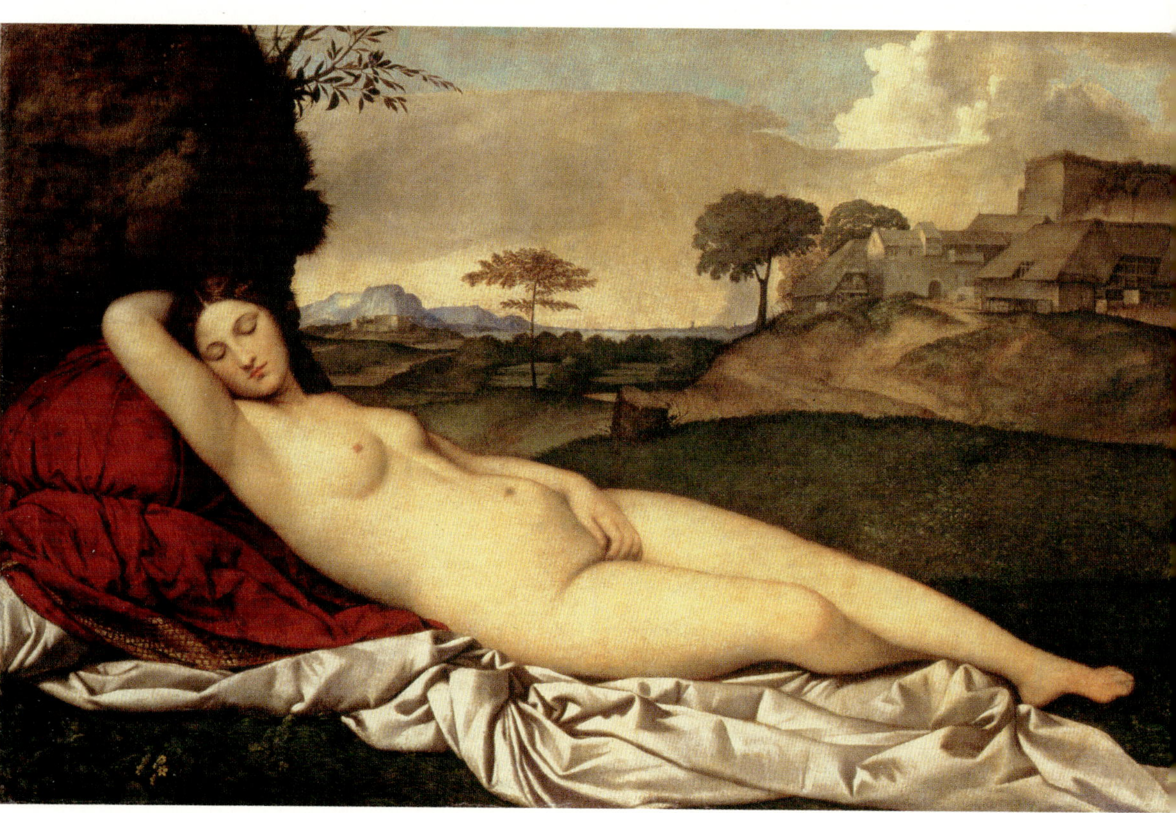

and *Sleeping Venus* in those of Taddeo Contarini and Girolamo Marcello respectively. These three Venetian collectors knew or were related to one another, indicating that Giorgione worked for a close-knit patrician circle that actively encouraged him to make paintings reflecting their overlapping interests in natural and occult philosophy, the classical world, pastoral poetry and sensual eroticism. Though literary humanism had been slow to take root in Venice, it had been stimulated by the establishment of Aldo Manuzio's printing press in 1494, which had recently published such early monuments of classicizing secular literature as Francesco Colonna's *Hypnerotomachia Poliphili* (1499), a meandering story of a young man's quest for love; and Pietro Bembo's *Gli Asolani* (1505), a dialogue on the same subject by an associate of Giorgione's patrons, set in the contemporary landscape of the *terraferma*.

In Giorgione's *Sleeping Venus*, the goddess is shown asleep in a soft and luxuriant setting that consciously recalls the literary descriptions in contemporary pastoral poetry (FIG. 54). The poetic association between love and landscape is expressed by the way that the gentle undulations of the goddess's body are repeated in the folds of greenery beyond. Also typical of Giorgione is the inclusion of a farm building at the background right, a motif that links classical allusion to the contemporary world of the *terraferma*, where the kind of patricians who most enjoyed his work owned large and productive estates.

Giorgione's patrons were less interested in explicit religious or patriotic meanings than in works which could stimulate conversation, or *discorso*, or which made a connection with a renowned work of classical antiquity. The sensuous body of the goddess in *Sleeping Venus* was modelled on a well-known Roman sculpture (the so-called *Sleeping Ariadne* now in the Vatican Museum), while the *Tempest* recalled a lost masterpiece featuring a thunderbolt by the ancient Greek painter Apelles, as recorded in Pliny the Elder's *Natural History*. A literate patron such as Marcello would have enjoyed Giorgione's further allusion to a woodcut illustration in the *Hypnerotomachia Poliphili* in his *Sleeping Venus* (FIG. 55). However, if Giorgione followed the illustrator's lead in placing his nude in the foreground of the painting,

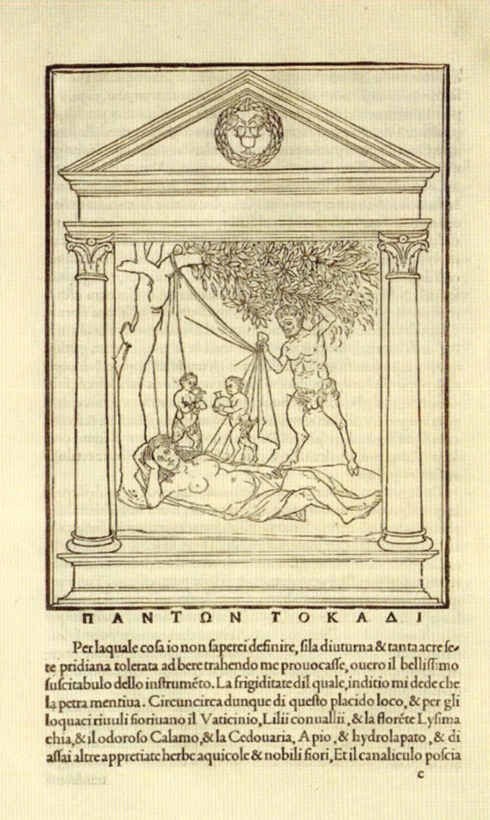

Per laquale cofa io non faperei definire, fila diuturna & tanta acre fete pridiana tolerata ad bere trahendo me prouocaffe, ouero il belliffimo fufcitabulo dello inftruméto. La frigiditate dil quale, inditio mi dede che la petra mentiua. Circuncirca dunque di quefto placido loco, & per gli loquaci riuuli fioriuano il Vaticinio, Lilii conuallii, & la floréte Lyfima chia, & il odorofo Calamo, & la Cedouaria, Apio, & hydrolapato, & di affai altre appretiate herbe aquicole & nobili fiori, Et il canaliculo pofcia

c

Fig.55
Page from *Hypnerotomachia Poliphili* by Francesco Colonna

1499. Woodcut, sheet 24.5 × 18.4cm (9⅝ × 7¼in). Herzog August Bibliohtek, Wolfenbüttel.

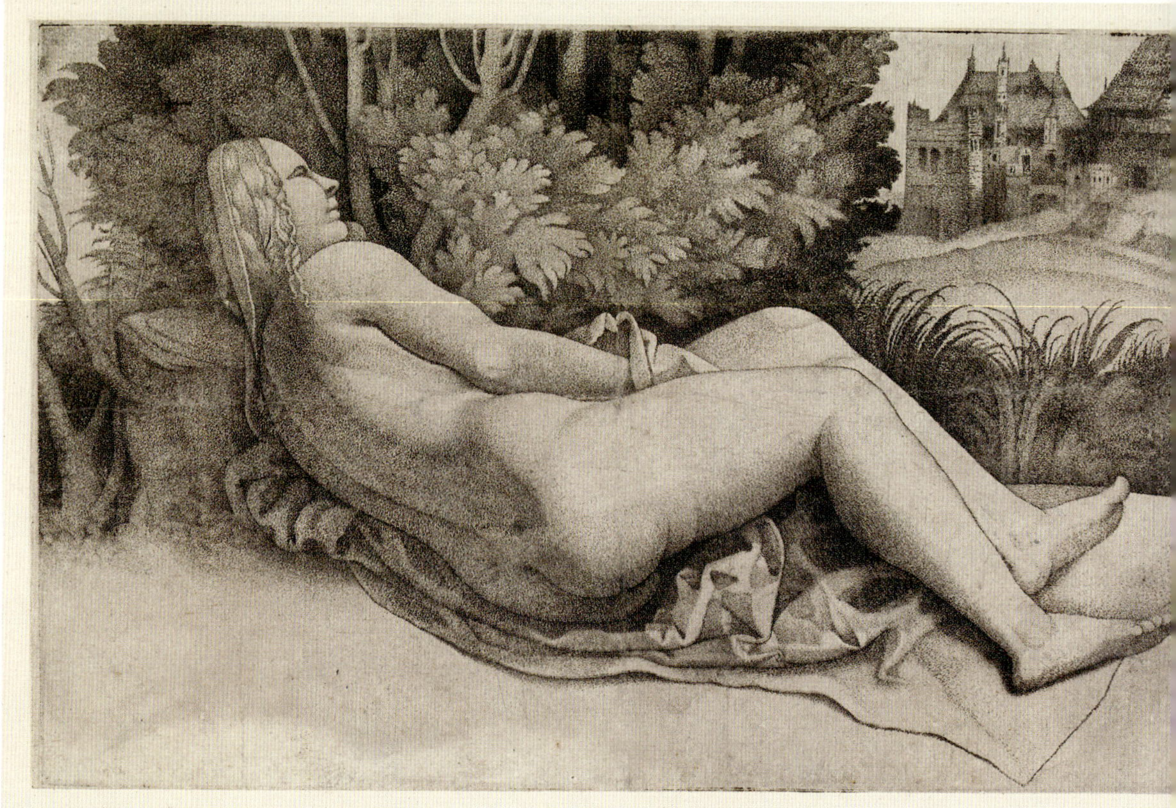

he also decorously ignored the aroused satyr who approaches her, a figure who was perhaps too obvious a proxy for the viewer's excited response. Nonetheless, the connection of Giorgione's art with the burgeoning culture of printed books and printmaking in the city is highly significant. And if Giorgione drew on the sometimes more explicit imagery to be found in these small-scale productions, then artistic printmakers such as Giulio Campagnola (ca. 1482–after 1515) also popularized the Giorgionesque approach, offering works with poetic and erotic meanings for sale to a wider audience. In contrast to the linear crudity of the *Hypnerotomachia* woodcut, Giulio's *Nymph in a Landscape* is a self-consciously 'artistic' production, carefully emulating the pictorialism of Giorgione's fluid painting technique through its unusual use of small dots or stipple engraving (FIG. 56). The sources suggest that Giulio followed a lost painting by Giorgione recorded by Michiel, which featured a female nude seen from behind: a work which may have provided a deliberate contrast to the frontal arrangement in the *Sleeping Venus*. However this may be, Giulio's print is more earthy and erotic than anything in

Giorgione. The very low viewpoint, like the woman's unawareness of being seen, and the suggestive movement of her right hand between her legs, indicate that we have a necessarily voyeuristic relationship with her, although this is not judged or commented on. Recalling again the woodcut from the *Hypnerotomachia*, Giulio casts the viewer in the role of an aroused satyr seeking out a beautiful nymph in the woods.

Landscape, love and war

The intimacy and eroticism of these works suggests that they had little to do with the public world of Venice, and perhaps that they were created expressly to offer an escape from its pressing utilitarian demands and darker realities. It may be that the new appeal of the Giorgionesque world of eroticized landscape was a response to the dire political situation of the Republic, which was, from 1508, at war with the so-called League of Cambrai: a powerful array of enemies from across mainland Italy and beyond, determined to reverse the 'dangerous' westward advance of Venice over the preceding century. Giorgione and his followers became vitally interested in the *terraferma* landscape just at the point when Venice lost control of it. Given the intense political and financial pressures on leading patricians, as well as the apparently imminent destruction of the Republic itself, Giorgione's patrons may have found solace in nostalgic representations of sunlit afternoon landscapes, with their promise of sensual pleasure and enjoyment. The *Tempest* perhaps makes a more direct kind of reference to the contemporary political situation. It has sometimes been understood as an allegorical representation of the famous siege of Padua of 1509, when leading Venetian patricians (led by the future doge, Andrea Gritti) joined the Republic's mercenary forces in an attempt to halt the rapid progress of the enemy just 40 kilometres (25 miles) or so from Venice itself. The inclusion of a coat of arms over the entrance of the background city appears to identify it as Padua, while the thunderbolt above might allude to the 'storm of war'. Such references were deliberately made oblique, however, and the depicted city remains determinedly generic. Even if some viewers did read the painting as a political allegory, Giorgione made this a matter of choice, perhaps to be debated with others who understood it as a more general evocation of an atmospheric landscape. Special acknowledgement of the viewer's input into the visual image was, in any case, an important aspect of Giorgione's fluid technique. It can be measured by the abbreviated or cursive brushwork he developed, with its requirement that the viewer 'reads in' to complete the meaning of the work.

A few years later Sebastiano del Piombo finished a painting in which the consequences of the war may also be referred to, although the presentation remains a matter of Giorgionesque poetic analogy (FIG. 57). Following a story in Ovid's *Metamorphoses*, Sebastiano shows Venus mourning the death of her mortal lover Adonis; but the city beyond is most certainly Venice itself, over which dark clouds gather. In the foreground scene of death and tears, it is hard not to see Adonis as a symbol of the recent Venetian losses; or the weeping goddess Venus – long identified with Venice since she too was 'born from the sea' – as an image of its present distress. Sebastiano moved to Rome in 1511, and later became a fervent follower of Michelangelo. Even before his move, he often combined Venetian painterly elements with a sculptural and monumental sense of form more typical of art in early sixteenth-century Rome. His early paintings can be seen as precursors to the more programmatic attempts to integrate Venetian colour (*colore*) with Central Italian design (*disegno*) later in the century. In the *Death of Adonis*, Sebastiano features a sequence of nudes whose bodies evoke the texture of smooth marble. Placed together in a single narrow plane

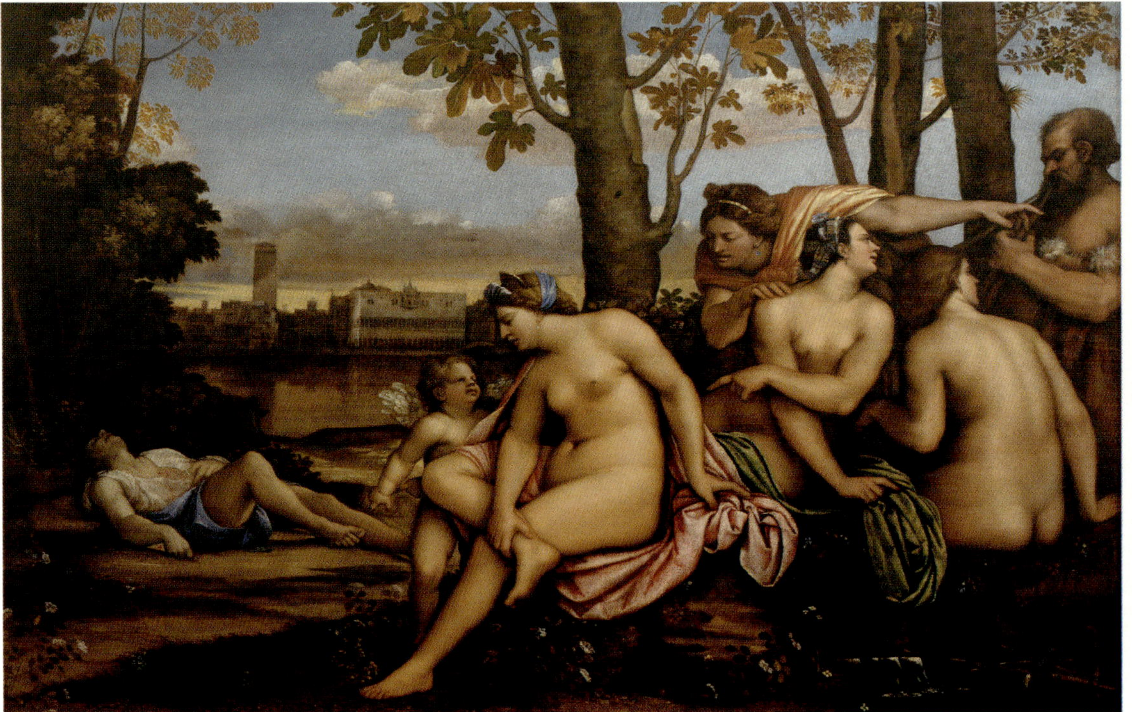

Fig. 57
Sebastiano del Piombo
Death of Adonis

ca. 1512. Oil on canvas, 189 × 285cm (6ft 2⅜in × 9ft 4¼in). Galleria degli Uffizi, Florence.

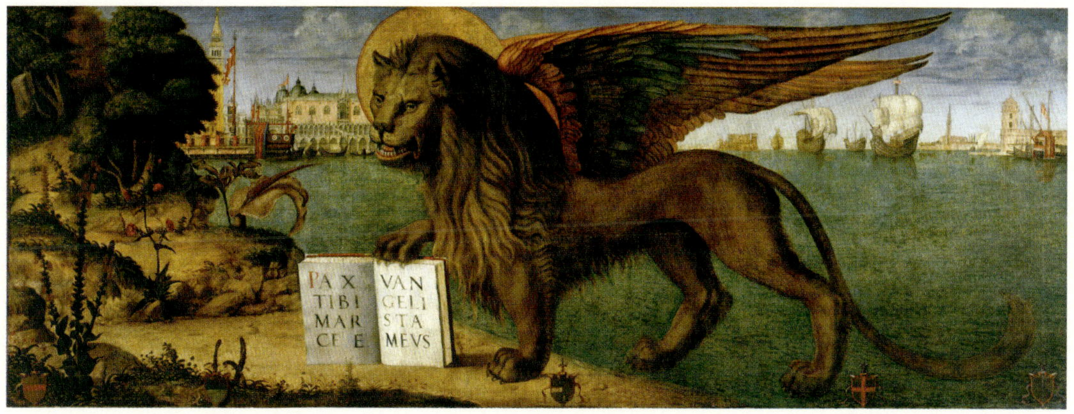

Fig.58
Vittore Carpaccio
Lion of St Mark

1516. Oil on canvas, 130
× 368cm (4ft 3⅛in × 12ft
⅞in). Doge's Apartments
(Sala delle Volte), Ducal
Palace, Venice.

of space, as if in a classical frieze, many are shown in a Roman profile and make the kind of rhetorical gestures familiar from ancient sculpture. The figure of Venus is closely modelled on a recent engraving after Raphael (1483–1520), indicating Sebastiano's knowledge of the most up-to-date *all'antica* art in Rome where the work may, in fact, have been painted. But the soft tones of the landscape, with its delicate blue evening sky lightening to gold towards the horizon, still powerfully recall the paintings of Giorgione.

Within a few years Sebastiano's classicizing vision of a fallen Venice must already have appeared as outmoded in a historical sense, even if its eclectic and proto-academic style speaks to the future. Venetian fortunes had quickly recovered when the various parties of the League began to argue among themselves, and by 1516, the year when Carpaccio painted his *Lion of St Mark* for the Palazzo dei Camerlenghi (Treasurer's Palace), the city had largely recovered both her lost territories and also her position as a powerful city state (FIG. 58). Carpaccio's all-confident work is tellingly also a return to a more traditional kind of imagery, offering the viewer a sense of continuity and reconnection with the Venetian past of the pre-war period. Both paintings take their viewpoint from the low weedy island of San Giorgio opposite the main entrance to the city. However, Carpaccio substitutes the elegiac mourning of Sebastiano's classical actors with the familiar winged lion of St Mark, patron saint of Venice. The patriotic beast easily out-scales all the other forms in the painting, powerfully reasserting a sense of the city's divine destiny. He bestrides land and sea, as if to express his command of these two essential domains of the Venetian empire: the Stato di Terra and the Stato di Mar. And perhaps his movement, from sea to land, east to west, refers more precisely to Venice's recent recovery of the *terraferma*, as also to the future direction of its political ambitions.

The erotics of portraiture

The above discussion has already indicated the extent to which painting predominated over other visual media in Venice in these decades, as also the way in which these latter sought to emulate painting's new expressive power. The mature work of Tullio Lombardo consistently indicates his concern to make sculpture match the fluid appearance of contemporary painting. Although Tullio continued to produce large-scale public sculptures, he also created a series of smaller 'painterly' double portraits that are every bit as suggestively ambiguous as the contemporary work of Giorgione and his followers. In a work known as *Bacchus and Ariadne* of ca. 1505, it is not clear whether we observe portraits proper or mythological imagery with the appearance of portraits (FIG. 59). A Giorgionesque interplay between past and present is made central to the effect. Though the semi-naked busts in high relief clearly evoke the imagery of classical antiquity, especially Roman wedding and funerary portraits, the woman sports a carefully observed early sixteenth-century brocaded headdress. Only the vine leaf garland of her lover indicates that he may be Bacchus, the Ancient Roman god of wine. The frame-like border may have been included to evoke a more direct *paragone* (comparison) with illusionistic painting: the placement of the overlapping figures in front of this feature, on the viewer's side, suggests their superior naturalism. With their truncated limbs, the busts

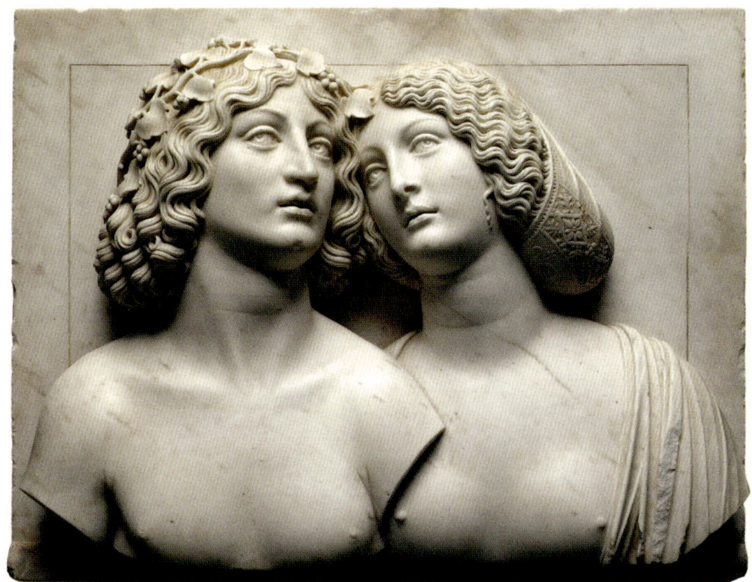

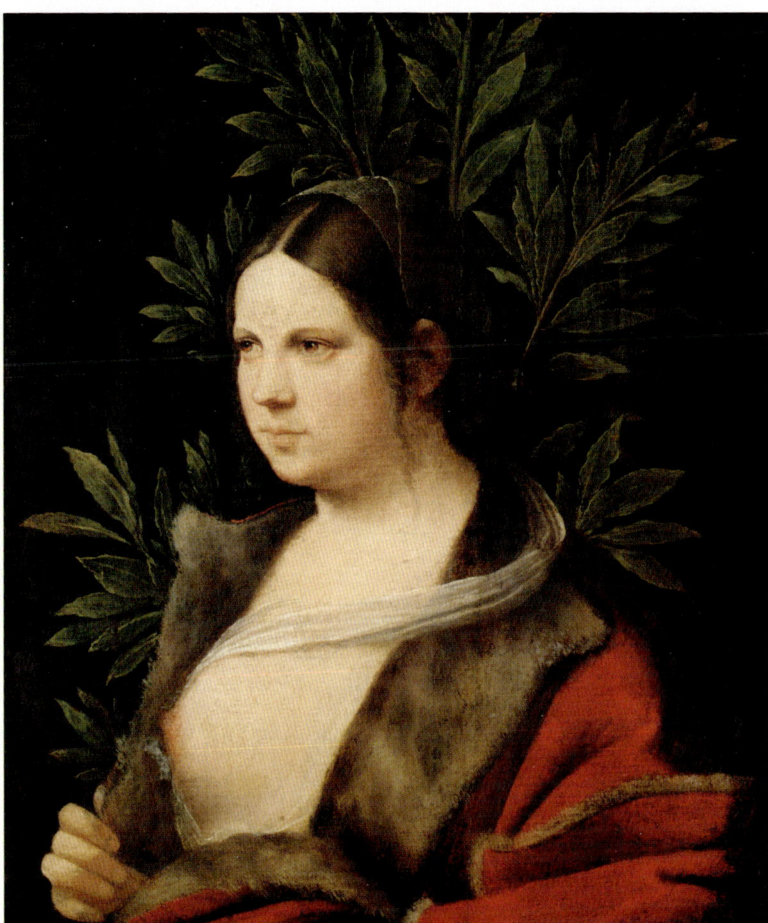

Fig.60
Giorgione
Laura (?)

1506. Oil on canvas over panel, 41 × 33.5cm (1ft 4in × 1ft 1in). Kunsthistorisches Museum, Vienna.

appear to have been made to recall antique sculptural fragments, but they are at the same time brought to life by modern details, such as the expressively parted lips and intricately carved eyes that roll in their sockets to create restless preoccupied gazes. Tullio was not directly influenced by a Giorgione work, but the elegiac yearning and sensuality of his relief is broadly similar to that found in many of the painter's productions, and may suggest the spread of a wider taste for such poetically ambiguous works among elite circles of the Venetian patriciate.

A near-contemporary painting by Giorgione features a sitter who may or may not be a real, contemporary individual, and thus again challenges the apparent identity of the work as a portrait (FIG. 60). As in Tullio's sculpture, the sitter is in a state of half undress, making it hard to imagine that the work was commissioned in the usual way by the woman's family or husband, or as a record of her marriage. Her placement in front of a laurel bush suggests that she is in some way connected with poetry, and is perhaps to be identified as 'Laura', Petrarch's poetic muse in his much-read *Rime sparse*,

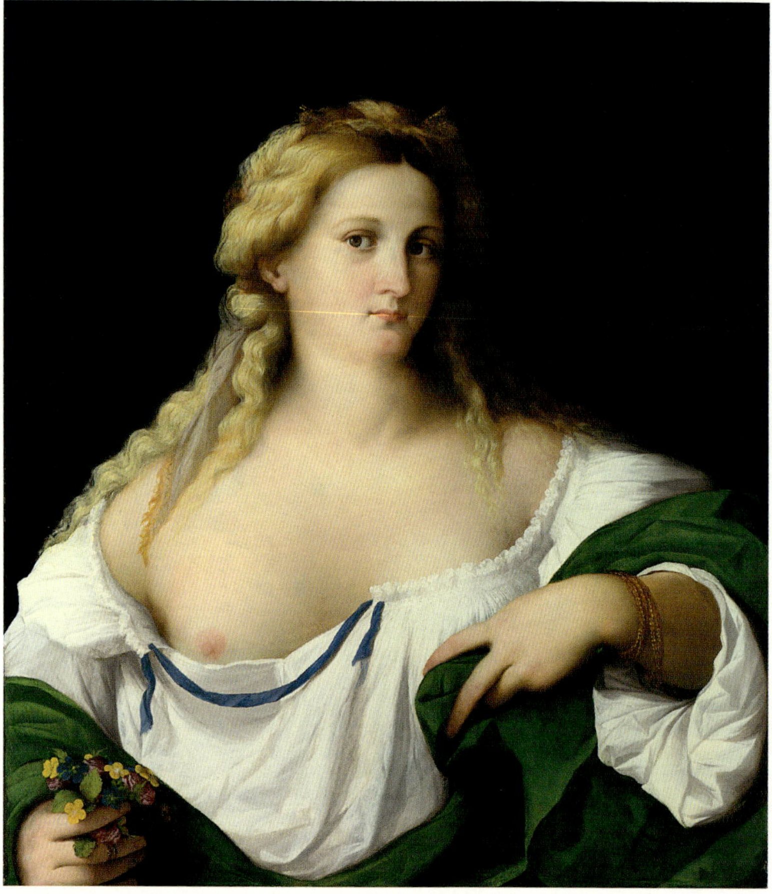

a new edition of which had been published by Manuzio in Venice in 1501. Yet the intimate details of the painting also suggest that she is something more than an abstract personification of poetry. As she opens her oversized jacket (perhaps belonging to a male lover) to expose her right breast, the young woman releases a powerful erotic charge based on the analogies between the softness of the fur and her breast and nipple. The casual sensuality of the movement, made more apparent by the lack of the usual parapet at the front, brings the image into the present in a way which has few precedents in Venetian painting.

The *Laura* shares an essential quality of ambiguity with many other works by Giorgione, its poetic and erotic elements indicating that it was meant to be understood, above all, as an original and suggestive work of art. The still insistent reference to portraiture may imply the truth of what was being represented, and certainly draws attention to the illusionistic skill of the artist, but the meaning of such works was clearly very different from the conventional public or documentary functions of portraiture in Venice. It is no coincidence that Giorgione's painting features a sexually alluring young woman, and thus one whose role within the patriarchal culture of Venice and its imagery had remained strictly circumscribed. Giorgione offers a glimpse into an altogether more private world, in which sex and desire predominate over patriotism or piety. At the same time, this feminine world could provide a link to poetic values and to classical antiquity. Younger painters such as Titian and Palma Vecchio (ca. 1490–1528) were quick to exploit these possibilities, painting beautiful young women (*belle donne*) in a state of undress along the lines of Giorgione's prototype. Juxtaposing hair and flesh in the same erotic manner, these works continue to suggest that they are portraits even as their status as images of generic beauty, or their literary identity as the types or followers of Venus, becomes increasingly apparent.

In the Palma illustrated here (FIG. 61), the fashionable white underclothing or *camicia*, golden bracelet and dyed blond hair reveal the sitter as a real woman of the present day, while her euphemistic offer of flowers to the viewer and her suggestive glance might indicate that she is a courtesan. Venice had become famous for these high-class prostitutes, a few of whom rose rapidly up the social order to become local celebrities, while others had their poetry published. Yet Palma's nods in the direction of contemporary reality do not disturb the overriding sense that his painting is an ideal artistic invention: the beauty of the sitter serves as a visual metaphor or figure for its status as a perfect work of art. Neither do they contradict the painting's generic classicism. Although Flora, goddess of flowers, does not occur in the usual classical literary or visual sources, Palma's reference to antique art is, if anything, more insistent than Giorgione's. Thus the exposed breast first introduced in the *Laura* now more directly recalls well-known classical Roman sculptures featuring the 'Venus Genetrix' ('Mother Venus'). While Palma's painting is not a deliberate recreation of a specific antique work, it nonetheless offers itself as a new kind of pagan mythology that supposedly replicates those typical of the classical world.

Although Giorgione's most groundbreaking portraits feature women, he had also suggested a similarly private and sensual domain for his male sitters in works such as the *Portrait of a Young Man* (ca. 1503–5, Gemäldegalerie, Berlin). From his earliest years, Titian built on Giorgione's example in portraiture, producing images of refined young male sitters who take up dreamy poses and possess a certain remoteness of mood. While these were typically commissioned works featuring named sitters, they still have a generic quality

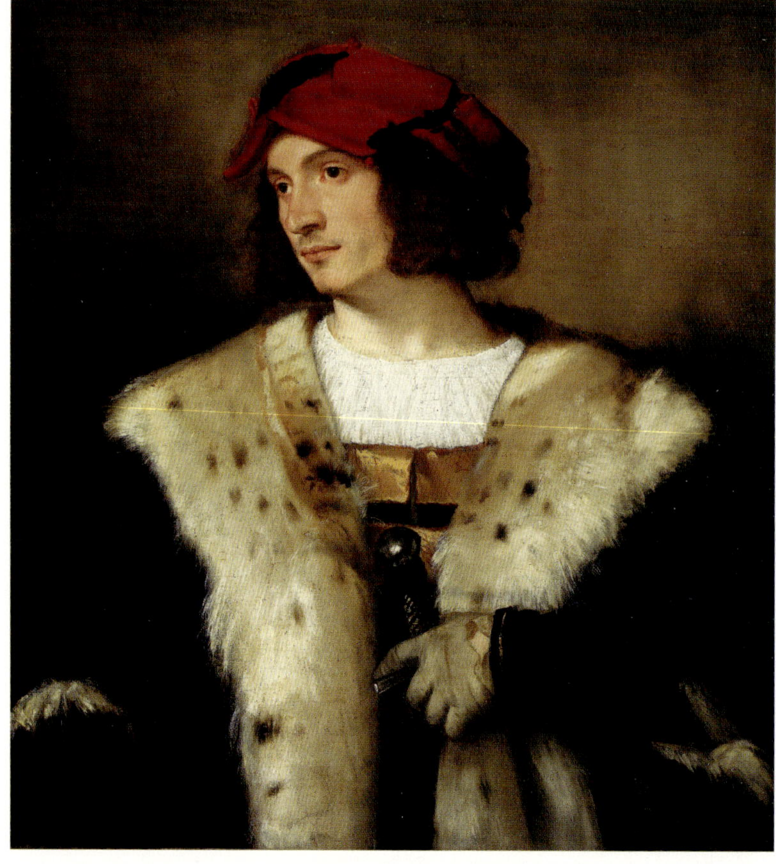

which brings them close to the depictions of beautiful young women discussed above. Titian's 'handsome men', sumptuously bedecked in furs and satins, and often with an intimate glimpse of underclothes against luminous flesh and with soft hair falling to the neck, also have a feminized or androgynous quality. Features such as the soft kid gloves, which cover the delicately extended fingers, are at once an expensive fashion accessory, a reference to Petrarchan poetry, and a sexual hint.

Such sensual works contradicted the determinedly masculine portraiture of the Bellini (*see* FIGS 39, 40), with its emphasis on dutiful attachment to the patriotic values of the state. In works such as the *Portrait of a Man in a Red Cap* (FIG. 62), the emphasis falls on superficialities of appearance, on a parade of sensuous surfaces and materials, and on a refined elegance of emotion. Rather than physical or moral strength, Titian's new kind of male identity draws on attributes traditionally ascribed to women. This stood in a potentially antagonistic relation to the contemporary official idea of masculinity promoted within the public culture of Venice, where the newly formed Provveditore alle Pompe attempted to control conspicuous consumption and sartorial display, including the puffed sleeves often featured in Titian's early portraits. These moves against personal extravagance had their immediate context in the struggle for the very survival of the Republic during the Cambrai war. When Titian's luxuriant portraits of young patricians from this period are seen against this background of self-repression we can gain a sense of just how far the young master was from expressing official Venetian values. From the second decade of the century onwards, the main focus of Titian's interest was already moving away from Venice towards the north Italian courts, where he received repeated commissions for portraits and mythologies. In his *Tommaso de' Mosti* (?), which probably features a follower of the d'Este court at Ferrara, the intense local coloration of works such as the *Portrait of a Man in a Red Cap* gives way to carefully balanced tonal modulations of black and white (FIG. 63).

Titian's change of palette around 1520 must owe something to the new taste for Spanish-style sobriety at court. In Baldassare Castiglione's social etiquette book, *Il Cortegiano* ('The Courtier', Venice, 1528), the aspiring courtier was tellingly advised to wear only black in order to understate his true rank and to cultivate nonchalance, or *sprezzatura*. Castiglione's key concept appears to be paralleled in the relaxed posture adopted by the sitter, one which fittingly draws on Raphael's recent portrait of the writer. In this new internationalized kind of portrait, Titian's partial suppression of Venetian-style *colore* coincided with an increased stress on the inner qualities of the sitter, moving the emphasis away from what can be seen of his appearance to what can be implied about his 'noble' inner qualities. The new priority given to de' Mosti's head encapsulates this kind of development of the portrait as a vehicle for the suggestion of non-sensual qualities of refined individual character. Such a development has relatively little to do with the traditional self-suppressing public culture of Venice.

Titian transforms Venetian mythological painting

In three so-called 'Bacchanals' of 1518–23 for the Camerino d'Alabastro ('small alabaster room') in the palace of Alfonso d'Este, Duke of Ferrara, Titian set a new expressive benchmark for Renaissance mythological painting. Although in certain ways this was to follow through on the lead given by Giorgione and his followers, these innovative works cannot be closely ascribed to Venice or to Venetian artistic models. Titian's approach in works such as the *Bacchus and Ariadne* (FIG. 64) is decisively different from earlier examples such as Tullio's double portrait or Giorgione's *Sleeping Venus*, replacing their dreamy poetic nostalgia with a riotous romp that imagines intense sensual pleasures and excitements. Titian had, in fact, finished Giorgione's *Venus* shortly after the older master's death, adding a vibrant and lively swath of drapery below the sleeping goddess, which twists and turns in on itself, as if it were a proxy for the viewer's excited response near the area where her fingers disappear between her legs (FIG. 54). Much later, in 1529, Titian was asked by Alfonso to rework and update Giovanni Bellini's original contribution to the Camerino, the *Feast of the Gods* (1514, National Gallery of Art, Washington DC) in accordance with the more dynamic style of his Bacchanals. Titian now added a towering and dramatic wooded mountain which contradicted the flattening effect of Giovanni's original row of trees, and was probably

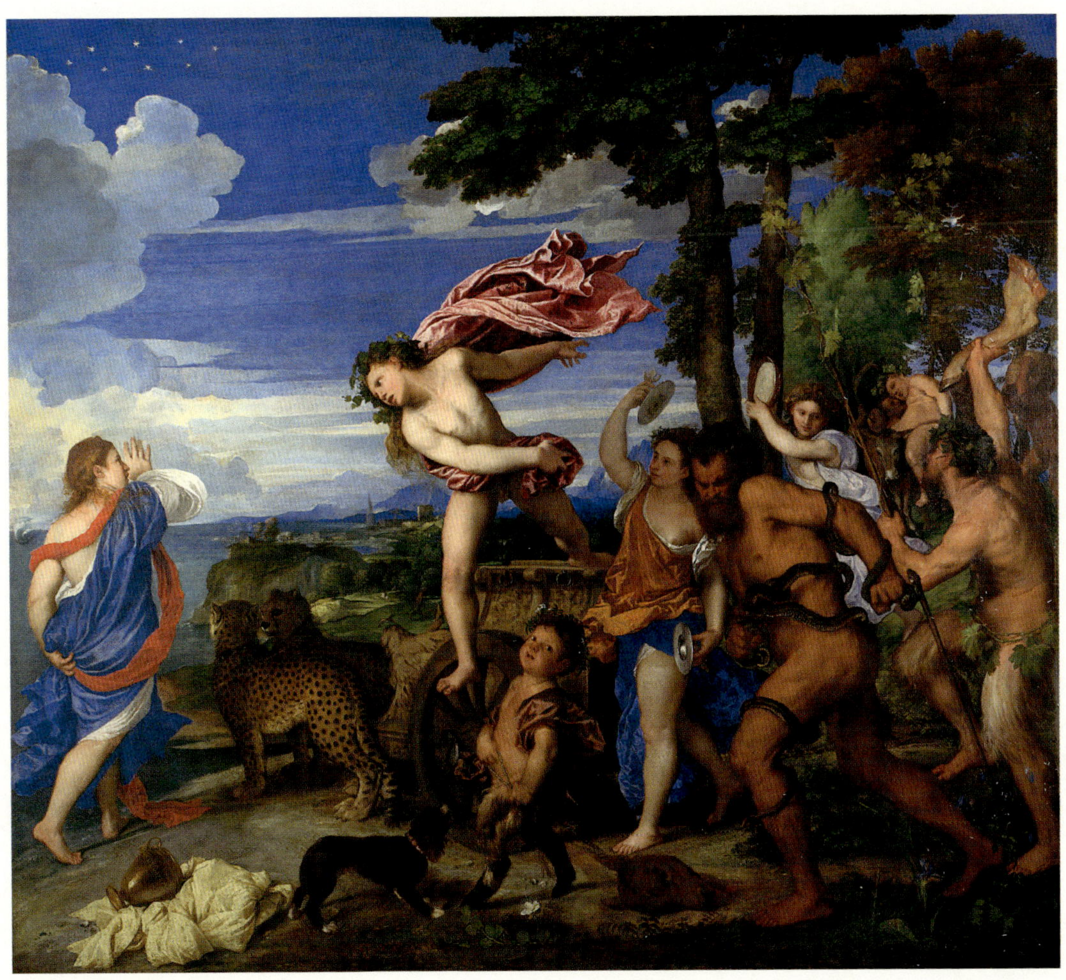

Fig. 64
Titian
Bacchus and Ariadne

1520–3. Oil on canvas,
176.5 × 191cm (5ft 9½in × 6ft
3¼in). National Gallery,
London.

Titian's reference to the
Laocoön in this painting
may have been encouraged by
a similar quotation in one
of the marble reliefs by
Antonio Lombardo (ca. 1458–
1516), Tullio's brother,
which had also been placed
in the Camerino.

intended to offset the now outmoded stillness and solemnity of the overall presentation.

Titian's appropriative additions to the mythologies by Giorgione and Bellini indicate his very self-conscious sense of his progression beyond their examples. In the Bacchanals for Ferrara, Titian also moved beyond the confines of Venice, and the supremely confident style of his paintings can be seen as a response to his position on a newly expansive artistic stage. A pan-Italian purview of Renaissance art had, in fact, been central to Alfonso d'Este's plans for the Camerino, which was originally to have displayed representative works by leading masters from Venice, Florence, Rome and Ferrara. Though it was Titian alone who came to dominate the commission, the style he developed may always have been intended to be seen as an eclectic, internationally orientated manner. Vital to this was the way in which his Bacchanals were presented as wholly distinct from the still-predominant existing tradition of religious imagery. If Bellini's solemn gathering in the *Feast of the Gods* still recalls older conventions in sacred art, then Titian's presentation of his subject in the *Bacchus and Ariadne* is unshrinking and unapologetic in its emphasis on fleshy corporality. Highlighting knowing references to antique Roman sculptures, such as the recently discovered *Laocoön* (in the heroically proportioned bearded man at the foreground right), and twisting figures in vigorous interlocking movements, Titian's painting recalls the effect of a classical sculptural relief. But intense coloration – featuring a dazzling array of subtly differentiated blues, reds, greens and yellows – also presents the fashionable artistic *paragone* (comparison) with sculpture, suggesting the final superiority of Titian's artistic medium.

The assertive secularity of Titian's Bacchanals was undoubtedly inspired by his (and his patron's) sense of them as 'accurate' recreations of the lost paintings of pagan antiquity. Titian drew closely on literary descriptions in classical texts by Philostratus, Ovid and Catullus in the *Bacchus and Ariadne*. However, the appearance of his painting was not a necessary outcome of those texts, and should be seen as a wholly unprecedented *visual* performance. Titian's mythological actors pay no attention to past or future, and in this way they lead a life that is free from the demands of Christian morality (with its required deferral of pleasure) or public duty and responsibility. Titian's new approach allowed him to focus directly on the physical beauty of the corporeal human body in a way that is unrivalled in painting since classical antiquity. This is exemplified in Bacchus' astonishing mid-air leap, which does something more than merely indicate his ability (as a god) to fly. It, too, expresses the absolute primacy of the transforming moment in accordance with the theme of the painting. The mortal Ariadne wanders on the shore of the island of Naxos, having been abandoned by her lover Theseus, who disappears out of sight in the tiny boat on the horizon. Bacchus's arrow-like dart towards her appears like an outward expression of her inward psychological change, as her preoccupation with a past lover is obliterated by the sudden appearance of another.

While dismembered animals, semi-naked music-making maenads, a snake charmer, and the drunken old Silenus on his donkey, form part of Bacchus's train, the fulsome life of the senses this noisy group introduces is presented in wholly non-moralistic fashion. Paradoxically, Titian's invention of a sensual classical past in this painting facilitated a return to the secular pleasures of the Ferrara court in the early sixteenth century, if only by way of analogy.

Titian probably intended the Duke of Ferrara to identify himself with Bacchus. Alfonso was famed for the fine wines grown in his vineyards, and his menagerie included leopards like those drawing Bacchus' chariot. Indeed, the Bacchanals can be seen as visual metaphors extolling the 'golden age' of Alfonso's rule in Ferrara. Titian's intuitive sensitivity to the sensual preoccupations and enjoyments of the court he served was reflected in the immediate success of these works with the Duke and his courtiers. This once again marks the distance of this new kind of courtly painting from Venice itself, with its still-predominant traditions of patriotic and sacred art made in the service of the Republic.

Developments in altarpiece design

Private and sometimes esoteric small-scale works of art certainly became more widespread and popular in Venice in these decades, but it would be a mistake to think that public religious works of a more established type were no longer commissioned. Even if the war

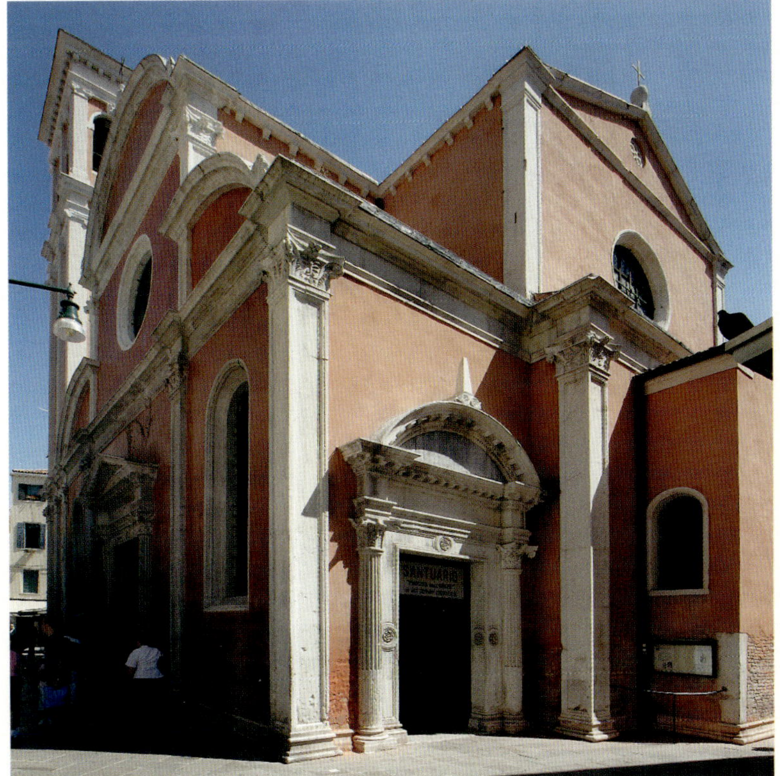

Fig. 65
Mauro Codussi
San Giovanni Crisostomo

1497–1504. Venice.

The relative plainness of the facade (to the left) may be a reaction to the extreme narrowness of the site of this church on one of the main thoroughfares of Venice. Many of its features repeat those on San Michele, although Codussi did exaggerate the architectural decoration of the portals in order to give his new building a more classical effect.

ca. 1507–9. Oil on canvas,
100 × 165cm (3ft 3⅜in ×
5ft 5in). San Giovanni
Crisostomo, Venice.

The oblique arrangement
of the architecture in
Sebastiano's painting, with
a landscape view to one
side, may have been based on
a recent altarpiece by Cima
da Conegliano (*Virgin and
Child with Saints Michael
and Andrew*, ca. 1496–8,
Galleria Nazionale, Parma).

radically curtailed the financing of expensive large-scale projects, developments in altarpiece design, in particular, continued apace, beyond the pioneering example of Giovanni Bellini's painting for San Giobbe. New architecture typically remained tied to the models of the late fifteenth century. Mauro Codussi's San Giovanni Crisostomo (FIG. 65), for example, closely revisited the design of San Michele in Isola of some 30 years earlier (*see* FIG. 34). Its Greek cross design, undoubtedly encouraged by the narrowness of the site, and also by the dedication of the church to a Greek saint, still reflects the neo-Byzantinism of earlier decades, but the three works commissioned to decorate its main altars indicate again the more progressive pattern we have noted in many of the figurative works discussed in this chapter. Tullio Lombardo produced a determinedly painterly altarpiece in marble relief; and in a late painting featuring St Jerome in the wilderness, Giovanni Bellini showed that he too was able to move boldly beyond his own earlier prototypes on occasion.

The High Altarpiece by Sebastiano del Piombo maintained the quattrocento type of the *sacra conversazione* but departed from the symmetrical arrangement preferred in many earlier examples (FIG. 66). While St John Chrysostom remains seated in a raised position at the centre of the composition, with three saints to either side, the architecture is now shown obliquely and in a sharp foreshortening, as if we have approached the painting from an angle of 45 degrees. Sebastiano's painting is infused with the discoveries of the new century, displaying his typical combination of Venetian and Central Italian elements. The saints are gathered on a Roman-style pavement before an early Christian basilica with enormous columns extending beyond the frame of the painting. If the colossal *all'antica* architecture and oval-shaped classical heads of the female saints reflect Sebastiano's fascination with the art of ancient Rome, then the shadowed introspection of the central figure of St John Chrysostom, the sensual over-the-shoulder glance of the soldier saint at the extreme right, and the soft light of the background landscape all strongly recall the art of Giorgione.

Titian's own contributions to the upright altarpiece type in Venice in this period drew on the progressive examples of Tullio, Bellini and Sebastiano at San Giovanni Crisostomo, but were more dramatic still. Though his *Assumption of the Virgin* is usually seen as bringing the Venetian tradition to a glorious climax, it is also possible to see this work as a further departure from the ways of the past (FIG. 67). It is true that in the upper part of his painting Titian includes an intensely supernatural golden glow reminiscent of the mosaics in St Mark's, and that his ascending Virgin, with her arms

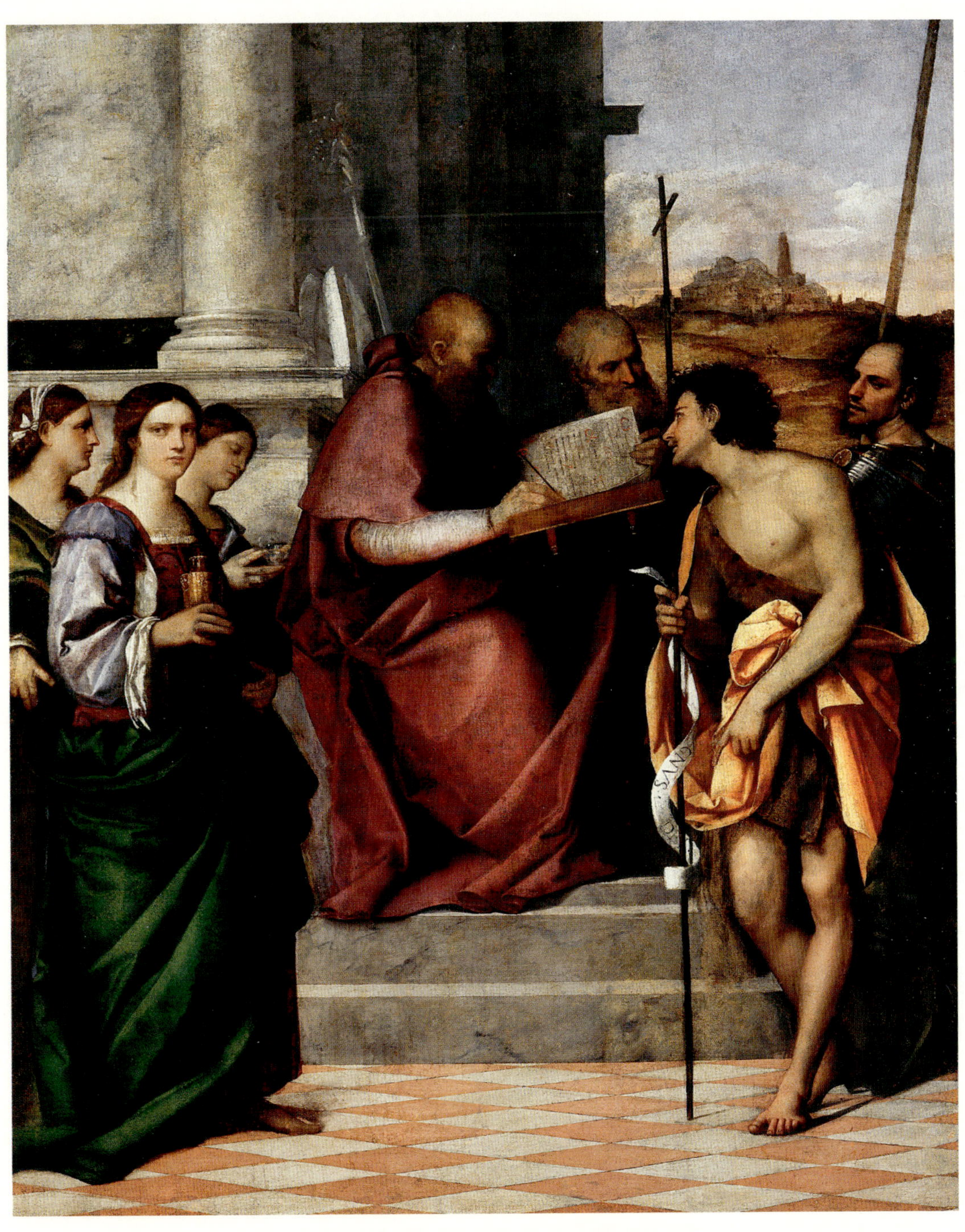

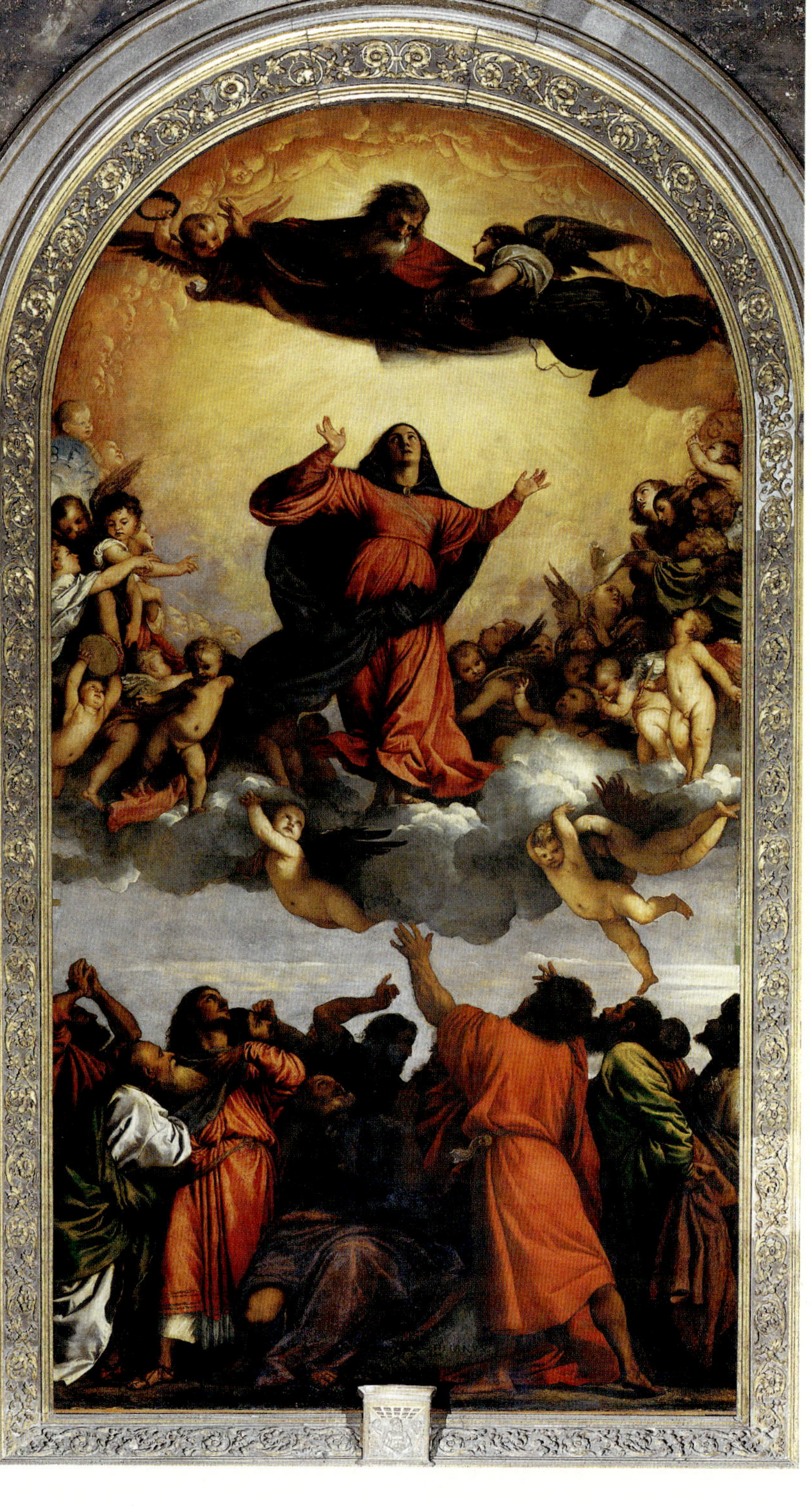

open in the traditional Orans position, draws on a medieval relief on the facade of the same building. But something of the surprise or even dismay felt at the unveiling of the painting at the Frari in 1518 is recorded in a sixteenth-century dialogue on art: the *Dialogo della pittura* by Lodovico Dolce (Venice, 1557). Dolce notes that the painting 'was grossly maligned' by 'the clumsy artists and dimwit masses who up till then had seen nothing but the dead and cold creations of Giovanni Bellini, Gentile and Vivarino'. Another early source tells us that the commissioning Franciscan prior, Fra Germano, was greatly disturbed by the sheer size of Titian's figures. And this was, indeed, one of the most extraordinary aspects of the new work, where the dynamic twisting movements of the bodies of the actors effectively generate the composition, unaided by any architectural support.

Titian's approach was evidently perceived as offering a challenge to the local models for the altarpiece, rather than as a continuation of their style, probably because he took the example of Raphael rather than Giovanni Bellini as his primary model. Abandoning Bellini's box-like architectural perspective, Titian generated a towering vertical composition in which the viewer's eye is kept close to the picture surface. Both the Virgin herself and the stretching foreground apostle with his back turned to us draw closely on figures in Raphael's recent paintings. In keeping with his innovations in mythological painting, Titian presents the Virgin's ascent as if it were happening in the present moment, abandoning the usual image of still and timeless spiritual reflection. In a further altarpiece, commissioned by the patrician and military commander Jacopo Pesaro for a side altar in the Frari, Titian's departure from the quattrocento conventions of the Venetian altarpiece was less immediately apparent, but also more subtly subversive (FIG. 68). In this work, Titian deliberately referred to the Bellinesque model insofar as he included an enthroned Virgin and Child surrounded by saints. He also drew on Sebastiano's Crisostomo Altarpiece in placing these sacred figures outdoors against a monumental classical architectural facade, shown from an oblique angle, with outsized columns ascending beyond the picture space towards heaven.

It is often noted that the skewed space of the composition reflects the position of the altarpiece on the left wall of the nave of the Frari, accommodating the mobile and decentred viewpoint of an observer approaching from the left through the main entrance of the church. Equally, the swivelling spatiality of the painting can be seen as laying new emphasis on the patron himself, who is introduced as a kneeling portrait at the foreground left, and around whom the entire composition appears to revolve. The Virgin and St Peter look towards him, while the group of his brothers appears to pray to him, rather than to the sacred figures. Although St Francis at the right draws the Infant Christ's attention to this family group, the prime focus is always on Jacopo Pesaro himself. This determines the selection of saints, chosen to refer to his military success in the service of the papal forces in the early years of the century. A connection with Rome rather than Venice is evident from the inclusion of St Peter, while the armoured St Maurice (who holds a flag featuring the papal arms of Pope Alexander VI) alludes to Pesaro's victory at the Battle of Santa Maura (Lefkada, Greece) in 1502. Such donor portraits had occurred very rarely in earlier altarpieces in Venice, and Titian's other innovations effectively served to privatize the traditionally public space of the altarpiece. If, in pioneering works such as the San Giobbe Altarpiece, Giovanni Bellini had used a centralized perspective to establish connection with the devotional community kneeling in prayer before his work, Titian now reimagined the picture type as a kind of individualized votive painting, focussed primarily on the person of his noble patron.

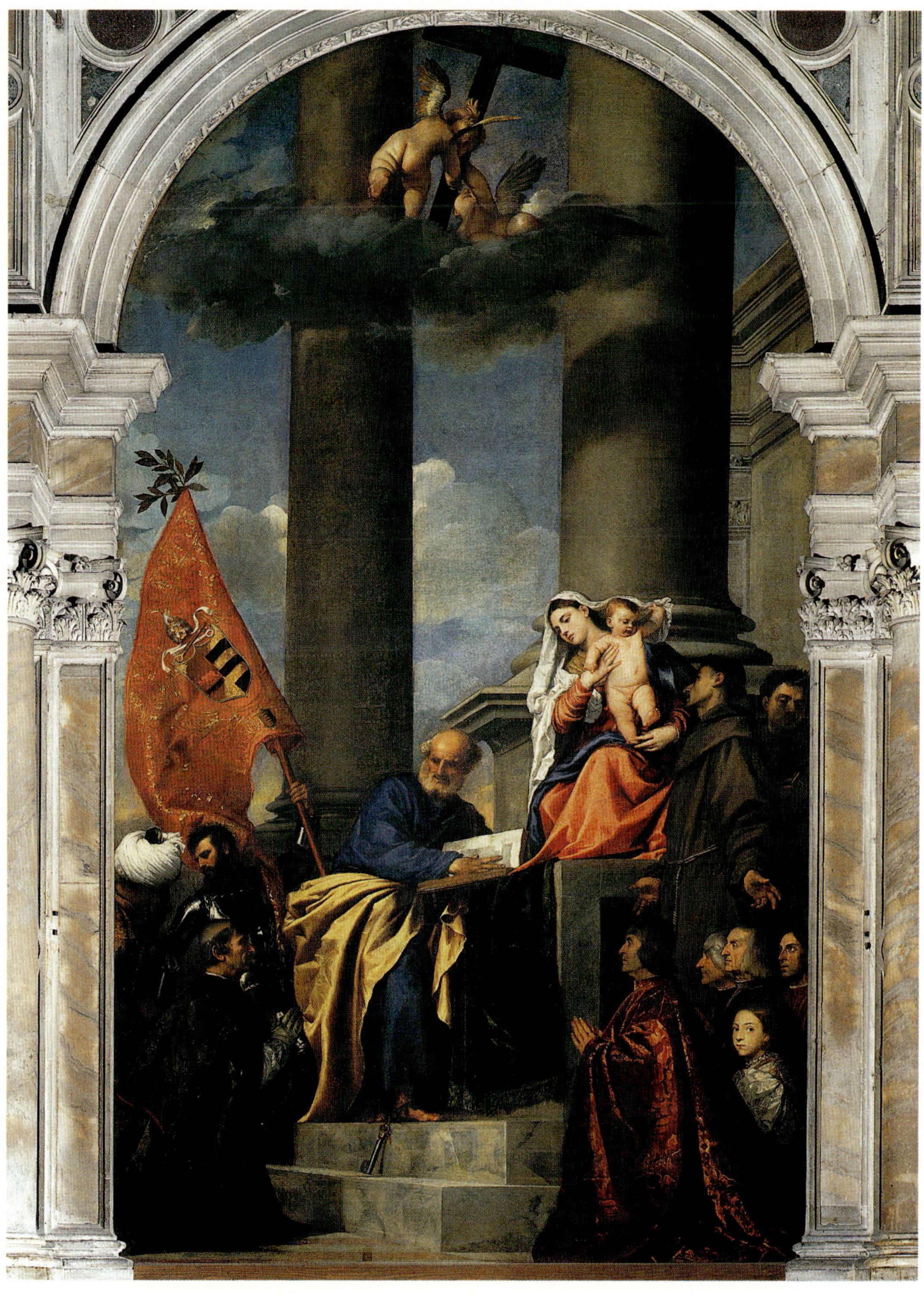

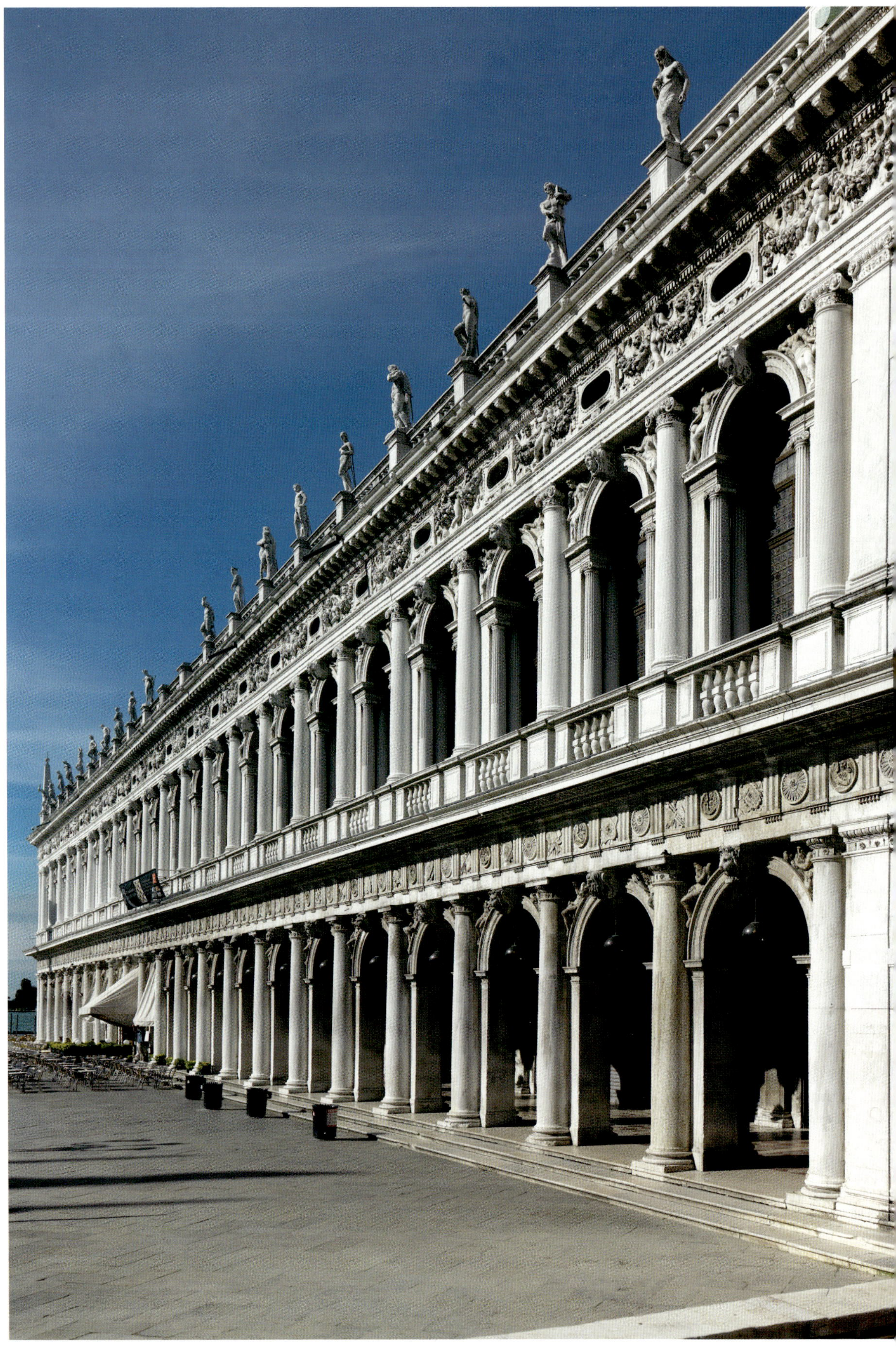

5

Romanism, Rank and Rivalry: 1526–50

Painting had taken a leading role in Venetian art in the early decades of the sixteenth century, but it temporarily lost ground after 1525, as innovative work in the fields of architecture and sculpture came to the fore. The display of Cardinal Domenico Grimani's famous collection of classical sculptures in the Ducal Palace from 1523, and the residence of the influential Bolognese architectural theorist Sebastiano Serlio (1475–1554) through the 1530s, encouraged this turn towards three-dimensional artistic media. The arrival of the sculptor and architect Jacopo Sansovino (1486–1570) from Rome in 1527 was more significant still. Sansovino went on to erect an impressive sequence of official buildings around St Mark's Square. The Zecca, or Mint, facing the waterfront (begun 1538), the Libreria Marciana (Library of St Mark's) opposite the Ducal Palace (begun in 1537), and the Loggetta (1537–46) at the foot of the bell tower, effectively transformed the centre of Venice, lending it an imperial grandeur that could rival the ancient Forum in Rome. The new buildings were entrusted to a single architect, and were conceived in relation to one another, representing a centralized program of urban planning that was unprecedented in Venice. With the support of the patricians appointed to look after the fabric of St Mark's and

Begun 1537.

The Library was built to house the treasured collection of Greek manuscripts donated to the city by Cardinal Bessarion in 1468. The final bays at the southern end of the Library were added by the architect Vincenzo Scamozzi (1548–1616) between 1588 and 1591.

its immediate environs (the Procurators of St Mark's), Sansovino worked in systematic fashion to produce a coherent and impressive public space at the political and religious heart of the city that deliberately contrasted with the haphazard multiplicity of the existing urban complex. Drawing on his wide knowledge of antique and recent buildings in Rome and elsewhere, Sansovino now introduced an architectural style that showed a clear connection with the modern Renaissance values prevalent in many other parts of Italy in the sixteenth century.

Sansovino and the *renovatio urbis*

Like earlier architects working in Venice, Sansovino modified his new architecture in accordance with local models, particularly the existing official buildings around St Mark's Square and the Piazzetta. The closely repeated architectural mouldings in the upper storey of his new Library (FIG. 69), for example, extend the approach already established in the facade of the so-called Procuratie Vecchie on the north side of the piazza, begun in 1513, while the open arcade at ground level mirrors that of the Ducal Palace opposite. Nonetheless, the insistent classicism of Sansovino's new buildings was a marker of change in Venice. His architecture was central to the so-called *renovatio urbis*: the political and cultural movement by which Venice demonstrated its recovery from the Cambrai war, through an ambitious programme of urban renewal and regeneration. Sansovino's official projects in Venice can also be seen as a response to the Sack of Rome in 1527, when the mutinous troops of the Holy Roman Emperor, Charles V, ran amok, killing a quarter or more of the population and destroying many churches and monasteries. With typical pragmatism, the Venetians saw an opportunity to present their city as a natural successor: Sansovino's *all'antica* architecture gave perfect expression to the idea that Venice was 'another new Rome'.

A further aspect of the *renovatio* was the 'renovation' of the patriciate of Venice itself. Members of the powerful group of families most closely associated with the movement typically enjoyed close political and personal ties with Rome. Patrician oligarchs from leading families such as the Grimani, Cornaro and Barbaro shared a developing sense of themselves as noble princes who had much in common with the cosmopolitan and courtly culture of the Eternal City. The dynamic doge Andrea Gritti (reigned 1523–1538), who played a key role in driving the *renovatio* forward, tellingly had himself commemorated as *principe* or 'prince' in a large inscription placed on the facade of the Palazzo dei Camerlenghi at the Rialto. These patrician *papalisti* ('papalists') were especially keen to abandon their more humdrum traditional Venetian identity as seafaring merchants in favour of a model of nobility based on the disavowal of trade and a clearer distinction from the non-noble majority in the city. The Sansovino building that gives best expression to these aspirations is the Loggetta (FIG. 70). The architect again took careful note of the existing buildings nearby. Though initially conceived as a kind of adjunct to the Library, the new building also owed something to the Ducal Palace, and more especially to the Porta della Carta (*see* FIG. 7). Sansovino suggested continuity by using parti-coloured marbles and a combination of niche sculpture and architectural mouldings. But the Loggetta nonetheless has little in common with the Gothic delicacy or verticality of the quattrocento gateway. Its block-like horizontal format, featuring free-standing columns, offered a bravura example of Renaissance architectural vocabulary and recalled the appearance of a classical triumphal arch. We have seen how Gambello had already used such an allusion to suggest Venetian economic and military might in his gateway to the Arsenal (*see* FIG. 22). Now Sansovino brought the idea of Roman-style triumph right to the

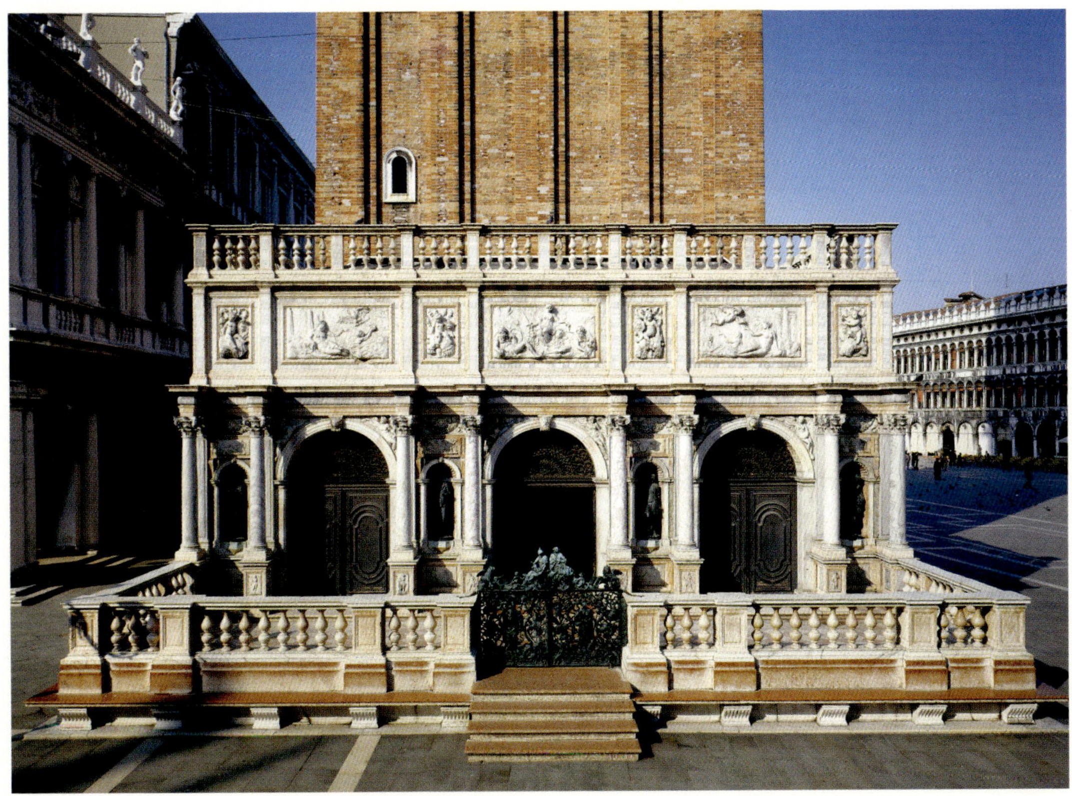

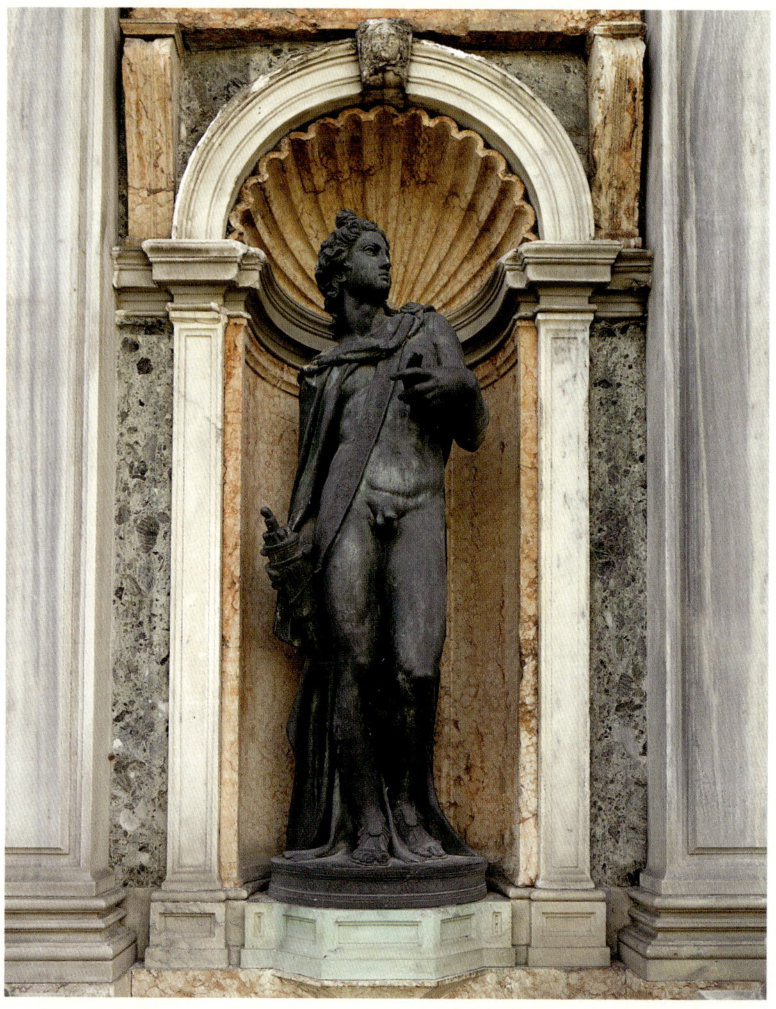

political and religious heart of the city, and more directly associated it with the ruling patrician caste itself, who were to use the Loggetta as a meeting place.

Instead of the sacred and votive imagery featured on the Porta della Carta, Sansovino presented a combination of Attic marble relief sculpture with bronze statuettes in the niches below. The usual Christian figures were replaced by pagan gods, who serve as secular personifications of the ideal qualities of the Venetian state. Classical deities had already appeared in works such as de'Barbari's patriotic map of 1500 (*see* FIG. 42), but their new predominance in large three-dimensional sculptures placed in St Mark's Square nonetheless marks a point of cultural change. The taste for classical art had sometimes showed itself before in the public or official context in Venice, but Sansovino's sculptures now presented the pagan gods as if they were a common language of art that could be easily understood by the public. This certainly reflects the gradual spread of interest in classical antiquity through the population. Sansovino's semi-nude sculptures, however, also possess a telltale 'artistic' quality which can be seen as a residue of their origin in more private and elite contexts of aesthetic appreciation. They take up sensuous *contrapposto* poses that insistently recall famous antique or Renaissance sculptures from Rome and Florence. The figure of *Apollo* for example, who represents Music and thus the internal harmony of Venice, pointedly recalls the renowned late antique sculpture known as the *Apollo Belvedere* in Rome, albeit with reference to Raphael's modern response to it in a figure in his *School of Athens* in the Vatican (FIG. 71). Learned recognition of its artistic heritage becomes an important aspect of appreciation of the work.

Sansovino's persistent use of such visual references indicates his concern to acknowledge the more specific Romanist tastes and knowledge of his patrons. To this extent, it can be seen as the intrusion of a more elite, though also international, kind of *all'antica* culture into the domain of official art in Venice. His sculptural style suggests that his patrician patrons sought to identify ever more fully with the political and cultural mainstream of mainland Italy. The success of Sansovino's classicism can be seen as reflecting a new stage in the on-going geopolitical reorientation from East to West that now decisively superseded the Byzantinizing phase of the later fifteenth century. It might also be seen as a signal of an internal change in Venetian social values, away from the communal or collective ideals that had previously predominated in the Republic. Sansovino's schemes of official building and sculpture may have helped to establish a clearer distinction between the newly aristocratized ruling caste and those lower down the social hierarchy. It is no accident that the erection of the Library coincided with the removal of the plethora of small traders who had previously run stalls, shops and taverns on the site. Just as the post-*renovatio* patrician sought to suppress his older merchant identity, so too the newly classicized environment at the heart of Venice was to be cleansed of any direct association with the trading activities of the lower echelons of society. It was now to serve as an idealized backdrop for displays of political power. Long before its rebuilding, the Loggetta had functioned as an exclusively patrician meeting place. Sansovino's aggrandizing architecture supplied it with a newly monumentalized theatrical quality that provided a suitable backdrop against which the 'renovated' nobility could play out its civic rituals of state to an admiring audience of the wider public.

Titian's imperial portraiture

The broad progress of Titian's career can also be seen as indicative of this political and cultural reorientation towards the West in Venice, and might also reflect the move towards greater social exclusivity noted above. Many of Titian's portraits from the 1530s and 1540s, especially those for foreign court dignitaries, have a masculine and martial tone and often feature men in armour with subordinate figures or animals in the lower areas of the painting. On several occasions, his portraits were conceived in the manner of *istorie* or history paintings, referencing specific events, their status as imaginative artistic inventions insisted upon. Titian also had a habit of subtly changing the look of his sitters in order to improve their appearance. His patronage from the Italian courts was now augmented by new commissions from the Habsburg family, the most powerful royal house in Europe. Titian's first meeting with the head of the family, Charles V, in Bologna in 1530 was undoubtedly a decisive event in his career. He quickly painted several imposing portraits of the young Emperor, in which his sitter's congenital deformity in the area of his lower jaw was cleverly concealed through a deft use of chiaroscuro. Following these successes, Charles formalized the new relationship by ennobling Titian on 10 May 1533. Earlier Venetian artists such as Gentile Bellini had enjoyed similar honours from foreign dignitaries, but Titian's elevation nonetheless gave his mature and later career an international dimension unmatched by any other painter in Venice in the period. Although he remained free to work for other patrons, both at home and abroad, the patent of nobility established an exclusive and lasting tie to the Habsburg family, which played a key role into the painter's old age. According to its wording, the intimate relationship between Charles and Titian stood as the modern equivalent to that between Alexander the Great and Apelles in ancient Greece.

Titian's most successful depiction of Charles is undoubtedly the equestrian portrait that he painted on a trip to Augsburg to meet the Emperor in 1548 (FIG. 72). This work is also the most overtly historical of his portraits of the Habsburg rulers and appears to commemorate a specific event. Charles is shown charging into battle for the Catholic cause at Mühlberg on 24 April 1547, where he won a decisive victory against the rebellious German princes of the Protestant Schmalkaldic League. The historical aspects of the presentation, however, are offset by others suggesting that we view a work abstracted from the immediacies of time and place in the manner of a traditional portrait. Thus, the calmness and benignity of the Emperor's expression already anticipates the victorious outcome of the

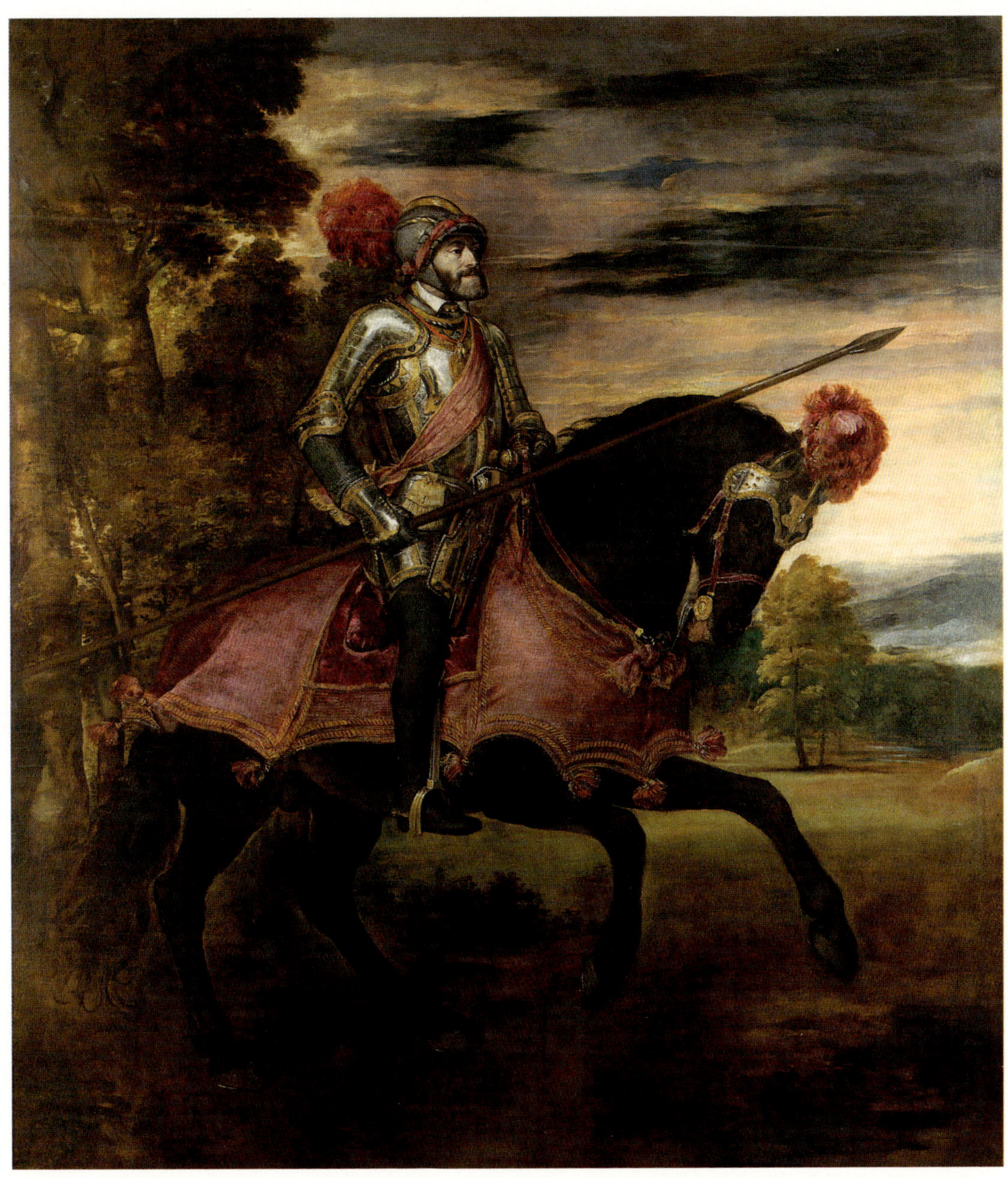

battle; and if the landscape is given a broad, diaphanous treatment, then the figure of the 'sitter' is handled more tightly, and appears to be lit from the front in a way that is not explained by the outdoor setting. While Charles sports the armour that he had worn on the day of the battle, his depiction is also given the kind of careful 'indoor' detail and resolution expected in a formal portrait likeness.

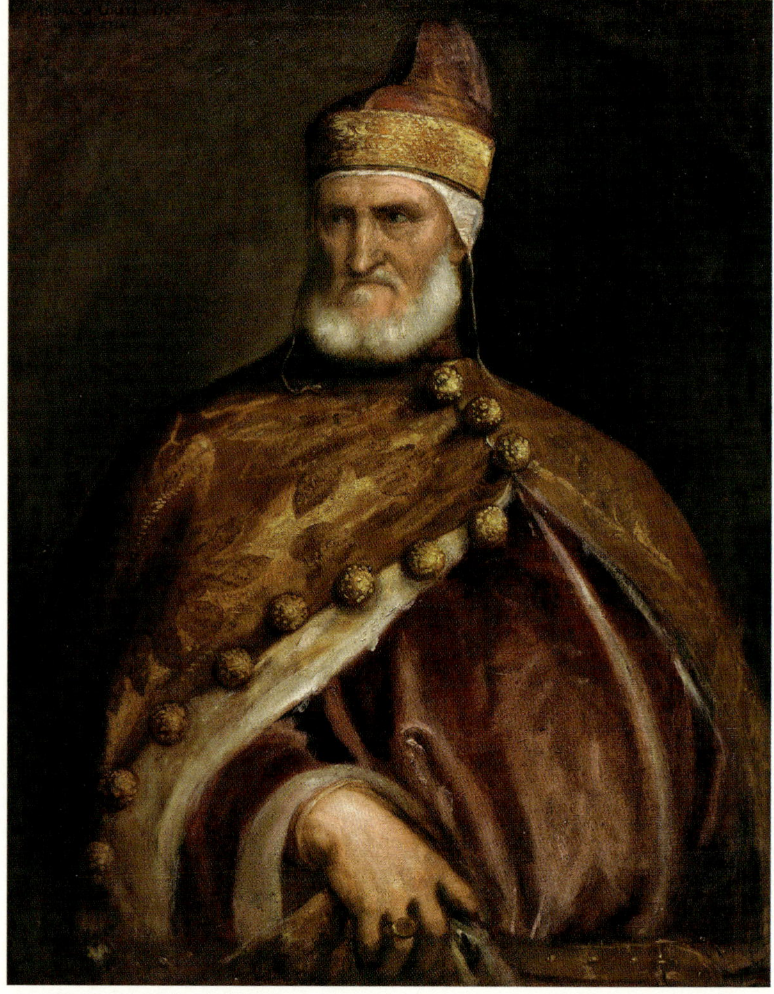

Titian brilliantly manipulated his formal and iconographic sources in this work. As a painter who had worked in Padua and Venice, he knew well the fifteenth-century equestrian statues by Donatello and Verrocchio (*see* FIGS 17, 41), but the association of his *Charles V* with the *Marcus Aurelius* monument of the second century CE, which he had recently seen in Rome, was more significant still. This connection was especially apposite, given its suggestion of a direct imperial link between Charles as the Holy Roman Emperor, and Aurelius, a Roman Emperor of antiquity revered for his Stoic moral rectitude and patience. At the same time, Titian's painting drew on more recent German prints of the ideal Christian knight shown seated on a horse, and thus expressed the religious aspect of Charles' identity, which distinguished him as superior to the pagan Emperors.

Titian's carefully constructed painting remains a portrait even as it co-opts certain aspects of the *istoria* into its visual armoury. It brought to a climax a sequence of portraits in which the qualities of sensuality, intimacy and equality evident in his earlier work give way to an ever more open assertion of personal force and leadership. The connection of this development to Titian's royal and court patronage is evident enough, and took its imperial tone from his association with Charles V in particular. However, in near-contemporary portraits for Venice, such as the *Doge Andrea Gritti*, Titian reinvented the traditional ducal portrait along similar lines (FIG. 73). In earlier works of this type, the emphasis was laid on constructing an abstracted ideal of state authority (*see* FIG. 39). In Titian's painting, on the other hand, the doge is granted new qualities of immediate physical presence and personal power. Titian places Gritti very high in the picture space, lowering the viewpoint so that he appears to tower above us, while enlarging his physical bulk so that his expansive figure is not quite contained by the picture frame. Titian's work probably dates from the period following his return from a visit to Rome in the mid-1540s. It owes an evident debt to Michelangelo's monumental sculpture of *Moses* which Titian had recently seen there: the forceful twist of Gritti's head away from his body, like the enlarged grasping right hand, owes a clear debt to Michelangelo's example. Yet the portrait also suggests a formal *paragone* or comparison with its sculptural source; the freedom of the brushwork in Gritti's clothing offers a claim for the artistic priority of Titian's painting over Michelangelo's sculpture. The bravura handling, including thick blobs of impasto on the buttons of Gritti's cloak and unmixed highlights on the crimson robe beneath, confidently asserts the superior lifelikeness and expressive power of Titian's oil medium over Michelangelo's cold and polished marble.

Titian's portrait was probably an unofficial commission painted years after Gritti's death, and this more private context may have encouraged him to create a freely invented kind of work that departed from the visual conventions of the ducal state portrait in Venice. But, as we have seen, Gritti was himself the powerful leader of a pro-Roman faction in Venice, who had played a key role in the ambitious remodelling of the city. Titian's revision of the traditional imagery of the dogeship was to this extent wholly fitting. Showing Gritti as a fiercely independent aristocratic ruler in the imperial mode he had developed for his courtly patrons abroad, Titian also gave visual expression to the cultural values of the *renovatio urbis* itself, with its new concern for individualized princely magnificence over the usual emphasis on the *mediocritas* of the dogeship in Venice.

A cultural triumvirate in Venice

The rise of Sansovino and Titian to dominance in the visual arts in Venice in these decades owed much to the larger-than-life figure of Pietro Aretino: the poet, playwright and man of letters who became the doyen of literary culture in the city in the decades following his arrival in 1527. The three men quickly struck up a close personal and professional friendship, supporting one another in seeking connections with patrons and publicity for their work. Aretino's reputation as 'the scourge of princes' belied his extensive connections with powerful figures in the foreign courts, and the rapid development of Titian's career in these contexts owed much to his influence. Aretino also carefully supported his Tuscan compatriot Sansovino in the development of his career in Venice. In return, Titian made flattering portraits of Aretino, including one which shows the poet in a similar way to *Doge Andrea Gritti*: as a man of bear-like physical power and fierce intellectual energy (FIG. 74). Aretino promptly sent the portrait as a gift to Duke Cosimo I de' Medici of Florence, probably with the intention of currying favour for both himself and Titian with the new autocratic leader of his native Tuscany. Sansovino, in his turn, carved portrait heads of himself with Titian and Aretino on the bronze door for the sacristy in St. Mark's which he began in 1546 (FIG. 75). The inclusion of sculpted portraits of contemporary artists and writers in such a hallowed interior indicates the unprecedented high profile and fame that the threesome now enjoyed in Venice. Interspersed with Evangelists and recumbent prophets at the margins of reliefs showing the *Entombment* and *Resurrection of Christ*, the portraits also appeal to the fashionable idea that artists were divinely inspired or godlike in their ability to create at will (the topos of the *divino artista*). But all this was a far cry from the original ideals of selfless anonymity in the service of religion and state at St Mark's, identified by Ruskin as its defining spiritual and cultural value.

The two heads towards the bottom of the door remain unidentified, but it may be that the young man opposite Titian on the middle level is Sansovino's son, Francesco, who was busy establishing himself as a significant literary figure in Venice. This identification would even up the numbers of artists and writers depicted on the door, with visual artists shown to the left and literary figures to the right. Looked at horizontally, each artist is visually linked to a writer, a connection that is reconfirmed by the turn of their heads towards one another, as if in conversation. This implied relationship may also be taken as showing the perceived intimacy and equality between the visual and literary arts. So much was, in any case, already implied

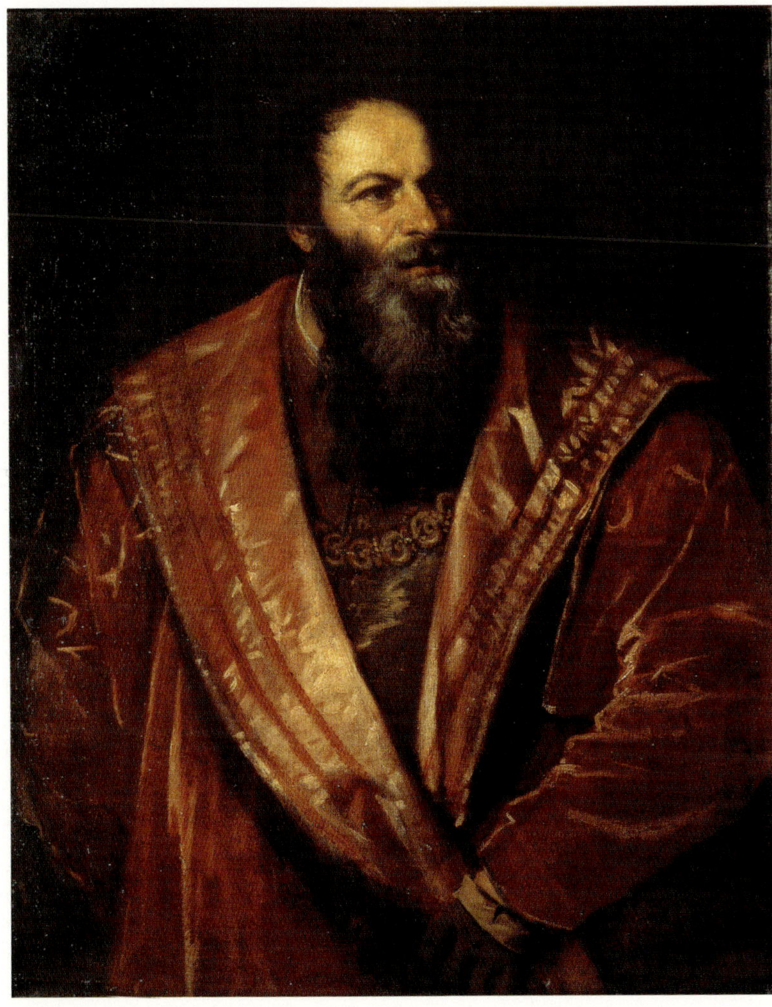

by the close relationship between Sansovino, Titian and Aretino. Aretino's avid interest in Titian's paintings, in particular, is evident from the frequent letters the poet published eulogizing the painter's work. In one of these from 1543, Aretino describes the vivid colours of a sunset over the Grand Canal as if it were a Titian painting: the sky was 'embellished by so beautiful a painting of lights and shades … such as those who envy you because they are not like you would wish to depict it'. This was a high accolade indeed, given its admission that the poet's experience of nature itself was directly shaped by Titian's illusionistic paintings. Equally significant is the way in which Aretino casts Titian's brilliance in painting within a context of fierce professional rivalry: as the cause of bitter 'envy' among those defeated by his artistic skill.

1546–69. Bronze, 216 × 117 cm
(7ft 1 in × 3 ft 10⅛ in). St
Mark's, Venice.

The complex arrangements of
the main narrative scenes
may reflect the impact of
Central Italian Mannerist
painters such as Giulio
Romano and Francesco
Salviati, whose work had
recently become very popular
in Venice. Sansovino's
fluid treatment, however,
may owe more to Titian's
increasingly free approach
to painting.

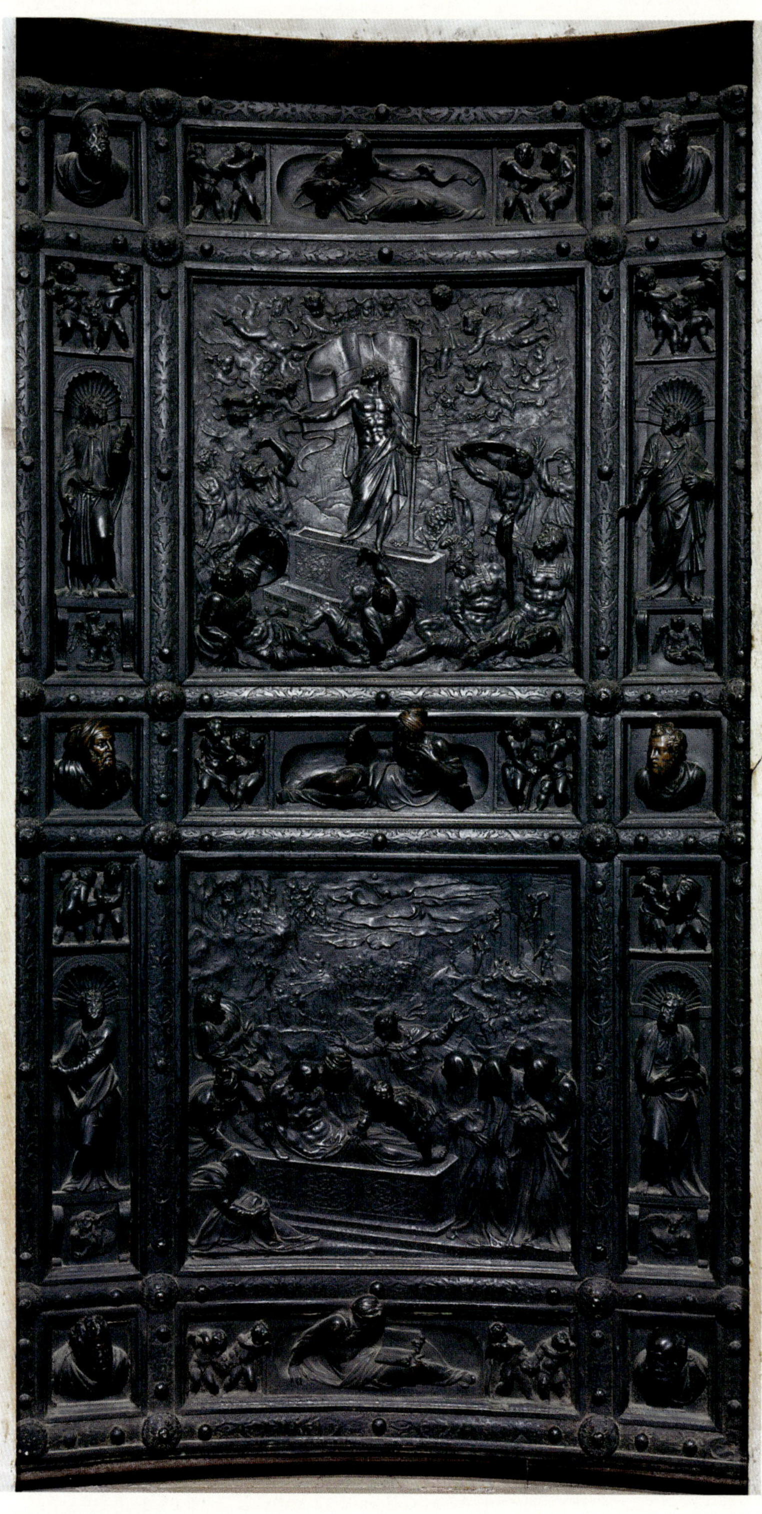

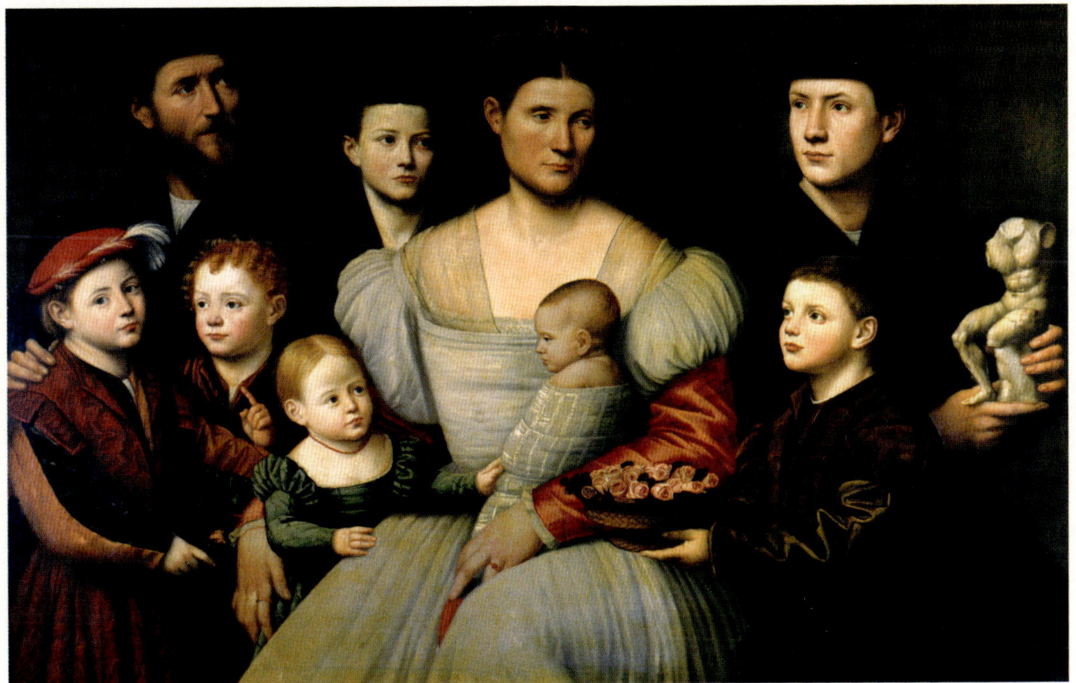

Sansovino, Titian and Aretino have often been described as an artistic 'triumvirate' that dominated in literary and artistic matters in Venice in the mid-sixteenth century. Still, if this aptly suggests that their exalted position was similar to that of leading figures in an ancient republic, it is equally important to note that they were not born in Venice, and operated, to some extent, as cultural colonizers and privileged outsiders in their adopted city. The internationalism that the 'triumvirate' developed played an important role in the *renovatio urbis*, and their vaulting ambition also reflected a move away from the older self-effacing values of Venice. So much can be seen from the contrast between Sansovino's hubristic portrait heads and a more local kind of work by the Venetian-born painter Bernardino Licinio (ca. 1490–ca. 1550; FIG. 76). Licinio's loving and careful depiction of his painter brother and his dependants indicates that family values continued to play a central role within the artistic culture of Venice in the age of the 'triumvirate'. In this painting, the bodies overlap intimately with one another in the narrow space of the picture, suggesting that the overall identity of the group remains more important than individualization. Thus, the painter and head of the family, Arrigo, is shown half-hidden by his younger children at the background left. The predominance of his wife, Agnese, seated in the brighter light at the centre, indicates the central role of the mother within the

Fig. 76
Bernardino Licinio
Portrait of Arrigo Licinio and his Family

ca. 1535–40. Oil on canvas, 102 × 165.1cm (3ft 4in × 5ft 5in). Galleria Borghese, Rome.

family. There is also a careful visual emphasis given to Arrigo's two sons to the right, both of whom went on to enjoy careers as visual artists. The elder of these, Fabio, holds up a statuette of the famous antique sculpture of the *Belvedere Torso*, probably to confirm his training as a goldsmith and sculptor. This was, of course, rather different to his father's occupation as a painter. But the two figures, father and eldest son and heir, are nonetheless made to mirror one another across the composition. The traditional value of continuity between father and son within the context of the Venetian family workshop is in this way made central to Licinio's image. The production of such a work as late as ca. 1535–40 indicates that the more individualistic and international ethos of the 'triumvirate' did not wholly encompass or determine the artistic field in Venice during these decades.

Continuity and revival in Venetian painting

Despite his domination, and although elements of his approach were certainly very influential, it is also true to say that Titian's work was increasingly divorced from that of other painters working in the city. No other artist could match his patronage from high-ranking foreign clients, or closely follow the sophisticated courtly and imperial artistic style he developed in their service. In Venetian painting these decades are characterized by a telling lack of stylistic unity or leadership. In contemporary Florence and Rome, art continued to develop around and through the towering examples of Michelangelo and Raphael, but the same cannot be said of Venice. Painting in the lagoon city did not cohere or progress in quite the same way, and often turned back to revive the approaches which Titian's example had apparently outmoded. It is characterized by stylistic plurality, with some works returning to the manner of the fifteenth century, while others were self-consciously progressive beyond Titian's example. Patronage was certainly a crucial factor in this regard, for example in the context of on-going commissions at the Meeting House of the Scuola Grande di San Marco, where Giovanni Mansueti (ca. 1485 –1527) worked on three large history paintings in a style that stuck fast to the manner of his master, Gentile Bellini (FIG. 77). Mansueti was an elderly man when he completed these works, and probably not in a position to creatively countermand his training and subsequent career as a Bellinesque painter. His continuing adherence to the oriental mode introduced by Gentile must also have been determined by an overriding concern to maintain the style established in earlier works for the cycle. The connection with the past that

Mansueti's style asserted can also be taken as having a more relevant contemporary significance. It was a reflection of the powerfully
Venetian cultural values of his *cittadini* (citizen) patrons, whose devotion to the Republic had been favourably contrasted with patrician
luxury and self-indulgence during the Cambrai war.

The key issue, here, may have been that of *Venezianità* or
Venetian-ness. While the main direction of Sansovino and Titian's
art was towards Romanism and courtly internationalism, other artists prolonged or revived a style that was more distinctively local,
usually recalling the work of leading artists from the period before the rise of Titian. From our modern perspective, works such as
Mansueti's inevitably appear *retardataire*, or out-dated, but in their
original context they may have been perceived as possessing qualities
of cultural authenticity and moral rectitude associated with the special loyalty to local values among the *cittadini*. Mansueti's old-fash-
ioned paintings express the values of a communal culture that was
now under threat from Western-orientated political, economic and
artistic developments. The patriotic imagery of his paintings, which
feature Venetian merchants mingling with turbaned Mamluks in Alexandria, may already seem nostalgic, given the inexorable rise of the

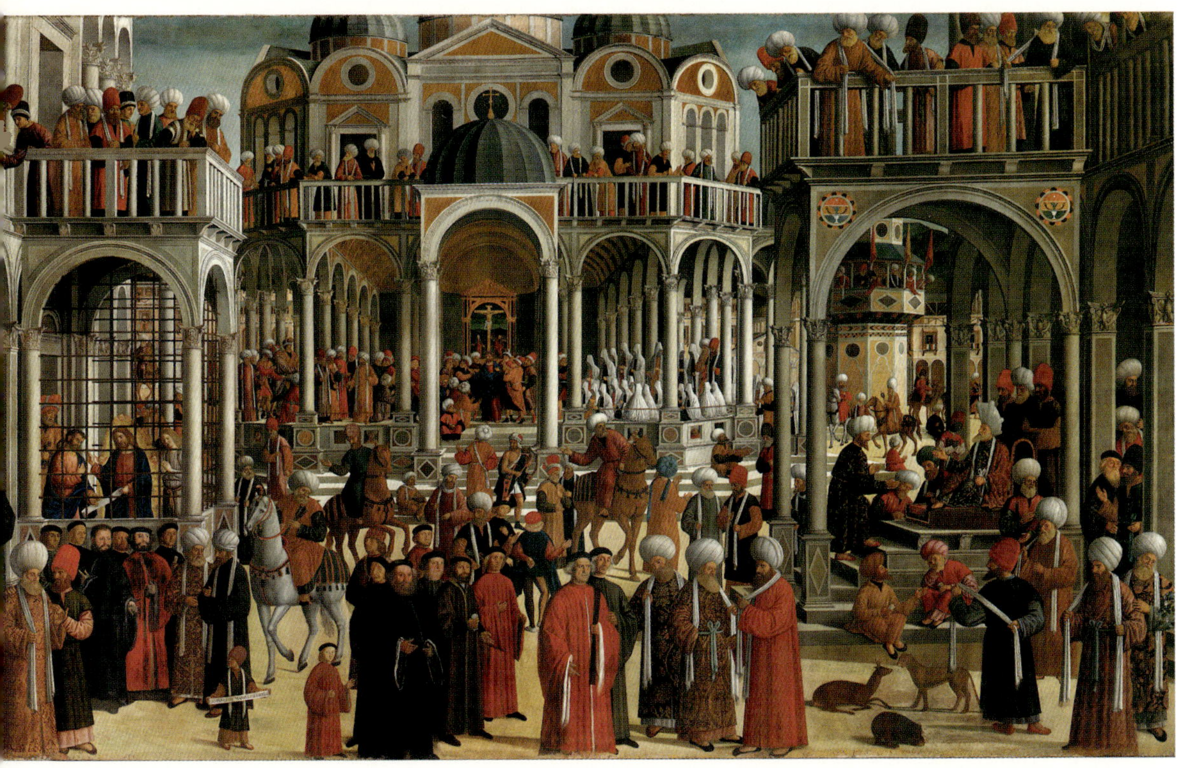

hostile and warlike Ottoman Turks, and the steady erosion of Venetian influence in Egypt and elsewhere in the eastern Mediterranean.

In smaller-scale or privately commissioned works, painters often returned to the poeticism and sensual allegory of Giorgione. This revival, which probably reflects the further development of private taste and collections across the city, as noted by Marcantonio Michiel, also marks a point of distinction from Titian's example, given that such works are typically characterized by qualities of intimacy and dreaminess quite different from his dynamic mode. In the *Warrior Adoring the Infant Christ and the Virgin* by Vincenzo Catena (active 1506–1531), which may originally have hung in the *portego* (main living space) of a Venetian palace, the painter maintains a scrupulously quattrocento-style planar approach, and this gives his work an air of timeless tranquillity (FIG. 78). The work combines reference to examples of votive and allegorical painting by Giovanni Bellini with the poetic ambiguity and warm tonality of Giorgione. Against the backdrop of a pastoral landscape, an unidentified warrior approaches the Holy Family wearing European armour, but equipped with objects, such as the horse's bridle and the knife and scabbard attached to the wall, from the Islamic world. The picture may show a Christian convert from Islam who approaches the Virgin and Child to be baptized: a theme which would reflect Venetian anxieties regarding its Eastern trading empire, and related hopes for the religious conversion of the belligerent Sultan, Suleiman I.

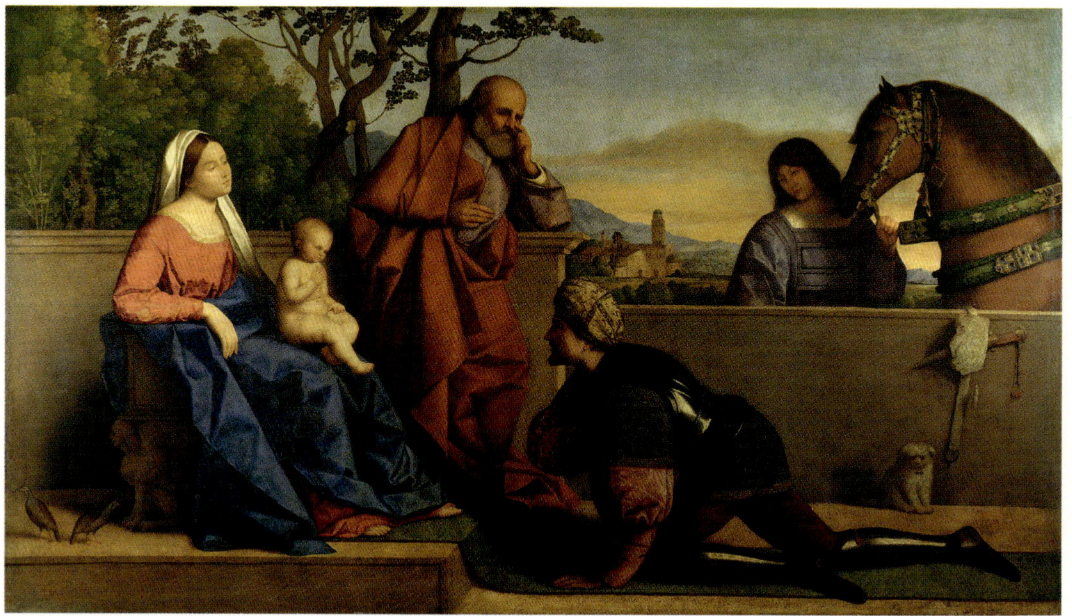

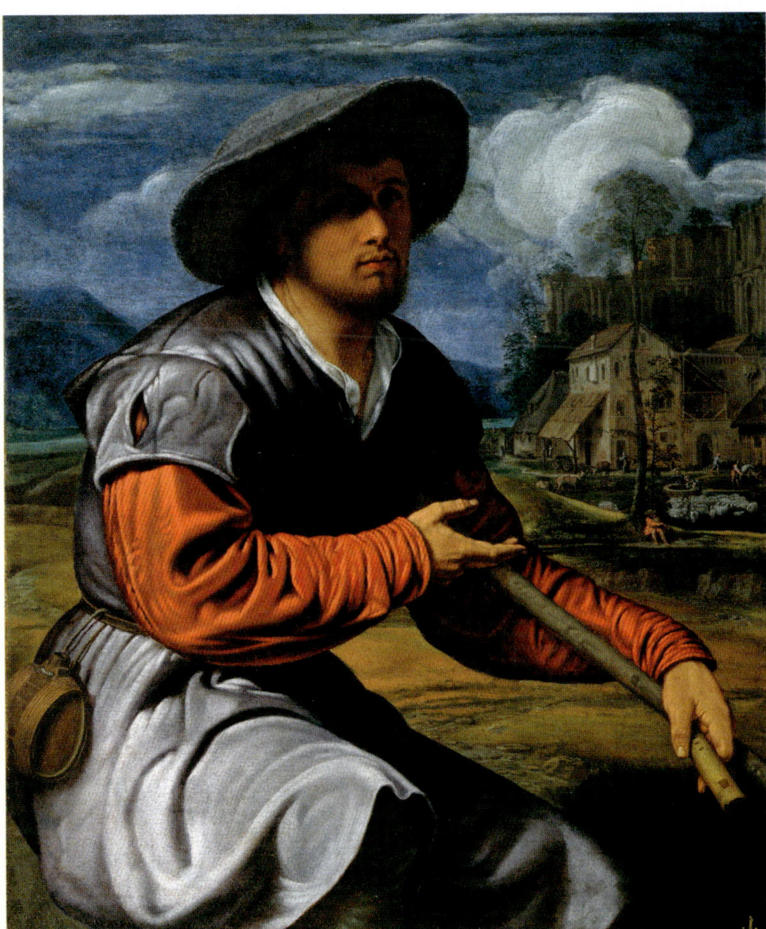

When set against Titian's ambitious example, Catena's static style appears knowingly archaic or retrospective, pointedly recalling an earlier phase of Venetian artistic culture in a period of rapid change. Catena is named as a 'colleague' of Giorgione in an inscription on the back of the *Laura* of 1506 (*see* FIG. 60), and it may be that he continued to see himself in that light until his death in 1531.

The careful way in which Michiel records the presence of Giorgione's paintings in patrician collections in the 1520s, and the evident revival of his poetic style in the work of painters such as the Brescian-born Giovanni Girolamo Savoldo (ca. 1480/5–after 1548), indicates that Catena was by no means isolated or eccentric in his preferences. In Savoldo's memorable *Shepherd with a Flute*, the painter draws on Giorgione's own depictions of musical shepherds, as also on the idea of visual ambiguity, with the viewer left uncertain whether the work is a portrait or a generic 'poetic' image (FIG. 79). Given the measure of individuation allowed to the sitter's face, it seems likely that the painting was a commissioned portrait, showing a young nobleman in the guise of a shepherd.

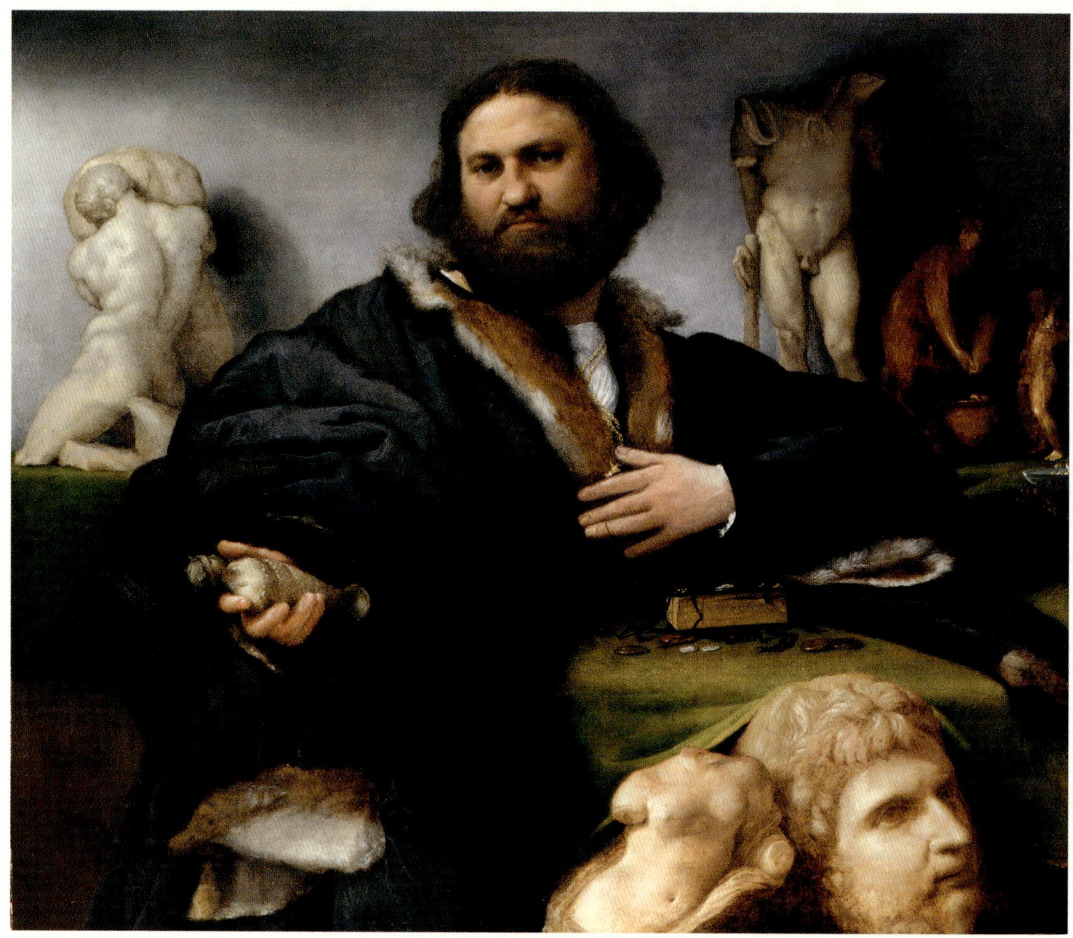

In his *Il Cortegiano* of 1528, Castiglione had advised that a true courtier should always be recognizable, even when dressed as a shepherd, and this comment might have encouraged the disguise. With his meticulous and literal technique, Savoldo depicts a landscape of agrarian productivity rather than pastoral sensuality in a work that appears more like a precursor to Jacopo Bassano's rural scenes than a close rendition of Giorgione. Nonetheless, Savoldo's many other paintings featuring Giorgionesque subjects for private patrons in Venice and the Veneto indicate the continuing popularity of the older master among leading collectors. And this marked a point of difference from the contemporary mode of Titian, as also from the wider cultural movement of the *renovatio*.

The sharp contrasts of light, clever use of silhouette, and intense local colouring also suggest that Savoldo responded to recent paintings by the peripatetic Lorenzo Lotto, who returned to Venice from Bergamo in 1525. Lotto now produced a number of innovative portraits which superficially recall Titian's style of the 1520s, but are actually very different in their meaning and orientation. If Titian developed portraiture towards an expression of ineffable courtly noblesse, detaching the sitter from immediate interaction with the viewer (*see* FIG. 63), Lotto insisted on direct and passionate interaction as a core condition of the work. In his depiction of the art collector *Andrea Odoni* (FIG. 80), Lotto marked the difference again by using an unusual broad landscape format that allowed him to provide a setting for his *cittadino* sitter, who is surrounded by the plaster casts of antique sculptures that he owned. In contrast to Titian's withdrawn ultra-aristocratic sitters wrapped within a mysterious dignifying penumbra, Lotto's Odoni is shown in more open and accessible fashion, at home and at ease among his cherished collection. At the same time, Lotto introduces an insistent – and distinctly non-Titianesque – element of moralization into his portrait: one that, as we saw in the previous chapter, was typical of his painting more generally. The decapitated, dismembered and chaotic fragments of classical casts which surround the sitter offer a commentary on the destruction of the pagan world, and form a telling contrast with the intensely expressive figure of Odoni himself. While the collector offers a classical statuette of Diana, goddess of nature, to the viewer, he also holds a cross to his heart with his other hand, as if to indicate his deeper commitment to a more lasting Christian piety.

Mannerism and Titian's authority in Venice

It may be that the spread to Venice of a highly artificial and ornate version of central Italian classicism, known as Mannerism, also served to limit the extent of Titian's artistic authority in these decades. The presence of well-travelled and experienced painters such as Lotto, and the arrival from Florence in the late 1530s of Giovanni da Udine (1487–1564), Francesco Salviati (1510–1563) and Giorgio Vasari (1511–1574) to work in the Palazzo Grimani at Santa Maria Formosa, offered sharp alternatives to Titian's approach to painting. And the circulation of drawings and prints after increasingly fashionable Italian masters from other leading artistic centres in Italy, such as Parmigianino (1503–1540) and Giulio Romano (1499–1546), also provided alternative models for the younger generation to follow. The newly complex *all'antica* style of this new wave of artists did not offer a clear departure from the Romanism of Sansovino; or from Titian's mature manner, with its own dynamic response to antique models

1527. Oil on canvas, 104.6 × 116.6cm (3ft 5⅛in × 3ft 9⅞in). Royal Collection Trust, London. © Her Majesty Queen Elizabeth II, 2015.

In this portrait, Lotto may have intended to flatter his non-noble patron by suggesting that Odoni's activities as an art collector were the modern-day equivalent to those of the Emperor Hadrian, whose sculpted head is featured at the lower right. Marcantonio Michiel saw the painting in the bedroom of Odoni's lavish palace on the Fondamenta del Gaffaro.

and Renaissance classicism. And yet it remains true that a keen interest in Mannerist art can often be taken as a measure of distance from Titian. To this extent, such progressive departures from his style can be understood as equivalent to the retrogressive ones noted above, even if the visual consequences were very different. Titian's frequent work abroad, like his rivalrous attitude and apparent lack of interest in teaching pupils and followers in his workshop, exacerbated this disintegrated situation among artists working in Venice.

The career of Paris Bordone (1500–1571) is a case in point. He was apparently a pupil of Titian who, according to Vasari's *Lives of the Artists* (Florence, 1568), was uninterested in teaching him and went so far as to steal a commission for an altarpiece at the church of San Nicolò ai Frari that Bordone had been awarded. Whether or not these stories are true, Bordone quickly turned to Giorgione's style in his earlier work of the 1520s. Like other painters, such as Lotto, he apparently struggled to gain many important commissions in the city, and his subsequent career was largely shaped by work for private and foreign patrons, including the French court around 1560. To this extent, Bordone's career followed the trajectory of Titian himself, but his successes abroad were with less high-ranking patrons and were comparatively minor and short-lived, and he died in relative obscurity in his home town of Treviso. The remarkable difference between the styles of master and pupil may be indicative of the hostility and distance between them. By the 1540s, Bordone had developed a highly finished and artificial Mannerist style, featuring intense but non-naturalistic colour schemes, twisting sculptural figures, and stage-set architectural perspective backdrops that are very different from the contemporary style of Titian. In a painting for a Milanese nobleman, Carlo da Rho, he drew on a woodcut illustration in Serlio's recently published *Libro II dell'Architettura* (Paris, 1545) depicting the architectural backdrop deemed suitable for the 'Tragic Scene' in contemporary theatre (FIG. 81). This may have been fitting enough for a depiction of Bathsheba at her bath. King David sent the heroine's faithful and patriotic husband Uriah away to die in a war, so that he could possess her, though the lovers were subsequently punished by the death of their son. David and Uriah are, in fact, glimpsed as miniscule figures among the stage-set architecture in the background. The tragic narrative, however, is evidently much less significant than the display of Bordone's strange pictorial invention for the composition, in which the exaggerated movements of the figures serve as artistic showpieces, rather than being determined by the needs of the story. The painfully self-conscious stylishness of the work becomes, in effect, its main meaning.

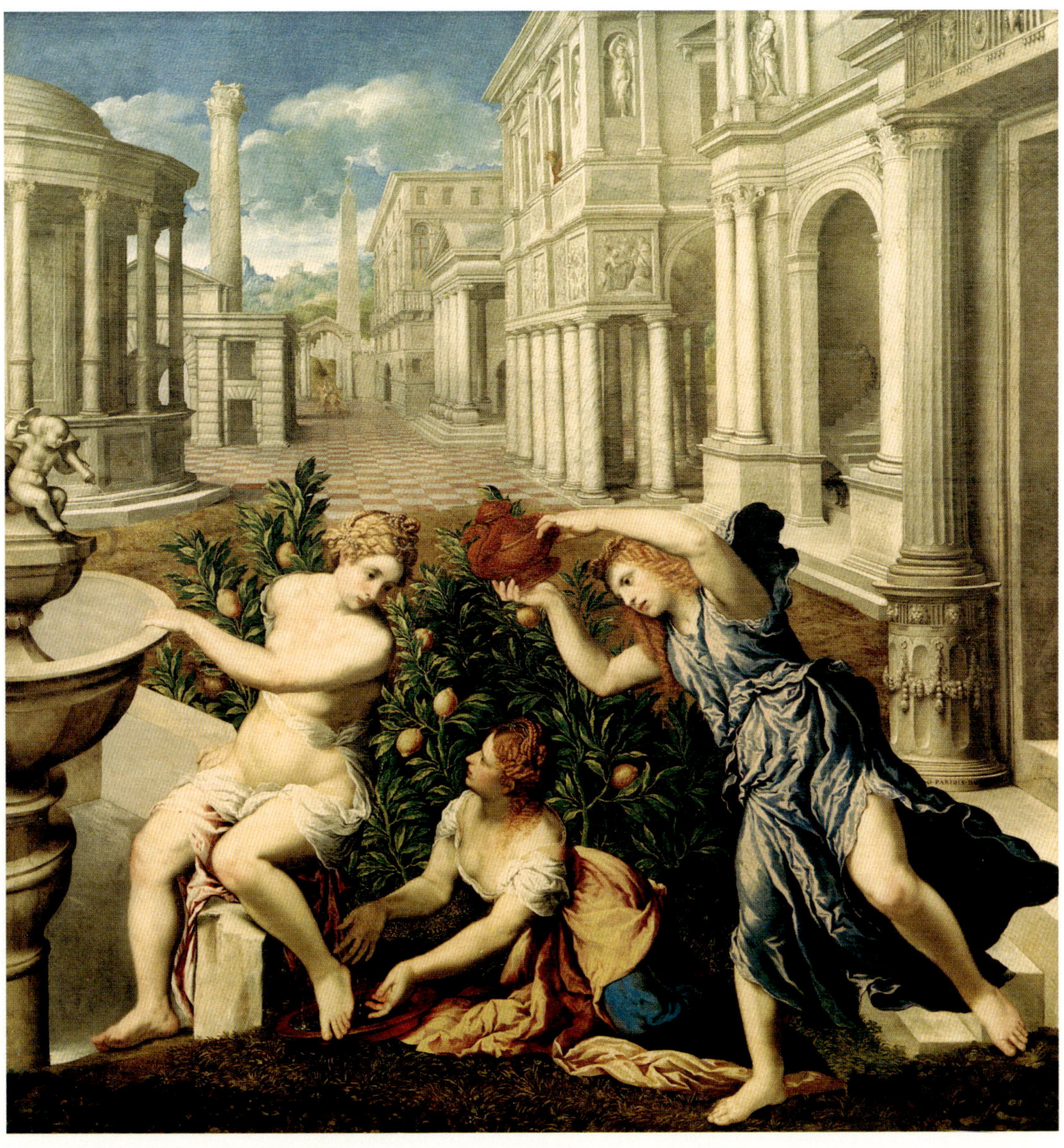

The growing division between Titian and other painters in Venice is also evident from the development of contrasting attitudes to Michelangelo in this period. From the outset of his career Titian had made a habit of referring to the great Tuscan's works, and this reached a high point around the time of his visit to Rome in 1545–6, as we have seen in the portraits featuring *Pietro Aretino* and *Andrea Gritti*. The exaggeratedly monumental figure-types in Titian paintings from these years suggest the intensified impact of his rival at this point. After a visit to Titian's temporary studio in the Belvedere in the Vatican, Michelangelo is said to have praised the colouring of Titian's *Danaë* (1545, Museo di Capodimonte, Naples), in which the body of the heroine was based, in part, on his own works. According to Vasari,

Fig.81
Paris Bordone
Bathsheba in her Bath

ca. 1545–8. Oil on canvas,
324 × 217cm (10ft 7½in × 7ft
1⅜in). Wallraf-Richartz-
Museum, Cologne.

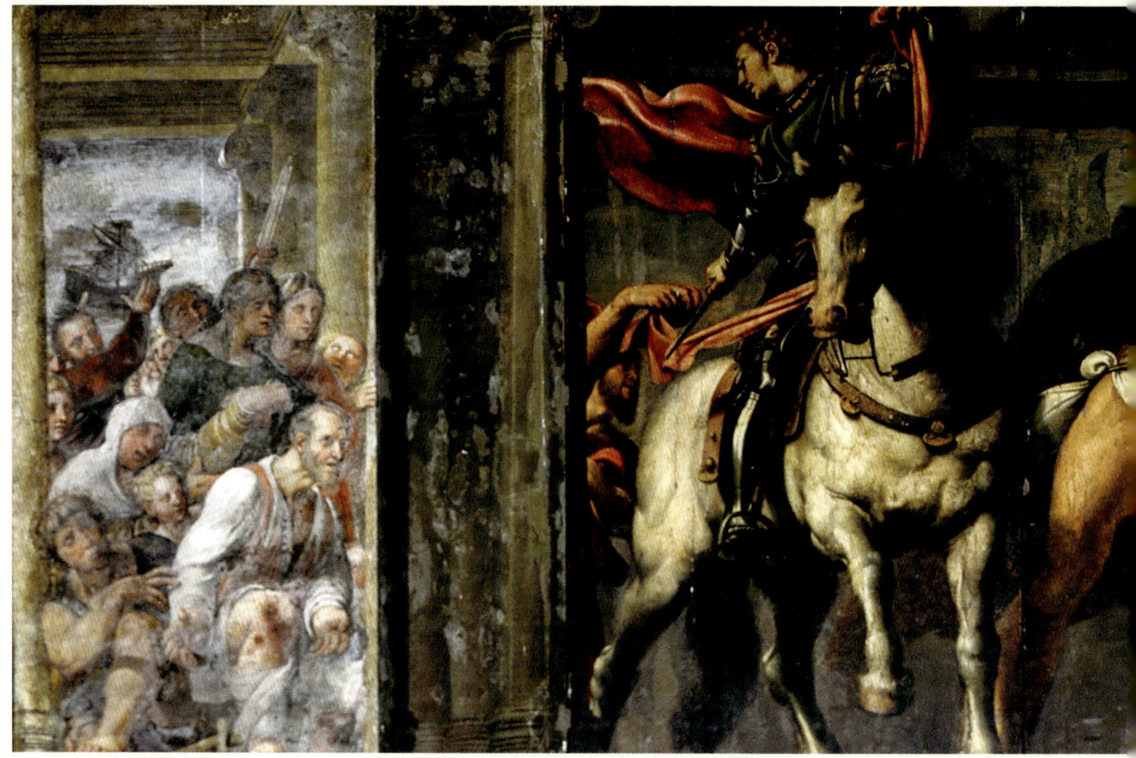

though, Michelangelo took the opportunity to criticize Titian's lack of *disegno*, pronouncing that 'if this man had in any way been assisted by art and design, as he is by nature, no one could do more or work better'. Shortly afterwards, Aretino published a letter castigating the nudity in Michelangelo's *Last Judgement* fresco in the Sistine Chapel (1536–41): the battle lines were drawn. While we do not know exactly what Titian himself thought of Michelangelo's work, his friend Lodovico Dolce soon published the dialogue mentioned in the previous chapter, in which 'Aretino' explains that Titian is superior because he excels in all the aspects of visual art (design, invention and colour), whereas Michelangelo is excellent only in the first category.

If Titian and his circle became more critical of Michelangelo, others in Venice were increasingly enthralled by his example. Their repeated and ever more explicit reference to his works took on a polemical edge against the example of Titian. Through much of the 1530s, Titian had faced a fierce rivalry of this kind from the Friulian painter Giovanni Antonio da Pordenone (ca. 1483/4–1539), who had developed an exaggeratedly Michelangelesque style even before his arrival in Venice in 1527. In the *Saints Martin and Christopher* he painted on a cupboard door in the church of San Rocco, Pordenone

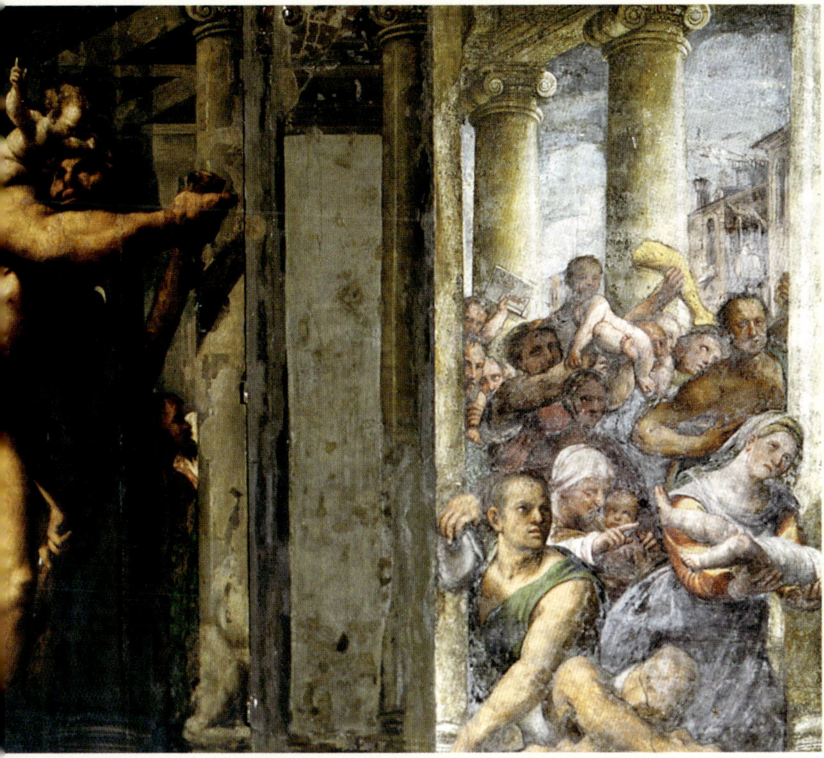

featured enormous striding figures whose massive forms are revealed by a raking light (FIG. 82). Pordenone's giant saints were more convincingly sculptural than any Titian had so far managed, even if the figure of St Christopher was modelled on Titian's recent depiction of the saint in the Ducal Palace. Titian was shortly to create his own highly dramatic Michelangelesque group in the lost *Death of St Peter Martyr* Altarpiece of 1528–30. It may be the astonishing foreshortenings and formal energies of that work were a response to Pordenone, who had unsuccessfully competed with Titian for the commission, and whose preparatory drawing for it, featuring an equivalent display of artistic difficulty (*difficoltà*) in the struggling figures, still survives. In the 1530s, Titian retreated from the local artistic melting pot of Venice as his career developed abroad, but it is a measure of his rival's influence in the city that the Venetian Senate thought seriously about transferring Titian's commission for a battle painting in the Ducal Palace to Pordenone. It may only have been the latter's death in 1539 that saved Titian's position as the leading painter in the city.

If Titian dominated in the medium of oils and in all the best-established picture types commissioned in Venice, other artists developed their careers in more marginal visual media and pictorial

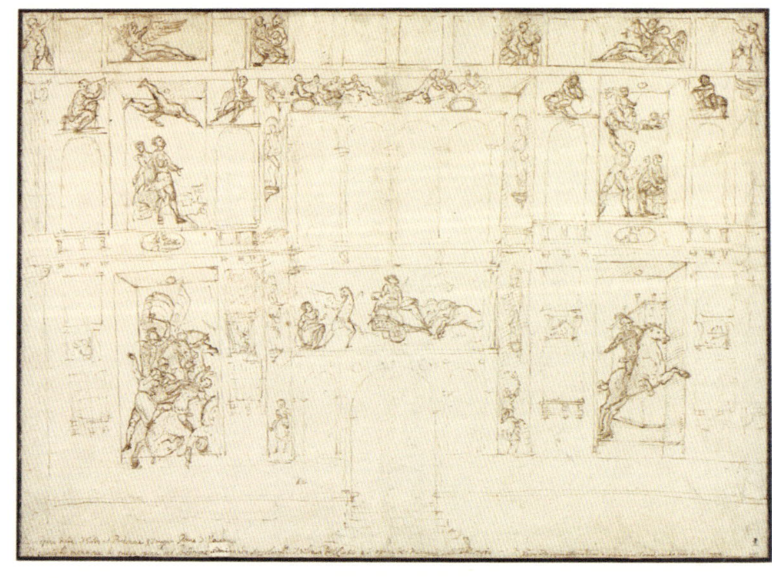

contexts. The fresco medium, for example, had been superseded by the rise of oil painting over the past half-century, especially because of its vulnerability to the salty climate of the lagoon. Nonetheless, it remained popular, especially as a cheap alternative to sculpture on palace facades. True or *buon* fresco was closely associated with Michelangelo, who proclaimed it the highest medium for painting, given that it was also the most difficult to handle. Pordenone was particularly drawn to this kind of work, painting frescoes in Venetian churches, and also on palace facades. Though the cycle he painted at Palazzo d'Anna on the Grand Canal has vanished, a design for the work survives (FIG. 83). Pordenone featured a brilliantly conceived sequence of outsized and sharply foreshortened figures that appear to move freely within relatively narrow fictive spaces. In the four scenes featured on either side of the ground floor entrance and the *portego* level above, massive figures plunge into or topple out of the picture space, and the sense of vertiginous illusionism is heightened by the narrow window-like framing imagined as seen in perspective from a low central viewing point.

Certain other painters collaborated with carpenters in the production of painted furniture, a practice which brought legal action from the painter's guild on occasion. This kind of domestic painting also had a good pedigree in the city, however, and provided a vehicle for the further survival of the Giorgionesque tradition of pastoral or poetic mythological and allegorical painting into the mid-sixteenth century. The style employed in such works stood quite apart from the Romanism evident in more mainstream picture types. For emergent young painters such as Andrea Schiavone (ca. 1515–1563) and Jacopo Tintoretto (1518–1594), the intimate scale of their work on wooden marriage chests known as *cassoni* provided opportunities for the development of a new kind of dynamic brushwork, in which the fluidly conceived figures appear to have been rapidly drawn in paint. In a pioneering treatise on painting published in Venice in 1548, Paolo Pino described the unfinished style of the furniture painters as a kind of 'smearing' that reflected their supposed careless haste to complete a work, and announced that this kind of low-grade commission should be avoided at all costs. Pino also expressed the idea that the combination of Titian's colour with Michelangelo's design was most desirable in art. And it is clear from Schiavone's quivering touch in *cassone* paintings such as *Diana and Callisto* (FIG. 84) that this lowly pictorial context could be used to create an improvised style which did indeed bring colour and form together in a new way.

Schiavone's cursive calligraphy both threatens and suggests form in an informal manner that is refreshingly far from the cold and mannered artificiality of Bordone, or the inflated ponderousness of Pordenone. In the painting illustrated here, the delicate arabesque figures are elegantly fluid carriers of flickering colour, intense emotion and also thematic meaning. Visualizing an Ovid story of sudden change and transformation from the *Metamorphoses*, Schiavone shows the nature goddess Diana imperiously pointing out the unwanted pregnancy of her supposedly chaste nymph Callisto to the right. Callisto, in response, struggles to conceal herself, but seems already about to lose her human shape, as if in anticipation of her imminent transformation into a bear for the hunt. The painting

Fig.84
Andrea Schiavone
Diana and Callisto

ca. 1548–9. Oil on canvas, 18.6 × 49cm (7¼in × 1ft 7¼in). Musée de Picardie, Amiens.

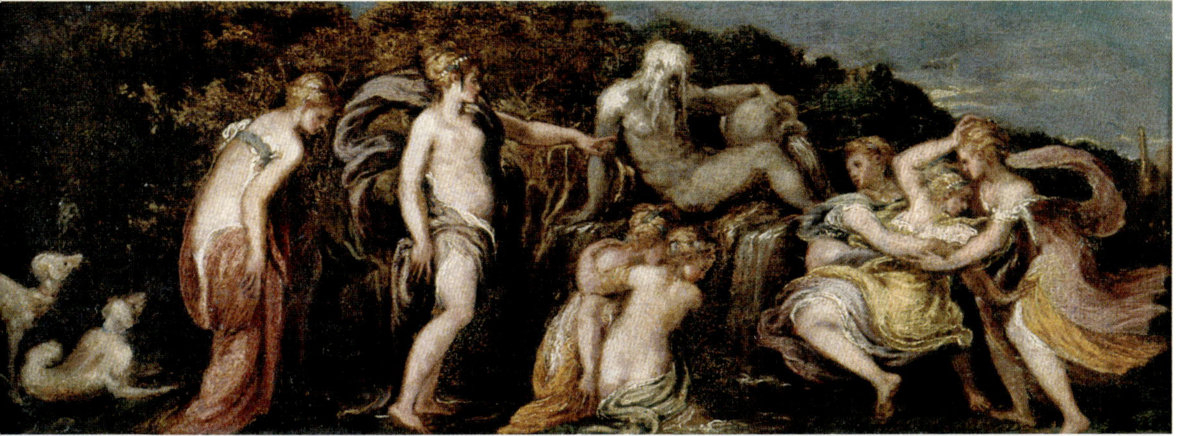

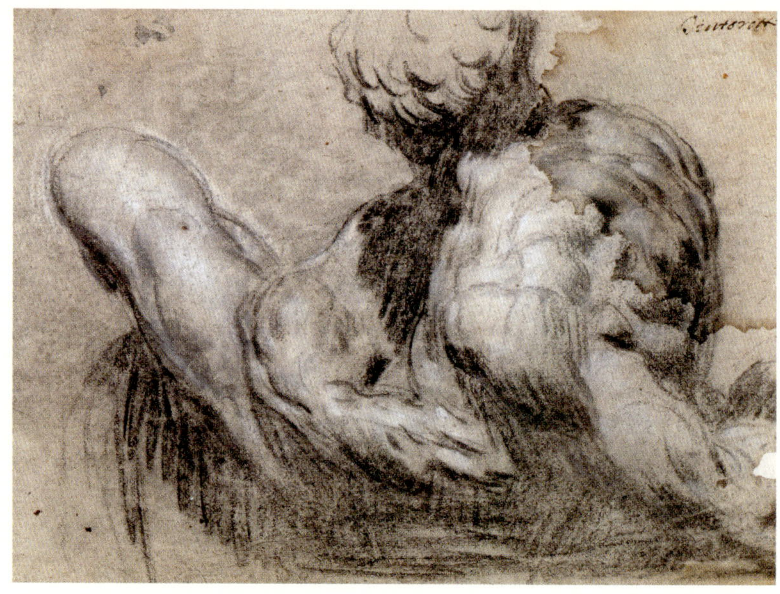

was probably made for a piece of bedroom furniture, and thus had a very private context. It nonetheless had a discernible impact on Titian himself, who referred to Schiavone's composition in his own much larger version of the subject painted some years later for the king of Spain.

According to an early source, the young Tintoretto pinned a notice over his studio door proclaiming his artistic ambition to combine 'the drawing of Michelangelo and the colour of Titian'. We are also told that after spending a short time as a pupil of Titian he was expelled from the workshop, either because his style was considered too eccentric, or because his talent made Titian jealous. The story suggests the existence of an antagonistic relationship between the painters that may have lasted for decades. In the early 1540s Tintoretto apparently turned to *cassoni* painting alongside Schiavone, and was also very active painting facade frescoes, probably because his dispute with Titian was making more prestigious commissions hard to come by. In a series of such paintings for the Palazzo Gussoni on the Grand Canal, Tintoretto paid the most explicit homage to Michelangelo yet seen in Venice, displaying large-scale paintings that were closely based on the Tuscan's four great allegorical sculptures in the Medici Chapel. He also made numerous drawings in this period, as if to distance himself from Titian's habit of by-passing this stage of the artistic process. Many of these are based on the small statuette copies after Michelangelo's sculptures that he owned, and indicate that the young painter sought to explore the spatial possibilities of three-dimensional sculptural form (FIG. 85). The small scale and movable qualities of the casts he worked from were also vital to the kind of expressive effects in which he was interested. The odd, sharply angled and steeply foreshortened viewpoints from which he drew freed up the sculptures' relation to the surrounding space, an effect which was immediately carried over into his large-scale paintings. At the same time, Tintoretto's habit of suspending small wax models in wooden boxes, strongly lit from the side, has the effect of breaking up the outlines or monumental integrity of the given form, and of generating a vibrating tension between surface and depth.

Tintoretto's *Miracle of the Slave*, painted for the Scuola Grande di San Marco in 1548, possesses a similar kind of visual dynamism worked between *colore* and *disegno* (FIG. 86). The extreme contrast this *istoria* offers to Mansueti's retrospectively orientated contributions to the same cycle, or to those by the Bellini from still earlier in the century, provides a clear measure of the young Tintoretto's stylistic radicalism in the Venetian context, and it is no surprise that

1548. Oil on canvas, 415 × 541cm (13ft 7⅜in × 17ft 9in). Gallerie dell'Accademia, Venice.

Although the miracle depicted occurred in Provence, in the south of France, Tintoretto shows several turbaned, obviously Eastern figures, including the main executioner. Their presence continues the theme established in earlier *istorie* for the cycle at the Scuola Grande di San Marco, and must again reflect cultural anxieties over on-going conflicts with the Muslim Turks.

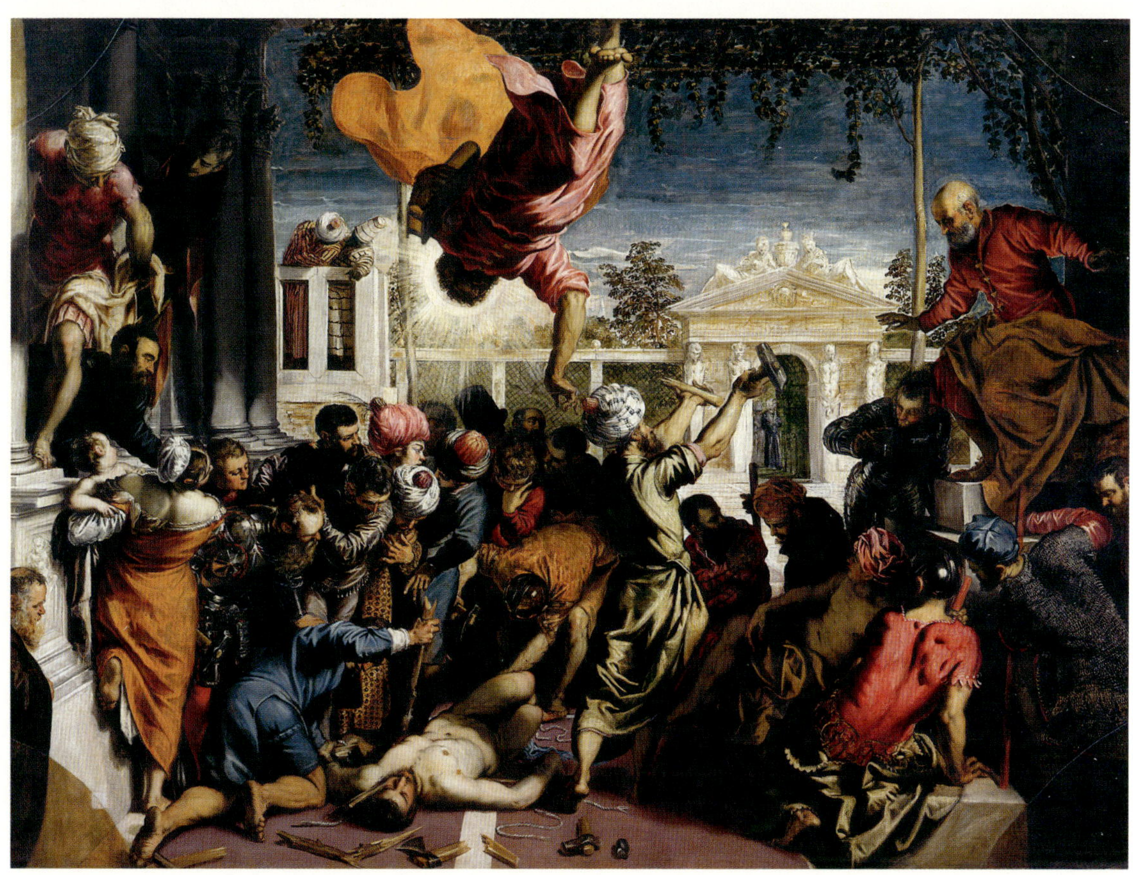

the painting was initially returned to the painter as unacceptable. It features an episode from St Mark's heavenly afterlife, showing the saint swooping down to relieve the torture of a Christian slave. Tintoretto's visual presentation appears as the very opposite of the earlier Bellinesque *istoria*, in which the narrative moment is buried within an unchanging and undisturbed surrounding environment. Every pictorial element is marshalled to intensify the drama which is imagined as happening in the immediate here and now, and as overturning all expectations. The watching group is wound up like a coiled spring, each figure straining to understand the sudden miraculous intervention against nature, as the instruments of torture break into pieces before their eyes. Only the slave sees the hurtling figure of the saint above him, his foreshortened body mirroring that of the supernatural visitor to suggest spiritual connection and interaction.

Titian's own approach to narrative in works such as the lost *Death of St Peter Martyr* Altarpiece undoubtedly provided a model for Tintoretto's stress on the dramatic exigencies of the present moment. But significantly, Tintoretto drew more inspiration from the work of his erstwhile master's rivals. His virtuosic *pièce de résistance*, the dynamic airborne figure of St Mark, was based on a similar figure at the upper left of Pordenone's Palazzo d'Anna facade (*see* FIG. 83). The cool acerbic colours and sharp contrasts of black and white in the folds of the draperies support the poised energies of the forms and must remind us of relief sculpture rather than the warm tones of Titian's painting. Tintoretto had the clumpy classicism of a recent relief by Sansovino for St Mark's featuring the same subject as a possible model. His early masterpiece, however, owes far more to Michelangelo's recently unveiled fresco in the Vatican featuring the *Conversion of St Paul*: a work that had rapidly become known in Venice following the publication of a reproductive print in 1547 (FIG. 87)

Tintoretto's Michelangelism in the *Miracle of the Slave* is also evident enough in the details of certain of the seated and sprawling figures based on his individual studies after the Medici nudes. Such repeated references might well have been understood by contemporaries as a limitation to the artistic authority of Titian. In response to the *Miracle*, Titian's great advocate Aretino wrote a public letter praising Tintoretto's naturalism in the work, while at the same time criticizing the young painter's undue 'haste to have done' (*prestezza del fatto*). This was probably a reference to Tintoretto's lightning-quick speed of execution: an aspect that was allied to an emergent business strategy, based on high turnover of paintings, low price, and an inclusive approach to patronage by a local clientele. Such a proceeding was destined to present another kind of marketing challenge to Titian's primacy in Venice, contrasting as it did with the older master's habits of slow production, high pricing and the prioritization of an exclusive circle of foreign courtly patrons. More widely, the discussion in this chapter has highlighted the increasing rivalry between artists, who developed deliberately differentiated styles, techniques and approaches to subject matter in order to compete against one another effectively in the pursuit of commissions and artistic renown. The formal differences this competitive situation generated, based on a keen sense of aesthetic value beyond the immediate demands of patron or subject matter, were very different in kind to the pluralistic diversity of art favoured in Venice in previous centuries.

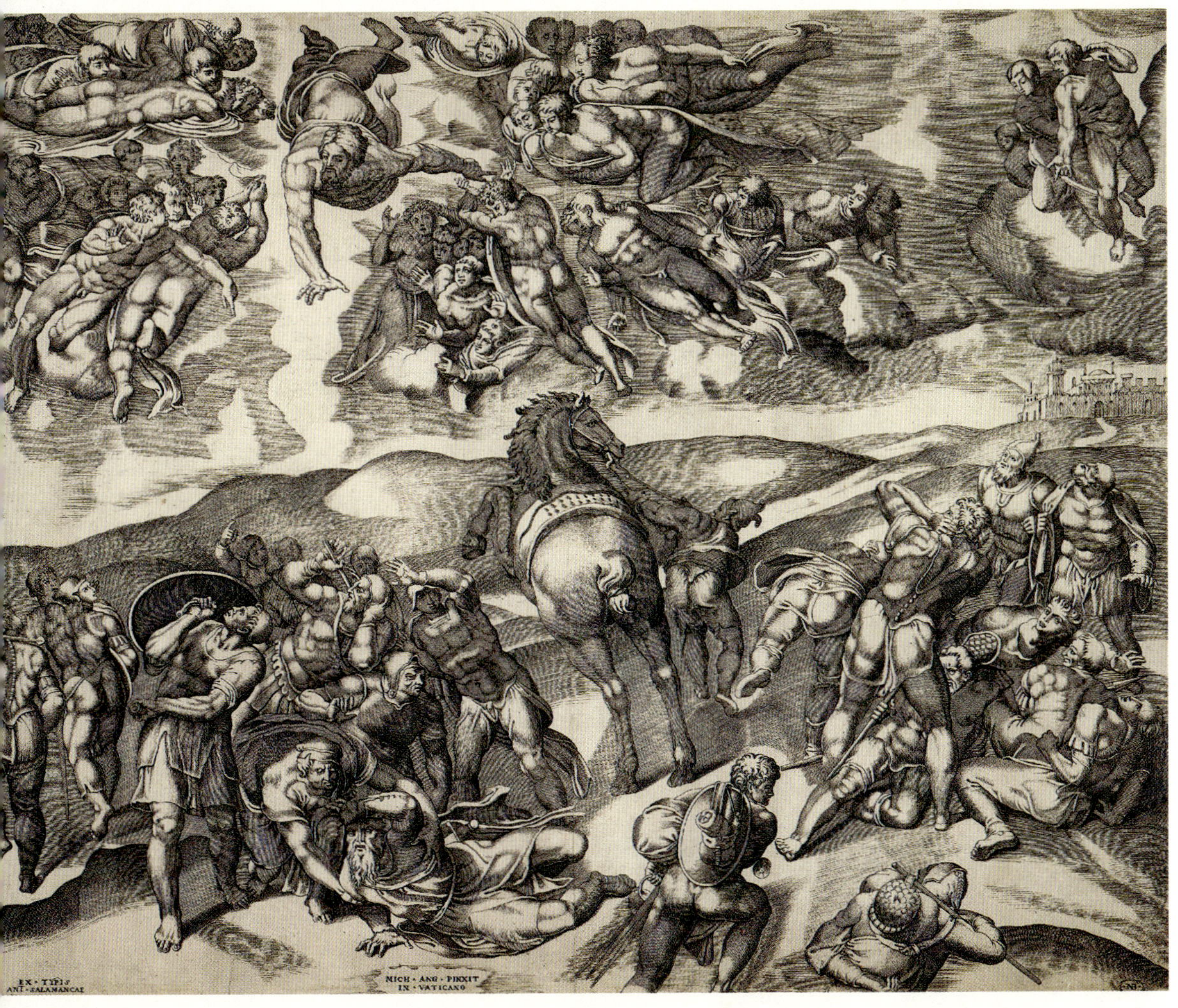

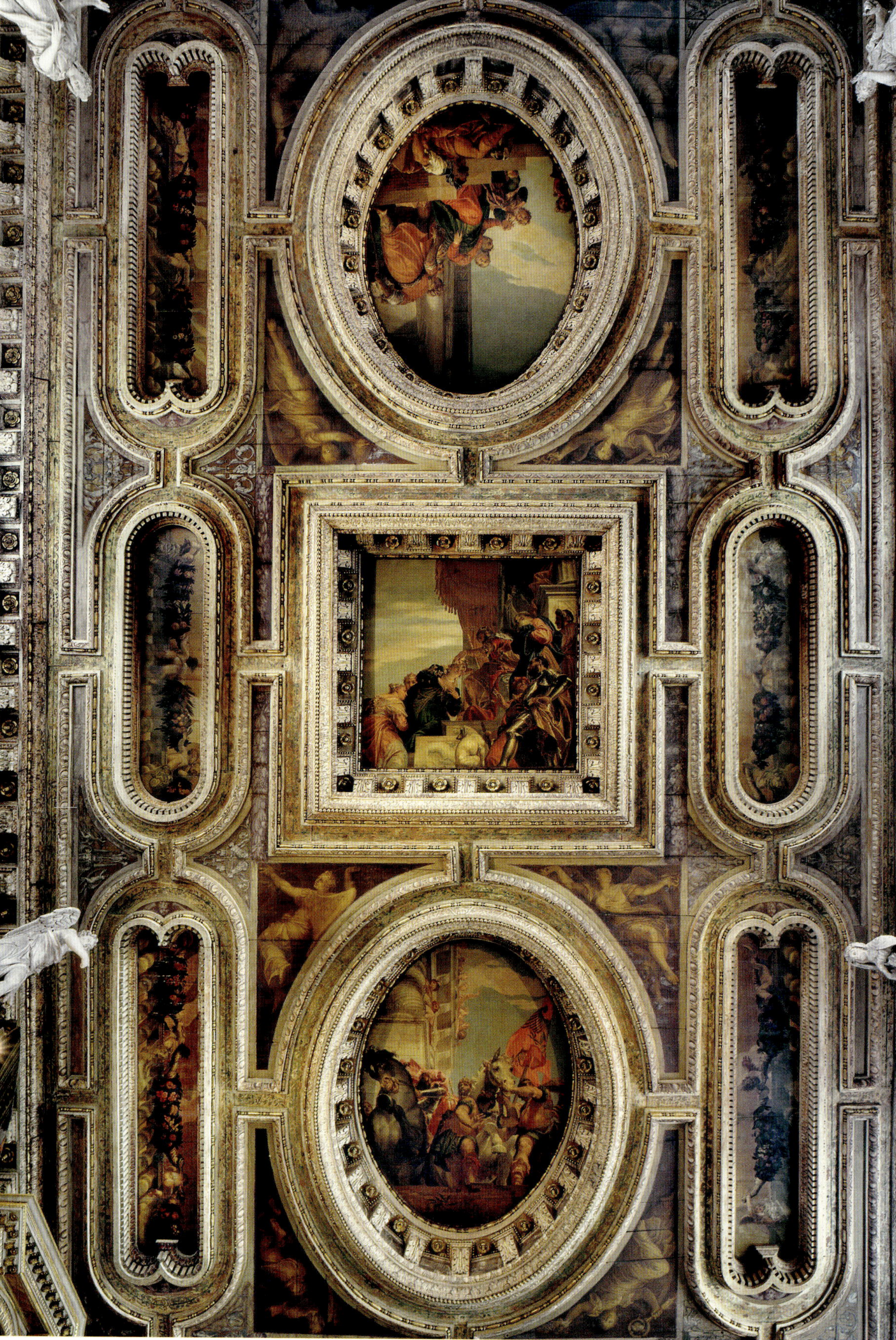

6

The Victory of Art: 1551–75

itian remained the leading figure in Venetian art in the decades after 1550. Although elderly he was still experimental, developing further the kind of free painterly style already indicated in works such as his portraits of *Andrea Gritti* and *Pietro Aretino* (*see* FIGS 73, 74). In this period, too, he established a new relationship with King Philip II of Spain, son and heir of his old patron Charles V. Commissions from Philip were key to Titian's later career up until his death in 1576. He frequently sent works abroad to the Spanish court and his paintings became known across Europe through the constant production of workshop copies and reproductive engravings. However, Titian's international commitments also meant that he was at an ever-increasing remove from on-going artistic developments in the city itself. He painted only rarely for the Venetian state, and while many younger artists saw him as 'the father of art', they may also have felt that his increasingly strange and personalized late style was difficult to emulate or follow. Art in Venice was, in any case, rapidly evolving in new directions. Paolo Veronese (1528–1588) arrived from Verona around 1555, and quickly established himself as a favourite painter among the cream of the city's art patrons. Following his struggle for recognition in the 1540s,

ca. 1556–8. San Sebastiano, Venice.

Veronese's extensive commissions at San Sebastiano apparently took shape through his relationship with the prior of the commissioning Hieronymite monastery, Fra Bernardo Torlioni, who was also from Verona. The vertiginous compositions featured in the three main panels of the nave ceiling were subsequently very influential on eighteenth-century Venetian rococo painters, such as Giovanni Battista Tiepolo (1696–1770).

Tintoretto now emerged as a powerful new rival to Titian, adroitly exploiting the old master's preoccupation with foreign clients to build a powerful patron base of his own centred in Venice. In contrast to the socially exclusive Titian, Tintoretto gained a reputation for working quickly, cheaply and for all comers.

The sophisticated international look of art in Venice established in previous decades was continued, with artists drawing on a wide range of visual sources. It was fashionable to quote well-known contemporary and antique works from Rome, Florence, Mantua, Parma and elsewhere in Italy; or to reference the naturalism featured in still-lives and landscapes by Flemish or German artists. The subject cities of the Venetian *terraferma* (mainland) had an ever more significant influence on developments in art and architecture. The nickname 'Veronese' proudly identified Paolo Spezapreda's origins in Verona as a selling point in Venice. Jacopo dal Ponte (ca. 1510–1592) was simply known as 'Bassano', after the small town some 72 kilometres (45 miles) northwest of Venice where he ran his workshop. It is no accident that the careers of the architects who now came to the fore, Michele Sanmicheli (1484–1559) and Andrea Palladio (1508–1580) developed (respectively) in Verona and Vicenza. From

Fig. 89
Jacopo Sansovino
Mars and Neptune

1554–67. Marble, height 440cm (14ft 5¼in). Ducal Palace, Venice.

Sansovino's figures stand at the entrance to the Ducal Palace at the top of Antonio Rizzo's late-fifteenth-century staircase. Mars originally held a sword in his right hand, while Neptune had a trident.

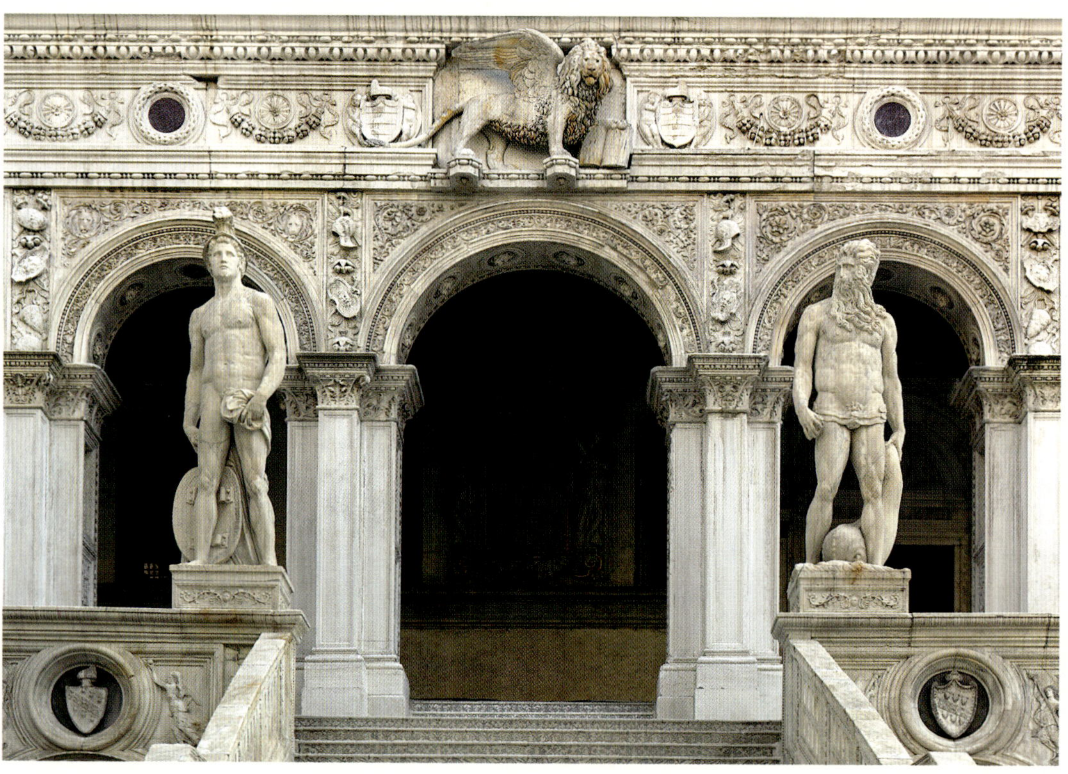

the artistic point of view, though, the new level of interaction between Venice and the *terraferma* was less a matter of domination from the centre than of a fluid two-way process of artistic import and export.

Artistic commissions multiplied as visual imagery became all-pervasive in Venice. Art was carefully and elaborately produced, even when it was understood that it would not survive. When the new king of France, Henri III, arrived for a state visit in 1574, a triumphal arch designed by Palladio was erected on the Lido, near to the entrance to the city from the sea, featuring paintings by Tintoretto and Veronese; but this was a temporary feature and was rapidly dismantled following the royal visitor's departure. The expendability of art was, in fact, another measure of its new ubiquity and predominance. Long-standing traditions of fresco, furniture, mosaic and manuscript painting were continued, alongside numerous commissions for oil paintings featuring portraits, mythologies, allegories and religious subjects. A new taste for paintings set into elaborately carved wooden or stone ceilings emerged, and in Venetian churches horizontally shaped wall paintings, known locally as *laterali*, were commissioned to supplement the altarpieces.

Imagery of the Republic

In these decades the traditional values of the Venetian Republic were most closely reflected in art commissioned by the state. In this context, many of the visual conventions and meanings established for official art in earlier periods were continued, albeit with the innovations of the classicizing *renovatio urbis* incorporated. In two large sculptures placed outside the Ducal Palace, Sansovino further developed the programme of decoration initiated in previous decades, again presenting the classical gods as personifications of state (FIG. 89). The exaggerated muscularity of these *giganti*, or giants, as they were known locally, deliberately recalled the enormous sculptures (*colossi*) of the Ancient Roman Empire, indicating again that Venice was its natural heir. Sansovino's sculptures were conceived as exemplars of heroic physical strength, and placed to either side of a more traditional winged lion of St Mark. Neptune references Venice's Stato di Mar, and Mars its Stato di Terra. The new sculptures display a more thought-through adaptation of mythological pagan imagery to the demands of the official context. The sculptures possess little of the lithe elegance or sensuality of their predecessors on the Loggetta. Sansovino's pagan henchmen now take on an almost archaic frontality, and their genitals are decorously covered. Drawing on the example of monumental patriotic nudes by Michelangelo and Baccio Bandinelli (1493-1560) at the entrance of the Palazzo Vecchio in Florence, Sansovino confidently defined his pagan gods as muscular guardians of the public safety of the state.

The classical gods were also pressed into state service in the interior of Ducal Palace itself, most notably in the ceiling paintings for the room of the Council of Ten, Venice's main security committee, where Veronese painted the central panel showing *Jupiter Expelling the Vices* around 1555. Such mythological figures became popular in official art because they allowed key political ideas to be presented in a non-direct or euphemistic way. Venetian state imagery did not often tackle contemporary political or social realities. Official portraits and votive paintings remained more conservative still, harking back to the artistic conventions of earlier centuries. In Tintoretto's *Madonna of the Treasurers*, for example, the painter studiously abandoned the spatial aerobatics and sudden plunges of perspective that characterize many of his non-official works (FIG. 90). The composition, which very deliberately recalls the kind of compositional arrangement of sacred paintings featuring the Adoration of the Magi, shows three patrician officials (Michele Pisano, Marin Malipiero and Lorenzo Dolfin) worshipping the holy figures to the left. Tintoretto uses an orderly

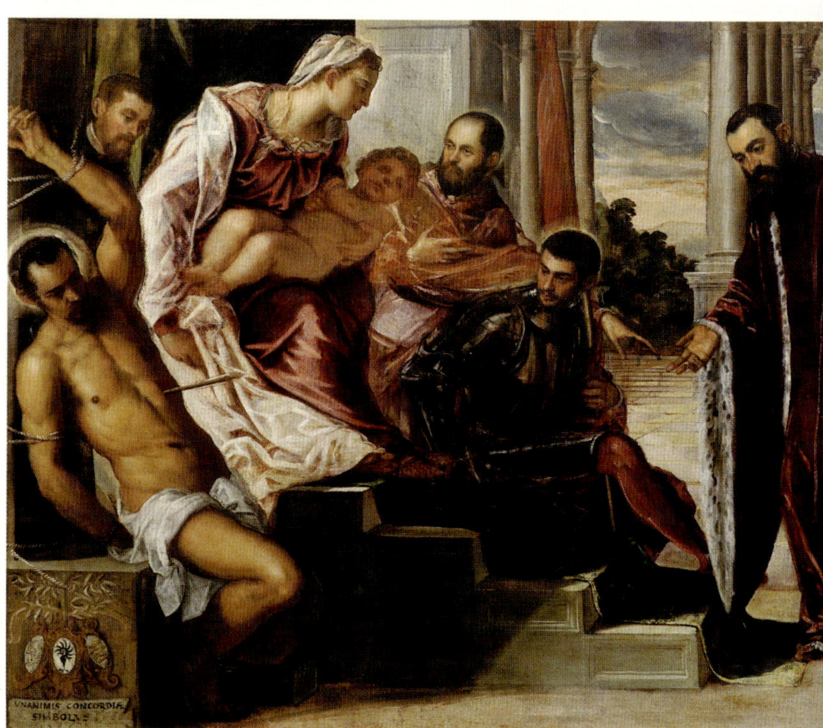

and measured planarity similar to the kind of ritalized figural move-ment found in late-fifteenth-century narrative paintings by painters such as Carpaccio (*see* FIG. 46).

The work is a group portrait: but Tintoretto is very careful to downplay the individualization of the figures. The patricians' red silk robes with lynx-fur-trimmed sleeves overlap, as if the three men shared a single gown of office. Their physiognomies are also made similar in support of their choreographed movements, which appear as part of a single pious response to the sacred figures. Tintoretto's painting expresses the hierarchical patterning of the social order in Venice. The intimacy between the patricians and the Virgin is par-ticularly significant, given that the foundation myth of the city had established her long-standing connection with Venice. Her inclined posture, mirroring that of the worshippers, creates a figural arch that expresses the connection between divine and social orders. The three *cittadini* (citizen) civil servants to the right are at one remove, towards the picture margins, but their actions emulate the pious movements of their patrician masters. If they are more literal in their offer of a well-stuffed money bag to the holy group, their self-suppressing black outfits and similar physiognomies confirm their uncomplaining and selfless loyalty to the divinely sanctioned patrician state.

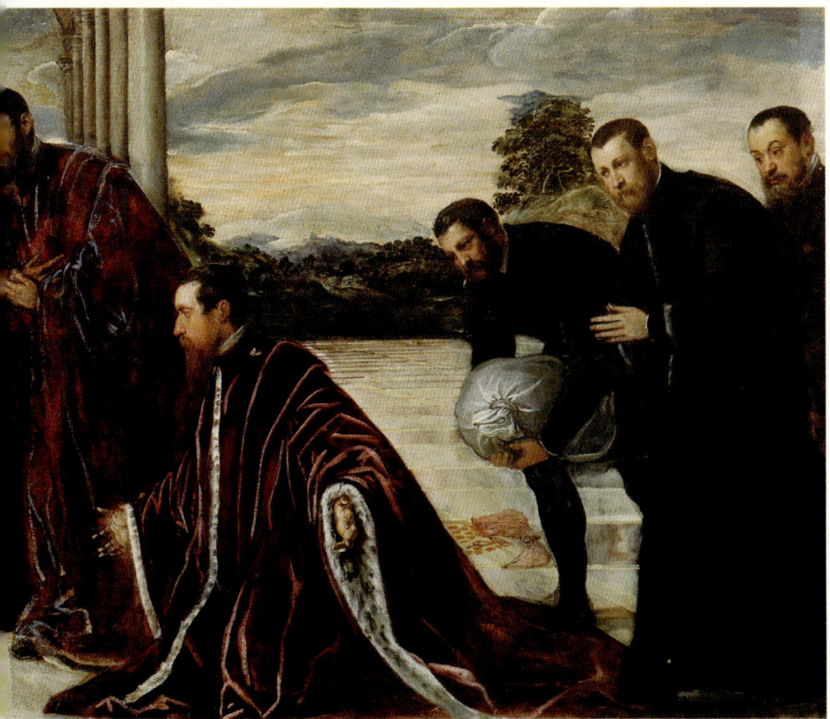

Impact of the *terraferma*

Such traditionalism was, however, much less apparent away from the sphere of state patronage. In the non-official context the well-established patrician taste for all things classical only intensified. This was most noticeable in the fashion for building farmhouses, which took on the appearance of antique villas, on the *terraferma*. The buying up of productive landed estates was an indication of Venice's ever-closer relationship with its mainland territories to the west – now something of a necessity, given the Republic's loss of territory and economic control in much of the eastern Mediterranean. As we saw in the previous chapter, such a reorientation produced and reflected a refashioning of the social identity of the Venetian ruling caste. The traditional 'merchant-nobleman' of Venice now attempted to present

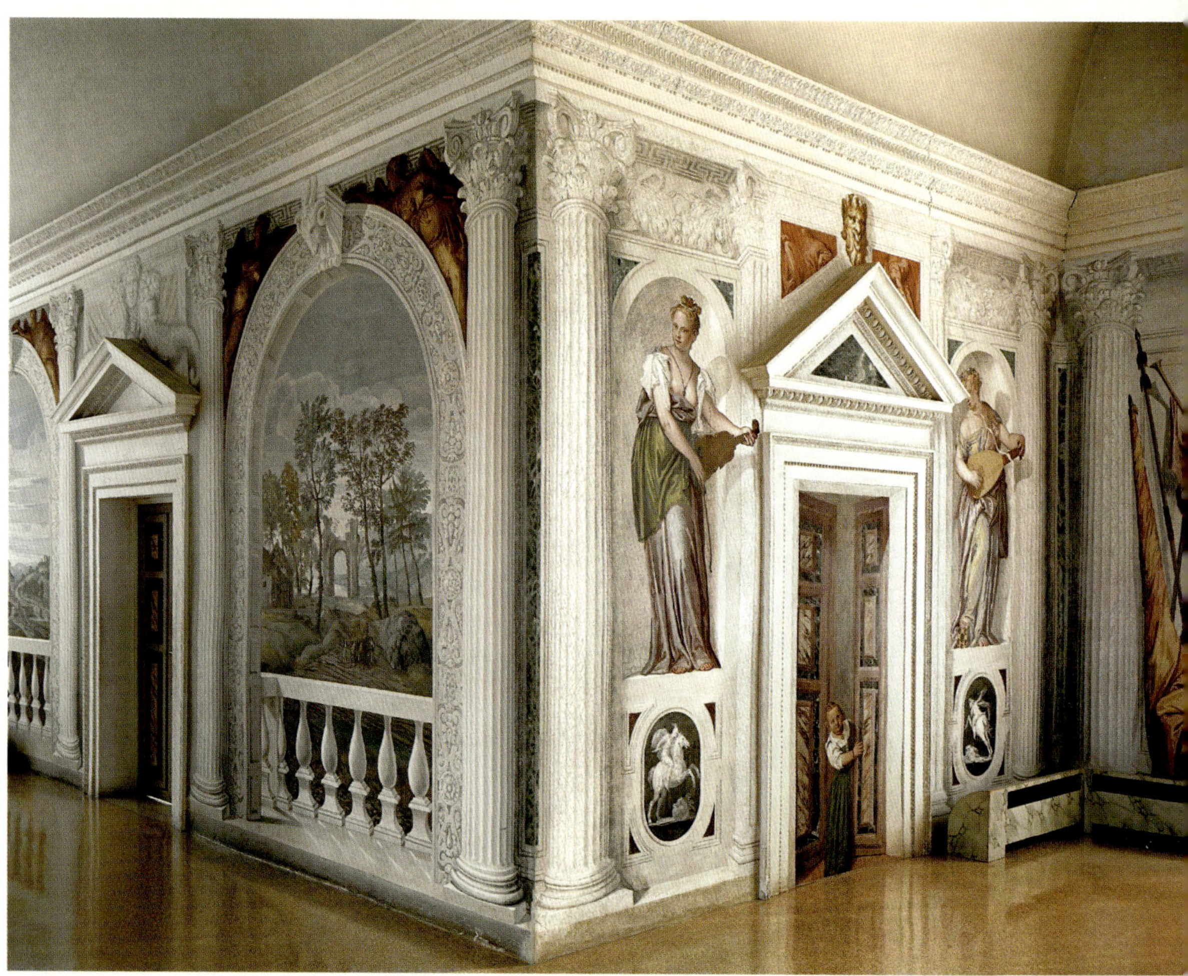

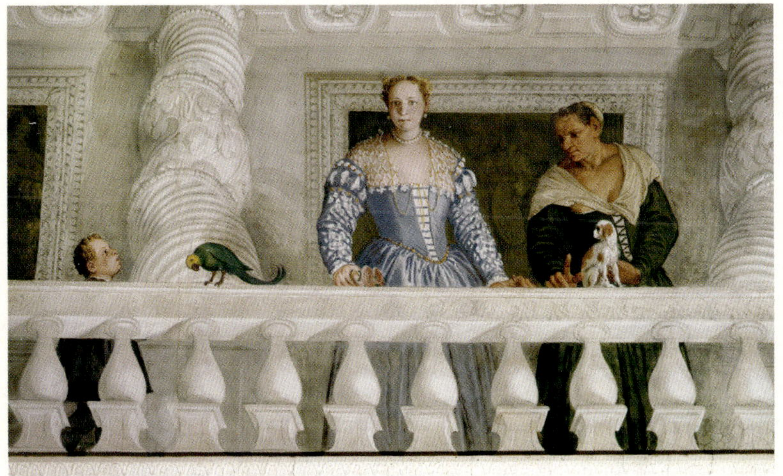

himself as more akin to the old feudal aristocrats, whose wealth and power depended on the ownership and cultivation of land. On their productive *terraferma* estates patricians felt freer to cultivate themselves, self-consciously emulating a princely taste for conspicuous expenditure and opulence, or referring to the key courtly concept of *otium*, or leisure. In doing so, they could draw on the example of villa culture in the ancient Roman Campagna, as recounted in fashionable ancient books such as those by Pliny and Vitruvius. An example is the villa near Asolo that Palladio completed for the patrician brothers Marc'Antonio and Daniele Barbaro in 1559. The interior decoration, with frescoes by Veronese, was apparently finished just two years later.

Veronese's frescoes feature a grand *trompe l'oeil* fictive architecture that references Palladio's facade, though it is more expansive and fantastical. His paintings offer an illusion of spaciousness to the relatively cramped villa interior, indicating numerous further openings through the evocation of painted balconies, doorways and windows. The fictive stonework is punctuated by classicizing or astrological allegories of agrarian production and cosmic harmony, in keeping with the patrons' learned interests and the wider function of the farmhouse. Veronese's paintings also feature more personalized imagery (though still laden with classical association and allegorical meaning) that reference the on-going life of the Barbaro family, including its children, servants and pets. The area of the hallway crossing includes painted archways with balustrades giving onto classical-looking landscapes inspired by contemporary engravings (FIG. 91). A smiling child appears at a fictive doorway between two allegorical music-makers. Elsewhere, a woman who may be Marc'Antonio's

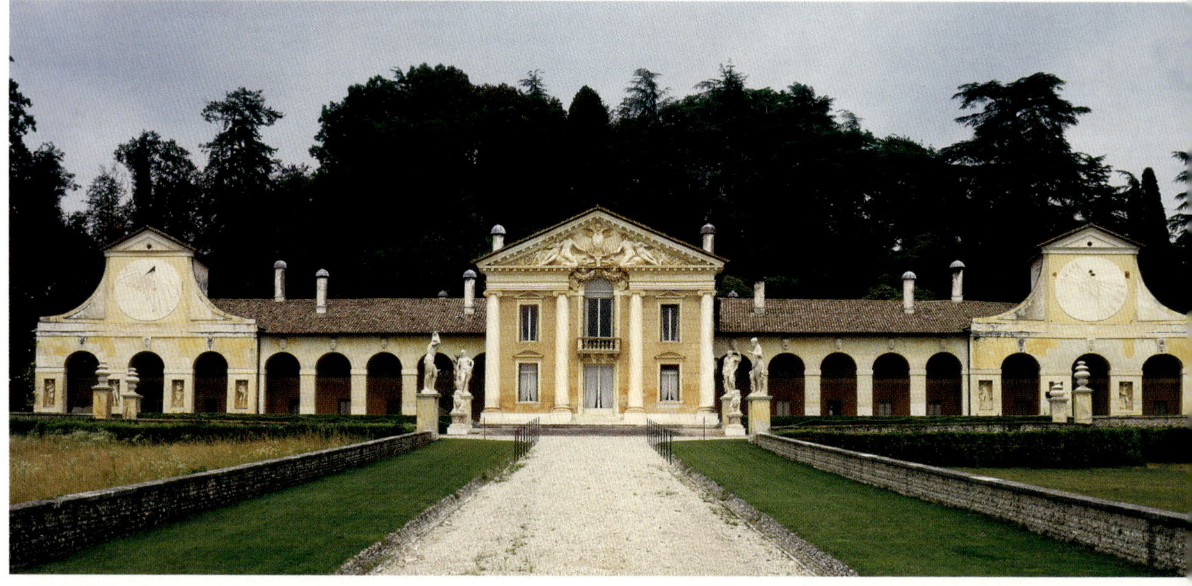

wife, Giustiniana, leans out informally over a painted balcony as if she has stopped momentarily for a brief conversation with her husband below. Resplendent in her fashionable blue satin dress, she quite literally puts her servant into the shade (FIG. 92).

Veronese's paintings were intended to complement Palladio's architecture, which features a similarly restrained yet monumentalized style of classicism, based on the architect's first-hand study of architectural antiquities in Rome. On the facade, Palladio used a limited number of architectural features, while simultaneously enlarging them and clarifying their relation to one another (FIG. 93). Four giant half-columns extend upwards across the two storeys, and appear to hold up a pediment above, evoking a Greek or Roman temple. The temple front was a much-favoured feature in Palladio's architecture. His Villa Capra (known as 'La Rotonda', begun 1567) has one on each of its four sides, and his late church of the Redentore in Venice evokes as many as five on a single facade. While the wide lateral extension of the side arcades and dovecotes was determined by the working realities of the farmhouse, the grand scale and symmetrical ordering of the features, like the fine quality of the pale stone itself, conceals these quotidian realities. The impersonality of the classical features is offset by repeated reference to the villa's occupants themselves: a personalizing approach which is reiterated in Veronese's allusions to the life of the family in the fresco decorations. The facade highlights the Barbaro coat of arms as a deeply carved feature probably by the sculptor Alessandro Vittoria (1525–1608), which draws attention to itself by breaking through the lower edge of the pediment directly above the entrance (FIG. 94). Inscriptions in the friezes on the facades of the villa and the family chapel, known as the Tempietto, built a little to the east, are equally prominent, giving the names and offices of the two brothers, Daniele and Marc'Antonio, and their father. Freed from the restrictions of the more self-restraining culture of the urban metropolis of Venice itself, the patricians were able to manifest themselves and their individual presence in more assertive ways. From the period of the *renovatio urbis* onwards, a penchant for self-display was also evident in Venice itself. Newly commissioned domestic buildings in the city, such as Michele Sanmicheli's Palazzo Grimani a San Luca on the Grand Canal, share certain of Palladio's formal concerns in his villa architecture (FIG. 95). Sanmicheli's palace is also related to recent classicizing examples by Sansovino, such as the Palazzo Corner (begun ca. 1545), insofar as it applies a determinedly Romanizing architectural vocabulary to Venetian domestic palace design. Sanmicheli's monumentalizing approach, however, owes more to Palladio than to Sansovino. Taking liberties with local conventions, Sanmicheli now reduced the number of horizontal bays on the facade to just five, generating a towering verticality that was quite alien to local traditions of building (*see* FIG. 10). As with much of Palladio's architecture, the simultaneous reduction and enlargement of architectural elements makes the Palazzo Grimani appear much larger than it really is. The facade is a kind of outsized architectural illusion that juts beyond the top of the palace behind, and is divorced from

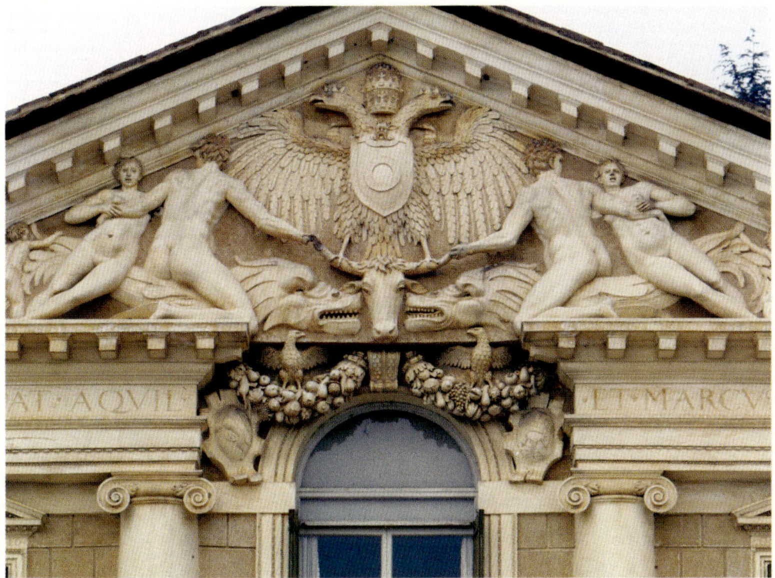

Fig. 94
Alessandro Vittoria (?)
Detail of the Barbaro coat of arms on the tympanum

1560–61. Villa Barbaro, Maser.

This illustration shows the tympanum with relief sculptures probably by Vittoria. Male and female nudes astride dolphins support the family's coat of arms, while the Latin inscription in the frieze below advertises the names of the patrons and their father: 'Daniele Barbaro, Patriarch of Aquileia and Marc'Antonio Barbaro, sons of Francesco'.

the layout of the interior living space. It is, in fact, the widest part of the palace, which narrows rapidly behind in accordance with the irregular constraints of the site.

The theatrical and illusionistic architecture of Palazzo Grimani suggests that innovations made on the *terraferma* now had a ready impact on building in the city itself. Palladio initially struggled for success in Venice, perhaps because of his attachment to the more courtly context of the mainland, but he was awarded a key commission on a prominent site near to the centre of Venice in 1565, when work on the Benedictine church of San Giorgio Maggiore began (FIG. 96). It is the readiness of the Venetians to accommodate Palladio's uncompromisingly non-local style that is most significant. Though his building has certain features in common with Codussi's San Michele in Isola (*see* FIG. 34), its monumental scale, with its facade based on the intersection of two illusionistic temple fronts, represents a very deliberate intervention against earlier architecture in Venice. Palladio radically simplified his design, abandoning the repeated domes and apses featured at St Mark's, visible from San Giorgio on the opposite side of the Bacino. Palladio's uncompromising suppression of such Veneto–Byzantine features in its turn allowed the symbolic whiteness of his Istrian stone facade a new prominence. Even though the facade was not erected until 1607–11, Palladio's design was closely followed, and the feature immediately formed its crowning glory. It radically reduced the impact of the single crossing

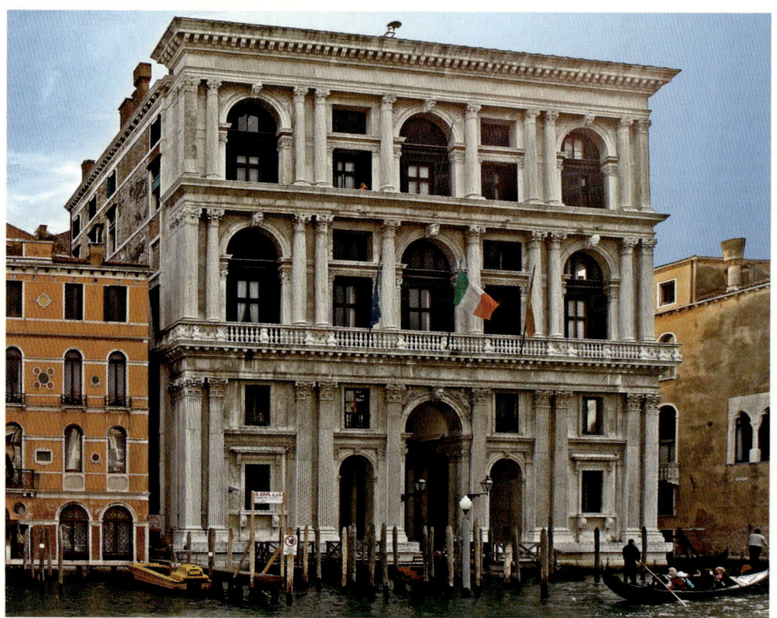

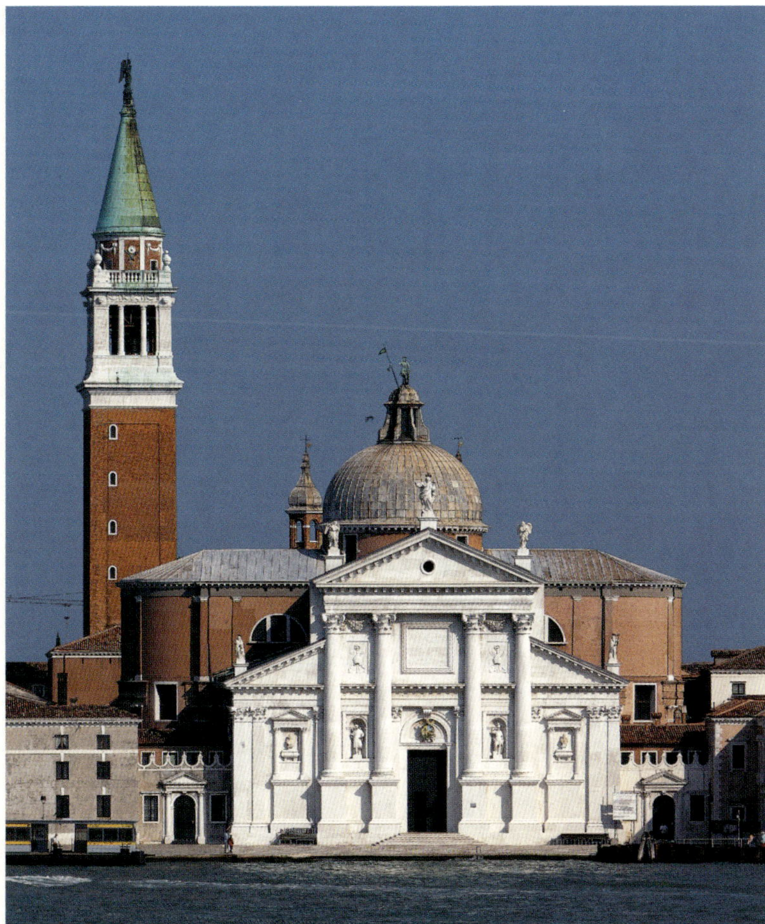

dome and traditional brickwork of the transepts behind, providing a visual focus that effectively responded to the open prospect of the site. The facade out-scaled the Gothic buildings in the vicinity, always anticipating the more distant view from across the wide expanse of water of the Bacino. Its imperious quality, established by the use of outsized giant half-columns and bases, brought a new kind of architectural self-consciousness to Venice that is the equivalent of the individualistic styles developed by leading painters in the same period.

The increasing overlap between the culture of the *terraferma* and that of Venice itself is also evident from the success of Jacopo Bassano in this period. Bassano had initially come to Venice in ca. 1533–5 to be trained in the busy humdrum workshop of Bonifazio de' Pitati (1487–1553), but significantly returned to his home town shortly afterwards. His development of a fashionable style based on the latest models available in Venice and Central Italy during the 1540s is often contrasted with the more local naturalistic idiom he developed in the following decades. Yet Bassano's decision to make his career away from Venice was hardly a matter of failure, and it

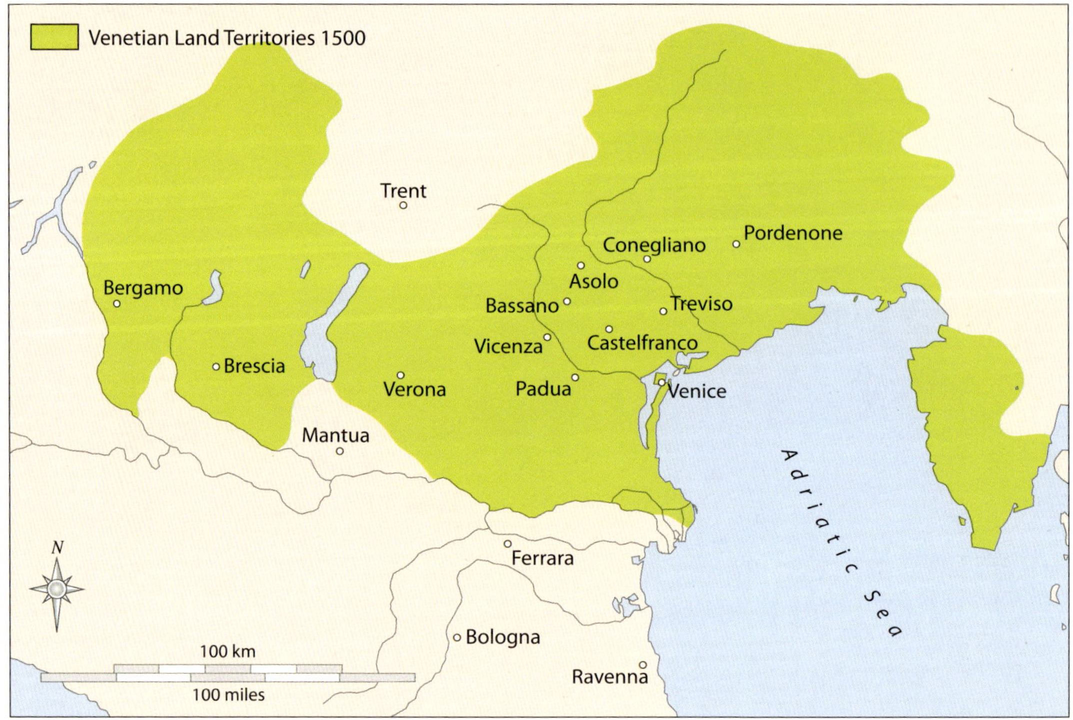

would be a mistake to understand his mature style as parochial or unknowing. Bassano's development of simple subjects featuring peasants and animals was, in fact, a sophisticated ploy by an artist very well versed in the international dimensions of contemporary visual art and taste. Although the majority of his commissions came from the local area and nearby towns on the *terraferma*, some of his most lowly rural subjects were exported directly to patrician collectors in Venice. By the early 1570s, Bassano was able to rely on this kind of non-local support in his production of scenes depicting rural life, typically with a distant view of Monte Grappa to suggest the locality. A series of paintings depict *The Seasons*; these works are closer to contemporary examples of Flemish genre painting by Pieter Bruegel (ca. 1525–1569) or Joachim Beuckelaer (ca. 1534–1574) than to the dramatic and meaningful subject paintings favoured in Venice and elsewhere in Italy during the sixteenth century.

One of Bassano's paintings from this series, *Summer* (FIG. 98), stresses the typical peasant pursuits of the time of year: sheep shearing, wheat threshing, and outdoor feasting. It is not quite true to say that it has no subject at all. On a mountain ridge at the left, Abraham makes ready to sacrifice his son Isaac, while an angel swoops down to hold back his hand. The inclusion of this background scene from the Old Testament, which goes wholly unnoticed by the peasants, does not mean that the lives of these latter are mocked or understood as ungodly. Their labours may be the inevitable result of Original Sin, but these peasants are not presented in moral terms. Bassano's meticulous attention to their rustic appearance and environment (faces, dress, animals, utensils and habitations) determines the content in a way that must remind us of the penchant for close pictorial description in the northern Renaissance tradition of painting, with which Bassano was familiar through paintings and prints in local collections. At the same time, the soft and generalized lighting of the broadly painted landscape still recalls the Giorgionesque pictorial tradition in Venice: an adjustment that might reflect Bassano's accommodation to the tastes of the high-ranking collectors from Venice. Such paintings were sophisticated exercises in artistic naturalism, rather than moralistic satires, and were understood in this way by his early supporters, such as the local writer Lorenzo Marucini, who noted in 1577 that Bassano 'alludes, whenever he

ca. 1576. Oil on canvas, 78.5 × 110.5cm (2ft 6⅞in × 3ft 7½in). Kunsthistorisches Museum, Vienna.

This painting, along with two others showing spring and autumn, also now in Vienna, are often attributed to Jacopo's eldest son, Francesco. But their original conception and confident handling indicates that they are works by the father rather than the son.

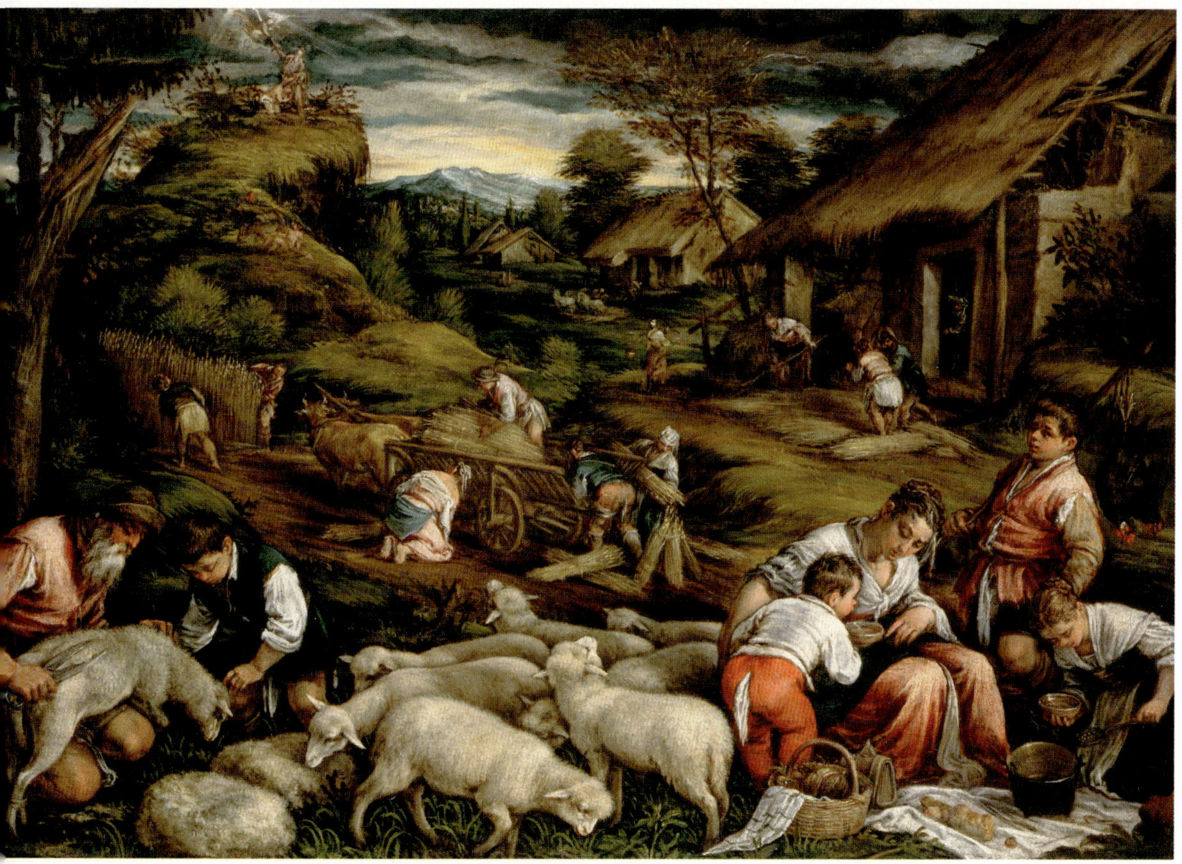

wants, to both men and animals, by portraying from nature what they are most like … and his paintings resemble them so well that men run from every direction to admire his things'. In Venice, mean-while, leading painters such as Titian, Tintoretto and Veronese were alive to the appeal of Bassano's works, readily including in their own paintings shepherds and animals that draw directly on his example.

A *cittadini* style

Some of the most striking and original works produced in Venice after 1550 were commissioned by the city's non-noble citizens, some of whom, at least, were particularly keen to distinguish themselves from the population at large (the *popolani*). Though these *cittadini* had originally emulated patrician tastes when commissioning art,

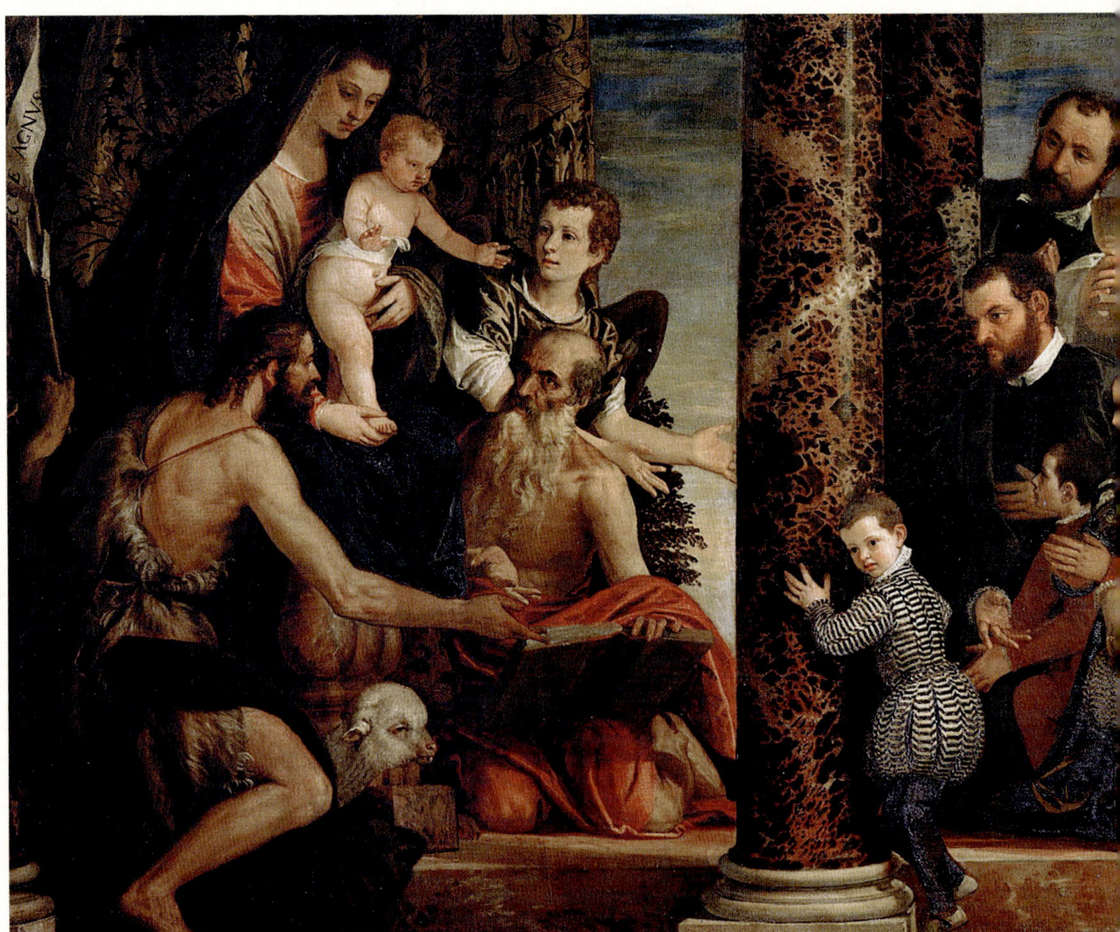

they gradually became more independent. They had always been somewhat distanced from the more learned and classical tastes of the nobility. In the works they now commissioned, portraits and religious subjects typically predominated over mythologies or learned allegories. In these fields, at least, *cittadini* patronage provided a context for artistic innovation rather than passive emulation, and their commissions now played an important part in the general diffusion of art through the city. If earlier *cittadini* patrons had upheld the communal and self-repressing ideals of the Republic, the new status-conscious generations after 1550 wanted works featuring carefully personalized depictions of themselves and their families, and were quite ready to push the boundaries of the socially acceptable in this regard.

In Veronese's *Madonna and Child with the Cuccina Family* (FIG. 99), one of four large paintings commissioned for the *portego* (main living area) of the family palace on the Grand Canal, unreal

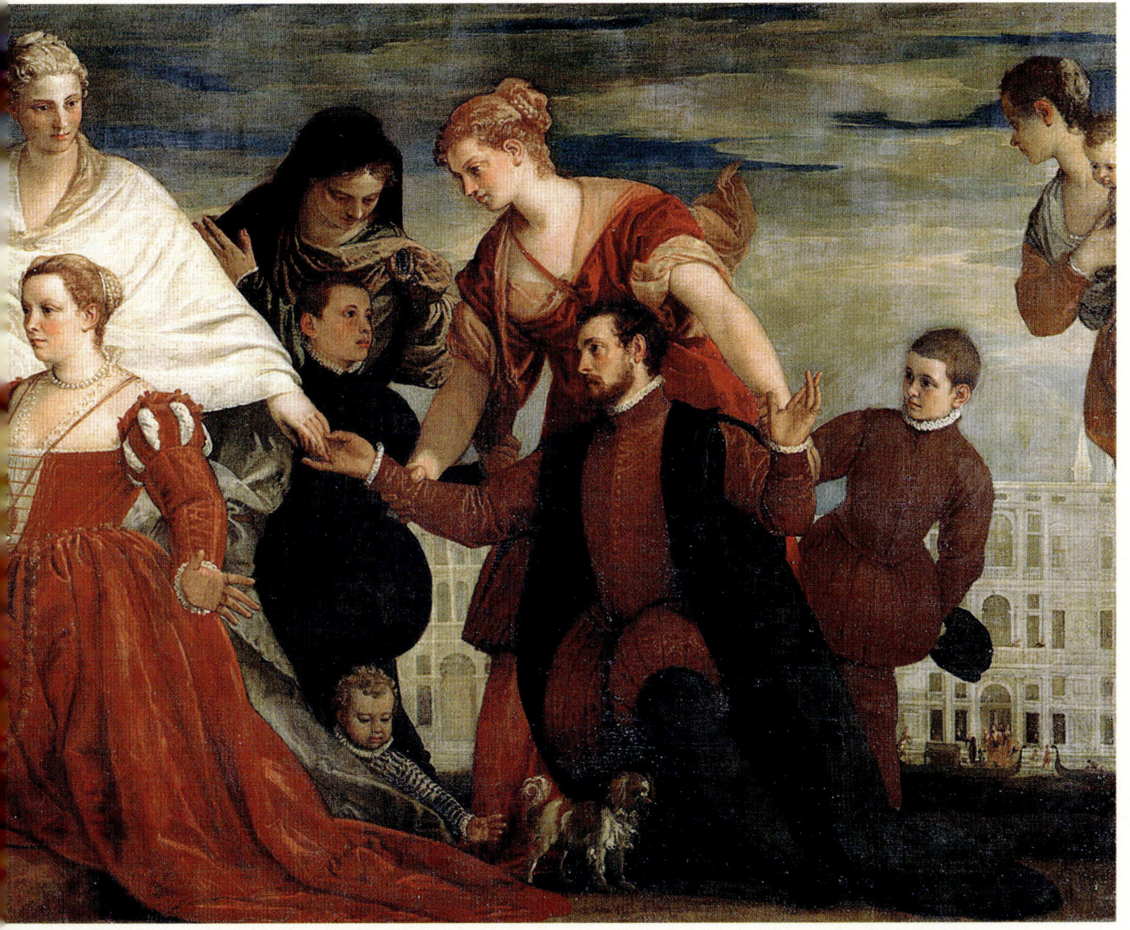

Fig. 100
Jacopo Sansovino and
Alessandro Vittoria
Monument to Tommaso Rangone

ca. 1553–7. Bronze, life-sized. San Giuliano, Venice.

Rangone paid 1,000 ducats for a new facade for the church, a work undertaken by Sansovino. In return, he was allowed to erect a bronze sculpture of himself by Vittoria, in which he is shown seated on a fictive funeral sarcophagus. Rangone was eventually buried in the church, which he evidently saw as his personal mausoleum.

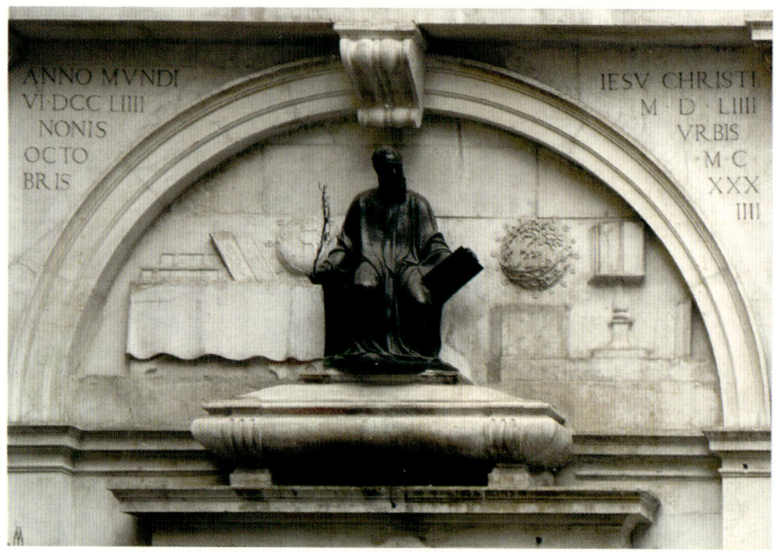

allegorical religious figures (Faith, Charity and Hope, reading from left to right) mix freely, and with symbolic import, with eleven members of Alvise Cuccina's family. To an unusual extent, women and children dominate the scene: especially Alvise's buxom wife, Zuanna di Mutti, who is glorified like a St Catherine at the centre foreground. Veronese's emphasis was undoubtedly encouraged by the original location of his work in the domestic (and therefore conventionally feminine) space of the family palace. He may also have followed earlier *cittadini* family portraits from Venice such as Licino's, discussed in the previous chapter, with its similarly dominant materfamilias (*see* FIG. 76). But Veronese's work is more grandiose and 'aristocratizing', its horizontal format recalling patrician votive paintings and their visual connection with sacred subjects such as the Adoration of the Magi (*see* FIG. 90). The Cuccina were relatively newly arrived in the city: as recently naturalized Venetian citizens, they were partially free from the usual ideological controls in their adopted home. Veronese's painting is, in fact, made the means of assertive self-promotion. The family are probably imagined as gathered before their private altar in Sansovino's fashionable new church of San Francesco della Vigna (finished in 1554), while a depiction of their palace on the Grand Canal appears at the background right.

After 1550 art became less circumscribed by traditional Venetian values, especially in the private context, or away from the politically charged and ritualized public spaces of the city. Even here, however, individualistic outsiders began to make their mark. The state did intervene to prevent the learned doctor and philologist Tommaso Rangone of Ravenna from erecting images of himself on the facades of high-profile public buildings around the centre of Venice. In the end, the official objections are less significant than the successes of this self-promoting *arriviste*. In the 1550s, for example, he managed to erect a portrait above the entrance of San Giuliano on the Merceria, a church close to St Mark's Square on the main mercantile street in the city (FIG. 100). With the help of the versatile sculptor, Alessandro Vittoria, Sansovino created an ideal- ized image of Rangone as a learned doctor and scholar in his study with saintly connotations. Rangone holds healing plants (sarsapa- rilla and guaiacum) with which he is said to have healed syphilitics and suffers of yellow fever, and is surrounded by the attributes of his learning, along the lines of a St Augustine or St Jerome. These sacred associations are reinforced by the placement of his figure within a semi-circular architectural moulding that suggests both a Roman triumphal arch and the dome of heaven.

Counter-Reformation

Non-noble patronage also played an important role in the field of religious painting after 1550, providing opportunities for artistic innovation that were unmatched in the field of official or patrician commissions. The city's ever more numerous Scuole were a particu- larly rich source of patronage in this regard, given that the *cittadini* who dominated them were especially alive to new developments in religious feeling or aspiration amongst the local laity. A number of Tintoretto's most striking works from this period were commis- sioned by confraternities known as the Scuole del Sacramento ('Schools of the Sacrament'), whose particular focus was the proper upkeep of the Holy Sacrament between the Masses in local churches. The rapid spread of these parish-based confraternities in Venice after 1550 coincided with the sitting of the Council of Trent (1545–63), the church committee convened to establish a response to the Prot- estant rebellion in Northern Europe, and can be taken as a marker of the gathering movement of Catholic reform within the city.

Such confraternities may have particularly appealed to non- noble parishioners keen to demonstrate their piety. They often had control of a Chapel of the Sacrament in which the reserved sacra- ment was kept, and commissioned pairs or sets of paintings with sacramental themes to decorate the walls on either side of the altar. In this context, Tintoretto developed a newly direct, even 'popular', style of sacred painting, combining realistic and visionary elements within a suggestive chiaroscuro treatment suggesting spiritual urgency or mystery. His *Last Supper* for the church of San Trovaso of ca. 1560 relocates the scene to a cluttered basement, with crudely made chairs and stools and piles of tattered books tumbling in a heap in the corner (FIG. 101). The naturalistic squalor of the foreground is alleviated as the eye moves into depth by a visionary arcade with mysterious figures behind Christ, perhaps raising the possibility of redemption that his upcoming death, recently announced to the apostles, will offer. The awkwardly skewed space of Tintoretto's painting was a response to its position on the right wall of the chapel, anticipating an obliquely positioned viewer, but it would be a mistake to assume that the lowly tone directly reflects the social rank of Tintoretto's patrons in the commissioning Scuola. The casual postures, rough clothing and bare feet of his apostles certainly

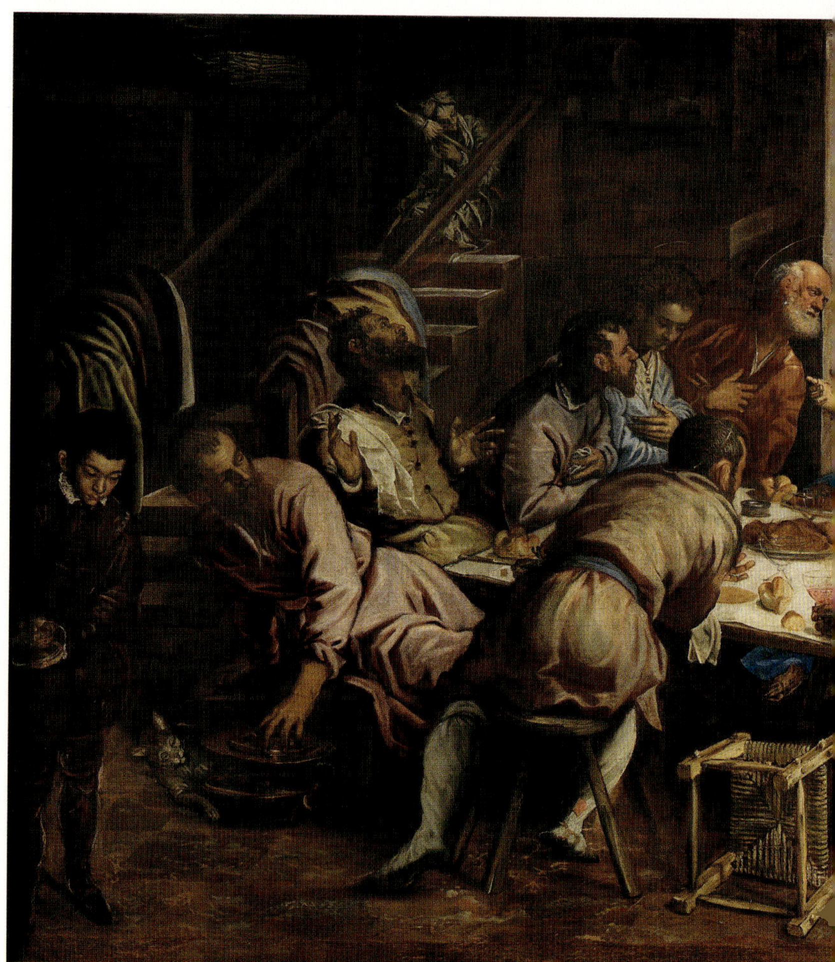

reference the appearance of the impoverished working people of Venice, the *popolani*, who formed the majority of the city's population but so rarely appear in its visual art. However, the relocation of the famous scene was motivated primarily by theological rather than social considerations. Tintoretto's presentation recalled the original emphasis on the humble social origins of the apostles in the Gospels: the contemporary appearances of Venetian lower-class life helped to establish a new emphasis on Christ's own 'sacred poverty', or *santa povertà*, one that expressed his core religious value of humility.

Works such as this reflect the rapid spread of the religious image in Venice beyond conventional picture types, such as the upright altarpiece. Another example of the expansion of religious imagery in the city is Veronese's lavish decoration of the church of San

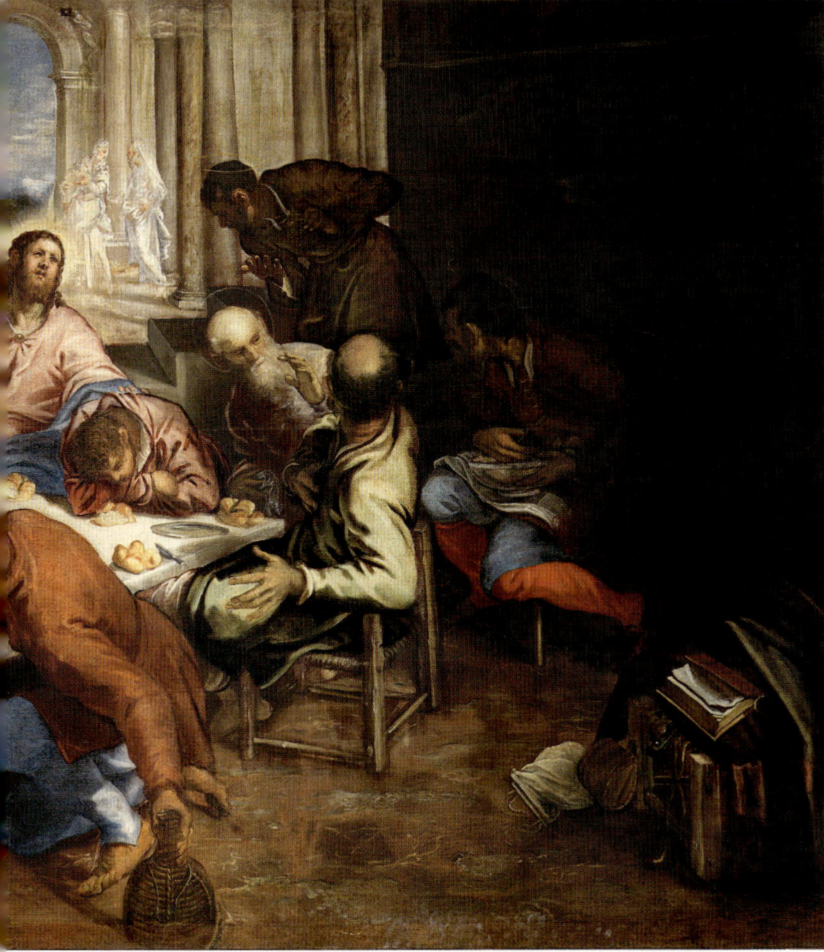

ca. 1560. Oil on canvas, 221 × 413cm (7ft 3in × 13ft 6⅝in). San Trovaso, Venice.

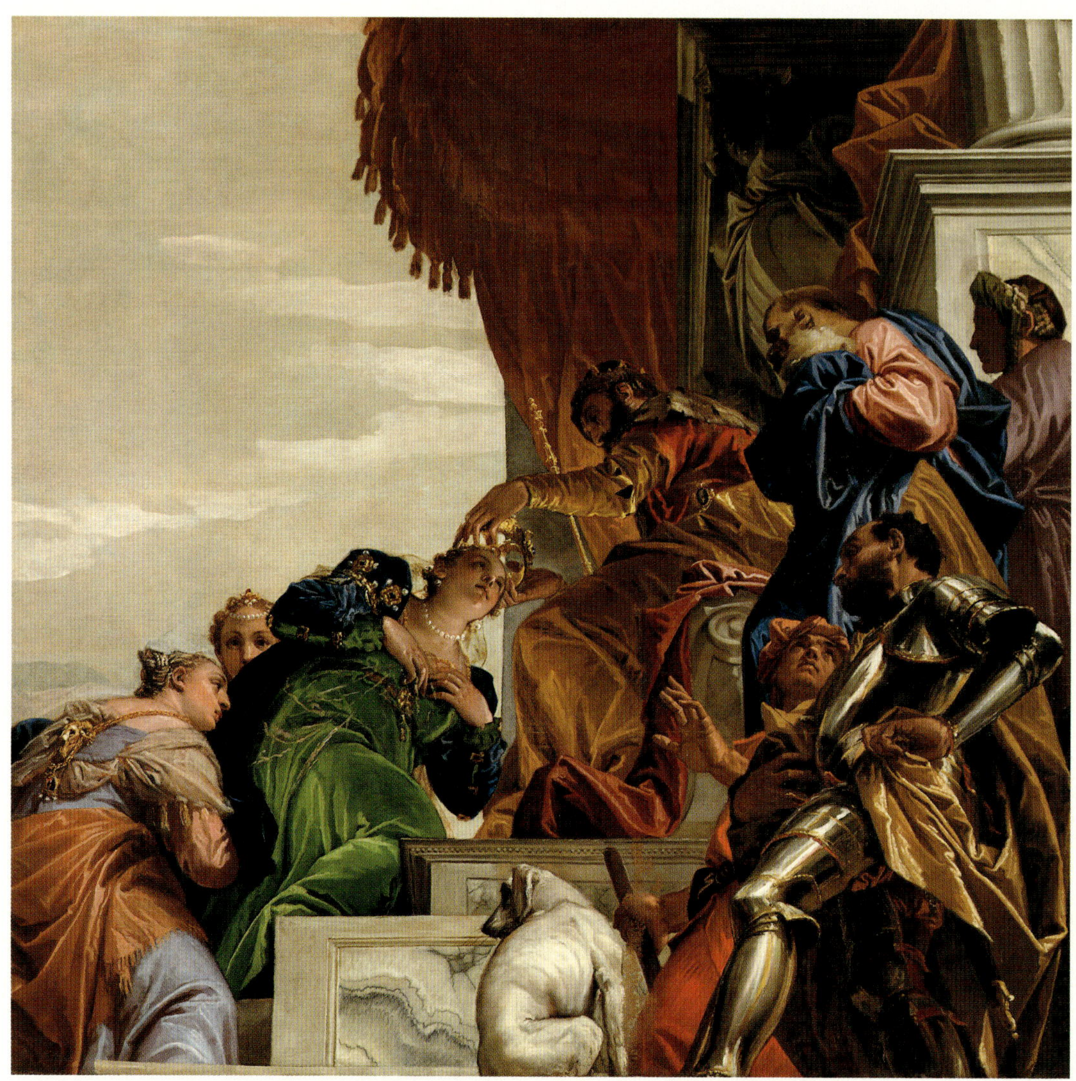

Sebastiano, which includes two painted ceilings. By the time he had completed his work in the church around 1570, the great majority of its available internal surfaces had been covered with religious paintings. The very extensiveness of these church decorations offered a rebuttal of the iconoclastic tendencies of the Protestants in Northern Europe, reconfirming as it did the central role of the visual image in Christian devotion. Having completed a set of paintings featuring the Virgin on the ceiling of the sacristy, Veronese went on to decorate the nave ceiling with three scenes from the Book of Esther in the main panels (*see* FIG. 88). The depiction of Old Testament scenes on the ceilings of religious buildings had important precedents in

Central Italy (including the Sistine Chapel painted by Michelangelo in Rome), but was a relatively recent development in Venice. Esther, a Jewish heroine, could stand as an Old Testament prototype for the Virgin, reconfirming the theological importance of 'The Mother of God' in the face of Protestant arguments to the contrary.

The sharp 'from below to above' (*di sotto in sù*) perspective sets the brightly coloured protagonists against delicately painted grey-blue skies, exploiting the expressive potential of the dramatic silhouette. The reception of bowing figures before enthroned ones was a familiar enough theme in Venetian Renaissance painting (*see* FIG. 46), but Veronese's flamboyant ceiling is difficult to square with its serious Counter-Reformatory meaning. Even in the wall paintings, featuring the martyrdoms of Saints Sebastian, Marcellinus and Mark, the tone is light-hearted and celebratory. The ceiling panels are presented as triumphal social pageants, and there is more than a whiff of courtly romance in the focus on King Ahasuerus' rejection of his first wife Vasti in favour of the beautiful Esther. The crowning of the heroine in the central panel (FIG. 102) sets up an Old/New Testament typology with the scene of the *Coronation of the Virgin* in heaven featured on the sacristy ceiling. But the panel is, nonetheless, worldly and secular by comparison. Dividing his protagonists along gender lines, with beautiful women on the left and handsome men on the right, Veronese lays emphasis on expensive drapery, elaborate coiffure and jewellery on the one side, and glinting polished surfaces of crown, sceptre and armour on the other. No dramatic intervention from above is included to indicate the controlling influence of heaven, and the event, set against a grand palace facade, is conceived in terms of the conferral of royal favour on an attractive young female heroine.

Veronese's ceiling at San Sebastiano was destined to be a favoured source for Rococo painters of the eighteenth century, perhaps because of its essentially theatrical and decorative presentation. In the more immediate context of the deepening Counter-Reformation in Venice in the 1560s and 1570s, however, this kind of visual pageantry in a religious work could prove problematical. After Veronese had completed a 'Last Supper' for the Dominicans of Santi Giovanni e Paolo, his inclusion of 'buffoons' and 'German soldiers' was immediately identified as objectionable by the religious authorities, given that such non-canonical figures obscured the meaning of the religious subject (FIG. 103). A surviving transcription of Veronese's subsequent interview with the recently formed Holy Tribunal of the Inquisition reveals that the painter was very far from naïve when asked to justify his pictorial approach. Veronese first referred to the artistic licence long enjoyed by painters in Venice when composing

ca. 1555-6. Ceiling painting. Oil on canvas, 450 × 370cm (14ft 9⅛in × 12ft 1⅝in). San Sebastiano, Venice.

religious paintings, before going on to point out that the subsidiary figures are all 'placed outside the space where Our Lord is shown'.

Veronese's second point is clearly backed up by the evidence of the painting itself. He had, in fact, frequently used painted architecture to establish divisions between sacred and secular actors in his paintings (*see* FIG. 99 for example). And this kind of pictorial decorum seems always to have been a part of his composition in the work under discussion. Christ is at the centre of the composition, silhouetted against a symbolic blue sky and separated off from the figures in the crowded foreground spaces by the giant columns of the fictive painted loggia. These arguments apparently held some sway with the inquisitors and the matter was quickly resolved by an agreement that Veronese change the subject through the addition of an inscription pronouncing that his painting showed the

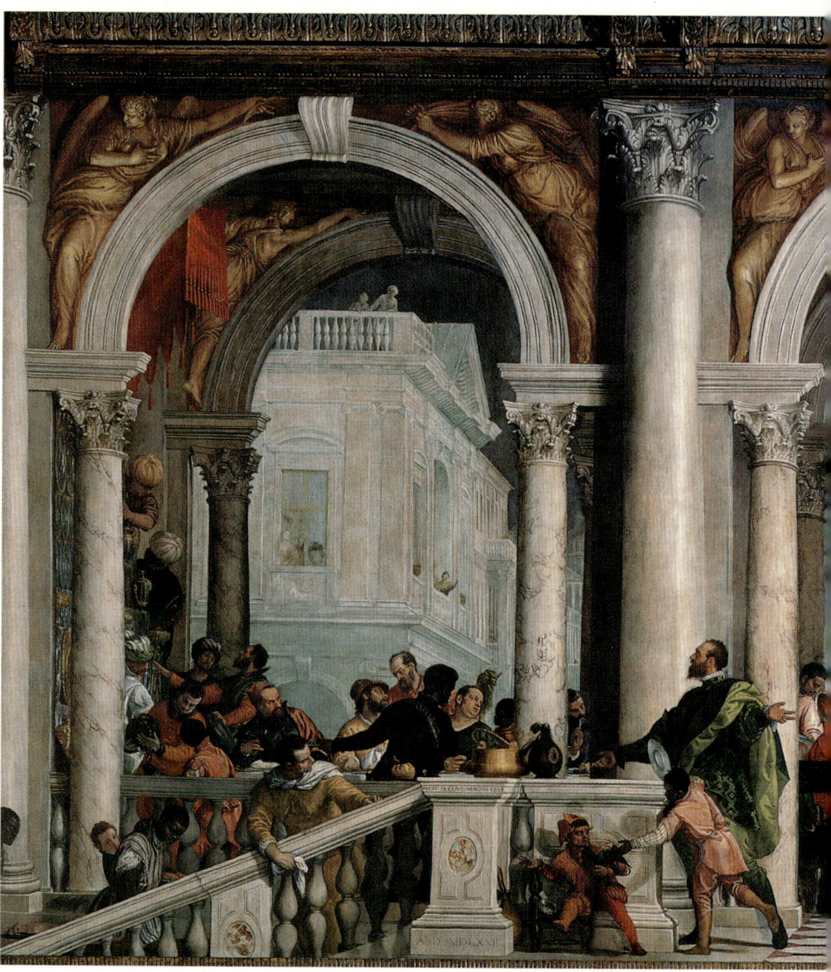

lesser subject of 'The Feast in the House of Levi'. In support of this re-identification, the painter also added the figure of Levi himself, dressed in red and seated in the foreground to Christ's right. But Veronese's painting, like his other feast scenes from these decades, is nonetheless very different in tone and setting from religious Supper scenes by Tintoretto. In contrast to his rival's works, with their references to the inclusive culture of the non-noble majority, Veronese presents his composition as an exclusive aristocratic feast. Such lavish presentations were typically painted for the walls of monastic refectories, rather than for chapels in parish churches, anticipating the gaze of feasting monks, who were often members of wealthy patrician families. The presence of servants and lesser minions towards the picture margins was, in a sense, a necessary result of this patrician conception. Like the grand classicizing architecture, such

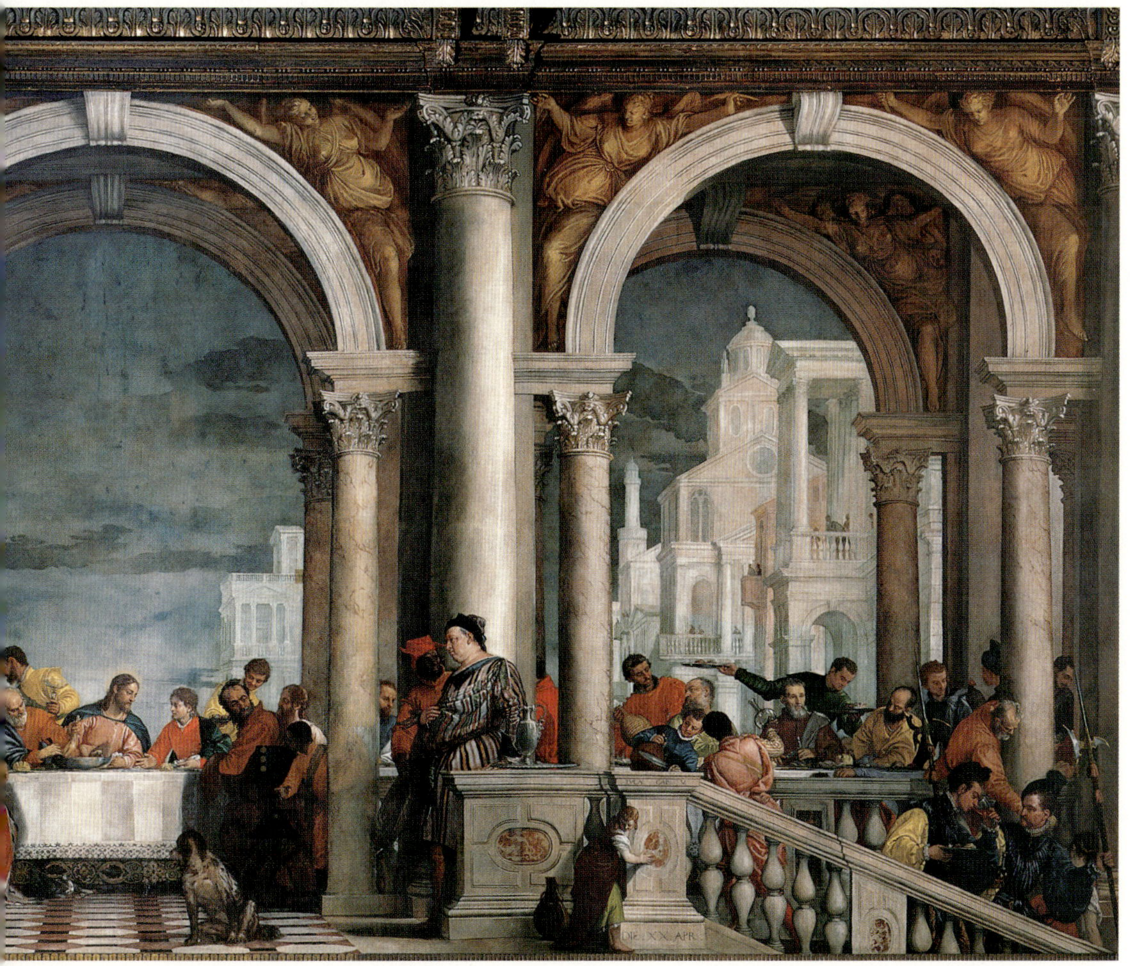

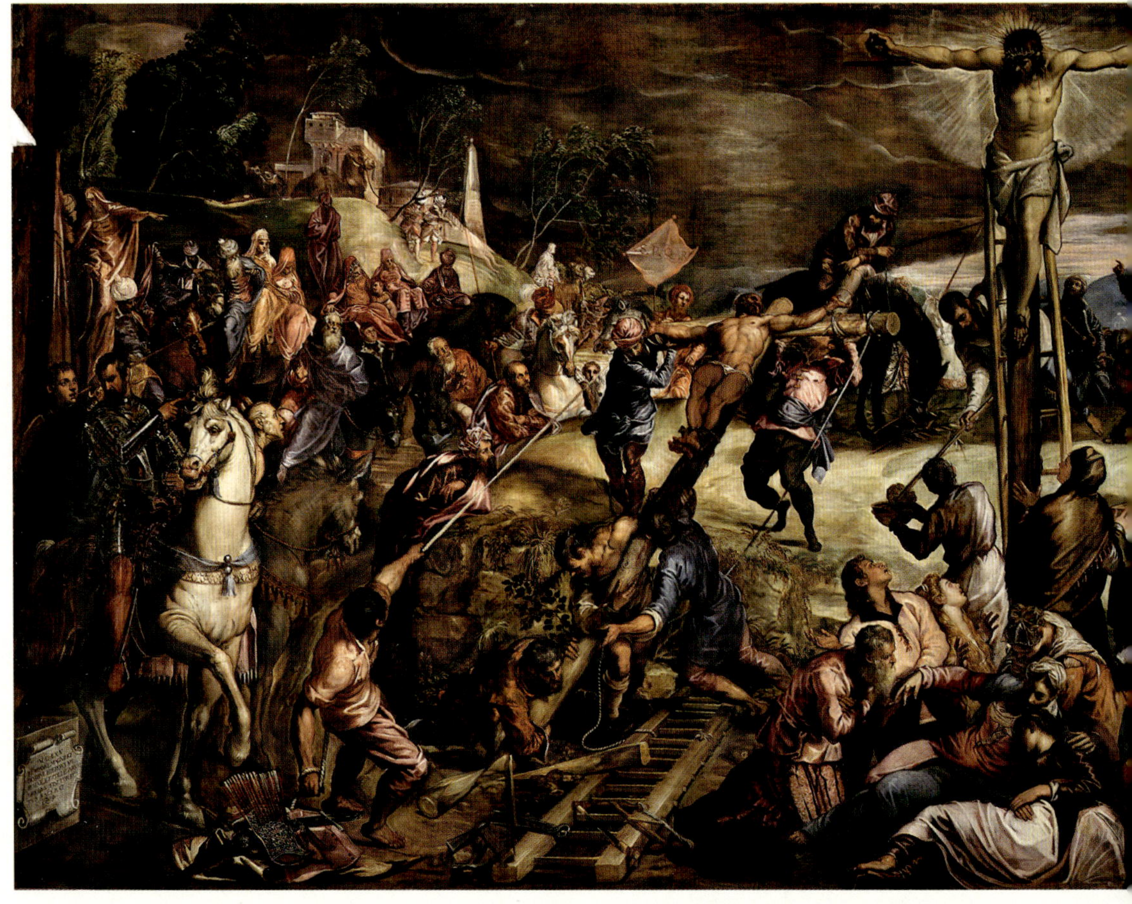

figures were a necessary part of the supporting scenery, and helped to establish the theatrical and elevated tone of the painting.

The Catholic Counter-Reformation certainly gathered pace in Venice, as elsewhere, especially after December 1563, when the Council of Trent finally proclaimed its ultra-orthodox rulings on the proper role of visual imagery in churches. Following the spirit, if not the letter, of the Council's decrees, a new emphasis on scenes showing the Passion of Christ, the life of the Virgin and the intercession and martyrdom of the saints is apparent in many commissions for sacred art. The Counter-Reformation in Venice cannot so easily be related to a given artistic style, and the divergent approaches to religious painting of Veronese and Tintoretto in these decades may both be considered as responses to the movement. When Tintoretto painted his *Crucifixion* for the Scuola Grande di San Rocco in 1565, he further developed the chiaroscuro-based manner he had already experimented with in earlier works for Venetian churches (FIG. 104).

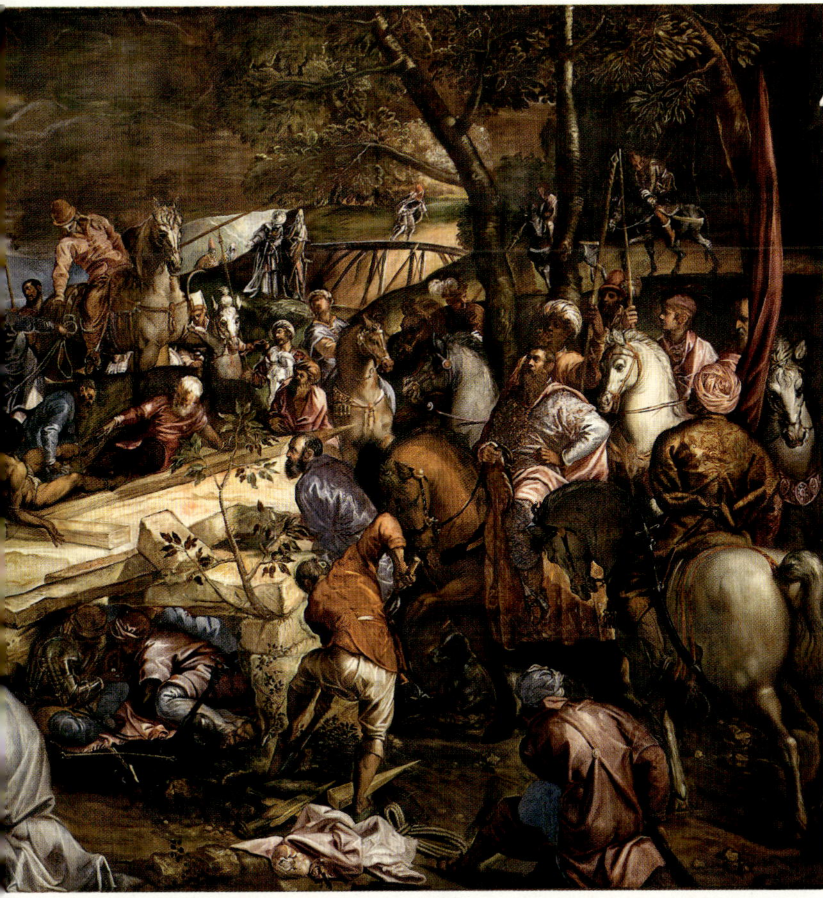

This astonishing painting is presented on an epic scale, and covers the entire wall of the board room (*albergo*) in the Scuola's Meeting House. Despite its crowdedness, Tintoretto's painting brilliantly intensified the focus on Christ's death by its novel combination of iconic and narrative elements. Christ's crucified body is placed at the upper centre of the composition, and is presented as the still central point around which the complex composition, organized into a flattened ellipse, revolves. His body lies along the picture surface in the manner of a religious icon, contradicting the foreshortenings and rapid movements to either side.

If the stillness and abstraction of Christ's body, with its implication of sacred timelessness, sets it apart from the busy everyday actions of the surrounding groups, then it is nonetheless always the unknowing focus of their activities. To left and right we witness two earlier stages in the raising of a cross, both of which refer ultimately to the Crucifixion of Christ himself. Tintoretto lays particular emphasis on the physical effort and mechanics of cross-raising, featuring again a group of rough-looking Venetian *popolani*. These working men, whose physical effort pointedly contrasts with the emotional response of the holy group at the foot of the cross immediately to the right, pull on ropes or struggle to dig the bole of the cross into the earth. Tintoretto nonetheless carefully distinguishes the two sides of the painting. On the viewer's left, but to the symbolic right hand of Christ, the cross is being successfully raised. This is presented as a triumphal elevation towards Christ himself, reminding us of the previous moment when Christ was successfully crucified, and thus fulfilled his mission of sacrifice for mankind. In keeping with this, the so-called 'good thief', well-known from religious devotional texts, is shown staring up at Christ in a moment of religious conversion. To Christ's left, on the so-called 'sinister' side of God, the 'bad thief' remains earthbound, struggling against his executioners with his back pointedly turned to Christ as an indication of his continued lack of spiritual awareness.

Mythologies

The seriousness of tone in a work such as Tintoretto's *Crucifixion* did not lessen the demand for sensual or erotic cabinet paintings with mythological subject matter in the decades after 1550. Titian regularly sent religious paintings to the Spanish court in Madrid through the 1550s and 1560s, but his main commission for Philip II was a loosely conceived series of mythologies illustrating scenes from Ovid's *Metamorphoses*. In his explanatory letters to Philip, Titian described these works as *poesie* ('poetries'), indicating that he thought of them as a kind of painted equivalent to Ovid's poetry in their richness of meaning and allusion. This idea might have arisen as early as the opening decade of the sixteenth century in Venice, under the impact of richly allusive Giorgionesque painting. Titian himself had further defined mythological painting as closely akin to poetry in his Bacchanals (*see* FIG. 64), but in his new mythological series, Titian showed the classical myths in a less benign or ideal light. If works such as the *Bacchus and Ariadne* presented a classical golden age of freely taken sensual pleasure and desire, then the *poesie* depict pagan antiquity as a more problematic sphere of pain, suffering and worldly transience.

At first sight, Titian's *Venus and Adonis*, sent to Philip in 1554 as a pendant to a painting of *Danaë* that he had sent a few years earlier, appears simply to follow his earlier approach to mythological painting, with a primarily sensual and erotic meaning (FIG. 105). The composition is focussed on a complexly arranged figural group, featuring in particular the twisted figure of Venus with her arms around the torso of her mortal lover Adonis. Titian pays his usual close attention to the variable bodily surfaces of his female nude, pointing up the subtle differences between the taut flesh of her shoulders and its softened or rumpled quality where her buttocks meet the hard surface of the seat. The interlocking but contrasting figures remind us of a complex antique relief, and it comes as no surprise to find that Titian based their forms on a well-known classical sculpture, the

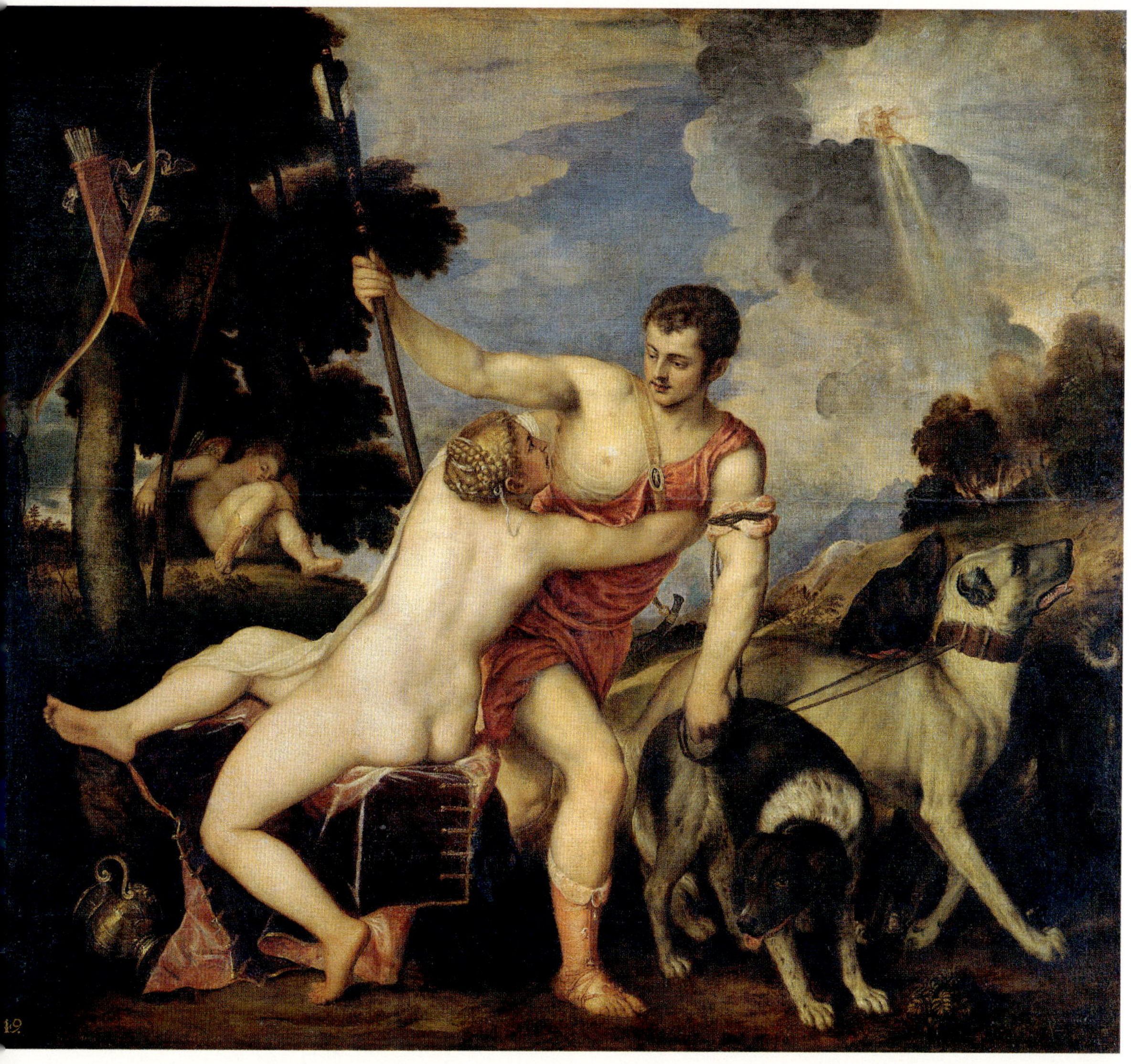

so-called *Bed of Polyclitus*, which he had recently seen in Rome. The almost impossibly 'difficult' pose that Venus assumes provides an opportunity for the painter to show off his illusionistic skill, and appears like a studied *paragone*, or comparison, demonstrating the superiority of his painted figure to the sculpture it was based on.

Titian also pointedly departed from Ovid's text to depict a moment in which the cheeks of the goddess glow puce in her desperate effort to hold back her mortal lover from the lure of the hunt. As a goddess, of course, she has foreknowledge of his coming death. The fateful spot where he will soon be gored by a boar is highlighted at the background right, where Venus reappears in her chariot in the heavens to highlight it with a shaft of light. Adonis' blindness to his future is indicated by the turn of his head away from this scene and by the blankness of his expression, which forms a poignant contrast to the goddess's urgent and pleading look. The sleeping cupid to the left, symbolic of the sudden demise of the goddess's power, reinforces the darker elements in the scene.

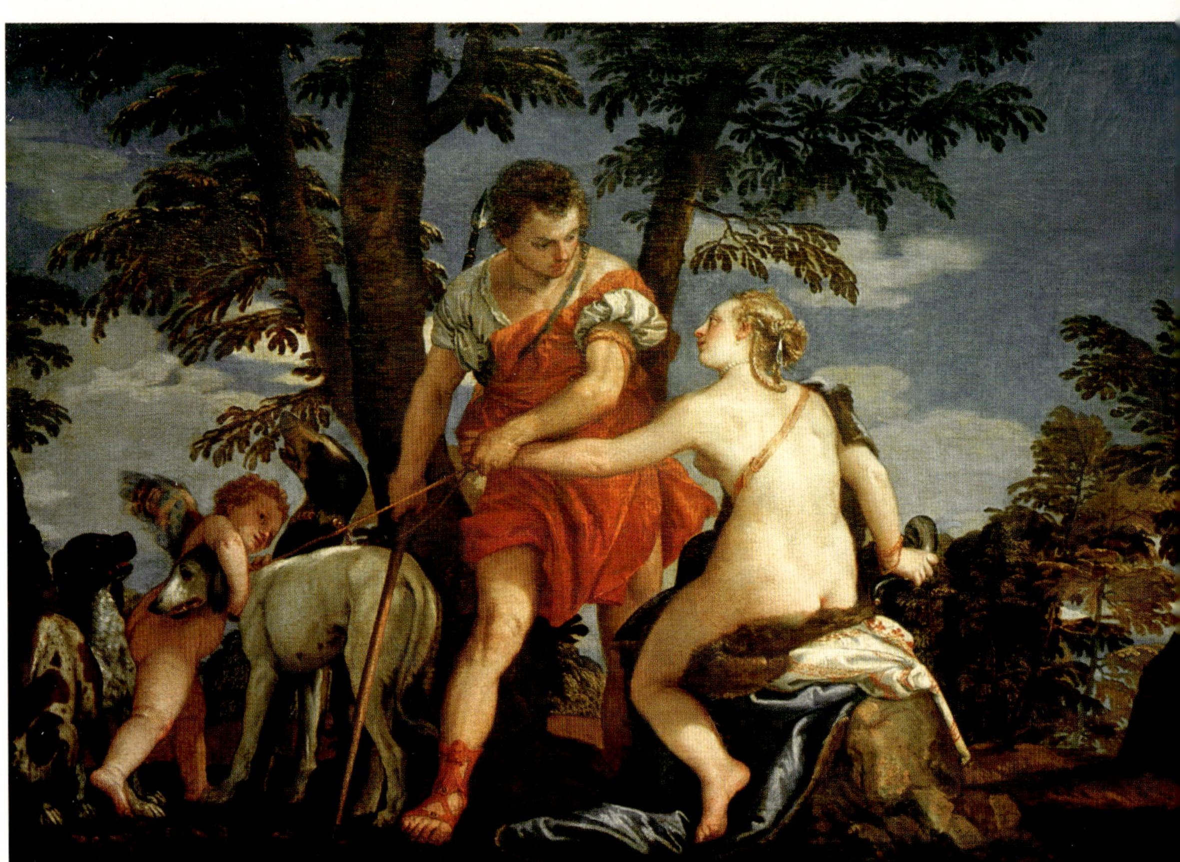

In *Venus and Adonis*, Titian appears both to suggest and to undermine the usual erotic or artistic meanings of Renaissance mythological painting. In the subsequent pair of *poesie* that he sent to Philip in 1559, featuring the harsh fate of two mortals at the hands of Diana, goddess of hunting and chastity, this dualistic approach is taken a step further. Titian's darkening tone in the *poesie* has sometimes been taken to mean that they were intended as moral allegories, aimed to educate or warn the young Philip against the dangers of sexual love. Others have understood the *poesie* as painted tragedies that can be explained with reference to the theoretical prescriptions for this dramatic genre given in Aristotle's *Poetics*; or as a response to contemporary performances of plays by Seneca and other classical tragedians, which were highly popular in contemporary theatre. Yet not all of Titian's *poesie* are so tragic in tone. Enjoyment of Titian's varied depiction of the young female nude in a wide variety of positions is, after all, encouraged in all the works from the series. While several of the paintings contain a disturbing new emphasis on the fragility of human love and desire, this is likely to have been based on Titian's long experience as a religious painter, rather than on a literary or dramatic category such as tragedy.

It is not surprising that painters of the younger generation in Venice found the *poesie* difficult to understand or assimilate. Veronese certainly referenced Titian's original idea of a contention between the lovers in a painting of the subject of ca. 1562 (FIG. 106). The future scene of the goddess's reappearance in the sky is dropped, however, and the outcome of the argument between the protagonists is thrown into doubt. As in many of Veronese's other mythologies, Cupid actively intervenes in support of his mother, holding back Adonis' hunting dog in a playful (if irritating for the dog) arm lock. Venus smiles confidently up at Adonis, whose uncertain expression betrays her continuing hold over his affections. The emotional urgency and physical effort emphasized in Titian's Venus is downplayed in favour of a more simplified and settled depiction in which the comic appears about to win out over any more tragic meaning. If Titian had challenged the commonplace that 'Love Conquers All' (*omnia vincit amor*), derived from Virgil's *Eclogues*, then Veronese already hints at its return. In his later mythologies, this concept quickly became the defining meaning, almost regardless of the more specific subject matter. Whether Veronese painted Venus with Adonis, Mars or some other lover, it is Love's victory that is made paramount. In keeping with his untroubled imagination, Veronese imagined the classical world in terms of a perfected sensual idyll that stood apart from the violence and suffering of the world beyond.

Fig. 106
Paolo Veronese
Venus and Adonis

ca. 1562. Oil on canvas, 122 × 178cm (4ft × 5ft 10⅛in). Städtische Kunstsammlungen. Karl and Magdalene Haberstock Foundation, Augsburg.

Artistic identity, style and theory

The work of many artists after 1550 is characterized by a new measure of confidence in what was a triumphant period of achievement in the history of art and architecture in Venice. The key model for the success of many artists was inevitably Titian, who by now enjoyed unprecedented high status as the richest and most famous painter in Europe. In a woodcut by Giovanni Britto (active 1530–1550) after a lost self-portrait (FIG. 107), Titian is shown drawing or sketching, as if to answer Michelangelo's complaint that he worked without due attention to *disegno*. His abstracted gaze might suggest that he looks beyond the specific motif in nature and is inspired, rather, by a pre-existing artistic idea in his mind. In contrast to his master Giovanni Bellini's medal (*see* FIG. 49), Titian's high forehead is exaggerated as if to identify the nature of his work as intellectual, and he wears the rich furs of an aristocrat, rather than a Venetian toga. Around his neck hangs the double gold chain awarded to him by Emperor Charles V in 1533, on the occasion of his elevation to the imperial nobility. Like the many other depictions of Titian in paintings, prints, medals and medallions that appeared after 1550, Britto's woodcut carefully shaped the great painter's artistic identity for the consumption of the wider public, both in Venice and (more especially) abroad. It served to identify Titian as a courtly aristocrat, whose social identity was closer to that of his high-ranking patrons than to the middling status traditionally ascribed to painters in Venice.

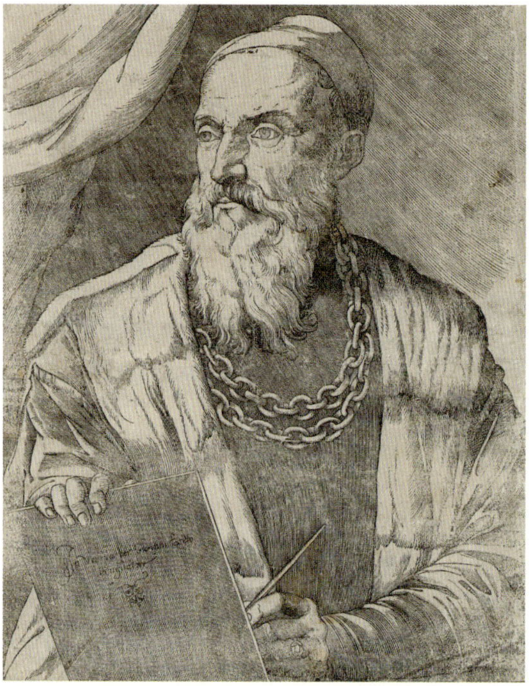

Fig. 107
Giovanni Britto
Portrait of Titian

1550. Woodcut on paper, 41.5 × 32.2cm (1ft 4⅜in × 12⅝in). Rijksmuseum, Amsterdam.

Following Titian, the younger generations also sought to challenge the relatively humble role traditionally ascribed to them in the city. Leading figures such as 'Paolo Caliari' (Veronese), 'Palladio' and 'Vittoria' adopted professional names that, respectively, suggest an aristocratic background; a connection with a guardian angel in a humanist poem; and a proof of victory in the field of art. 'Tintoretto', 'the little dyer' (whose real name was apparently Jacopo Comin) took a different approach, associating himself with the local working people of the city through his adopted nickname. We cannot simply take this at face value: it, too, may have been a marketing ploy, developed to distinguish the painter from professional rivals who sought association with the upper

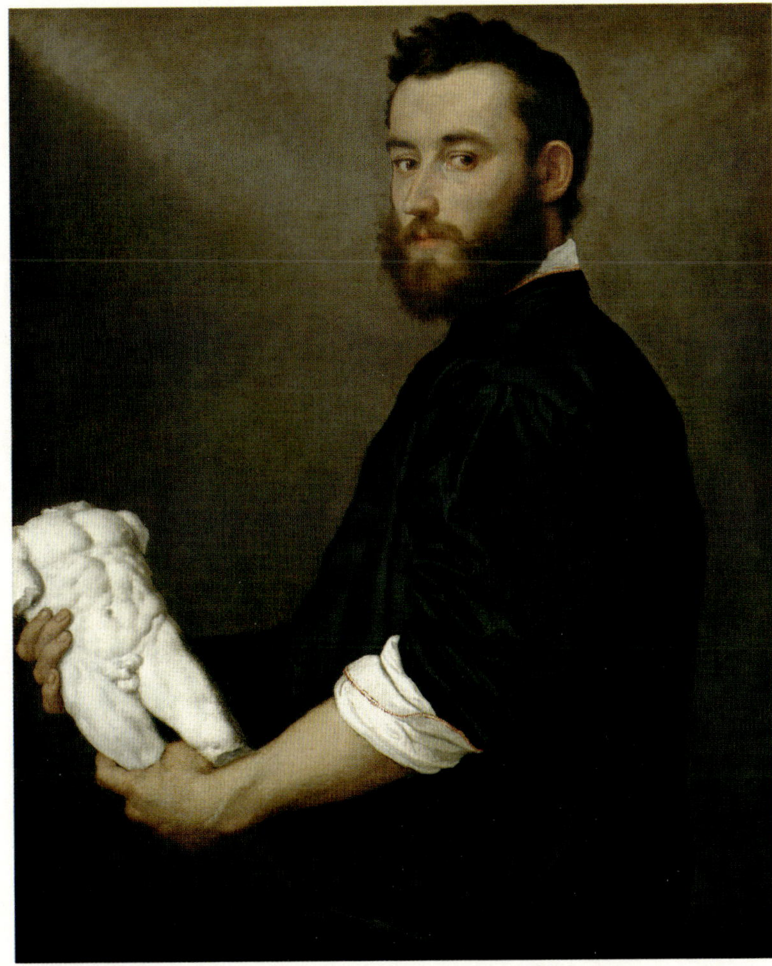

echelons of Venetian society. Many younger artists now followed Titian's example, producing boldly conceived self-portraits, or depicting their artist contemporaries. Tintoretto painted Sansovino's portrait, while Veronese and the *terraferma* painter Giovanni Battista Moroni (ca. 1525–1578) both depicted the vainglorious Vittoria, who is known to have built up an extensive collection of artist portraits and self-portraits. Moroni's portrait draws together the two apparently contradictory sides of Vittoria's identity: the sculptor's sleeves are rolled up in the manner of an artisan at work, but he wears the soft silks of a gentleman and holds a classical-looking cast in his hands, as might a learned art collector or connoisseur (FIG. 108). It was more typical for a painter to show himself alongside Titian, as his possible artistic son and heir. Veronese probably did so in the group of musicians in his *Marriage at Cana* of

ca. 1570. Oil on canvas,
116.8 × 149.9cm (3ft 10in
× 4ft 11in). Minneapolis
Institute of Art,
Minneapolis. The William
Hood Dunwoody Fund.

The young El Greco
apparently had some success
with his depictions of
this moralizing Counter-
Reformatory subject, and
repeated it in a number of
surviving versions. His
early style owes more to
Tintoretto than to Titian.

1562–3 (Musée du Louvre, Paris). Even outsiders, such as the young Domenikos Theotokopolous, now known as 'El Greco' (1541–1614), who arrived in Venice from Crete in 1567 as a fully matriculated icon painter, sought to make this connection. At the lower right of his *Purification of the Temple*, where one might expect to find a signature, he placed four artist portraits (FIG. 109). In a sense, these heads, featuring (from left to right) Titian, Michelangelo, Giulio Clovio (1498–1578) and (perhaps) a self-portrait, did serve a signature function, given that they suggest the young painter's style was a direct outcome or continuation of the array of proven old masters. But the strange spidery appearance of El Greco's painting renders this claim spurious, and it may be that he had relatively little to do with Titian. In common with many other images of artists from this period, El Greco's identification with 'the father of art' was essentially a matter of professional aspiration and ambition rather than a historical reality.

The new climate of artistic self-consciousness gave visual art a semi-independent and progressive life beyond the mere fulfilment of the specific demands or values of patrons. Artistic innovation after 1550 probably owed more to the continuation of the intense rivalry between leading practitioners, noted in the previous chapter. This competitiveness was, in part, a response to the professional attitude and practice of Titian himself. His towering example led the younger generations to develop carefully cultivated styles and identities that might either refer to Titian, or be self-consciously differentiated from him. Titian's success was not easily emulated, but his high profile did provide many opportunities. Visual art was now deemed worthy of attention in literary publications, and in 1557 Ludovico Dolce published his *Dialogo della pittura* already mentioned above. Dolce's treatise was a response to Giorgio Vasari's *Lives of the Artists* (1550), in which Titian had been omitted altogether, and the Venetian contribution generally denigrated in favour of Tuscan artists. It began a famous aesthetic argument between Florentine 'design' (*disegno*) and Venetian 'colour' (*colore*) that was destined to run on for centuries. The idea that colour can be seen as the defining characteristic of Venetian Renaissance art is open to question, however, and is actually more suited to Titian's example alone. Such considerations do not have much relevance to the monochrome marbles and bronzes of Sansovino or Vittoria; or, in architecture, to the shining white structures of Palladio and Sanmicheli. Titian may have used preparatory drawing (a key aspect of Central Italian *disegno*) increasingly rarely, but the practice of careful preparation through this means remained significant in the workshops of Tintoretto,

Veronese and Bassano. Although younger artists often still referred to Titian's works, they rarely attempted to emulate the extraordinary fluid technique, now often described as his 'late style'. The old Titian frequently changed his mind as he painted, leaving unresolved alterations (*pentimenti*) visible, and whole passages of brush work exposed to view, even if these rough marks were often placed next to others that were finished to more conventional standards.

The *Death of Actaeon* (*see* FIG. 111) remained in Titian's workshop until his death in 1576, but was begun as early as 1559, apparently as another *poesia* for Philip II. Titian's habit of painting 'in patches' (as Vasari now described it in the 'Life' he added to the new edition of his book in 1568) is evident enough. If the head of the vengeful goddess is relatively finished, then in the surrounding areas (the foreground bush, dog's head and foaming water) the coarse

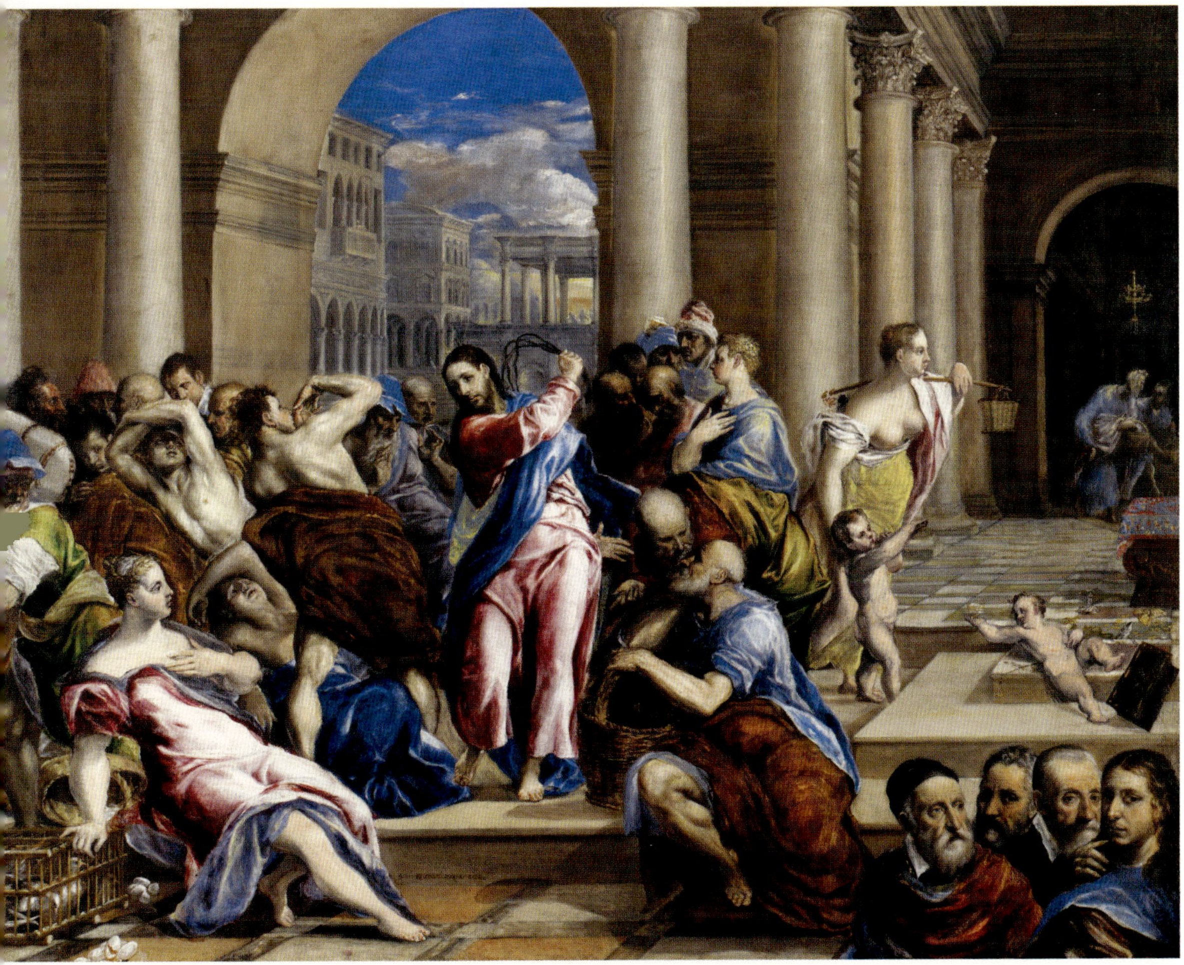

paint marks reappear, as if to deliberately reveal the fiction of an illusionistic painting. Throughout this work, the viewer is made aware of the materiality of the pigment lying on the picture surface, as a challenge to the effect of three-dimensionality. It is unclear how deliberate this revelation of the mechanics of painting was, given that Titian withheld the 'Diana' in the studio. But the surface is certainly densely worked, and the rough handling of paint, like the overall tonal unity, does consistently support the grim import of the subject matter: the death of the hunter Actaeon, who is transformed into a stag and hunted down by the goddess before being ripped apart by his own hounds. It may be that Titian's late style represents a self-conscious masterly display of the many expressive possibilities of oil painting itself. His new approach in old age, which had few predecessors in Venetian painting, and could not really be imitated, drew attention to the way in which 'colouring' (*colorito*), rather than mere colour (*colore*), could act as a shaping force in painting. It revealed the limitations of *disegno*, in which the execution of a work was made subordinate to the pre-conceived idea in the artist's mind.

Titian, with Dolce's help, published a personal emblem, or *impresa*, that encapsulated this idea in 1562. The image features a she-bear who licks her still unformed cub into shape (FIG. 110). Titian, we understand, does something similar as he 'licks' the raw material of nature into shape in his paintings. The title of the *impresa* reconfirms the point, proclaiming 'Art More Powerful than Nature'. The device confirmed Titian's superiority to his materials, but also expresses the common sixteenth-century idea that the modern artist goes beyond or improves nature itself in his production of the perfect work of art. This was a widely accepted tenet across much of Italy, where patrons would now expect artists to pursue their own unique style, or *maniera*. To some extent, the acceptance of this aesthetic imperative transcends the arguments over the relative merits of local Schools in Italy. Even if the younger generations of artists in Venice could not closely follow Titian's strange late style, they each developed their own carefully differentiated *maniera* and thus fulfilled the underlying demand for artistic individuality.

Titian's *impresa* can, in fact, be taken as a paradigm for the victory of art in Venice in the third quarter of the sixteenth century. Art's rhetorical fictions became all-pervasive in Venice, penetrating,

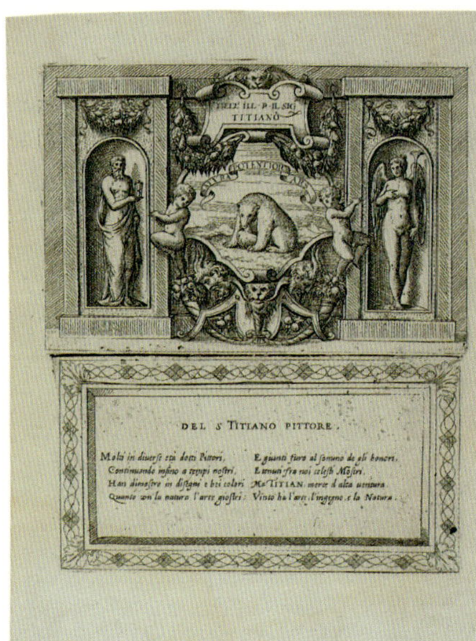

Fig. 110

Titian's *impresa*

1562. From Battista Pittoni, *Imprese di diversi prencipi* (Venice, 1562)

Dolce supplied the rhyming couplets beneath the image, while above it the epithet *natura potentior ars* is featured.

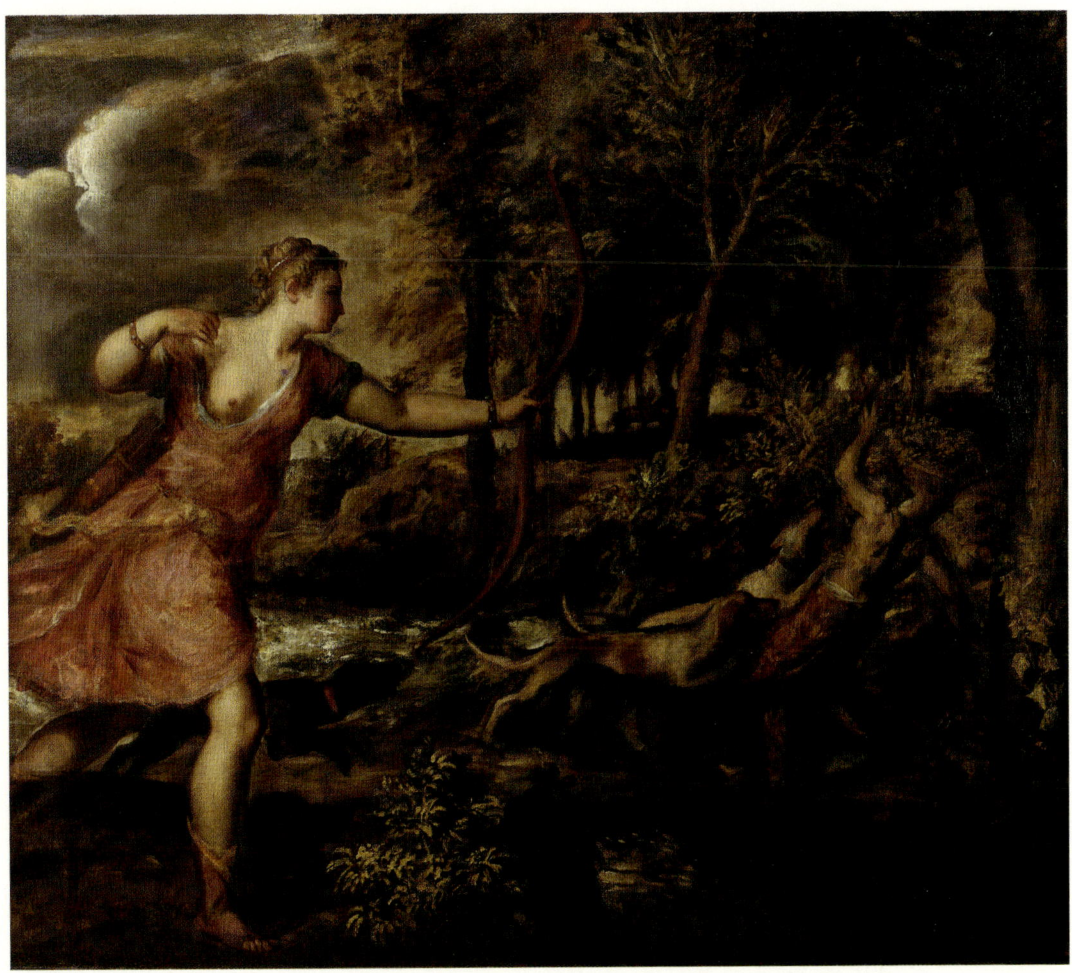

defining and constituting reality in ever more absolute terms. From an artistic point of view, these decades have long been understood as the high point or climax of the Renaissance in Venice. Though we (like the original patrons and audiences of Titian, Veronese, Tintoretto, Palladio, Bassano and others) might revel in the sheer range of artistic effect and invention, the victory of art may nonetheless be taken as a sign of the decline of the Venetian Republic. As the identities of patrons, publics and artists were shaped in and through the glorifying illusions of art, so their relation to reality became ever more tenuous. The new pervasiveness of art by 1575 may already reflect the beginning of the city's long slide into the fiction of its own myths.

1559–76. Oil on canvas, 178.4 × 198.1cm (5ft 10¼in × 6ft 6in). National Gallery, London.

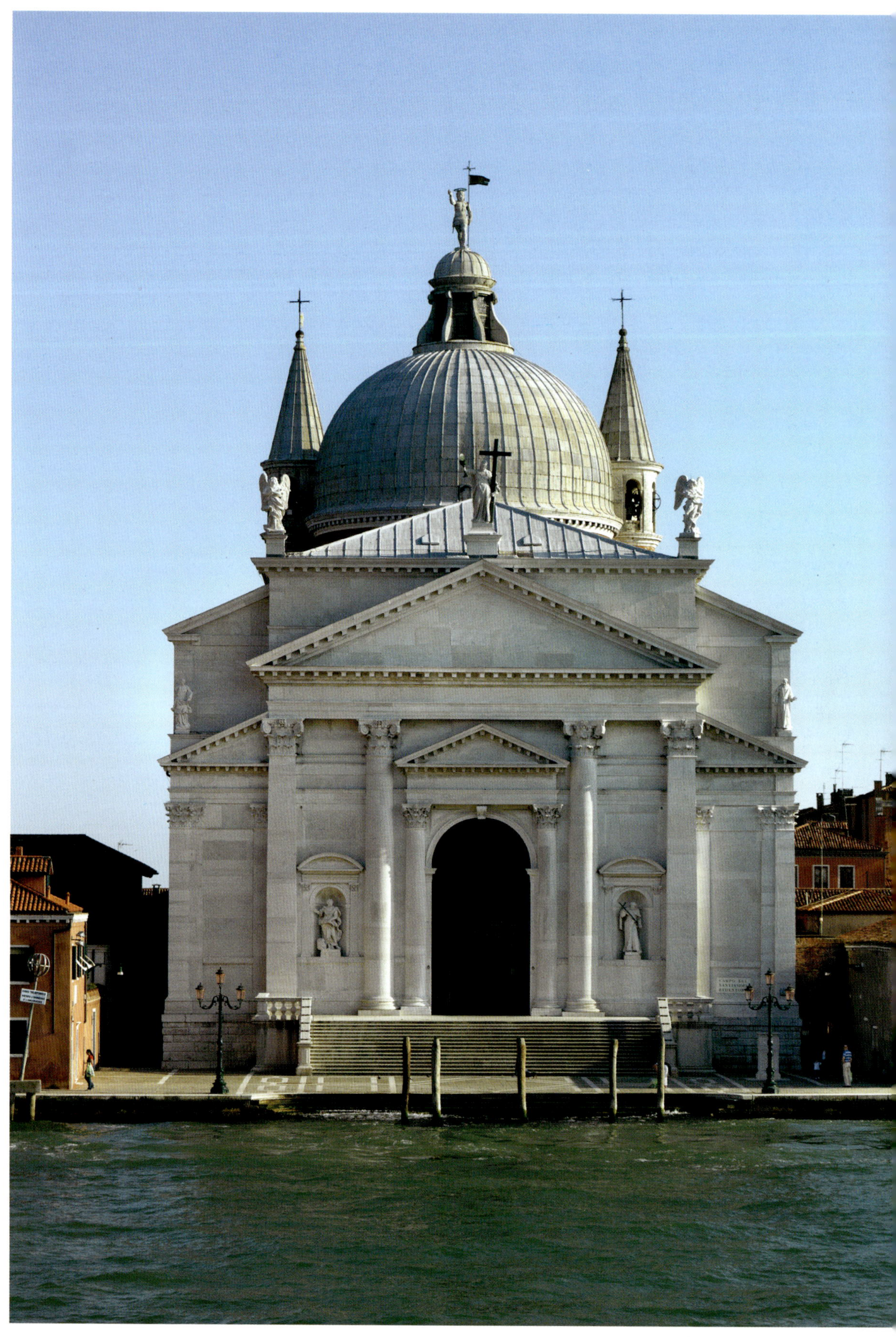

Adversity, Creativity, Retrospectivity: 1576–1600

Venice in the final quarter of the sixteenth century was a city marked by political adversity, economic decline and spiritual uncertainty. The exaggerated and over-optimistic outburst of patriotic fervour that followed the Venetian victory over the Turks at the Battle of Lepanto in 1571 is ultimately symptomatic of this worsening situation. The conflict had been stimulated by the Turkish threat to Cyprus, Venice's last remaining trading stronghold in the Levant; but within two years the island was lost to Venice for good, and the so-called Holy League binding the city to the papacy and to Spain had dissolved. Long-term economic degeneration was also to take its toll on the leadership of the patrician caste, even if it is true that official commissions came to the fore again, as the ruling group reconfirmed its grip on the city with new tenacity and determination. The patriciate beat a retreat from the boldly individualistic dimensions of the mid-century *renovatio urbis*, even as it also sought to appear more orthodox in religious matters, and to further extend its power over many aspects of Venetian cultural life. A group of families known as the *case giovani* ('young houses') came to the fore, and sought to revive the traditional principles of the Republic. This, however, was less a return to the confidently communal and inclusive cultural values of the past, than a withdrawal to ossified and hierarchical social order and convention. The new reactionary attitude offers a significant parallel to the Counter-Reformation itself, with its rigid restatement of the long-standing tenets and traditions of Catholic Christianity. Indeed, the way in which social and religious conservatism in Venice now found common cause can be seen as characteristic of these decades.

Responses to plague, fire and poverty

Two disastrous fires swept through the main state rooms of the Ducal Palace in 1574 and 1577, destroying the extensive cycles of *istorie* (histories), votive paintings and portraits that had been built up over the past 200 or more years, and that had formed a key part of the Venetian artistic patrimony. Following the destruction of the renowned Alexander cycle in the Sala del Maggior Consiglio (Council Hall), there was serious talk of demolishing the entire building, with Palladio's erstwhile patron, Marc'Antonio Barbaro, arguing that the architect should be commissioned to design a classical-looking replacement. In keeping with the deepening conservatism of the period, Barbaro's radical solution was quickly dismissed, and it was decided to restore rather than rebuild the palace. This provided new opportunities for many painters to participate in the creation of extensive schemes of pictorial redecoration. It is a sign of the times that this 'communal' effort proved to be something of a failure in artistic terms. It is nonetheless true that the manifold challenges of these years could offer a stimulus to innovative art. For example, the terrible plague of 1575–7, which killed as much as 30% of the city's population, resulted in the creation of a superb new church by Palladio on the island known as the Giudecca, in the south of the city. And at the Scuola Grande di San Rocco, the plague's devastating horrors provided imaginative impetus for the new cycles of ceiling and wall paintings by Tintoretto: works which are among the most important produced anywhere in Italy or Europe in the late sixteenth century.

Venice was less at ease with itself than at any other period described in this book, but cultural and spiritual discomfort could, on occasion, provide creative edge. Many works from these decades express a curious dialectic between older habits of patriotic self-celebration and self-justification, and a less familiar sense that the city was the subject of divine wrath and punishment. The proclivity of Venetians to identify themselves as God's chosen people, and their city as ultimately justified and victorious, was restated in no uncertain terms, especially in the domain of official patronage at the Ducal Palace. Yet as the disappointments, tragedies and adversities multiplied, a troubling conviction that Venice was being punished for sins of luxury and indulgence also emerged. A perceived need for urgent moral reform expressed itself in both art and architecture, and can be recognized by a pointed withdrawal from the traditions of rich colouristic display and free formal invention characteristic of earlier decades of the century. The more secular, sensuous and individualistic aspects of sixteenth-century artistic culture were questioned, as the city sought to return to its older conventions of restraint and pious devotion.

Redemption became a pressing cultural, artistic and spiritual concern in these decades, and certainly motivated the state's commission to Palladio to build a new church known simply as 'Il Redentore', or the Redeemer (FIG. 112). The direct emphasis on Christ himself, rather than on his many intercessors or adherents, was also a leitmotif of the period, one that reflects the wider impact of the Counter-Reformation. The very fact that the new church was commissioned by the state itself, rather than by a religious order, as had been the case with Palladio's San Giorgio Maggiore, is indicative of the changing cultural climate. In these decades, the state sought to show itself as a pious or even quasi-religious entity, in a manner that was quite different from the secularism of the *renovatio urbis*. Importantly, too, the Redentore was the result of a vow made by the Senate at the height of the plague, rather than in the period following it. The new building was born out of adversity and suffering, and conceived as an offering to an angry God, intended to assuage his displeasure. It was vowed that the doge and his Senate, along with the choir of St Mark's, would process annually to the church, on the date of the plague's eventual cessation, to express Venetian thanksgiving for God's protection and mercy.

Palladio's building, which was promptly begun in 1577, was thus understood as a votive temple, and this conception influenced its compact external appearance. Seen from across the Giudecca canal, the elaborate horizontal spread of the facade effectively conceals the thick buttressed walls of the nave, giving the illusion that the structure is centrally planned, as in many other votive temples. In reality, the church is Latin-cross in shape, a decision probably taken to maximize access and aid preaching and acoustics within. The illusion of as many as five interlocking temple fronts set in a narrow spatial recession on the facade reflects Palladio's on-going imaginative response to the Pantheon in Rome, as recorded in a woodcut illustration in his theoretical study, *The Four Books of Architecture*

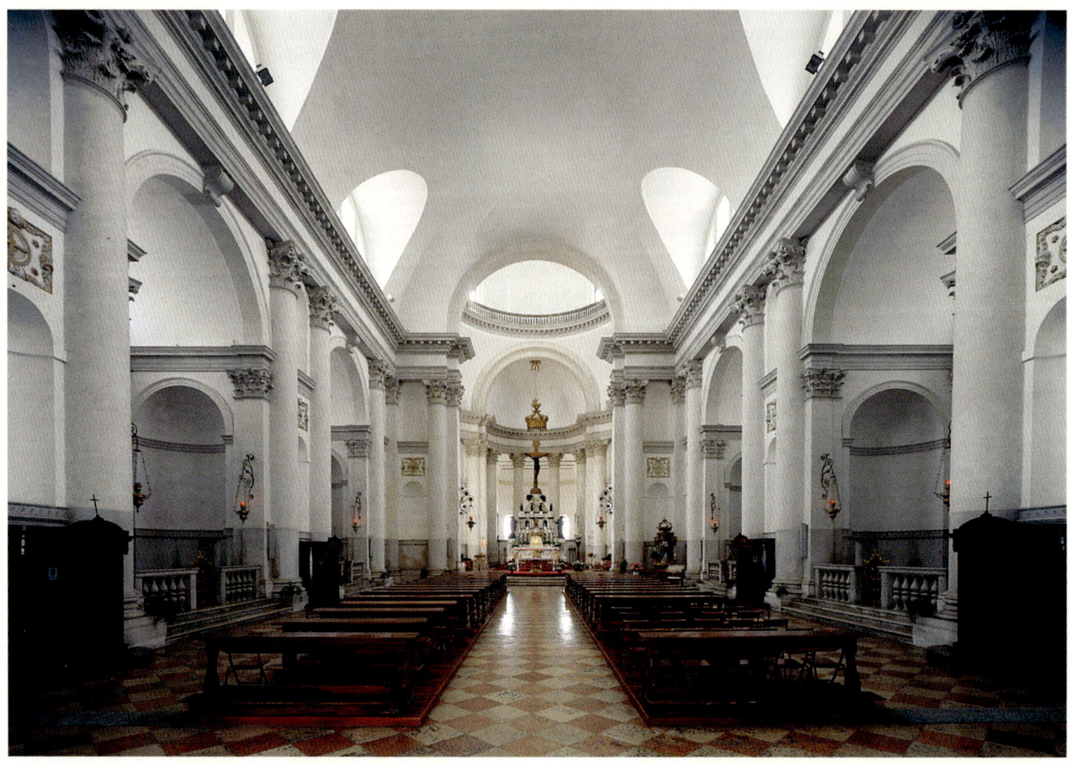

(*I quattro libri dell'architettura*), published in 1570. This work was destined to have a foundational impact on the development of classicizing Palladian architecture across Europe in the following centuries. The architect had not visited Rome for more than 20 years, however, and the inventiveness and originality of the new facade was perhaps a product of his increasing distance from his classical sources. In comparison with the San Giorgio facade (*see* FIG. 96), that of the Redentore is both more complex and more completely integrated with the structure behind it. The intersecting triangular pediments enter into a more intimate formal dialogue with the enlarged dome, which itself leads up to the elaborate lantern with the standing figure of Christ the Redeemer above.

Although the puritanical Capuchin friars who were housed in the church baulked at its grandeur, the simplicity and slow rhythm of Palladio's monumentalized classical architecture is evident enough. With its lack of coloration and reduction of decorative features, it expressed a sense of visual restraint common to many works of art in Venice from these decades, especially away from the Ducal Palace. In the interior, a single nave and side chapels were economically defined using a simple combination of Istrian stone and white-washed stucco to create an atmosphere of austerity quite different from the warm and mysterious golden glow of St Mark's (FIG. 113). Palladio's architecture at the Redentore represents a subtle adaptation of a Roman architectural vocabulary to the new imperatives of the Counter-Reformation, his retreat from the temptations of decorative colour and sensuality oddly comparable with the very latest religious paintings of Titian, including the stark *Pietà* (ca. 1570–6; Gallerie dell'Accademia, Venice), which the painter intended to place over his tomb in the Frari. Palladio's church and Titian's last painting share a solemn tone, as if the supreme artistry of their creators had been chastened by God's judgement against worldly presumption.

No such doubts explicitly appear in the triumphalist allegories of Venetian state power and worldly dominion that were now created for the lavishly refurbished Ducal Palace. Still, the sometimes vacuous hyperbole of the visual language employed tells its own story, and can be taken as further evidence of the decline of Venice as a political and cultural entity. The impressive votive painting by Veronese showing an *Allegory of the Victory of Lepanto* painted for the Sala del Collegio is to some extent the exception that proves the rule (*see* FIG. 115). Tellingly, however, Veronese's fussy patrons intervened in the course of his work on the painting to insist on a more

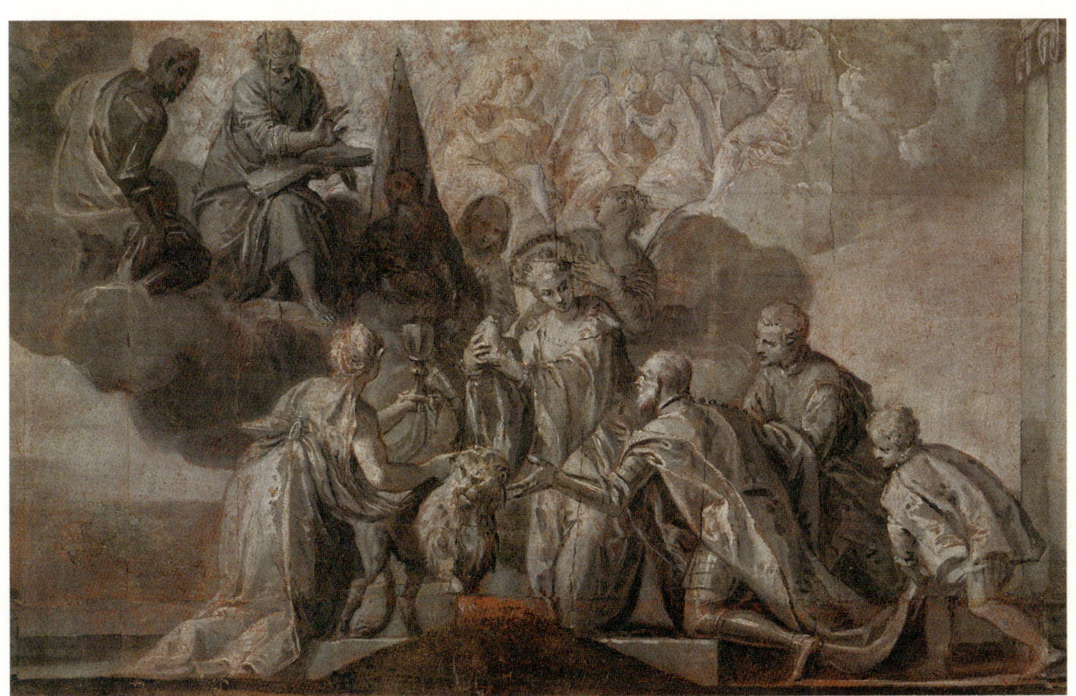

'correct' interpretation of the given theme. As we have seen, the defeat of the Turkish navy at Lepanto had come to have a disproportionate significance for Venetian self-esteem, and was understood by some as a turning point against the downhill slide in the city's political and economic fortunes. Publications and paintings were quickly commissioned to celebrate the victory, with little sense that it had so quickly proved to be hollow or pyrrhic. In Vincenzo Marostica's poem *Venetia trionfante* (Venice, 1572), the city is compared to the Immaculate Virgin, a pure woman free from sin, and it is said that God himself guided the sword of Sebastiano Venier, victorious general of the Venetian fleet. God the Father or Christ often appeared in prints showing the battle itself, which may explain the changes that Veronese was apparently required to make.

In an echo of the painter's brush with the Inquisition in 1573 over his 'Last Supper', Veronese was apparently instructed to replace the shadowy figure of St Mark in the heavens, featured in his preparatory drawing, with one of Christ himself (FIG. 114). If Venier, who had been elected doge in 1577, is allowed to dominate proceedings in the initial study, with the sacred and allegorical figures appearing

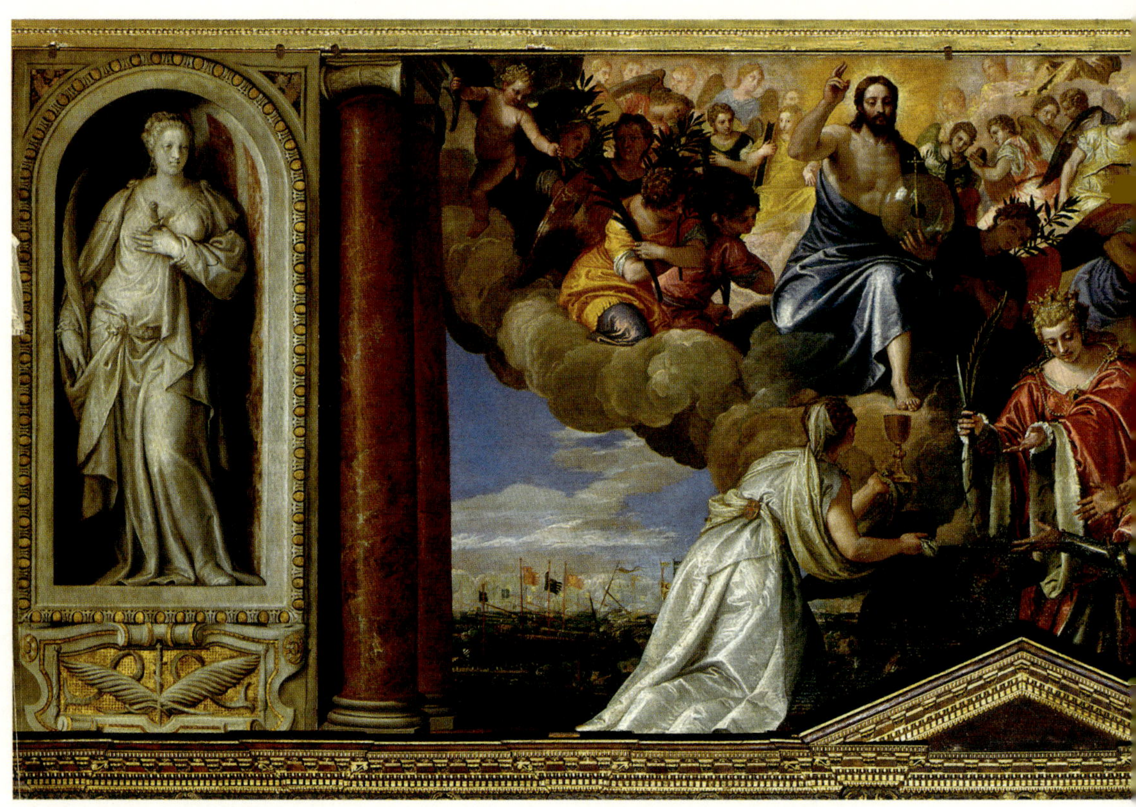

to revolve round him, then in the final painting he is made secondary to the explosion of the heavenly host above (FIG. 115). The all-
dominant Saviour holds a globe representing the world, while raising his other hand in a gesture of benediction. The rebalancing of
Veronese's votive composition between the person of the doge, and
the apparatus of heavenly power, probably reflects the influence of
the values of the *case giovani*, who were particularly keen to reinstate
the self-suppressing qualities of the previous centuries. One of their
number, the Ambassador to Rome, Leonardo Donà, went so far as to
proclaim in 1583 that he wished to be known 'in the Roman Curia
as Ambassador of Venice; and equally in Venice as senator of that
fatherland … and not by my private name'. But Veronese had only
followed local iconography in featuring Mark, patron saint of the
city, offering religious sanction to a kneeling doge below him (*see*,
for example, FIG. 7). The direct association of the state with Christ
himself had fewer precedents in Venetian patriotic imagery, but had
recently been confirmed at the Redentore, and had the advantage of
making the city appear to conform to the Christocentric values of
the Counter-Reformation.

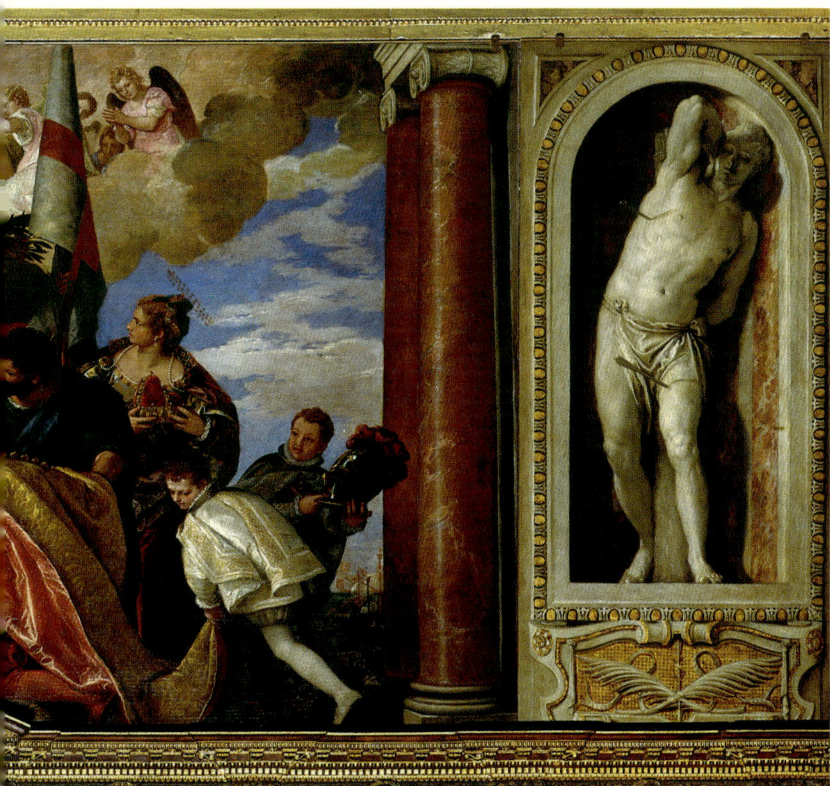

Fig. 115
Paolo Veronese
*Allegory of the Victory of
Lepanto*

ca. 1578–81. Oil on canvas,
285 × 565 cm (9 ft 4¼ in × 18 ft
6½ in). Sala del Collegio,
Ducal Palace, Venice.

In visual terms, too, Veronese's Collegio painting appears to retreat to a more simple and direct type of composition. Abandoning the more complex compositions of his earlier career, Veronese returned to the kind of pyramidal shape and centralized planar figure groups reminiscent of the art of the early sixteenth century. Special emphasis is also laid on making the earthbound group intersect with the heavenly one above, the shape of these interlocking social and heavenly domains mirroring one another to confirm their intimate connection. That Veronese was currently thinking about new ways of picturing Venice as the ideal state is evident enough from the great oval painting he shortly produced for the new ceiling in the Sala del Maggior Consiglio, showing the *Triumph of Venice* (ca. 1579–82). In a pendant painting, Palma Giovane (ca. 1548–1628) combined references to Veronese's work with elements drawn from Tintoretto's neighbouring ceiling panel to show *Venice Enthroned above her Conquered Provinces* (FIG. 116). Palma had recently spent seven years in Rome, however, and his hard-edged handling of forms, like the persistent visual quotations from Michelangelo's Sistine Ceiling (especially the foreground nude based on the *Jonah*), make his work appear as a barren exercise in stylistic eclecticism: one which is, in fact, more widely typical of the redecorations in the Palace. The commission for this ceiling, the most important in the entire Palace, involved the distribution of 35 paintings among as many as 10 named artists, all under the direction of the Veronese architect, engineer and cartographer, Cristoforo Sorte (1510–1595). This careful distribution of a major commission among a wider variety of artists and workshops, which was replicated in the other main state rooms, recalls the ways of the past, and may again reflect a reassertion (under the impact of the *case giovani*) of the Republic's original principles of stylistic diversity and resolution. In the event, however, the quality of the work produced, as the artists struggled to accommodate the elaborate allegorical programmes devised by leading patricians, was highly variable. Given that the return to *Venezianità* ('Venetian-ness') in the late sixteenth century was a result of social and economic uncertainty and cultural retreat, much of the new imagery in the Ducal Palace offered little more than uninspired and overblown visual rhetoric. With sometimes disastrous aesthetic effect, the individualistic and innovative styles of the city's leading artists were modulated towards a more generic manner to accommodate the special needs of a failing state.

The new emphasis on the piety of the state, which had encouraged Veronese's patrons to alter his votive painting, was supplemented by a parallel concern to demonstrate its active engagement in charitable activities. Contemporary writers such as Giovanni

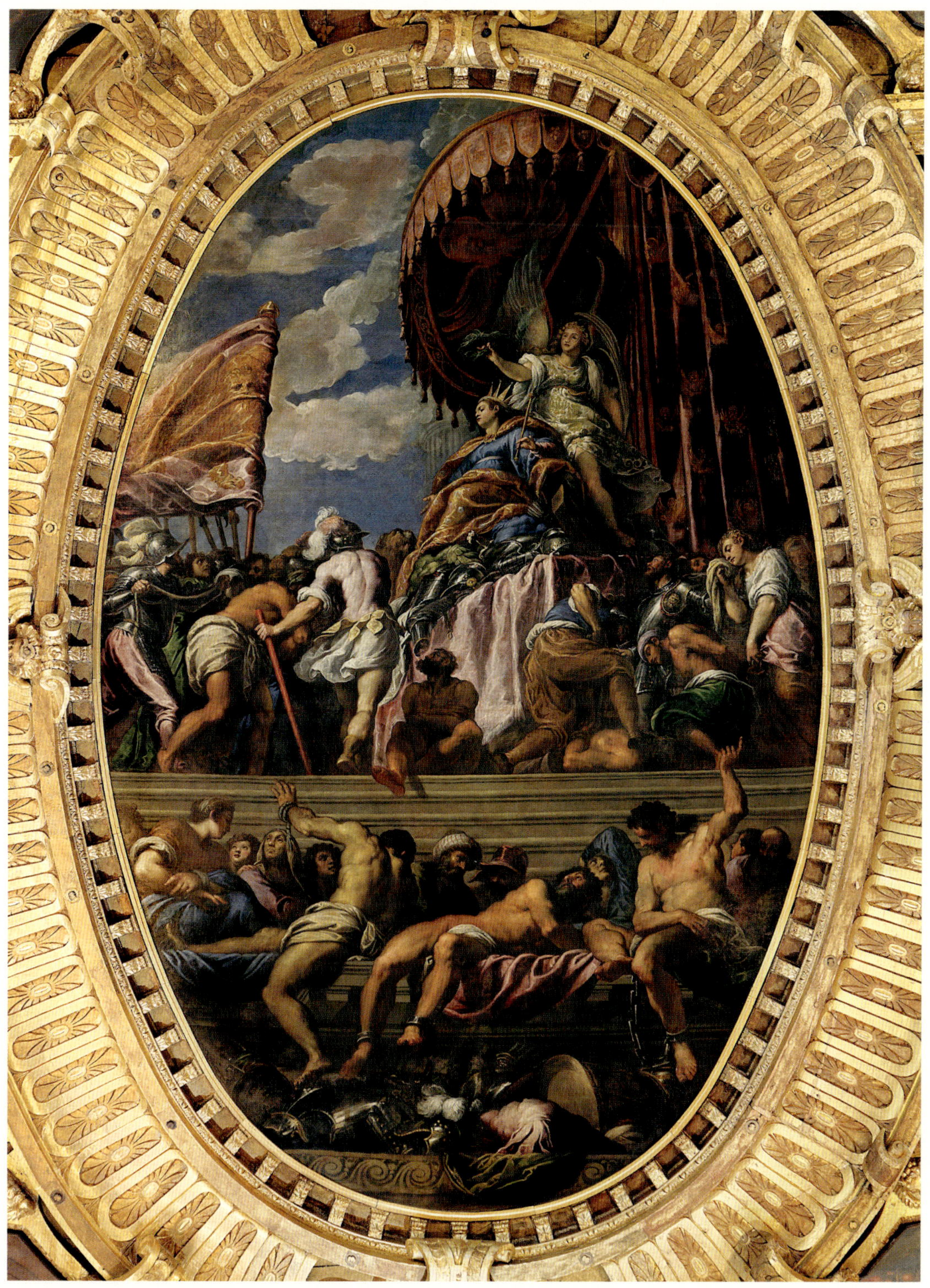

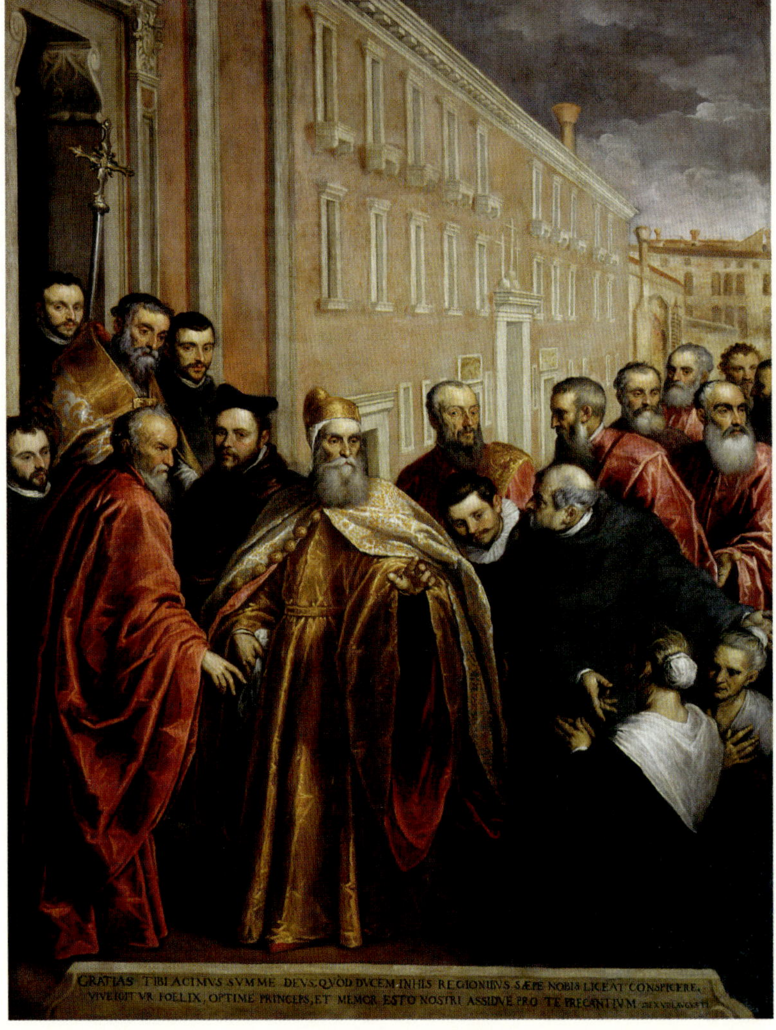

Botero laid emphasis on the 'public beneficence' of the Venetian state, while Giovanni Nicolò Doglioni claimed that 'few cities can equal Venice in piety and in the maintenance of alms'. In the 1580s, Palma Giovane painted a series of works for the hospital of the Crociferi that dramatize the growing official concern with poor relief in this period. Palma's paintings feature the prominent patrician, Pasquale Cicogna, showing his charity to the poor old women of the hospital both before and after his election as doge in 1585. In one painting, Cicogna is shown kneeling among the hospital inmates to receive the Mass. In another, he returns to the hospital oratory as doge, and although now dressed in full ducal regalia, pauses to notice the indigents once again (FIG. 117). Cicogna's charitable attitude, we understand, was unchanged by his rise to high office. But emphasis on Cicogna's personal piety is carefully offset in these paintings by elaboration of the wider institutional and official context. The doge is surrounded by red-robed patrician senators, suggesting that he is now seen as the representative of the state, which was the hospital's main funder. Perhaps more importantly still, Cicogna does not actually give alms at the oratory door. While visibly moved by the sight of the poor women, he does not succumb to his immediate emotional impulse to give charity. His benevolence will manifest itself, rather, through the state's continuing support to the institution, and in this way it will be supra-personal and rational in nature.

Palma's Crociferi paintings were much more successful than those he produced for the Ducal Palace, reintegrating elements of documentary-style realism which give more grounded and believable expression to the current ideals and actions of the state. If the suggestion that the doge and his government are on a procession through the city recalls long-established visual traditions in Venice (*see* FIGS 2, 44), then Palma's imagery is also original in its suggestion of different pictorial types, combining elements drawn from the *istoria*, the altarpiece, portraiture and even genre painting. At the same time, these works provide a demonstration of the state's direct intervention in the field of poor relief. Venice could show itself as properly 'Reformed' insofar as it demonstrated obedience to the core Counter-Reformatory dictates on the moral necessity of 'Good Works'. Yet, in a manner that went decisively beyond the reactive, crisis-generated and ad hoc approach taken to the problem of poverty in the city in the past, Venetian almsgiving was now understood as a matter of state-backed institutional control.

Tintoretto at San Rocco

In keeping with its newly heightened moral profile, the state acted in 1580 to curb the excessive amounts of money spent on paintings in its official buildings. Nevertheless, overall expenditure on art can hardly be said to have declined in this period. Though the Senate had initially granted a moderate sum of 10,000 ducats for the erection of the Redentore in 1577, the costs had escalated to more than 70,000 by the time of its completion 15 years later. As early as 1541, the *cittadini* (citizens) of the Scuola Grande di San Rocco had been publicly criticized in a book by the philo-Lutheran Alessandro Caravia for the huge amount of money consumed by their new Meeting House: 'they have spent 80,000 ducats when 6,000 would have been enough: The rest, which was spent in vain, could have been spent for the bare foot and naked who cry "alas"'. Tintoretto, who was an early associate of Caravia, and had taken his portrait, might still have had this stinging criticism in mind when he offered to complete 21 paintings for the ceiling of the Scuola's Sala Superiore (Upper Room) at a greatly discounted price in 1577 (FIG. 118). He quickly followed this up with a proposal of further discounts, offering to paint all further works required for the Meeting House (including the large wall paintings to go between the windows) in return for an annual salary of 100 ducats, and to deliver three works each year before the Feast of St Roch (16 August). Though Tintoretto's salary was for life, his conditions were nonetheless remarkably generous, given that large-scale paintings in Venice typically cost in the region of 100 ducats each, and took a year or so to complete. The artist had previously offered competitive prices and rapid production to other patrons in Venice, but there is no serious reason to doubt the genuineness of his claim in his petition that he now wished to work 'for the great love I have for our venerable Scuola, and for devotion to the glorious St Roch'.

Caravia had criticized the elaborate architecture of the Scuola from a Reformist point of view. Now Tintoretto developed a dramatically original 'San Rocco style' that in many ways reversed the extravagant ultra-classicism of the building's exterior. His paintings feature a predominant chiaroscuro treatment, and include large areas of barely worked shadow: qualities which certainly reflect their rapid production and low cost. The radically abbreviated forms often feature slashing white highlights that reveal the rapid and broad movements of Tintoretto's brush over the picture surface, and are partially disconnected from the underlying forms that they suggest. Despite the freedom of his expression, Tintoretto's technique is very different from the visual expansiveness of much earlier painting in Venice, with its attention to sensuous or decorative colour and to the individual textures of objects and surfaces. Downplaying such naturalistic conventions, Tintoretto developed a new kind of pictorial roughness, which might also have provided an answer to any Reformist charge regarding the unnecessary material luxury of his work. The element of visual reduction or restraint in Tintoretto's paintings at San Rocco may have something in common with other works from these decades; but it also helped him to arrive at a newly epic, serious and even apocalyptic tone that has few precedents or parallels in Venice, and that can be seen as expressing a core spiritual value of 'sacred poverty' or *santa povertà*.

The subject matter of Tintoretto's new cycles of paintings was developed as a continuation of those he had already completed in the board room (*albergo*) of the Meeting House in the mid-1560s, featuring Christ's Passion (*see* FIG. 104). On the ceiling of the Sala Superiore he depicted scenes from the Old Testament, focussed especially on episodes from Exodus, which served as the antitypes to those from the life of Christ depicted in the *albergo* and on the walls below. Downstairs, in the so-called Sala Terrena, he painted a further cycle of eight wall paintings between 1581 and 1586, showing episodes from the life of the Virgin and the infancy of Christ. The choice of such core universal Christian subjects was itself a departure from the more locally derived subjects featured in many earlier Scuole cycles in Venice, and must again reflect the wider impact of the Counter-Reformation. However, Tintoretto's astonishing pictorial invention at San Rocco cannot really be ascribed to the universalizing theological orthodoxies of this wider movement. In the three main ceiling panels, the painter took radical liberties with form and space,

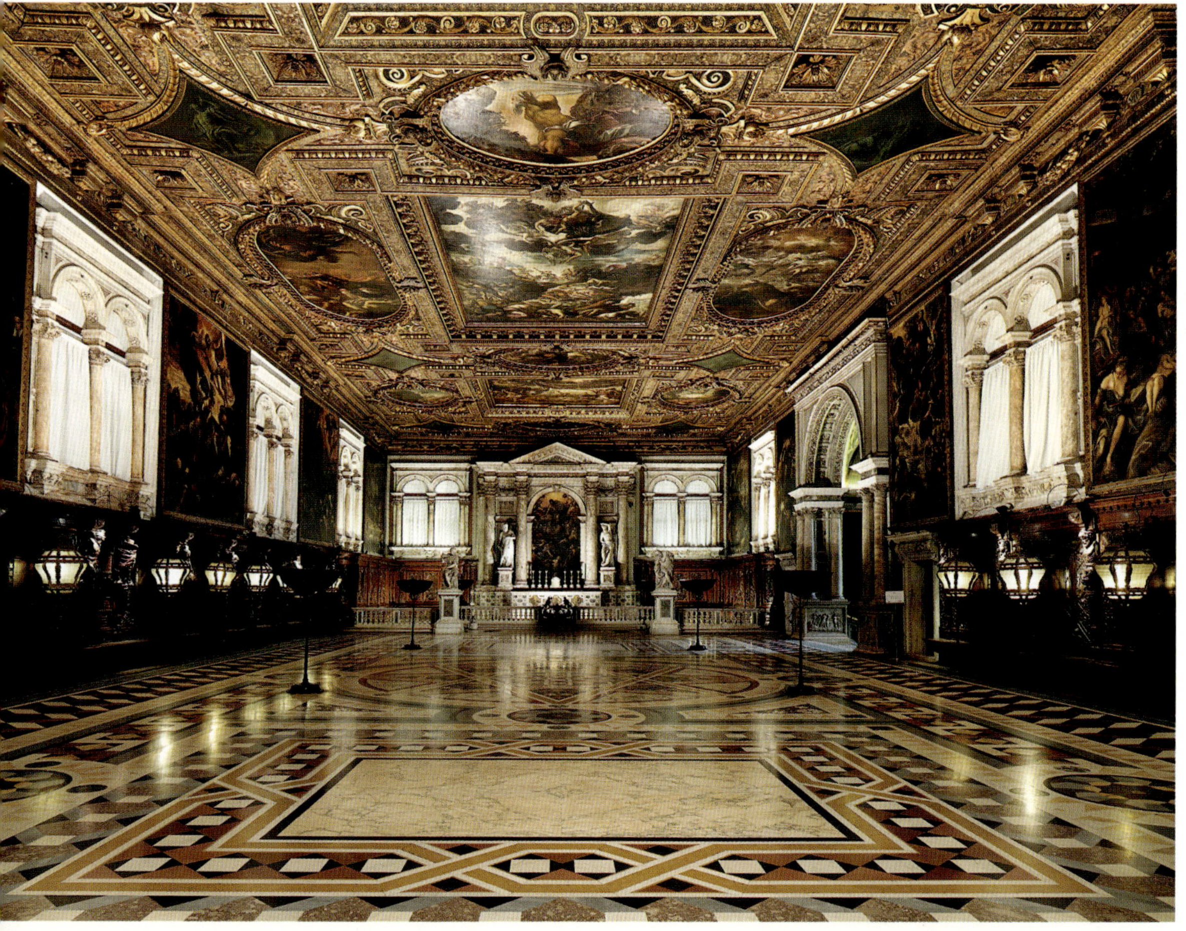

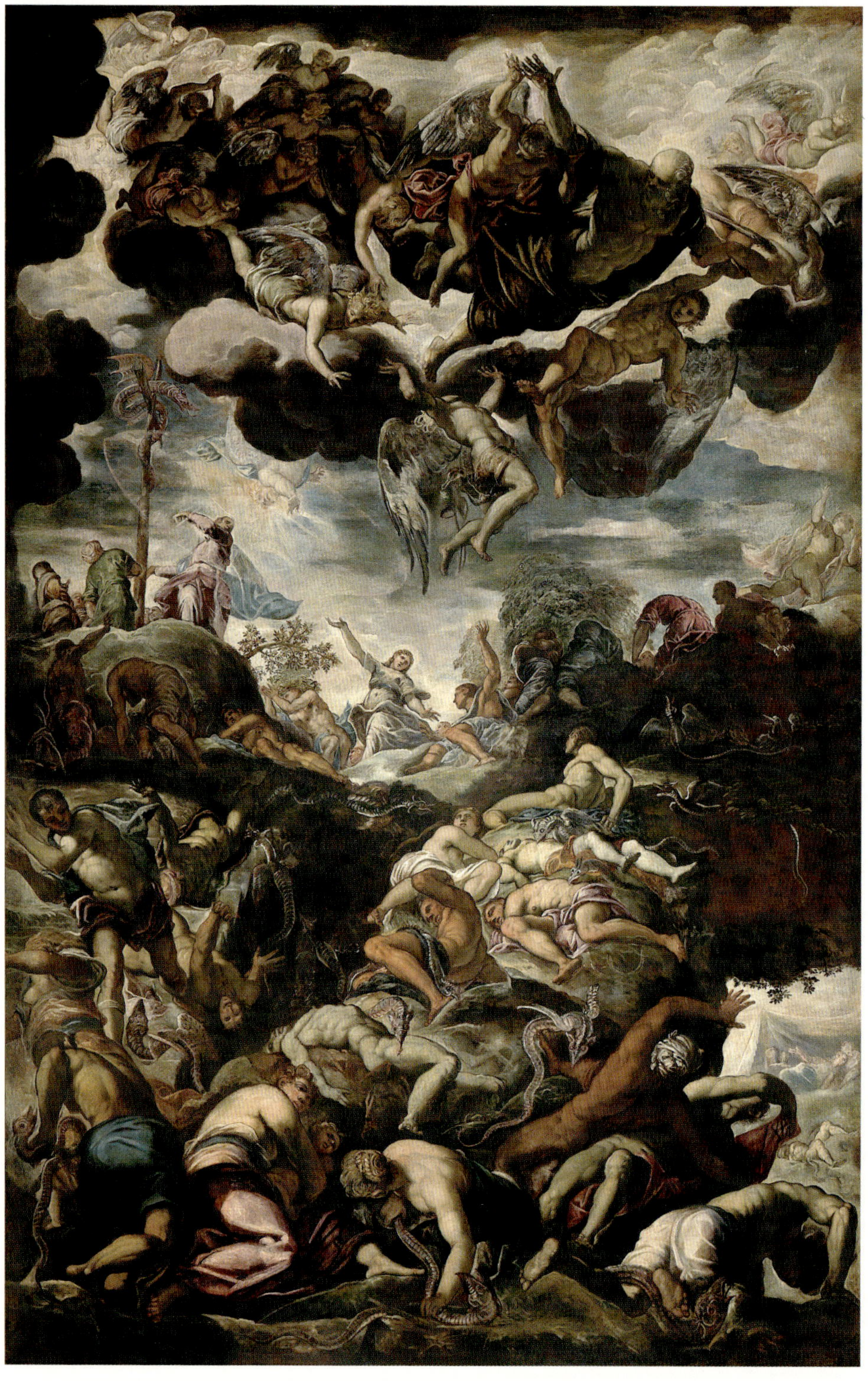

generating idiosyncratic spatial chutes and tunnels through his juxta-positions of writhing bodies, painted using the kind of visual short-hand noted above. Although Michelangelo's Old Testament scenes on the ceiling of the Sistine Chapel may have been in the painter's mind, Tintoretto's expressive use of spatial disintegration to indicate God's overriding supernatural authority was essentially original. In accordance with their setting on a ceiling, Tintoretto imagined each scene as occurring in an elevated quasi-heavenly domain, and this may have encouraged him to splinter the space of his paintings to suggest the power of God's frequent interventions. Both the creation and the collapse of pictorial space are made a matter of God's com-mand alone, alternatively expressing the power of his divine wrath or merciful intervention. This approach is very far indeed from the studious naturalistic perspective of fifteenth-century painters in Ven-ice, as it also is from the more unified or integrated spatial systems of the Baroque. It is the radical instability of space that is specific to Tintoretto's conception, serving as a pictorial expression of the ultimate power of the divine will over human comprehension or understanding.

Tintoretto began work on the main ceiling panel, featuring the *Brazen Serpent*, at the height of the plague in 1575 (FIG. 119). Its stern and apocalyptic tone must reflect this context, and was only to be softened in the scenes from the life of Christ below. The plague outbreak was widely seen as a kind of forerunner to the Last Judgement itself, and it is in this light that Tintoretto also conceived his central ceiling panel. The Israelites, to some extent identifiable by association with the plague-stricken Venetians, are attacked by snakes, as an act of divine retribution for their sins (God the Father gestures imperiously towards them at the top right). Tintoretto drew on harsh metaphors from St Paul, such as 'the sting of death is sin and the strength of sin is the law' (1 Corinthians 15:56), showing their bodies writhing in agony as they tumble out of the lower foreground of the painting, their physical descent trac-ing their spiritual fall. Others among the Israelites, however, have already seen the light, and appear to have been saved by their ap-parent understanding of the action at the upper left as a forerun-ner of Christ's Crucifixion: 'And as Moses lifted up the serpent in the wilderness, even so must the Son of man be lifted up: that whosoever believeth in him should not perish but have eternal life' (John 3:14–15).

Tintoretto also had in mind the famous antique sculpture of the *Laocoön*, which features an attack by snakes. The male figure in the central foreground, with his bent arm above his head, recalls this ancient source. The reference is more pronounced still in the depiction of *St Sebastian* (FIG. 120) which Tintoretto went on to paint on the wall of the Sala below, next to an image of *St Roch*. These two were well known as the city's plague saints, and were regularly invoked to protect the populace from the ravages of the disease. In order to confirm the connection, Tintoretto showed the saints peering up towards the central ceiling painting with evident consternation, as if understanding their own afflictions as directly equivalent to those of the Israelites, and indicating their readiness to intercede on behalf of the sufferers. It was typical of Tintoretto's approach to make the paintings on the walls connect actively with those on the ceiling, generating a formal interaction across the real space of the Sala that intensifies both visual effect and theological meaning. All the same, Tintoretto's writhing *St Sebastian* is a very far cry from earlier depictions of the saint in Venice (*see* FIG. 32), his restless writhing form presented as if in the throes of continuing physical agony or torment. The only release from this appears to lie in the unerring faith expressed in the upward turn of his body towards God, depicted in the ceiling paintings above. The powerful light which falls on the saint, apparently from this source, is, though, already a direct reflection of God's recognition and favour. The Gospel of St John was Tintoretto's main biblical source here, with its constant play on the fundamental metaphor 'God is light'. Throughout the cycles at San Rocco, light is made an attribute of the divine, evoking direct association with the Word or Logos, and indicating the infusion of grace. But Tintoretto's light frequently becomes incandescent fire, with the power to break apart and dematerialize the physical forms of the world.

It is not quite accurate to say that Tintoretto's spiritualized chiaroscuro replaced colour in the San Rocco cycles. Subtle tones of crimson, lilac, blue and green still lurk beneath the luminous veil, adding visual lustre to his paintings. But even if the wall paintings are more worldly than those on the ceiling, they still appear as if scorched or seared by God's all-consuming power, particularly in works such as the *Baptism* and the *Resurrection*. In other paintings, the reduced shapes that survive express worldly suffering and want. In the

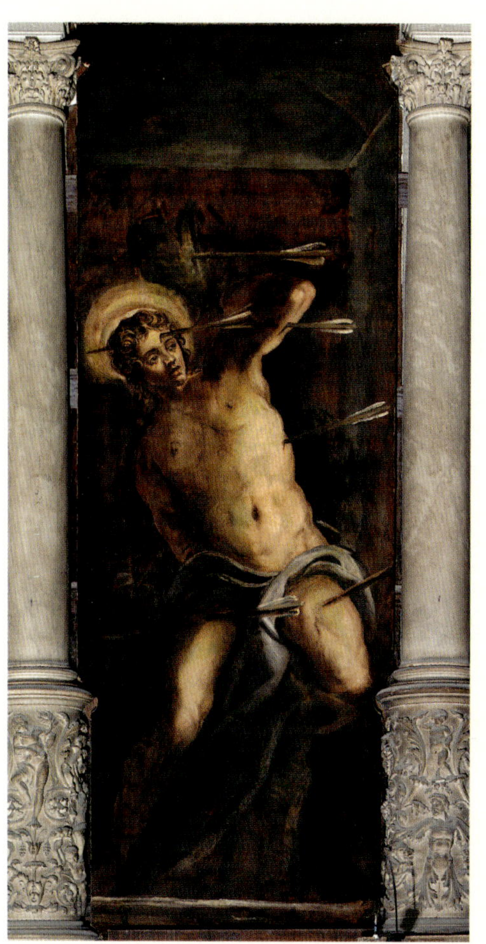

Fig. 120
Jacopo Tintoretto
St Sebastian

1578–81. Oil on canvas, 250 × 80cm (8ft 2⅜in × 2ft 7½in). Sala Superiore, Scuola Grande di San Rocco, Venice.

Miracle of the Loaves and Fishes (FIG. 121), Tintoretto followed John's account of the boy who brings the reviving food to the hungry, as, too, the help Christ received in its distribution from St Andrew (6:1–13). In keeping with the ceiling painting directly above it, showing the *Gathering of Manna*, the wall painting refers to the charitable activities of the Scuola itself, although only by way of analogy. More significant here is the way in which Christ and Andrew are shown at some distance, and are made difficult to identify. Christ, to the

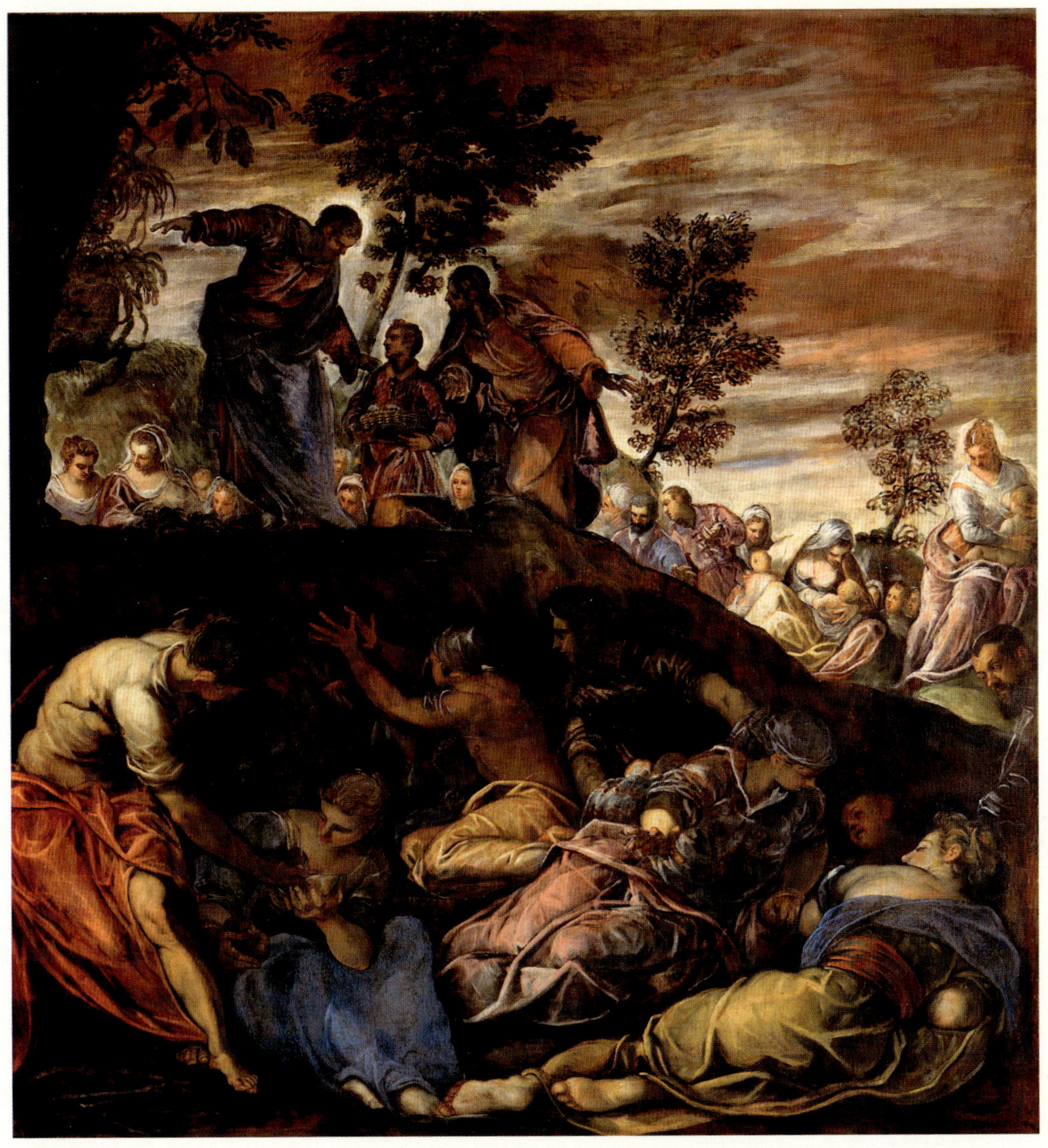

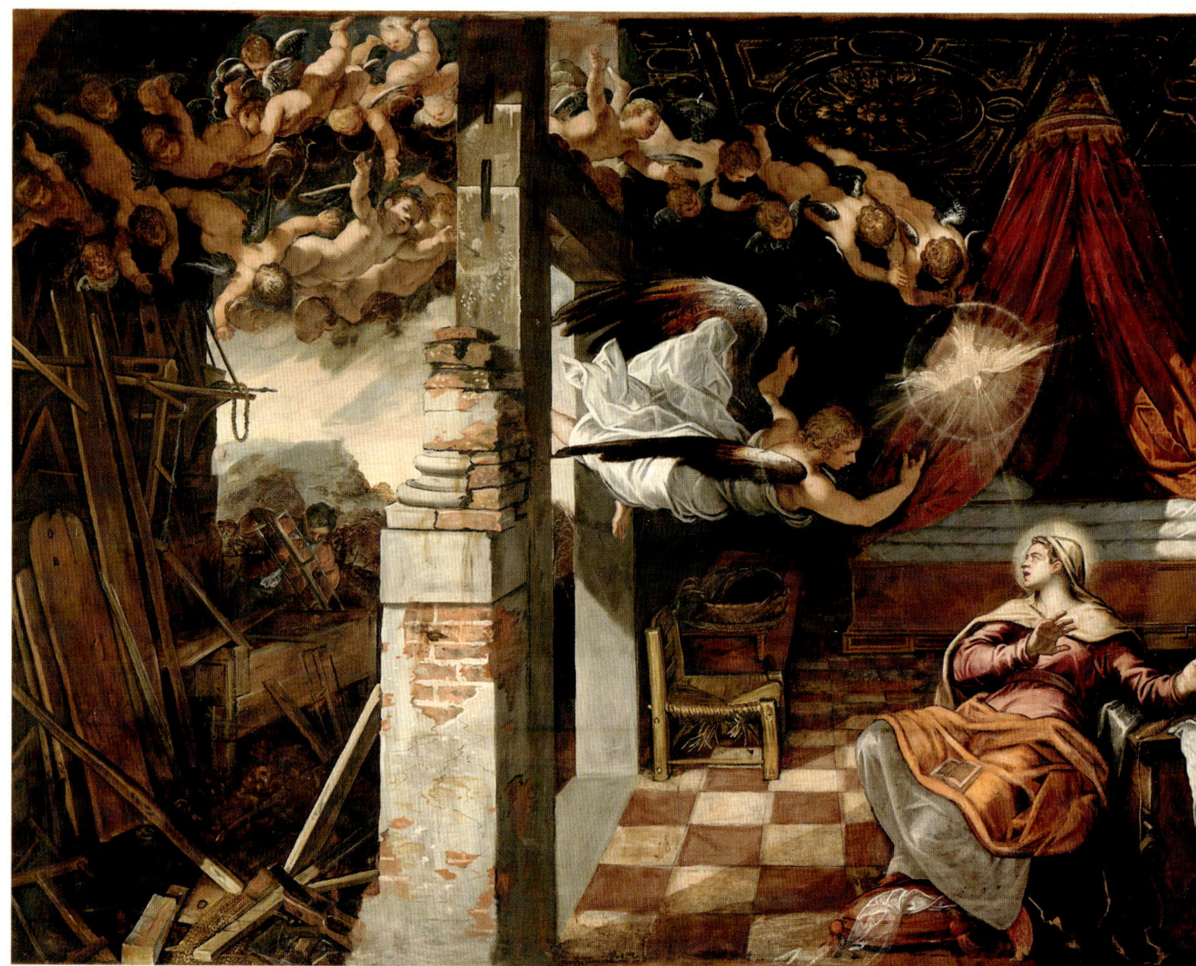

left, is only slightly distinguished by his more upright posture. He is anonymized by his similarity to Andrew, by the fall of shadow across his form, and by his integration into the surrounding crowd. This might superficially recall the 'eyewitness' style of earlier history paintings for the Venetian Scuole (*see* FIG. 44), but in this work the displacement of the protagonist serves to make a different spiritual point, demonstrating Christ's essential quality of humility.

In several paintings from the Sala Terrena cycle begun in 1581, the physical dilapidation of the buildings and objects represented serves more directly still as a metaphor for the transience of the world. Yet poverty is also more clearly defined as a sacred value, or as a confirmation or guarantor of spiritual integrity. This is the case in the painting of the *Annunciation*, fittingly hung to the immediate left of the main entrance (FIG. 122). While many earlier versions of this subject painted in Venice showed the Virgin in a pristine environment that reflected her purity, a naturalistic artistic language is employed in this work to catalogue the details of the collapsing and decaying world in which Mary and Joseph live. With a Venetian eye, well used to the excoriation of the surfaces of the city's buildings by its harsh salty climate, Tintoretto carefully records the weathering of the once-decorative classical column in the foreground back to its crude stone core. The broken wicker of the chair and the discoloured tiles, like the grime of Joseph's workshop, and the depiction of the Virgin herself as a simple woman of the *popolani*, reconfirms the overall impression of social and economic deprivation. Yet this context of worldly decay appears almost to invite or precipitate God's intervention. In a manner which recalls the early *Miracle of the Slave* (*see* FIG. 86), Tintoretto's drama is worked around the miraculous appearance of a divine airborne figure to save one who is at the bottom of the social order. Gabriel powers through the open aperture – apt metaphor for the miraculous Incarnation of Christ in the Virgin's womb – accompanied by a host of heavenly putti, and the dove of the Holy Spirit. This dynamic heavenly invasion does not so much contradict the material poverty of the Holy Family as answer its call.

Late works by Veronese and Bassano

In a number of religious and mythological paintings from the 1580s, Paolo Veronese, perhaps chastened by the criticism of his work at Santi Giovanni e Paolo and the Ducal Palace during the previous decade, attempted to modify his earlier decorative and flamboyant style in keeping with the more sombre and serious tastes of the period. For several decades Veronese had developed and maintained a style that contrasted with the deepening emotion and spiritual values of his main rivals. The 'noble' actors and actions set on his stage-like prosceniums, monumental facades or vertiginous architectural ledges keep the viewer at a distance. Faces and expressions may vary, but the kind of intense psychological interchanges or full bodily responses that feature in contemporary works by Titian and Tintoretto are studiously avoided. Veronese evidently disliked violent drama of the kind increasingly demanded for sacred painting, and had often seemed relatively unconcerned with the tragic import of his subject-matter. Now, however, Veronese's colours began to darken, and chiaroscuro was admitted into his pictorial armoury, not always with the best results. A successful example of his late style is the *Martyrdom and Last Communion of St Lucy*, in which he skilfully adapted to the imperatives of the Counter-Reformation (FIG. 123).

The Council of Trent had demanded simplicity and directness in sacred imagery, so that the given work could be easily understood by the viewer, and serve to stimulate pious thoughts regarding its sacred prototypes (without ever, of course, being confused with them). In the *St Lucy*, Veronese abandoned the elaborate apparatus of complex architecture and supporting cast of observers typical in his earlier works. Instead, he focussed attention on the essential protagonists in the drama, who are placed close to the picture plane at the front of the space. Though a residual classicizing architecture is still present, this is reduced to sketchy unreality away in the background. The secondary scene, set in this hazy distance, is the earlier moment in Lucy's martyrdom, when an unsuccessful attempt was made to drag her to a brothel. There is little, now, to distract us from the scene of her death in the foreground. Even in this work, however, Veronese's seemingly innate pictorial decorum leads him to distract our attention from the moment of Lucy's violent end. Thus, the executioner's knife thrust into her chest is cleverly concealed from our view by his hand, which also partially covers the blood that spurts from her wound. Instead, our attention is drawn to the action of the priest to the right who administers the last sacrament. Renewed emphasis on the active role of the clergy in the proper administration of the sacraments had been deemed of great importance at the Council of Trent, and Veronese's emphasis on this event expresses the key role of the Church at the point of death. As the priest holds up the sacramental wafer in his right hand, the saint turns her head decisively towards it, and away from her executioner and the worldly brutality he represents.

Both Veronese and (more especially) Tintoretto are sometimes thought to have been influenced by the very late style of Titian, with its serious tone, disturbing or tragic subject matter, and radically darkened palette. Titian's final works were probably more influential on Jacopo Bassano, who apparently knew the famous old master better than most, and would certainly have had access to Titian's studio at the Biri Grande, especially after his painter son Francesco (1549–1592) went to live there in the early 1580s. It used to be thought that the ageing Jacopo stopped painting altogether around 1581, due to a misreading of a comment in a letter by Francesco saying that his father 'by now does not draw any more'. However, an inscription on Jacopo's *Susanna and the Elders* bears the date 1585, and it is clear that he continued to paint up until shortly before his death in 1592. Works from this late period include a number accurately described by contemporaries as 'nocturnes' or as 'imitating night', featuring a radical suppression of the usual local colour-values of illusionistic painting. In these works, Bassano developed a dramatic contrast between obscure backgrounds and the shining bodies of human figures, whose luminosity remains unexplained from a naturalistic point of view. These forms are laid in using a few fluid brushstrokes left revealed on the surface, in a manner that can be paralleled in the late work of Titian. Admixtures of the non-colours of black and white are allowed to shape the darkening world Bassano depicts. The formal abbreviations of Jacopo's late paintings certainly indicate the essential correctness of Francesco's statement that his father (again like Titian before him) had largely abandoned preparatory drawing.

In the *Susanna and the Elders*, as in many of his other paintings from the 1580s, Jacopo Bassano also abandoned the comforting rural imagery through which he had made his name in earlier decades, moving towards a more dramatic narrative style (FIG. 124). To the right of the painting, a goat and a rabbit survive Bassano's

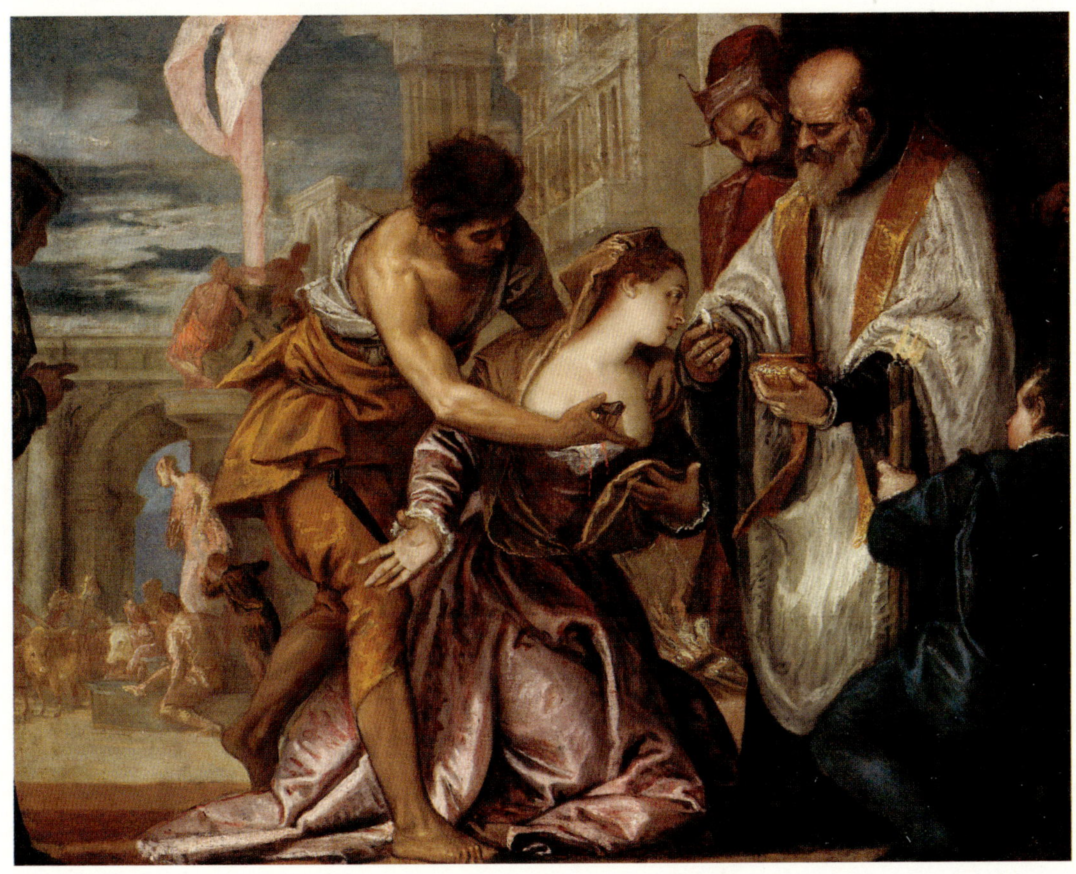

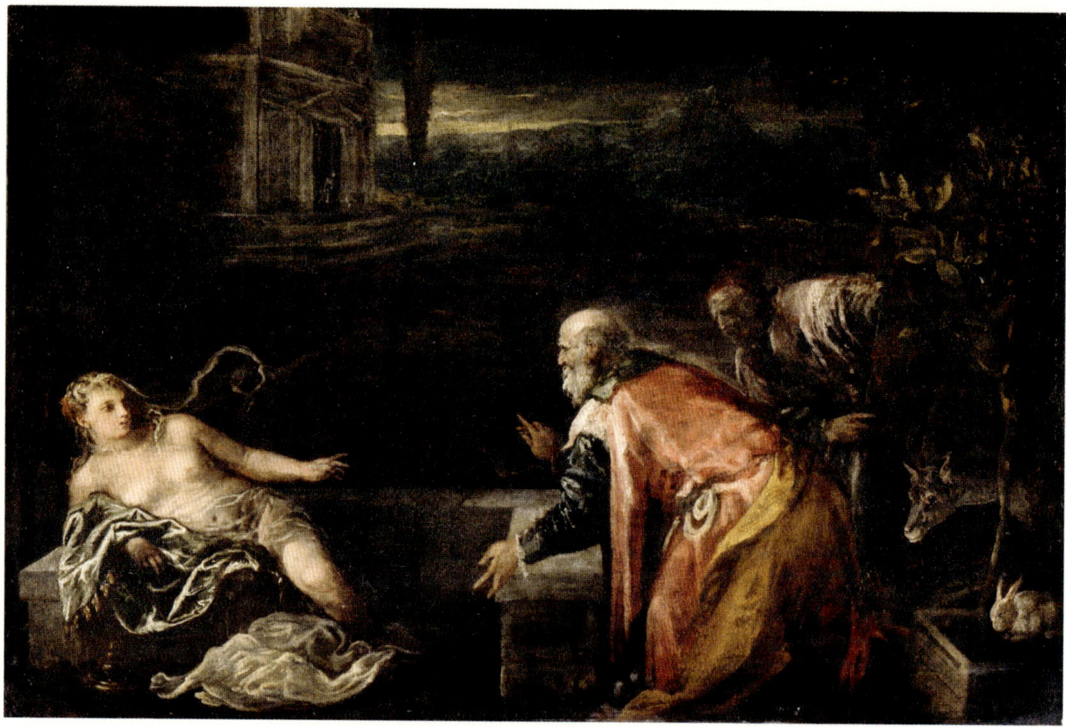

radical reduction of his usual country cast, but are now pressed into symbolic service, referring to the lust and lecherousness of the two Elders nearby. The landscape might still feature Mount Grappa in the distant background, but local flavour is now less important than the issues raised by the biblical subject matter itself. Visual attention falls solely on the significance of the interaction between the semi-naked young woman and the gesticulating old men in the foreground. Their contrary though also complementary actions, straining forward and recoiling backwards, define the actors' emotions, contrasting the surprise and shock of the pious wife Susanna with the penetrative or invasive lust of the Elders. In this way, Bassano captures the dramatic tension of the immediate moment in a masterly fashion, and with the minimum of pictorial fuss. His subject, though drawn from the Apocryphal Book of Susanna, was of great significance to a period much concerned with moral questions, especially around the issue of sexual desire and sensuality. It is hard not to see the great pool of darkness surrounding the figures as symbolic of the sinfulness of the world. Perhaps, too, Bassano's painting comments on, and critiques, a well-established visual tradition in Venetian painting. Even as she recoils from the Elders, Bassano's Susanna takes on something of the appearance of the reclining nudes so often featured in the art of

sixteenth-century Venice (*see* FIGS 54, 55, 56). But if many earlier artists confidently presented beautiful women as the legitimate objects
of desire, then in Bassano's painting any such relationship is forbid-
den by the theme. Indeed, it is a defining feature of his 'absorbed' depiction that the viewer is kept outside the drama, unacknowledged by
the actors themselves, who are so intensely engaged with one another.
As if to reinforce the importance of this lateral interaction, Bassano
extended a thin line of yellow-white paint across the picture surface,
which must be taken as a part of Susanna's veil or headdress. It coils
out in serpentine fashion from the beautiful young woman towards
the desperate old men, its curving hook-like shape echoing the soft
folds of her fleshy body, while appearing to reel in their desire.

In a work which might be his very last, Bassano made an oil-
sketch for an altarpiece (FIG. 125). Like the late Tintoretto at San
Rocco, Bassano used a dark ground which allowed him to build his

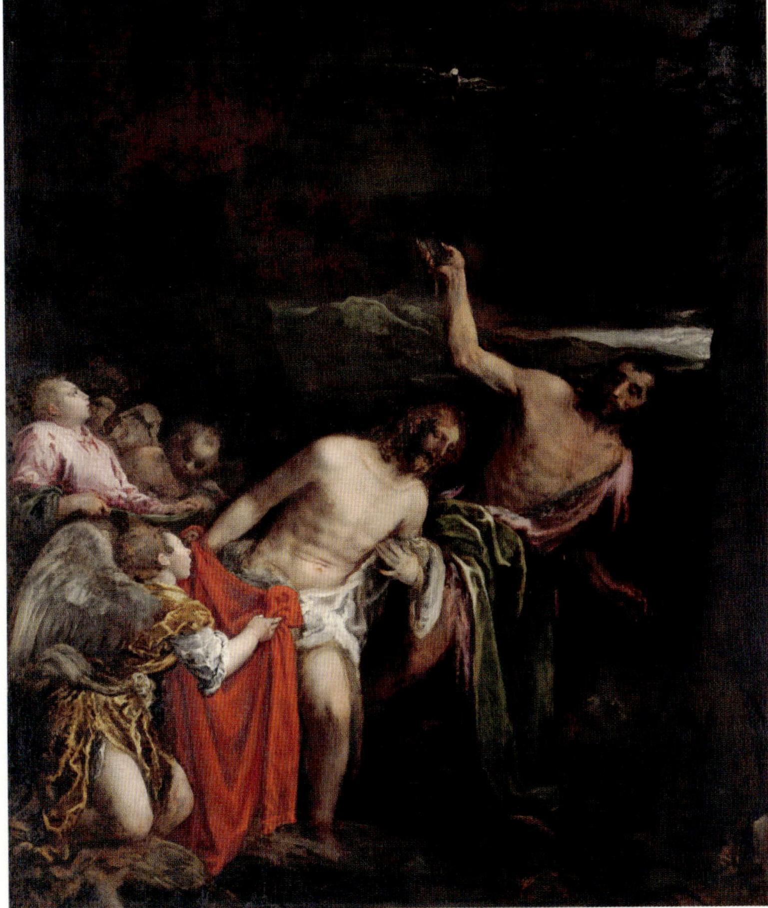

Fig. 125
Jacopo Bassano
The Baptism of Christ

ca. 1590. Oil on canvas,
191.8 × 160.3cm (6ft 3½in
× 5ft 3⅛in). Metropolitan
Museum of Art, New York.
Partial and Promised Gift
of Mr. and Mrs. Mark Fisch,
2012 (2012.99).

figures out of the surrounding shadowy penumbra. As in many of his other late paintings, Bassano's tone is tragic, a departure from the earlier tendency in sixteenth-century painting to present the Baptism of Christ as a celebratory subject. At San Rocco, Tintoretto had recently shown Christ in sacrificial fashion in the *Baptism*, kneeling and inert with head bowed towards the earth, as if ready for his upcoming Crucifixion. In Tintoretto's painting, however, the clouds billow apart to allow a cascade of golden heavenly light to stream down from heaven behind the dove of the Holy Spirit. Bassano allows of no such justification or sign of redemption from suffering. The dissolving fluidity of his brushwork does not tell us whether the painting is finished, given that the old artist had apparently sent similarly loosely painted works to patrons as completed. As in Titian's late work, the contrast between loosely painted and more carefully worked passages might have been quite deliberate. Bassano used excited broken brushwork for the three angels to lower left, but the scarlet cloth held up for Christ to wrap himself in is carefully finished, probably to emphasize its symbolic connection with Christ's blood in his upcoming Passion. This cloth is, in fact, the key to the entire meaning of the composition. It divides the heavenly figures to the left from the lonely Christ who, with the heaviness of his human flesh painfully evident from his awkward leaning posture, turns his back on the angelic consort. Only the angels turn up their faces to notice the descent of the dove of the Holy Spirit, while Christ lowers his head down towards the darkness of the earth below him, a delicate action which indicates sorrowful acceptance of his impending death.

Master and workshop

Much of the discussion so far in this chapter has focussed on unique late works by ageing masters, and has been framed around the extraordinary and original achievements of their final years. Without succumbing to the later romantic myth of the lonely and isolated genius, who works only for himself or for posterity, it is clear that the artistic individualism of Palladio, Tintoretto, Veronese and Jacopo Bassano in the final phases of their careers was real enough. In Venice, however, the tradition of the family-based artistic workshop had always been very strong, and the leading masters of the late sixteenth century continued to run them. One important function of these workshops was the transmission of artistic knowledge and ideas from the master to his pupils, or from father to son. In this way, the workshop might potentially secure the continuation of artistic tradition down the generations. At the same time, the work-shop assumed that visual art was a taught or learned activity, rather than a matter of God-given talent, and its communality also offset or counteracted the idea that artistic style is personal or unique. As we have seen, though, for much of the sixteenth century the practice of visual art in Venice had not really been based on such assumptions, and had become far more personalized than the workshop model presumed or accommodated. Although outwardly conforming to the communal tradition of the workshop, the unique qualities of the masters' artistic style and technique meant that they could not be imitated or effectively followed. The artistic malaise that emerged in Venice in the final decades of the century was to this extent a prod-uct of the powerfully individualistic trajectory of Renaissance art in the city from around 1500 onwards.

The key and in many ways defining figure in this regard was Titian himself. The old master was a staunch supporter of his painter son Orazio (ca. 1528–1576), and clearly envisaged that the young man would succeed him as an internationally famous artist. How-ever, the evidence suggests that Orazio, like the other members of Titian's workshop, was singularly unable to follow his father's pro-gressive example in painting, and that he was especially perplexed by the old master's astonishing 'late style'. Predicated, above all, on the old master's unique touch – he sometimes used his fingers rather than brushes – this was almost impossible to follow. Rumours cir-culated that Titian was, in any case, uninterested in teaching his pupils, and even that he locked his paintings away when he was abroad in order to stop them stealing his inventions. In the event, Orazio died of the plague a few weeks after his father in 1576, and the Vecellio workshop quickly ceased to exist amidst family infighting and thievery. Even had he survived to inherit Titian's painting em-pire, it is very unlikely that Orazio would have proved artistically equipped to purposefully continue, or progress beyond, the extraor-dinary artistic achievements of his father. Other family members, such as Titian's second cousin Marco Vecellio (1545–1611), contin-ued the house style in a number of large-scale paintings beyond the end of the century, signing himself as 'Marco di Tiziano'. He even completed an unfinished votive painting begun by Titian himself for the Ducal Palace. But like Orazio's, Marco's work proved to be nothing more than a timid and inept recapitulation of Titian's much earlier early style of the 1520s and 1530s.

In the artistic workshops of other leading masters, tensions around 'the genius in the workshop' were less immediately appar-ent. It is nonetheless true that very few of the progressively minded

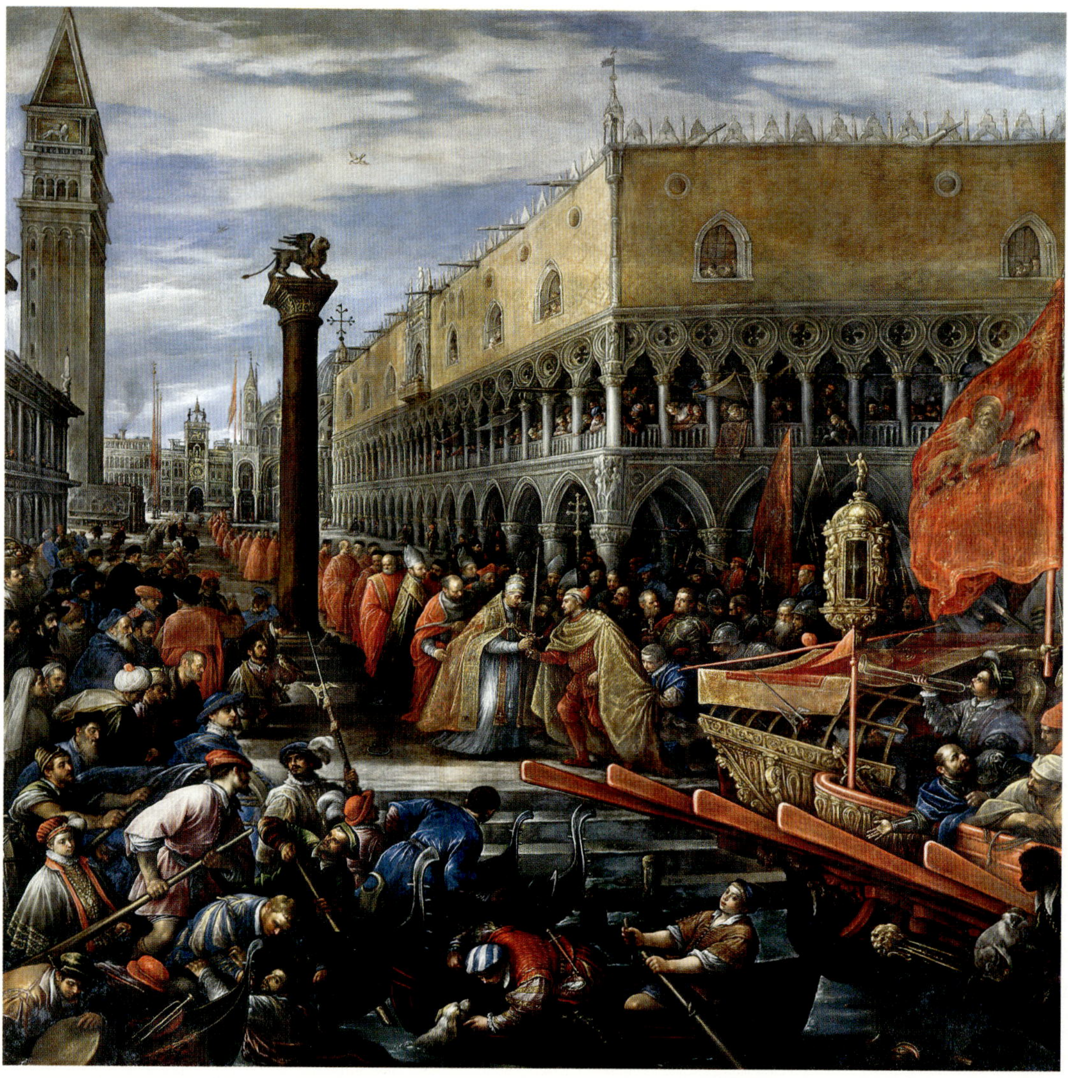

masters who dominated them ultimately succeeded in transmitting the secrets of their art to their painter sons or followers. Jacopo Bassano's elder son Francesco, mentioned earlier, moved to Venice in 1577, presumably in order to exploit the new opportunities on offer at the Ducal Palace following the fires. Although Francesco quickly gained employment on the redecorations, he was apparently poorly equipped to deal with large-scale patriotic history painting of the kind now required at the Palace. A more or less explicit accommodation to the demands of 'Venetian tradition' was, as we have seen, central to the ethos of this on-going official commission, and it may have been a tacit requirement that individualistic styles were downplayed in favour of direct reference to the earlier paintings in the Palace that had recently been destroyed. In a painting for the Sala del Maggior Consiglio, Francesco was apparently required to 'restore' Gentile Bellini's lost painting of *The Consignment of the Sword by the Pope to the Doge* (FIG. 126). The laboured painting he produced may also be a product of his earlier domination by Jacopo in the workshop at Bassano. While a surviving drawing and description show that Francesco attempted to closely follow Gentile's composition, his painting is nonetheless a weak mock-up of his father's style. Francesco makes only a slight reference to Jacopo's use of dark shadows and flashing white highlights in his contemporary works of the 1580s, and includes a genre-like scene at the lower foreground left, where a man and his dog have fallen into the water. This was a 'Bassanesque' addition to Gentile's composition that reflects Francesco's more typical humdrum employment in Jacopo's workshop, but does little more than distract attention from the famous historical scene beyond.

In the *Consignment*, Francesco made a faithful attempt to suggest the continuity of his father's favoured style with that of a 'great master' of the Venetian past. This also meant that Francesco's own contribution was largely occluded in the production of a painting that was unduly dominated by the art of the older generations. And this kind of debilitating 'retrospectivity' was more widely typical of paintings by younger artists from the leading workshops in this period. Given the domination of the old masters, one that was now reconfirmed in the domain of official patronage by the Venetian state itself, there appears to have been little scope for thinking beyond the artistic boundaries they had established. Francesco's tragic suicide in 1593 may be unrelated to this situation. Yet Francesco killed himself very shortly after his father's death, and the fact that he jumped from a window of Titian's old studio at Biri Grande seems especially resonant of this wider situation of creative and cultural impasse in Venice in the final decade of the century.

The works of the so-called 'Haeredes Pauli' or 'Paolo's Heirs', a business venture that comprised Paolo Veronese's brother Benedetto (1538–1598) and two sons Carletto (1570–1596) and Gabriele (1568–1631), ultimately proved little more successful in artistic terms. At the church of San Giacomo on the Giudecca, the Haeredes joined forces to produce a large painting that carefully reprises Paolo's lavish Supper scenes of the 1560s and 1570s, including the painting with the same subject discussed in the previous chapter (FIG. 127; *see* FIG. 103). While the warmer colours and imposition of a chiaroscuro treatment certainly reference the master's own late style of the 1580s, the more literal definition of form contrasts with Paolo's lightness and economy of touch. Recent restoration has confirmed that the painting was the product of more than one artist, and this is evident enough from the contrasting handling of forms between the right-hand and central areas. This determinedly collaborative 'workshop' attempt to replicate the manner of a master who had freely invented his own was doomed to aesthetic failure. Its vacuous monumentality appears to be an issue of the Haeredes' exaggerated sense of indebtedness to Paolo himself, as also of the essentially untranslatable quality of his style. The Haeredes' debilitating veneration of Paolo's work indicates once again that painting in Venice had reached the end of an era.

The above discussion has indicated that the individualism of the great Renaissance masters played an important role in the failure of art in Venice at the end of the sixteenth century. Only the lively and on-going Tintoretto workshop appeared to offer hope for the future. Jacopo Tintoretto had paid especially careful attention to the training of his sons and daughters in his workshop, especially his older son and heir, Domenico (1560–1635). The exceptionally long continuation of the business beyond Domenico's own death and into the later seventeenth century is a testament to Jacopo's care and attention in this regard. It appears that the father allowed his son an unusually active and quasi-independent role in both the

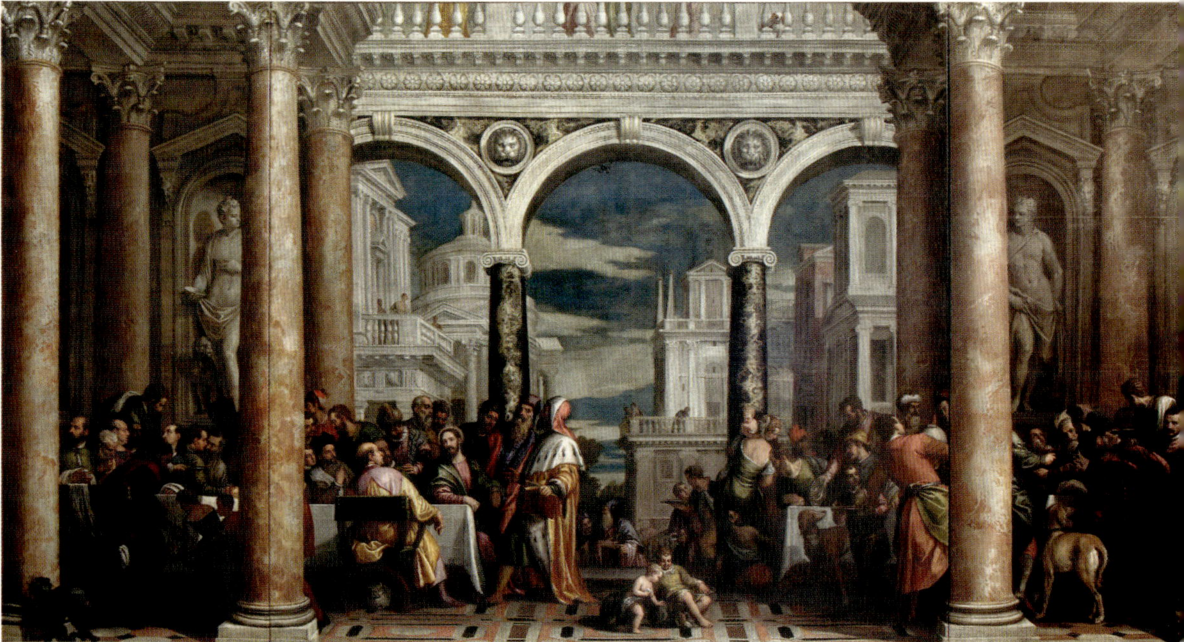

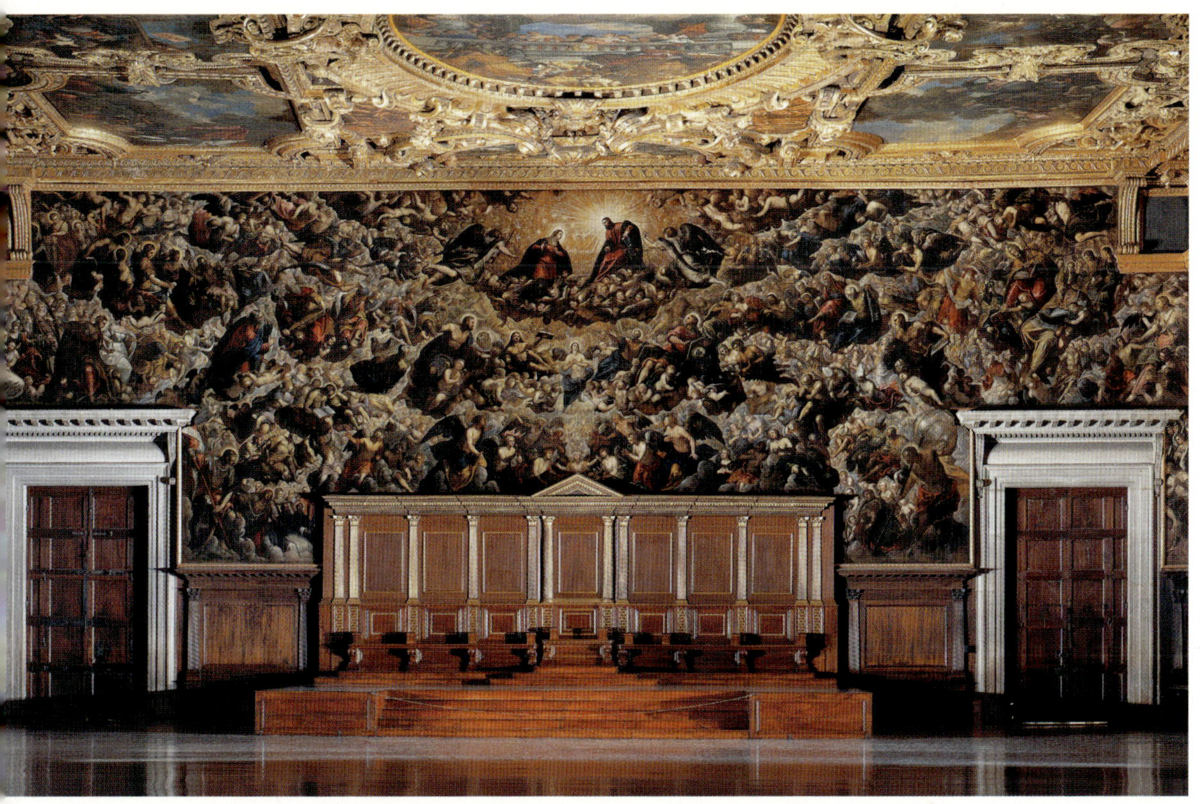

execution and planning of paintings from a very young age. The result is that many 'Tintoretto' paintings from the late 1570s onwards are in reality workshop productions, including major works such as the enormous *Paradise* in the Sala del Maggior Consiglio (FIG. 128). On this occasion, Domenico might have chosen to closely follow his father's earlier oil sketches for the painting, one of which was apparently made during an earlier competition for the commission between 1579 and 1582 (FIG. 129). But the marked differences between this sketch and the final painting indicate that Domenico assumed an unusual degree of freedom and authority during the completion of the work between 1588 and 1590. The series of concentric heavenly semi-circles on which the figures are arranged in Jacopo's dynamic sketch, carefully defined by darkened cloud-bases and open areas of golden light, are almost obliterated in the final work, as heaven becomes altogether more populous. Sacrificing his father's usual dynamic spatiality to an effect which makes it appear that the occupants of heaven are about to spill over into the Council Hall, Domenico responded with some pictorial intelligence to the specific demands of this highly charged commission. In what was

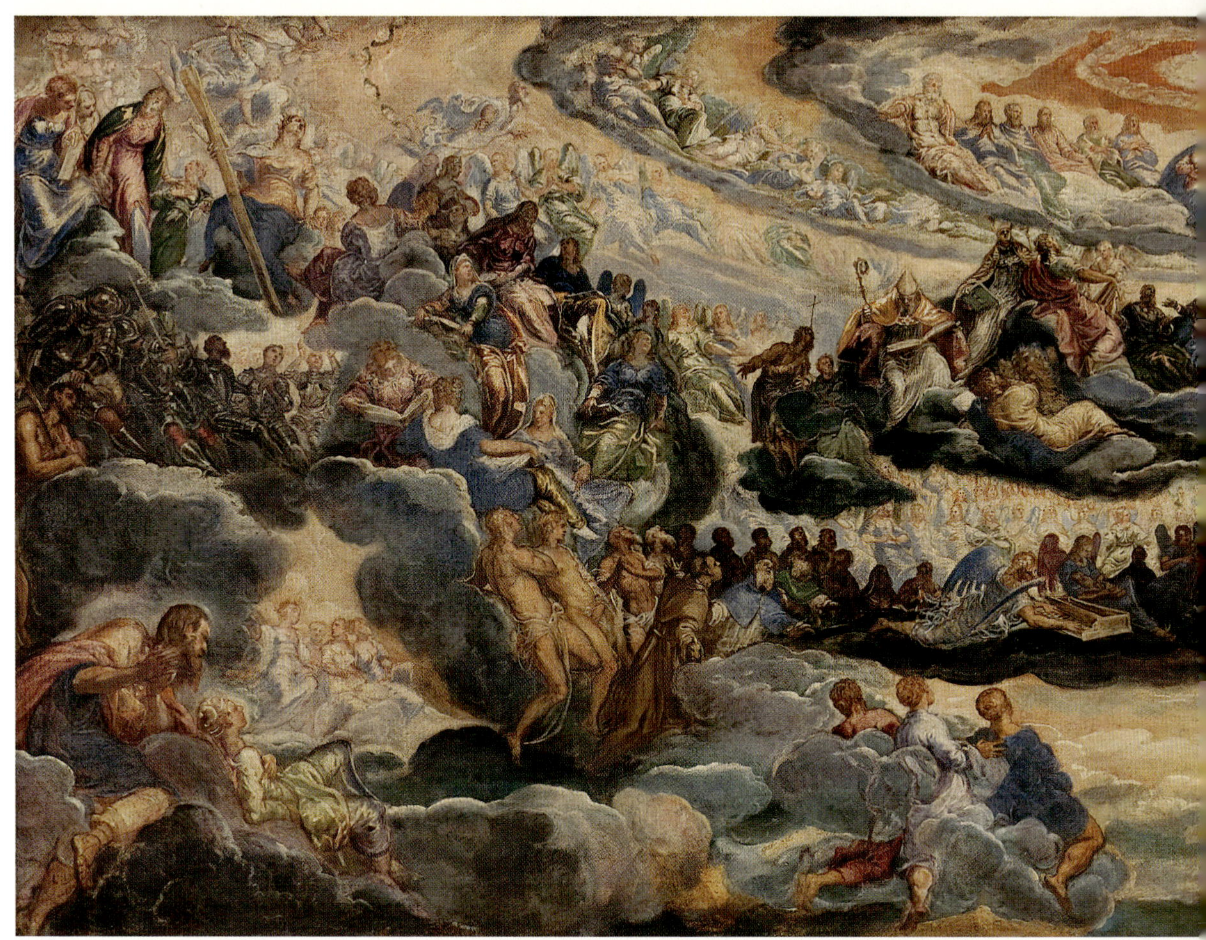

the largest oil-painting ever made in Venice, he produced a work that effectively offered to combine the realms of heaven and earth, allowing the doge and his councillors seated on the tribune below to appear to the assembled patricians in the hall as if they were already on the very brink of Paradise.

In subsequent large-scale and prominent commissions, such as the choir paintings in Palladio's San Giorgio Maggiore (1592–4), Domenico again excelled, producing works of such high quality that they are often taken as executed by Jacopo himself. On this occasion too, however, the old master might have provided designs to aid his son. And in the decades following Jacopo's death in 1594, Domenico's more literal and prosaic treatment of forms and surfaces, combined with his inability or unwillingness to explore new spatial possibilities, became ever more evident. Like the productions of the sons, relatives and workshop followers of the other leading painters

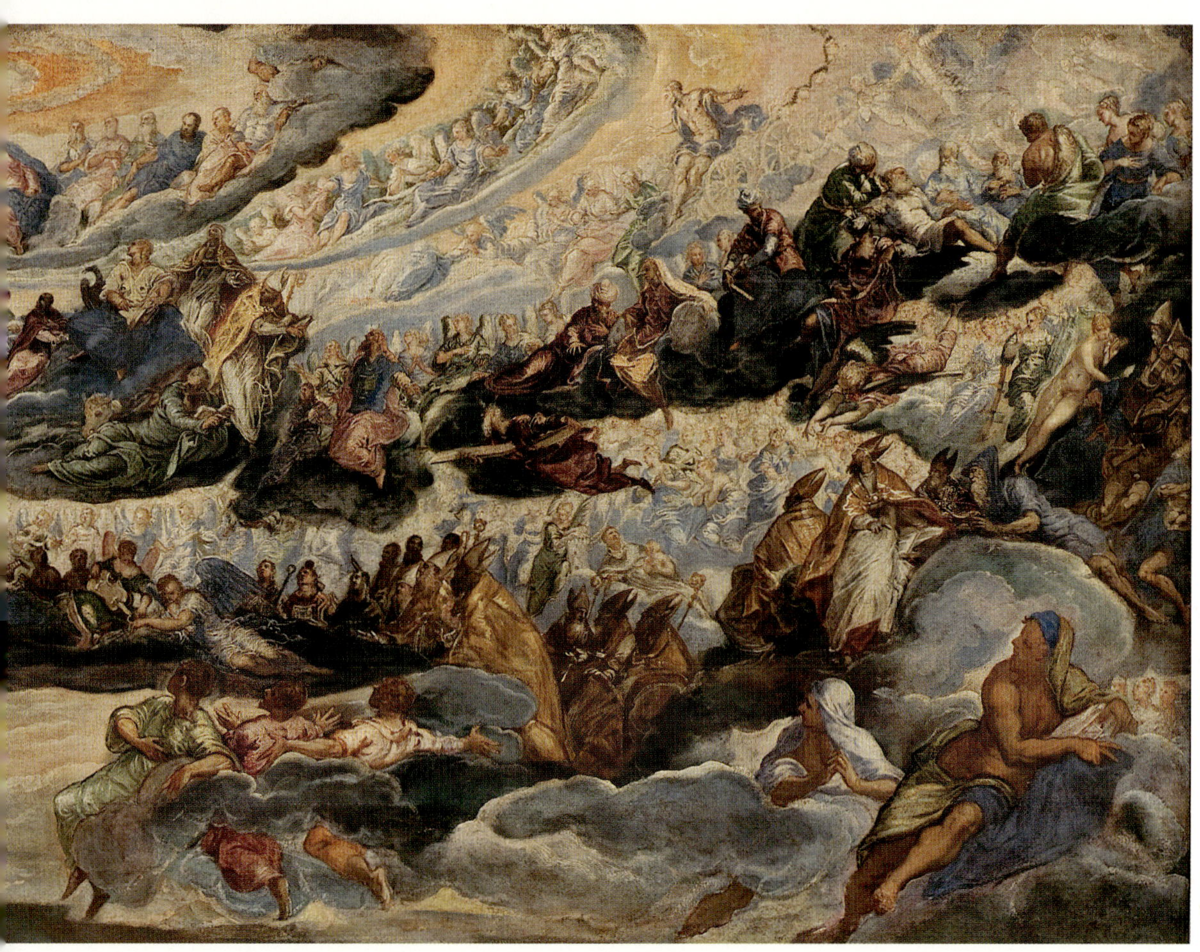

of the late sixteenth century, Domenico's paintings quickly became little more than tired and recherché renditions of the dynamic and individualistic Renaissance art of the previous generation.

1579–80. Oil sketch on canvas, 143 × 362cm (4ft 10¼in × 11ft 10½in). Musée du Louvre, Paris.

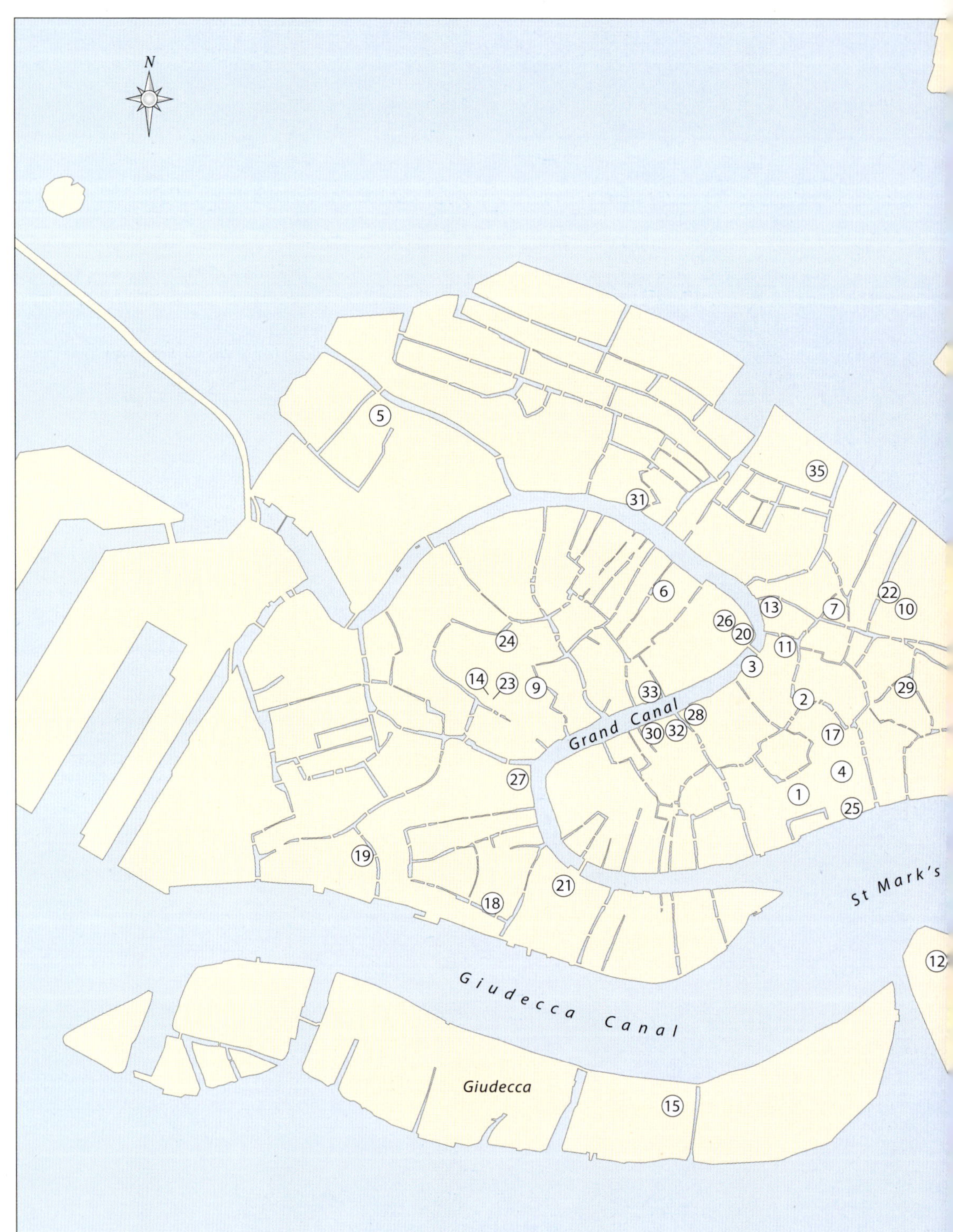

N
Grand Canal
Giudecca Canal
Giudecca
St Mark's

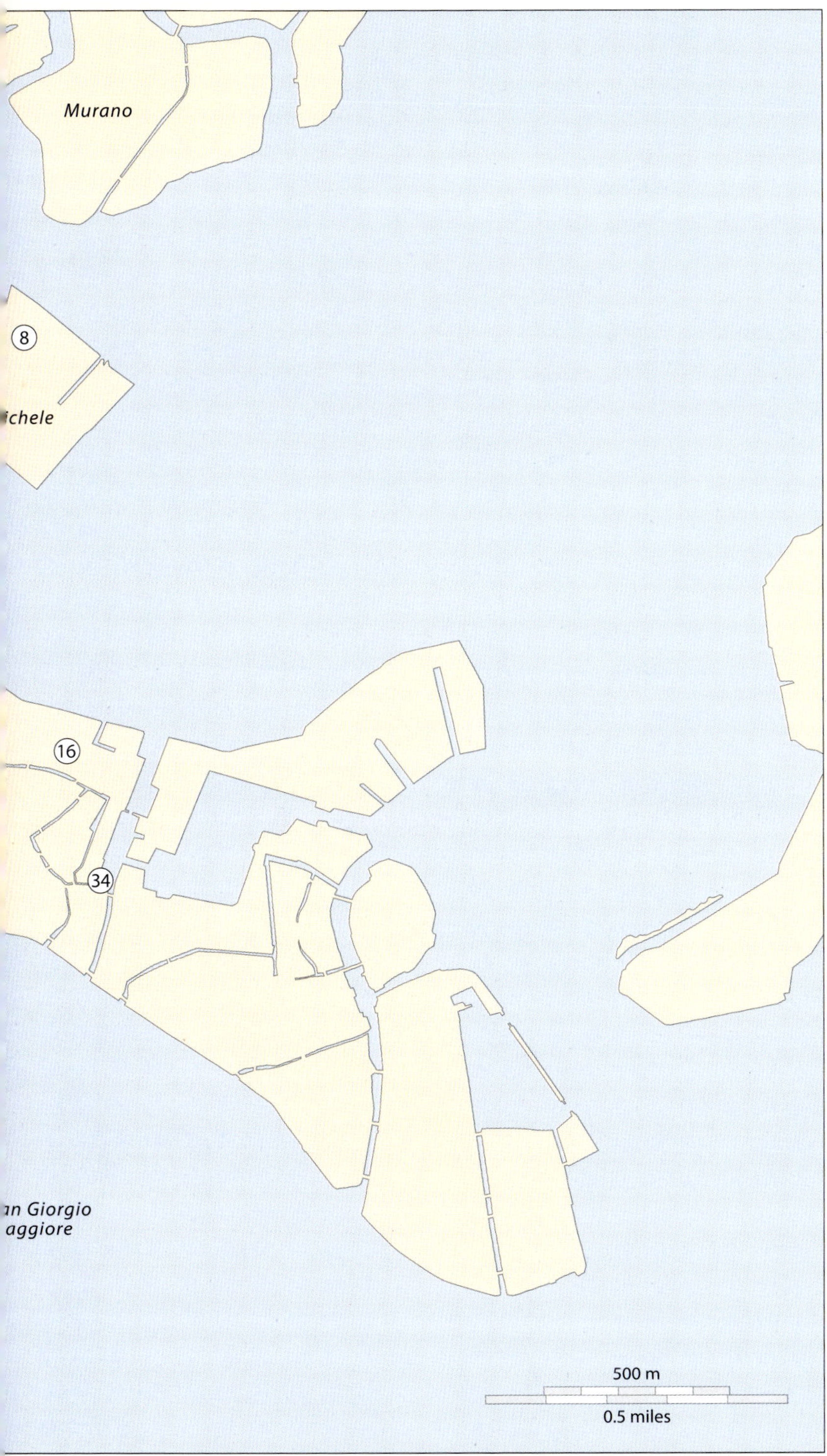

Fig. 130

Map of Venice

1. St Mark's Square
2. Merceria
3. Rialto
4. Basilica of St Mark's
5. San Giobbe
6. San Cassiano
7. Santa Maria dei Miracoli
8. San Michele in Isola
9. Sta Maria dei Frari
10. Santi Giovanni e Paolo
11. San Bartolommeo a Rialto
12. San Giorgio Maggiore
13. San Giovanni Crisostomo
14. San Rocco
15. Il Redentore
16. San Francesco della Vigna
17. San Giuliano
18. San Trovaso
19. San Sebastiano
20. Scuola dei Battuti della Carita
21. Scuola Grande di San Marco
22. Scuola Grande di San Rocco
23. Scuola Grande di San Giovanni Evangelista
24. Ducal Palace
25. Palazzo dei Camerlenghi
26. Ca'Foscari
27. Palazzo Grimani a San Luca
28. Palazzo Grimani a Sta Maria Formosa
29. Palazzo d'Anna
30. Palazzo Gussoni
31. Palazzo Corner
32. Palazzo Coccina
33. Arsenal
34. Crociferi Hospital

Bibliography

SELECTED GENERAL WORKS

Architecture, Art and Identity in Venice and its Territories, 1450–1750, eds Nebahat Avcioğlu and Emma Jones (Farnham, 2013)
PATRICIA FORTINI BROWN, *Venice and Antiquity: The Venetian Sense of the Past* (New Haven, CT; London, 1997)
PAUL HILLS, *Venetian Colour: Marble, Mosaic, Painting and Glass: 1250–1550* (New Haven, CT; London, 1999)
DEBORAH HOWARD, T*he Architectural History of Venice* (New Haven, CT; London, 1980) esp. pp. 73–208;
Venice and the Veneto, ed. Peter Humfrey (Cambridge, 2008)
EDWARD MUIR, *Civic Ritual in Renaissance Venice* (Princeton, NJ, 1981)
DAVID ROSAND, *Painting in Sixteenth-Century Venice: Titian, Veronese, Tintoretto* (Cambridge, 1997)
MANFREDO TAFURI, *Venice and the Renaissance*, trans. Jessica Levine (Cambridge, MA, 1985)

PRIMARY SOURCES

Venice: A Documentary History 1450–1630, eds D. S. Chambers and Brian Pullan (Oxford, 1992)
BALDASSARE CASTIGLIONE, *The Book of the Courtier* (1528), trans. George Bull (London, 2003)
FRANCESCO COLONNA, *Hypnerotomachia Poliphili: The Strife of Love in a Dream* (Venice, 1499), trans. Joscelyn Godwin (London, 2005)
LUDOVICO DOLCE, *Dialogo della pittura* (Venice, 1557): see Mark W. Roskill, *Dolce's Aretino and Venetian Art Theory of the Cinquecento* (Toronto; Buffalo; London, 2000)
MARCANTONIO MICHIEL, *The Anonimo: Notes on Pictures and Works of Art in Italy made by an Anonymous Writer in the Sixteenth Century*, ed. George C. Williamson, trans. Paolo Mussi (London, 1903)
PAOLO PINO, *Dialogo di pittura* (1548)
CARLO RIDOLFI, *The Life of Tintoretto* (1642), trans. Robert and Catherine Enggass (Pennsylvania, 1984);
The Life of Titian (1648), trans. Julia Conaway Bondanella and Bruce Cole (Pennsylvania, 1996)
GIORGIO VASARI, *The Lives of the Artists* (1550, 1568), trans. George Bull (Harmondsworth, 1965)

INTRODUCTION

PATRICIA FORTINI BROWN, *The Renaissance in Venice: A World Apart* (London, 1997)
PETER HUMFREY, *Painting in Renaissance Venice* (New Haven, CT; London, 1995)
NORBERT HUSE and WOLFGANG WOLTERS, *The Art of Renaissance Venice: Architecture, Sculpture and Painting, 1460–1590*, trans. Edmund Jephcott (Chicago; London, 1990)

CHAPTER 1: THE 'MOST SERENE REPUBLIC': VENICE AT THE OUTSET OF THE RENAISSANCE

FREDERIC LANE, *Venice: A Maritime Republic* (Baltimore, MD; London, 1973)
DAVID ROSAND, *Myths of Venice: The Figuration of a State* (Chapel Hill, NC, 2000)

Origins: Myths of Venice and the basilica of St Mark's
OTTO DEMUS, *The Church of San Marco in Venice: History, Architecture, Sculpture* (Washington DC, 1960); and *The Mosaics of San Marco in Venice*, 4 vols (Chicago, 1984)
JOHN RUSKIN, *The Stones of Venice* (1851–3), ed. J. G. Links (New York, 1960), pp. 25, 152–3

The Ducal Palace and the Porta della Carta
DEBORAH HOWARD, *Venice and the East: The Impact of the Islamic World on Venetian Architecture 1100–1500* (New Haven, CT; London, 2000), pp. 170–88
ANNE MARKHAM SCHULZ, 'The Sculpture of Giovanni and Bartolommeo Bon and Their Workshop', *Transactions of the American Philosophical Society*, vol. 68, no. 3 (1978), pp. 1–81
DENNIS ROMANO, *The Likeness of Venice: A Life of Doge Francesco Foscari 1373–1457* (New Haven, CT; London, 2007)

CHAPTER 2: INNOVATION AS TRADITION: 1440–75

PATRICIA FORTINI BROWN, *Private Lives in Renaissance Venice: Art, Architecture and the Family* (New Haven, CT; London, 2004)
DEBORAH HOWARD, *The Architectural History of Venice* (New Haven, CT: London, 1980), pp. 106–9; *Venice and the East: the Impact of the Islamic World on Venetian Architecture 1100-1500*, (New Haven, CT: London 2000), pp. 134–40
DONALD E. QUELLER, *The Venetian Patriciate: Reality Versus Myth* (Urbana-Chicago, 1986)
UGO TUCCI, 'The Psychology of the Venetian Merchant in the Sixteenth Century', in *Renaissance Venice*, ed. John Hale (London, 1973), pp. 346–78

Painting in two Venetian chapels of the mid-fifteenth century
PETER HUMFREY, *The Altarpiece in Renaissance Venice* (New Haven, CT; London, 1993)
MICHELANGELO MURARO, 'The Statutes of the Venetian Arti and the Mosaics of the Mascoli Chapel', Art Bulletin, 43 (1961), pp. 263–74
GARY M. RADKE, 'Nuns and Their Art: The Case of San Zaccaria in Renaissance Venice', *Renaissance Quarterly*, 54/2 (Summer, 2001), pp. 430–59

Space and figure in Jacopo Bellini's drawings
BERNHARD DEGENHART and ANNEGRITE SCHMITT, *Jacopo Bellini: The Louvre Album of Drawings* (New York, 1984)
COLIN EISLER, *The Genius of Jacopo Bellini: The Complete Paintings and Drawings* (New York, 1989)

Padua and its impact
SUSAN CONNELL, *The Employment of Sculptors and Stonemasons in the Fifteenth Century* (New York, 1988)
NORBERT HUSE and WOLFGANG WOLTERS, *The Art of Renaissance Venice: Architecture, Sculpture and Painting, 1460–1590*, trans. Edmund Jephcott (Chicago; London, 1990), pp. 134–42
RALPH LIEBERMAN, 'Real Architecture, Imaginary History: The Arsenale Gate as Venetian Mythology', *Journal of the Warburg and Courtauld Institutes*, LIV (1991), pp. 117–26
ANNE MARKHAM SCHULZ, *Antonio Rizzo: Sculptor and Architect* (Princeton, NJ, 1983)

Icons and images: early Giovanni Bellini
HANS BELTING, *Likeness and Presence: A History of the Image before the Era of Art*, trans. Edmund Jephcott (Chicago, 1994)
CAROLINE CAMPBELL and ALAN CHONG, *Bellini and the East* (London, 2005)
KEITH CHRISTIANSEN, 'Bellini and Mantegna' in *The Cambridge Companion to Giovanni Bellini*, ed. Peter Humfrey (Cambridge, 2004) pp. 48–74
RONA GOFFEN, 'Icon and Vision: Giovanni Bellini's Half-Length Madonnas', *Art Bulletin*, 57 (1975), pp. 487–518

CHAPTER 3: A PERFECTED IMAGE OF VENICE: 1476–1500

Oil painting and naturalism in Bellini's San Giobbe Altarpiece
LOUISA C. MATTHEW and BARBARA H. BERRIE, '"Memoria de colori che bisognino torre a vinitia": Venice as a Center for the Purchase of Painter's Colours' in *Trade in Artists' Materials: Markets and Commerce in Europe to 1700*, eds Jo Kirby, Susie Nash and Joanna Cannon (London, 2010), pp. 245–52
JOANNE WRIGHT, 'Antonello da Messina: The Origins of his Style and Technique', *Art History* 3.1 (1980), pp. 41–60

Pietro Lombardo and Mauro Codussi
RALPH LIEBERMAN, *The Church of Santa Maria dei Miracoli in Venice* (New York, 1986)
L. OLIVATO PUPPI and L. PUPPI, *Mauro Codussi e l'architettura veneziana del Primo Rinascimento* (Milan, 1977)
WENDY STEDMAN SHEARD, 'The Birth of Monumental Classicising Relief in Venice on the Façade of the Scuola di San Marco' in *Interpretazione veneziane: Studi di storia dell'arte in onore di Michelangelo Muraro*, ed. David Rosand (Venice, 1984), pp. 149–74

Two Venetian tombs
DEBRA PINCUS, 'The Tomb of Doge Nicolò Tron and Venetian Renaissance Ruler Imagery' in *Art, the Ape of Nature: Studies in Honor of H. W. Janson*, eds Moshe Barasch and Lucy Freeman Sandler (New York, 1981), pp. 127–50
JOHN POPE HENNESSY, *Italian Renaissance Sculpture* (London, 1958), vol. 1, pp. 106–17

Ruler imagery
CAROLINE CAMPBELL and ALAN CHONG, *Bellini and the East* (London, 2005)
JULIAN RABY, *Venice, Dürer and the Oriental Mode* (London, 1982)

The cultural dynamics of space: maps and history paintings
JUERGEN SCHULZ, 'Jacopo de'Barbari's View of Venice: Map Making, City Views', and 'Moralized Geography Before the Year 1500', *Art Bulletin*, 60 (1978), pp. 425–74

DEBORAH HOWARD, 'Venice as a Dolphin: Further Investigations into Jacopo de'Barbari's View', *Artibus et Historiae*, 18/35 (1997), pp. 101–11
PATRICIA FORTINI BROWN, *Venetian Narrative Painting in the Age of Carpaccio* (New Haven, CT; London), pp. 143–52

Carpaccio: past and present life
BROWN, *Venetian Narrative Painting*, pp. 279–82
SIMONA COHEN, 'The Enigma of Carpaccio's *Venetian Ladies*', *Renaissance Studies*, 19/2 (2005), pp. 150–84

CHAPTER 4: INDIVIDUALISM, INTERNATIONALISM, SECULARIZATION: 1501–25

New artistic identities
Bellini, Giorgione, Titian and the Renaissance of Venetian Painting, exh. cat., eds David Alan Brown and Sylvia Pagden (New Haven, CT; London, 2006)
JAYNIE ANDERSON, *Giorgione: The Painter of Poetic Brevity* (Paris, 1997)
JENNIFER FLETCHER, 'Bellini's Social World' in *The Cambridge Companion to Giovanni Bellini*, ed. Peter Humfrey (Cambridge, 2004), pp. 13–47
CAROLYN C. WILSON, 'Giovanni Bellini and the "Modern Manner"' in *The Cambridge Companion to Giovanni Bellini*, ed. Peter Humfrey (Cambridge, 2004), pp. 95–121

International cross-currents
Renaissance Venice and the North: Crosscurrents in the Time of Bellini, Dürer, and Titian, exh. cat., eds Bernard Aikema and Beverley Louise Brown (New York, 2000)
PETER HUMFREY, *Lorenzo Lotto* (New Haven, CT; London, 1997).

Poetic painting and printmaking
JAYNIE ANDERSON, 'Giorgione, Titian, and the Sleeping Venus', in *Tiziano e Venezia*, Convegno Internazionale di Studi, Venezia, 1976, eds Massimo Gemin and Gianantonio Paladini (Venice, 1980), pp. 337–42
SALVATORE SETTIS, *Giorgione's Tempest: Interpreting the Hidden Subject* (Chicago, 2004)

Landscape, love and war
MICHAEL HIRST, *Sebastiano del Piombo* (Oxford, 1981)
DEBORAH HOWARD, 'Giorgione's *Tempesta* and Titian's *Assunta* in the Context of the Cambrai Wars', *Art History*, 8.3 (1985), pp. 271–89
PAUL H. D. KAPLAN, 'The Storm of War: The Paduan Key to Giorgione's *Tempesta*', *Art History*, 9.4 (1986), pp. 405–27

The erotics of portraiture
Tullio Lombardo and Venetian High Renaissance Sculpture, exh. cat., ed. Alison Luchs et al. (New Haven, CT; London, 2009)
RONA GOFFEN, *Titian's Women* (New Haven, CT; London, 1997)
PETER HUMFREY, *Titian* (London, 2007); *Titian: The Complete Paintings* (New York, 2007)
TOM NICHOLS, *Titian and the End of the Venetian Renaissance* (London, 2013), pp. 87–95
PHILIP RYLANDS, *Palma Vecchio* (Cambridge, 1992)

Titian transforms Venetian mythological painting
CHARLES HOPE, 'The Camerino d'Alabastro of Alfonso
d'Este', *The Burlington Magazine*, 113 (1971), pp. 641–50
and 114 (1972), pp. 712–21;
*Bacchanals by Titian and Rubens: Papers Given at a Sympo-
sium in Nationalmuseum, Stockholm March 18–19, 1987*, ed.
Görel Cavalli-Björkmann (Stockholm, 1987)

Developments in altarpiece design
STAALE SINDING LARSEN, 'Titian's Madonna di Ca'Pesaro
and its Historical Significance', *Institutum Romanum Norvegiae*,
1 (1962), pp. 139–69
NICHOLS, *Titian and the End of the Venetian Renaissance*, pp.
64–72

**CHAPTER 5: ROMANISM, RANK AND RIVALRY:
1526–50**

MARILYN PERRY, 'Cardinal Domenico Grimani's Legacy of
Ancient Art to Venice', *Journal of the Warburg and Courtauld
Institutes*, 41 (1978), pp. 215–44

Sansovino and the *renovatio urbis*
BRUCE BOUCHER, *The Sculpture of Jacopo Sansovino*,
2 vols (New Haven, CT; London, 1991), vol. 1 pp. 73–88;
vol. 2 cat. no. 27
D. S. CHAMBERS, *The Imperial Age of Venice, 1380–1580*
(London, 1970), pp. 12–30
PAUL DAVIES, 'The Early History of Jacopo Sansovino's
Scheme for Piazza San Marco: A Proposal' in *Architecture,
Art and Identity in Venice and its Territories, 1450–1750*,
eds Nebahat Avcıoğlu and Emma Jones (Farnham, 2013),
pp. 51–70
DEBORAH HOWARD, *Jacopo Sansovino: Architecture and
Patronage in Renaissance Venice* (London, 1975), pp. 10–16;
Renovatio Urbis. Venezia nell'età di Andrea Gritti (1523–38),
ed. Manfredo Tafuri (Rome, 1984)
EDWARD MUIR, 'Images of Power: Art and Pageantry in
Renaissance Venice', *American Historical Review* 84 (1979),
pp. 16–52

Titian's imperial portraiture
TOM NICHOLS, *Titian and the End of the Venetian Renaissance*
(London, 2013), pp. 95–115
RUTH WEDGEWOOD KENNEDY, 'Apelles Redivivus' in *Essays
in Memory of Karl Lehmann*, ed. Lucy Freeman Sandler (New
York, 1964), pp. 160–70

A cultural triumvirate in Venice
JAYNIE ANDERSON, 'Pietro Aretino and Religious Imagery'
in *Interpretazione veneziane: Studi di storia dell'arte in onore
di Michelangelo Muraro*, ed. David Rosand (Venice, 1984),
pp. 284–7
BOUCHER, *The Sculpture of Jacopo Sansovino*, vol. 1 pp. 66–7;
vol. 2 cat. no. 23
JENNIFER FLETCHER '"Fatto al specchio": Venetian
Renaissance Attitudes to Self-Portraiture', in *Imaging the
Self in Renaissance Italy*, ed. Hilliard T. Goldfarb (Boston,
1992), pp. 45–60
PATRICIA FORTINI BROWN, *The Renaissance in Venice:
A World Apart* (London, 1997), pp. 165–6
CHARLES HOPE, *Titian* (London, 1980)
FRITZ SAXL, *A Heritage of Images* (London, 1970), pp. 71–88

Continuity and revival in Venetian painting
PATRICIA FORTINI BROWN, *Venetian Narrative Painting
in the Age of Carpaccio* (New Haven, CT; London), pp. 203–5
and 291–5;
PETER HUMFREY, Lorenzo Lotto (New Haven, CT; London,
1997), pp. 106-
PETER HUMFREY, *Painting in Renaissance Venice* (New Haven,
CT; London, 1995), pp. 164–83
GILES ROBERTSON, *Vincenzo Catena* (Edinburgh, 1954),
pp. 36–8, 68–9
CAROLYN C. WILSON, 'St Joseph and the Process of Decoding
Vincenzo Catena's *Warrior Adoring the Infant Christ and the
Virgin*', *Artibus et Historiae* 67 (2013), pp. 117–36

Mannerism and Titian's authority in Venice
*Da Tiziano a El Greco: Per la storia del Manierismo a Venezia
1540–1590*, exh. cat., ed. Rodolfo Pallucchini (Milan, 1981)
CHARLES COHEN, *The Art of Giovanni Antonio da Pordenone:
Between Dialect and Language*, 2 vols (Cambridge, 1996),
vol. 1 pp. 260–75, 390–99, 411–20
RONA GOFFEN, *Renaissance Rivals: Michelangelo, Leonardo,
Raphael, Titian* (New Haven, CT; London, 2004), pp. 265–338
HUMFREY, *Painting in Renaissance Venice*, pp.185–98
ROLAND KRISCHEL, *Jacopo Tintorettos 'Sklavenwunder'*
(Munich, 1991)
FRANCIS RICHARDSON, *Andrea Schiavone* (Oxford, 1980)
PAOLA ROSSI, *I disegni di Jacopo Tintoretto* (Florence, 1975)

CHAPTER 6: THE VICTORY OF ART: 1551–75

Venice and the Veneto, ed. Peter Humfrey (Cambridge, 2008),
section 3, pp. 207–326
ALESSANDRA ZAMPERINI, *Paolo Veronese*, trans. Grace
Crera-Bromelow (London, 2014)

Imagery of the Republic
BRUCE BOUCHER, *The Sculpture of Jacopo Sansovino*, 2 vols
(New Haven, CT; London, 1991), vol. 1, pp. 128–41; vol. 2,
cat. no. 35
TOM NICHOLS, *Tintoretto, Tradition and Identity* (London,
1999), pp. 114–26

Impact of the *terraferma*
JAMES S. ACKERMAN, *Palladio* (Harmondsworth, 1966)
BERNARD AIKEMA, *Jacopo Bassano and His Public:
Moralizing Pictures in an Age of Reform ca 1535–1600*
(Princeton, 1996)
RICHARD COCKE, 'Veronese and Daniele Barbaro: The
Decoration of the Villa Maser', *Journal of the Warburg and
Courtauld Institutes*, 35 (1972), pp. 226–46
TRACY COOPER, *Palladio's Venice: Architecture and Society
in a Renaissance Republic* (New Haven, CT; London, 2006)
DEBORAH HOWARD, *The Architectural History of Venice*
(New Haven, CT; London, 1980), pp. 183–6, 196–203
MICHELANGELO MURARO and PAOLO MARTON, *Venetian
Villas*, trans. Peter Lauritzen (Cologne, 1999), pp. 150–73

A *cittadini* style
BOUCHER, *The Sculpture of Jacopo Sansovino*, vol. 1 pp.
113–16, and vol. 2 cat. no. 31
TRACEY E. COOPER, 'Patricians and Citizens' in *Venice
and the Veneto*, ed. Peter Humfrey, pp. 151–205
BLAKE DE MARIA, *Becoming Venetian: Immigrants and the
Arts in Early Modern Venice* (New Haven, CT; London, 2010)

Counter-Reformation
PHILIPP FEHL, 'Veronese and the Inquisition: A Study of
the Subject Matter in the So-called Feast in the House
of Levi', *Gazette des Beaux-Arts*, 6/58 (1961), pp. 325–54
PAUL HILLS, 'Piety and Patronage in Cinquecento Venice:
Tintoretto and the Scuole del Sacramento', *Art History* 6
(1983), pp. 30–43
MADLYN KAHR, 'The Meaning of Veronese's Paintings in the
Church of San Sebastiano in Venice', *Journal of the Warburg
and Courtauld Institutes*, 33 (1970), pp. 235–47
JUERGEN SCHULZ, *Venetian Painted Ceilings of the
Renaissance* (Berkeley; Los Angeles, 1968), pp. 75–7
NICHOLS, *Tintoretto, Tradition and Identity*, pp. 162–8

Mythologies
THOMAS PUTTFARKEN, *Titian and Tragic Painting: Aristotle's
Poetics and the Rise of the Modern Artist* (New Haven, CT;
London, 2005)
DAVID ROSAND, 'Ut Pictor Poeta: Meaning in Titian's Poesie',
New Literary History 3 (1971–2), pp. 527–46

Artistic identity, style and theory
Tintoretto, exh. cat., ed. Miguel Falomir (Madrid, 2007)
MARY D. GARRARD, '"Art More Powerful than Nature?":
Titian's Motto Reconsidered' in *The Cambridge Companion
to Titian*, ed. Patricia Meilman (Cambridge, 2011), pp. 241–61;
Titian, Tintoretto, Veronese: Rivals in Renaissance Venice, exh.
cat., Frederick Ilchman et al., (Boston, 2009)

**CHAPTER 7: ADVERSITY, CREATIVITY,
RETROSPECTIVITY: 1576–1600**

Responses to plague, fire and poverty
BENJAMIN PAUL, '"And the Moon Has Started to Bleed":
Apocalypticism and Religious Reform in Venetian Art at
the Time of the Battle of Lepanto' in *The Turk and Islam
in the Western Eye, 1450–1750*, ed. James G. Harper
(Aldershot, 2011), pp. 67–87
STEFANIA MASON RINALDI, 'Le peste e le sue immagini
nella cultura figurativa veneta' in *Venezia e la Peste, 1348–
1797*, exh. cat. (Venice, 1979), pp. 209–24;
Palma il Giovane: L'opera complete, 2 vols (Milan, 1984), vol. 1
cat. nos 520–7
JUERGEN SCHULZ, *Venetian Painted Ceilings of the
Renaissance* (Berkeley; Los Angeles, 1968), pp.
107–11
STAALE SINDING-LARSEN, *Christ in the Council Hall: Studies
in the Religious Iconography of the Venetian Republic* (Rome,
1974)
W. TIMOFIEWITSCH, *The Chiesa del Redentore* (University
Park; London, 1971)

Tintoretto at San Rocco
GIANDOMENICO ROMANELLI, *Tintoretto: La Scuola
Grande di San Rocco* (Milan, 1994)
TOM NICHOLS, *Tintoretto, Tradition and Identity* (London,
1999), pp. 175–228
SCHULZ, *Venetian Painted Ceilings of the Renaissance*,
pp. 87–91

Late works by Veronese and Bassano
BEVERLEY LOUISE BROWN, 'Paolo Veronese's The Martyr-
dom and Last Communion of St Lucy', *Venezia Arti 2* (1988),
pp. 61–68; J
Jacopo Bassano c. 1510–1592, exh. cat., eds Beverley Louise
Brown and Paola Marini (Fort Worth, 1992), pp. 427–53

Master and workshop
ROBERT ECHOLS and FREDERICK ILCHMAN, 'Towards
a New Tintoretto Catalogue, with a Checklist of Revised
Attributions and a New Chronology' in *Jacopo Tintoretto:
Actas del Congreso Internacional*, ed. Miguel Falomir
(Madrid, 2008), pp. 91–150
JOHN GARTON, 'Paolo Veronese's Art of Business: Painting,
Investments and the Studio as Social Nexus', *Renaissance
Quarterly*, LXV/3 (2012), pp. 753–808;
Paolo Veronese: L'illusione della realtà, exh. cat., eds Paola
Marini and Bernard Aikema (Verona, 2014), pp. 314–63
JUERGEN SCHULZ, 'Tintoretto and the First Competition
for the Ducal Palace "Paradise"', *Arte Veneta*, 33 (1980),
pp. 112–26
GIORGIO TAGLIAFERRO, BERNARD AIKEMA, MATTEO
MANCINI and ANDREW JOHN MARTIN, *Le botteghe di
Tiziano* (Florence, 2009)

Index

Picture Credits

Details of collections are given in the captions. Additional information, copyright credits, and photo sources are given below. Numbers are figure numbers unless otherwise indicated.

Front Cover © Cameraphoto Arte, Venice

p.2 Image © The Metropolitan Museum of Art/Art Resource/Scala, Florence
pp.4–5 & 6 © Cameraphoto Arte, Venice
1 Folco Quilici © Fratelli Alinari
2 © Cameraphoto Arte, Venice
3 akg-images / Hervé Champollion
4 Photo Scala, Florence
5–7 & 9–12 © Cameraphoto Arte, Venice
13 Photo © RMN-Grand Palais (musée du Louvre) / Jean-Gilles Berizzi
14 © Trustees of the British Museum (1855,0811.30)
15 Photo © RMN-Grand Palais (musée du Louvre) / Gérard Blot
16, 17 © Cameraphoto Arte, Venice
18 KHM-Museumsverband
19 akg-images / Andrea Jemolo
20 Photo Scala, Florence
21 akg-images / Maurice Babey
22 Shutterstock/Brykaylo Yuriy
23 © Cameraphoto Arte, Venice
24 Photo Scala, Florence
25 Image © The Metropolitan Museum of Art/Art Resource/Scala, Florence
26 Pinacoteca di Brera, Milan, Italy / Bridgeman Images
27, 28 © Cameraphoto Arte, Venice
29 © The National Gallery, London/Scala, Florence
30 © Cameraphoto Arte, Venice
31 KHM-Museumsverband
32 © Cameraphoto Arte, Venice
33a akg-images / Schütze / Rodemann
33b © HelloWorld Images / Alamy
34–39 © Cameraphoto Arte, Venice
40 © The National Gallery, London/Scala, Florence
41,42a&b © Cameraphoto Arte, Venice
43 DeAgostini Picture Library/Scala, Florence
44a&b © Cameraphoto Arte, Venice
45 © Trustees of the British Museum
46a&b, 47 © Cameraphoto Arte, Venice

48 Courtesy Rijkmsuseum, Amsterdam
49 © Trustees of the British Museum
50 Photo Wilczyński Krzysztof/Muzeum Narodowe w Warszawie
51 Museo Thyssen-Bornemisza/Scala, Florence
52 Courtesy National Gallery of Art, Washington
53 © Cameraphoto Arte, Venice
54 Gemäldegalerie Alte Meister, Dresden, Germany / © Staatliche Kunstsammlungen Dresden / Bridgeman Images
55 © HAB Wolfenbüttel: 14 Astron. (http://diglib.hab.de/inkunabeln/14-astron/start.htm)
56 © Trustees of the British Museum
57 akg-images
58 © Cameraphoto Arte, Venice
59, 60 KHM-Museumsverband
61 © The National Gallery, London/Scala, Florence
62 © The Frick Collection
63 © Cameraphoto Arte, Venice
64 © The National Gallery, London/Scala, Florence
65 akg-images / Rabatti - Domingie
66–71 © Cameraphoto Arte, Venice
72 Image © Museo Nacional del Prado © Photo MNP / Scala, Florence
73 Courtesy National Gallery of Art, Washington
74 © Quattrone, Florence
75 © Cameraphoto Arte, Venice
76 Galleria Borghese, Rome, Italy / Bridgeman Images
77 © Cameraphoto Arte, Venice
78 © The National Gallery, London/Scala, Florence
79 J. Paul Getty Museum, Los Angeles
80 Royal Collection Trust © Her Majesty Queen Elizabeth II, 2015
81 akg-images
82 DeAgostini Picture Library/Scala, Florence/F. Ferruzzi

83 © The Victoria and Albert Museum. All rights reserved
84 Photo © RMN-Grand Palais / Agence Bulloz
85 Photo © RMN-Grand Palais (musée du Louvre) / Michèle Bellot
86 © Cameraphoto Arte, Venice
87 © Trustees of the British Museum
88–90 © Cameraphoto Arte, Venice
91 © Leemage/Corbis
92–94 © Cameraphoto Arte, Venice
95 Shutterstock/And_Ant
96 © Cameraphoto Arte, Venice
98 KHM-Museumsverband
99 akg-images / Erich Lessing
100-104 © Cameraphoto Arte, Venice
105 Image © Museo Nacional del Prado © Photo MNP / Scala, Florence
106 akg-images
107 Courtesy Rijkmsuseum, Amsterdam
108 KHM-Museumsverband
109 Minneapolis Institute of Arts, MN / The William Hood Dunwoody Fund / Bridgeman Images
110 Private Collection
111 © The National Gallery, London/Scala, Florence
112, 113 © Cameraphoto Arte, Venice
114 © The Trustees of the British Museum
115–122 © Cameraphoto Arte, Venice
123 Courtesy National Gallery of Art, Washington
124 Photo © RMN-Grand Palais / Gérard Blot
125 © 2015. Image © The Metropolitan Museum of Art/Art Resource/Scala, Florence
126 © Cameraphoto Arte, Venice
127 Verona, Museo di Castelvecchio, Archivio fotografico (foto Ottica Nodari di Caliaro Nereo, Verona)
128 © Cameraphoto Arte, Venice
129 Photo © Musée du Louvre, Dist. RMN-Grand Palais / Angèle Dequier